FairyCube

Vol. 3

Story & Art by
Kaori Yuki

CONTENTS

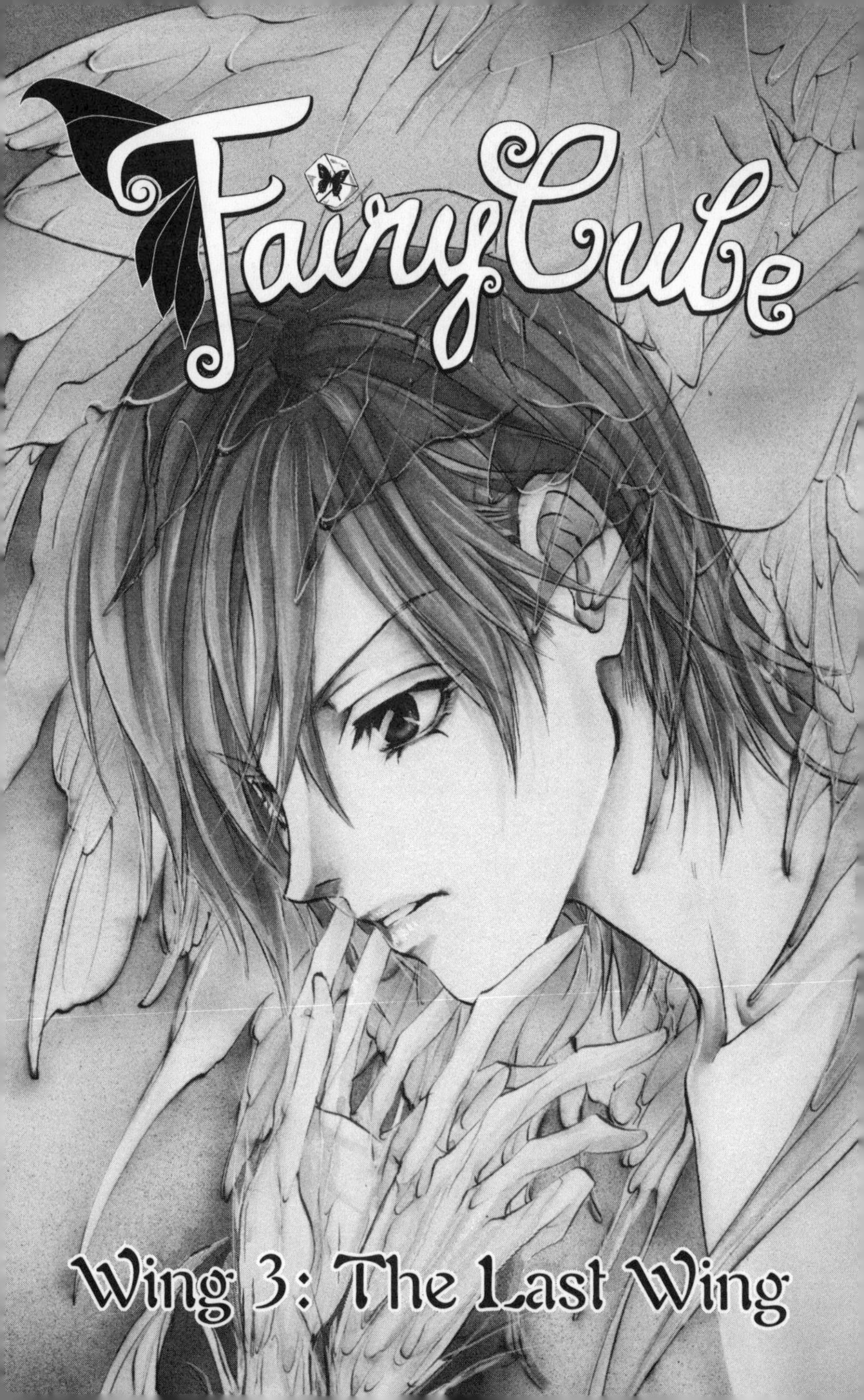
Fairy Cube
Wing 3: The Last Wing

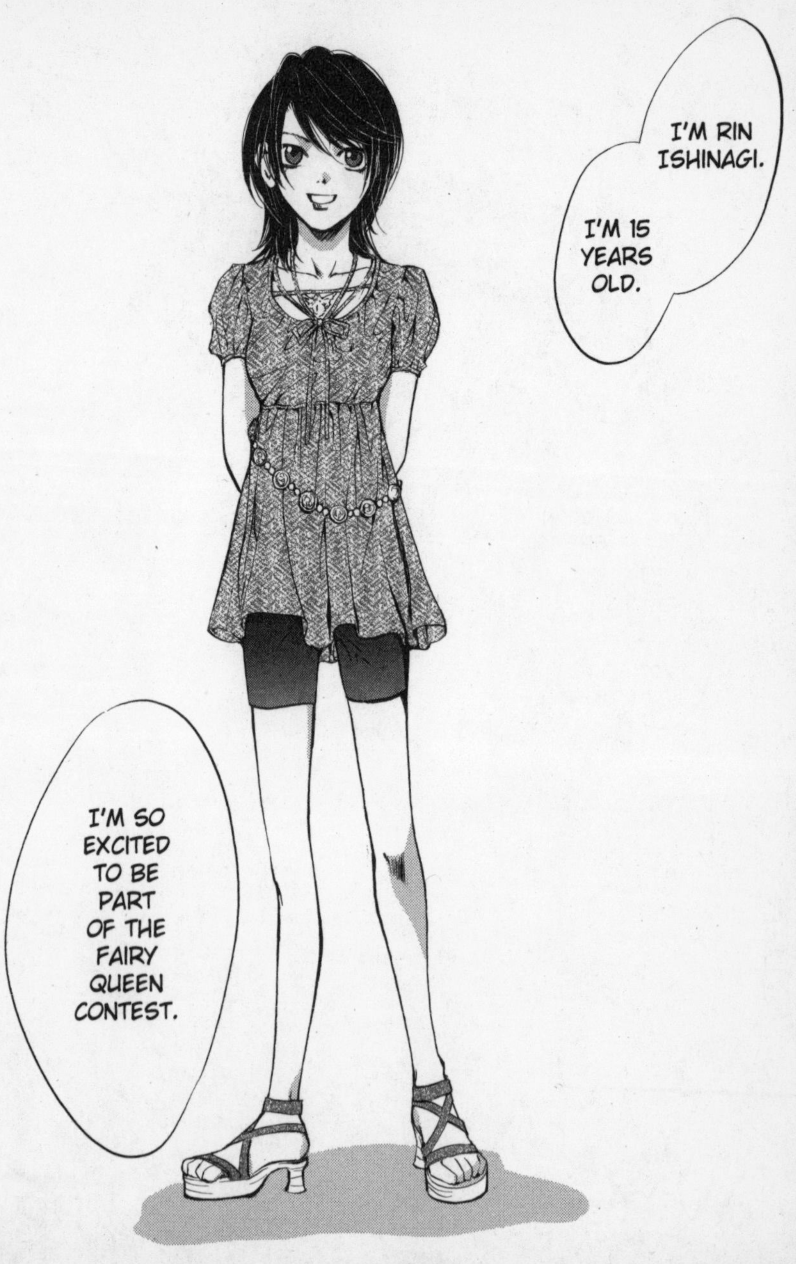
I'M RIN ISHINAGI.
I'M 15 YEARS OLD.
I'M SO EXCITED TO BE PART OF THE FAIRY QUEEN CONTEST.

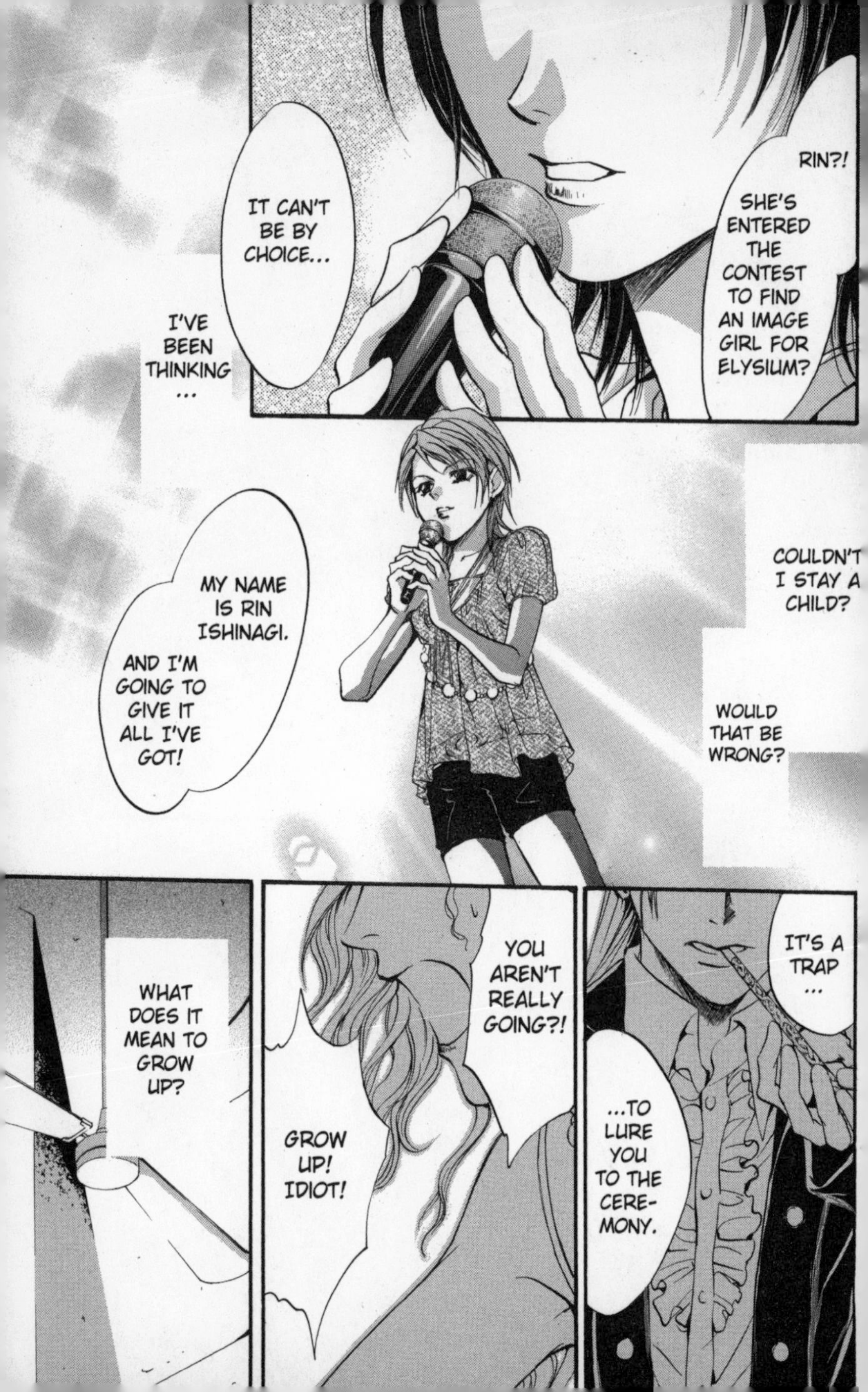
RIN?!
SHE'S ENTERED THE CONTEST TO FIND AN IMAGE GIRL FOR ELYSIUM?
IT CAN'T BE BY CHOICE...
I'VE BEEN THINKING...
COULDN'T I STAY A CHILD?
MY NAME IS RIN ISHINAGI.
AND I'M GOING TO GIVE IT ALL I'VE GOT!
WOULD THAT BE WRONG?
IT'S A TRAP...
...TO LURE YOU TO THE CEREMONY.
YOU AREN'T REALLY GOING?!
GROW UP! IDIOT!
WHAT DOES IT MEAN TO GROW UP?

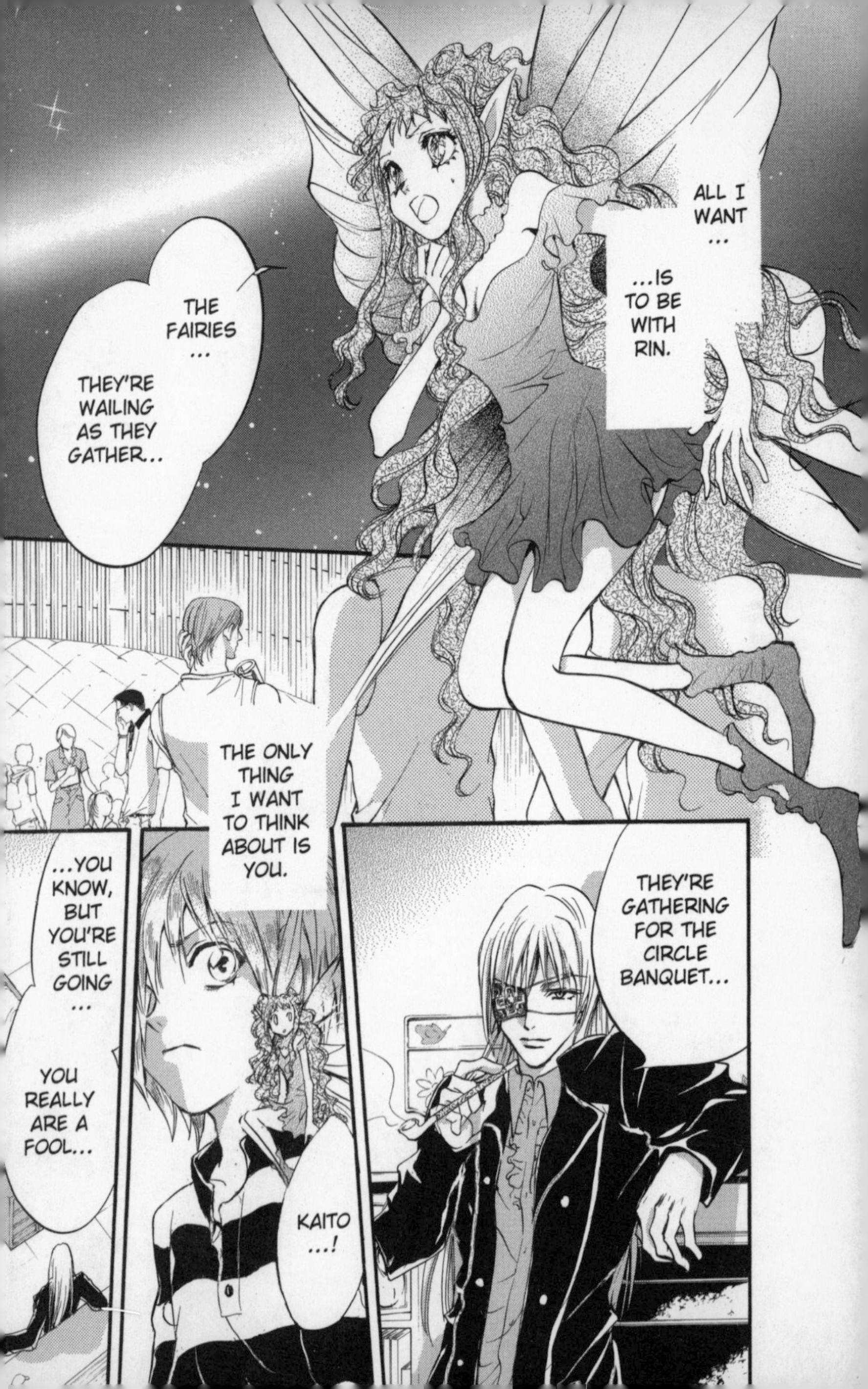
ALL I WANT...
...IS TO BE WITH RIN.
THE FAIRIES... THEY'RE WAILING AS THEY GATHER...
THE ONLY THING I WANT TO THINK ABOUT IS YOU.
THEY'RE GATHERING FOR THE CIRCLE BANQUET...
KAITO...!
...YOU KNOW, BUT YOU'RE STILL GOING... YOU REALLY ARE A FOOL...

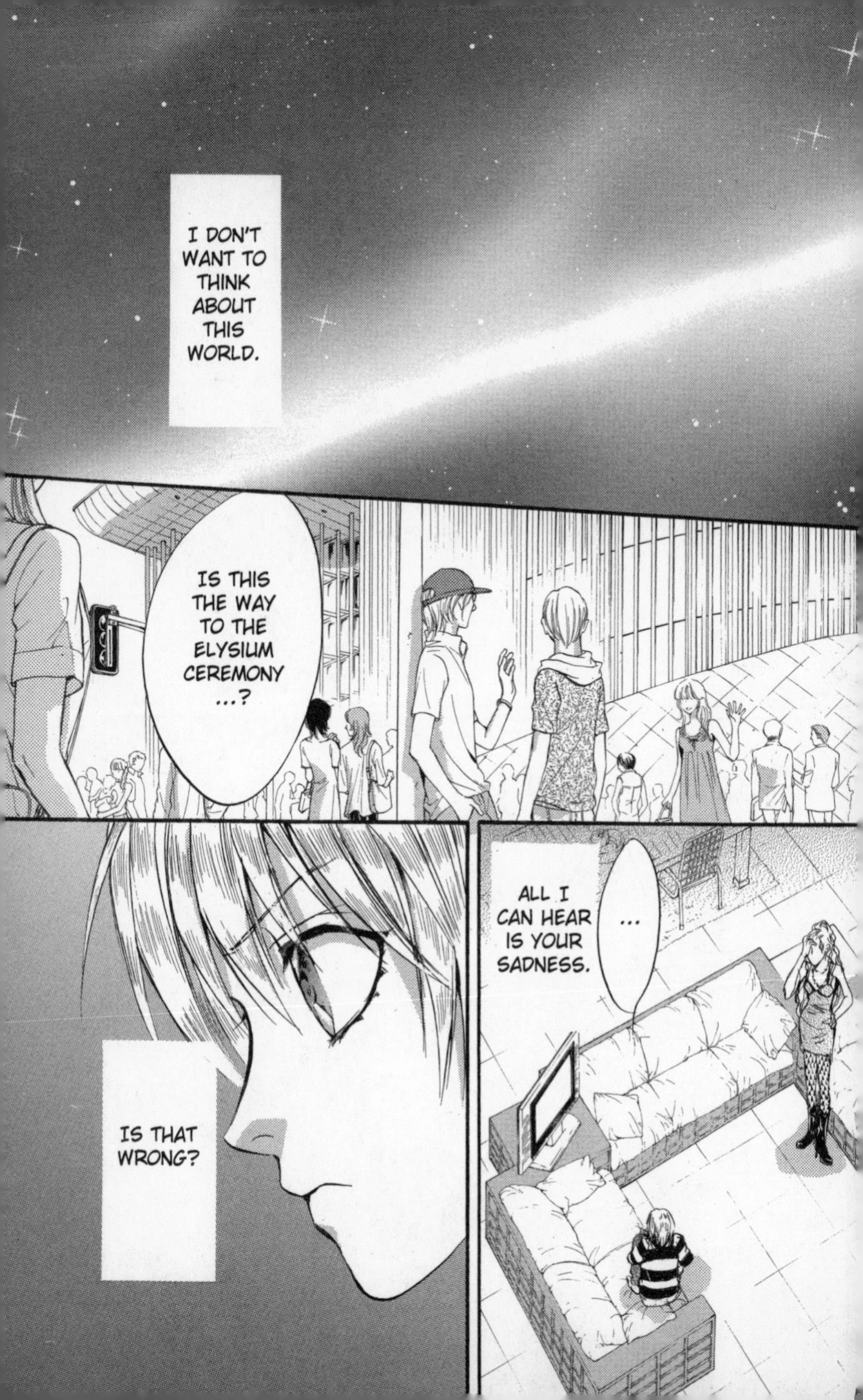
I DON'T WANT TO THINK ABOUT THIS WORLD.
IS THIS THE WAY TO THE ELYSIUM CEREMONY ...?
...
ALL I CAN HEAR IS YOUR SADNESS.
IS THAT WRONG?

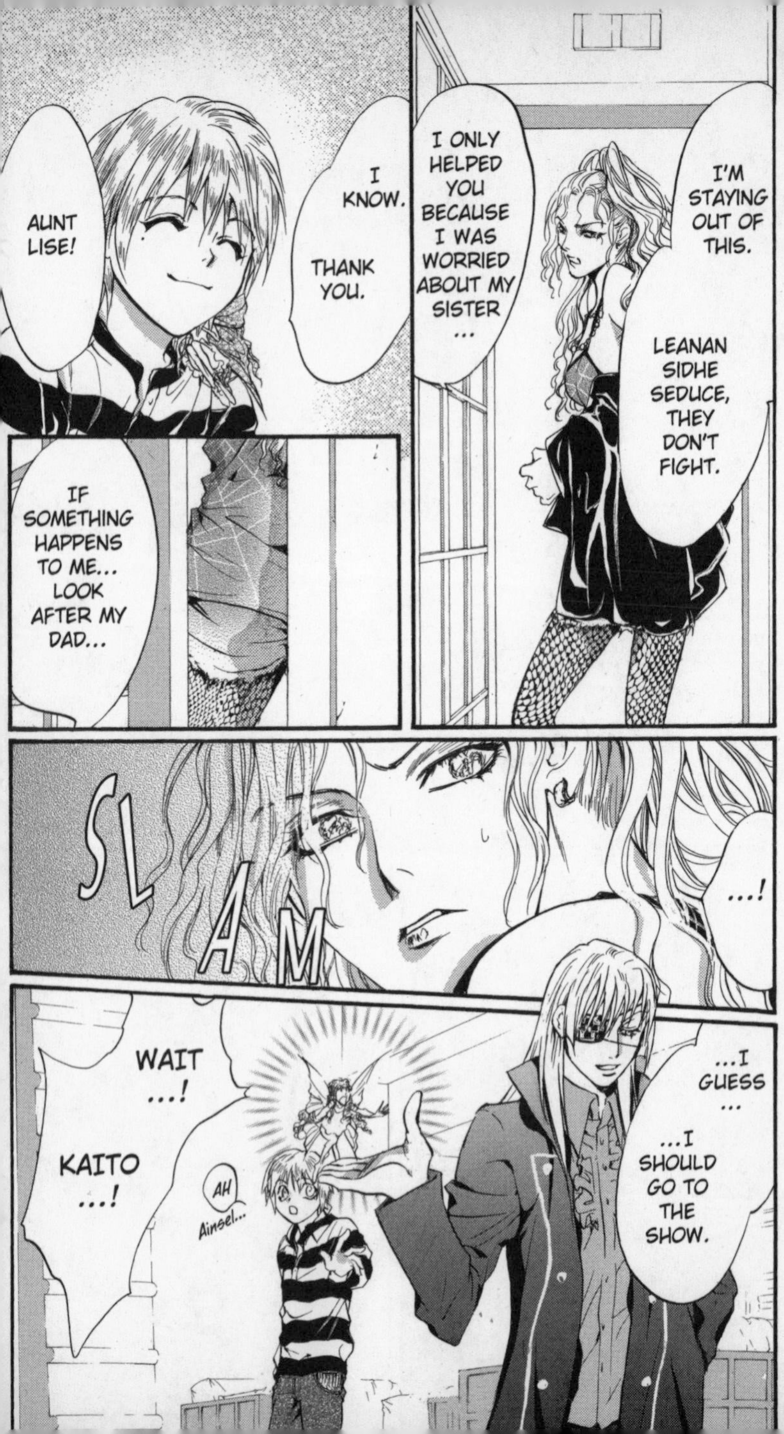
I'M STAYING OUT OF THIS.
LEANAN SIDHE SEDUCE, THEY DON'T FIGHT.
I ONLY HELPED YOU BECAUSE I WAS WORRIED ABOUT MY SISTER...
I KNOW.
THANK YOU.
AUNT LISE!
IF SOMETHING HAPPENS TO ME... LOOK AFTER MY DAD...
...!
SLAM
...I GUESS...
...I SHOULD GO TO THE SHOW.
AH
Ainsel...
WAIT...!
KAITO...!

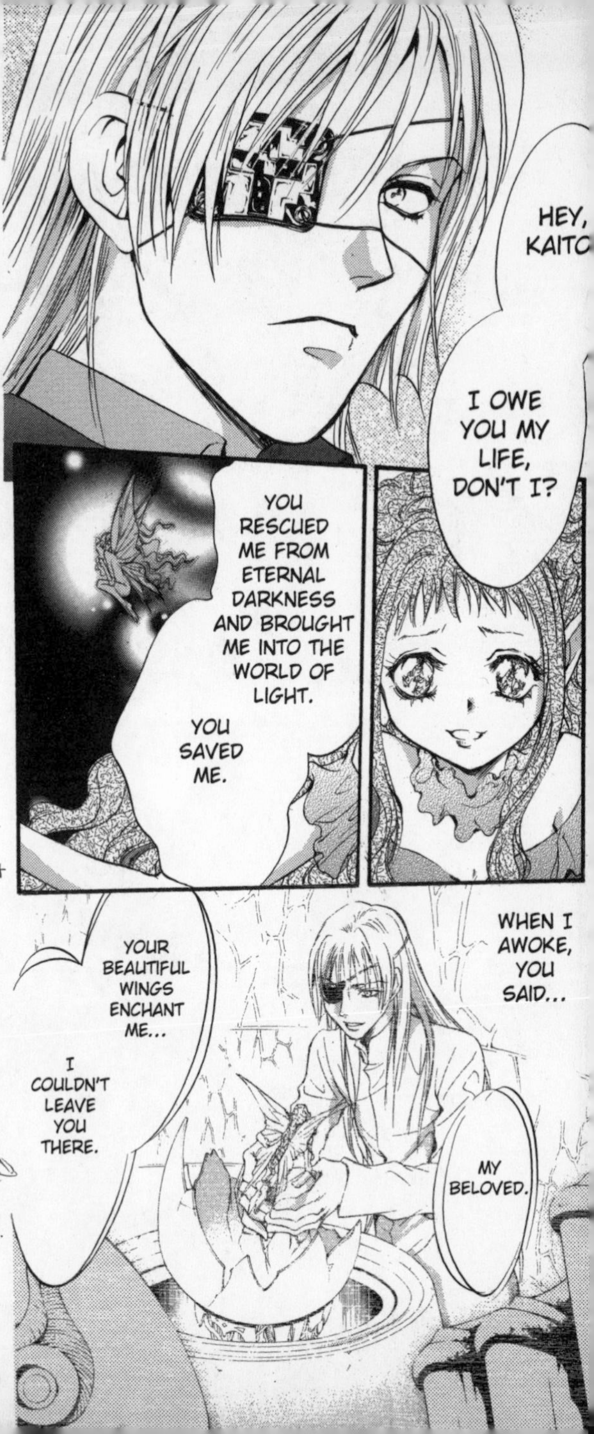
HEY, KAITO
I OWE YOU MY LIFE, DON'T I?
YOU RESCUED ME FROM ETERNAL DARKNESS AND BROUGHT ME INTO THE WORLD OF LIGHT.
YOU SAVED ME.
WHEN I AWOKE, YOU SAID...
MY BELOVED.
YOUR BEAUTIFUL WINGS ENCHANT ME...
I COULDN'T LEAVE YOU THERE.

Fairy Cube Volume Three The conclusion.

It was pretty difficult but I finished it. I hope you enjoy it.

I read that there have been more crop circles appearing in the U.K. recently.

Lots of people think that humans are making them, but it's only been proved in some cases. It's still a mystery.

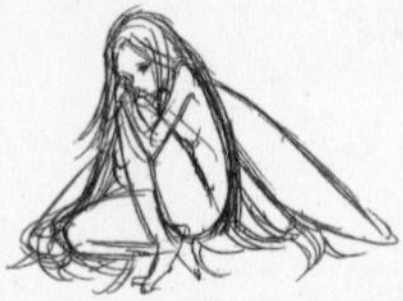

The fairy, Lumica.

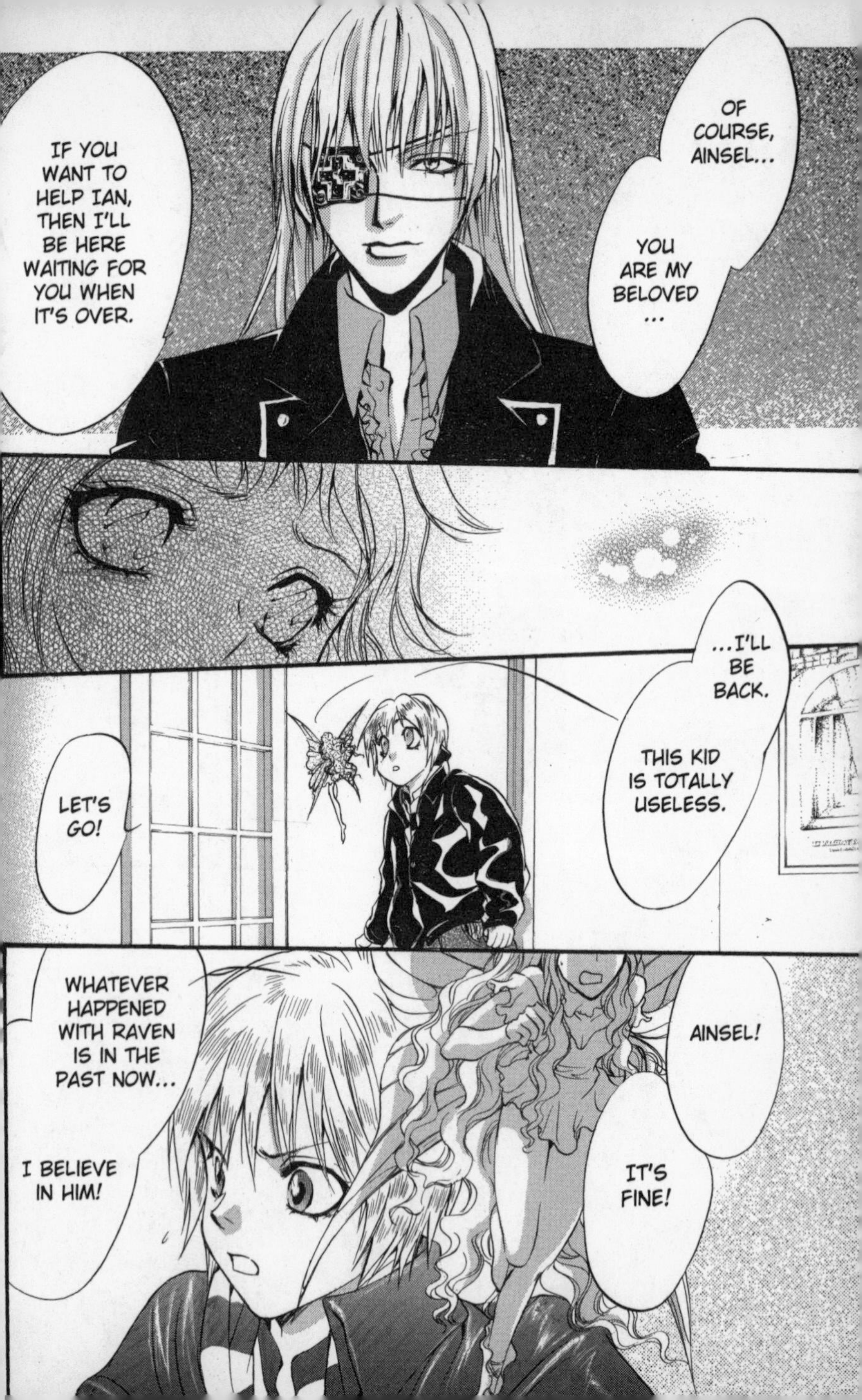
OF COURSE, AINSEL...
YOU ARE MY BELOVED ...
IF YOU WANT TO HELP IAN, THEN I'LL BE HERE WAITING FOR YOU WHEN IT'S OVER.
...I'LL BE BACK.
THIS KID IS TOTALLY USELESS.
LET'S GO!
AINSEL!
IT'S FINE!
WHATEVER HAPPENED WITH RAVEN IS IN THE PAST NOW...
I BELIEVE IN HIM!

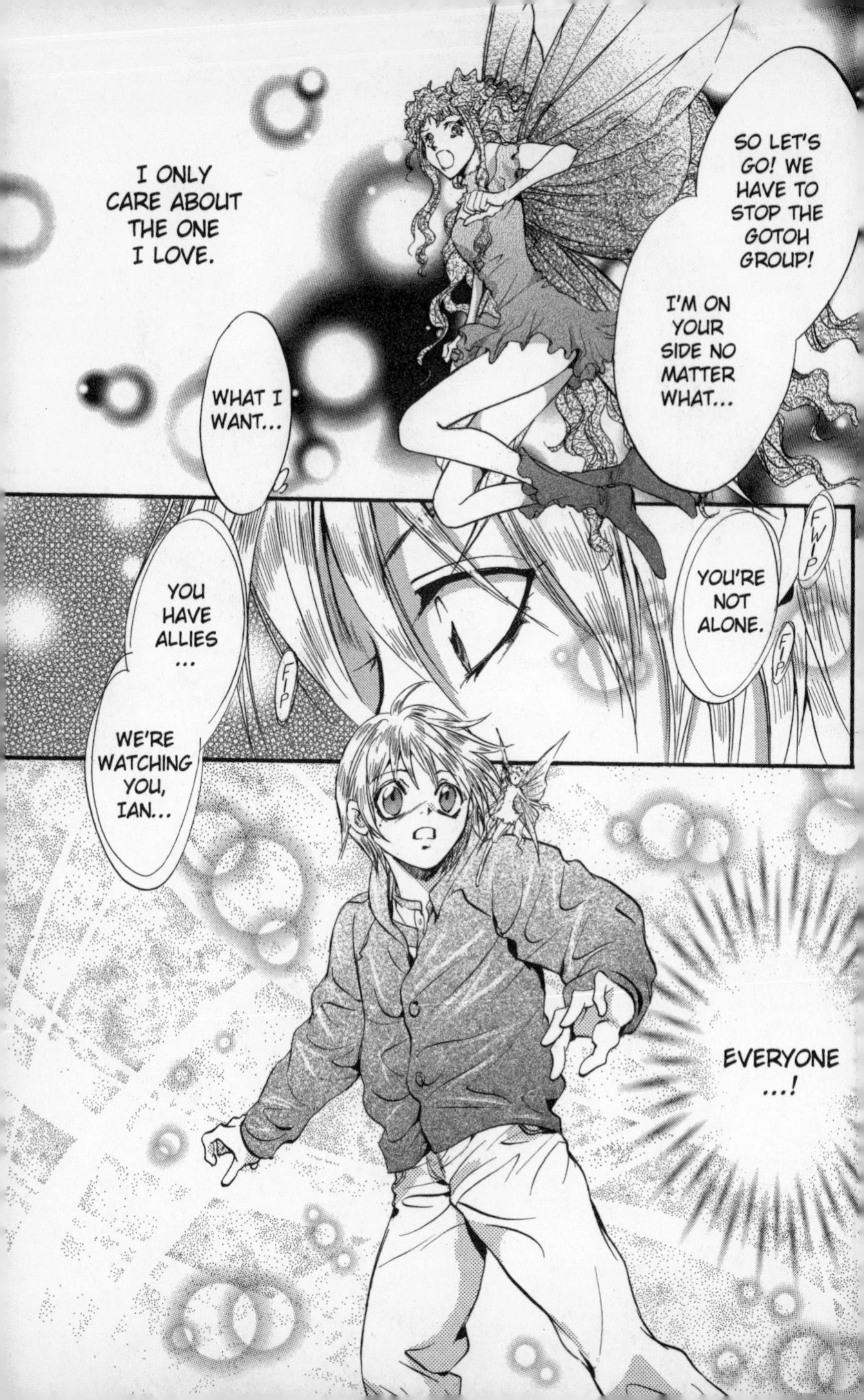
SO LET'S GO! WE HAVE TO STOP THE GOTOH GROUP!
I'M ON YOUR SIDE NO MATTER WHAT...
I ONLY CARE ABOUT THE ONE I LOVE.
WHAT I WANT...
FWIP
YOU'RE NOT ALONE.
FIP
YOU HAVE ALLIES...
FIP
WE'RE WATCHING YOU, IAN...
EVERYONE...!

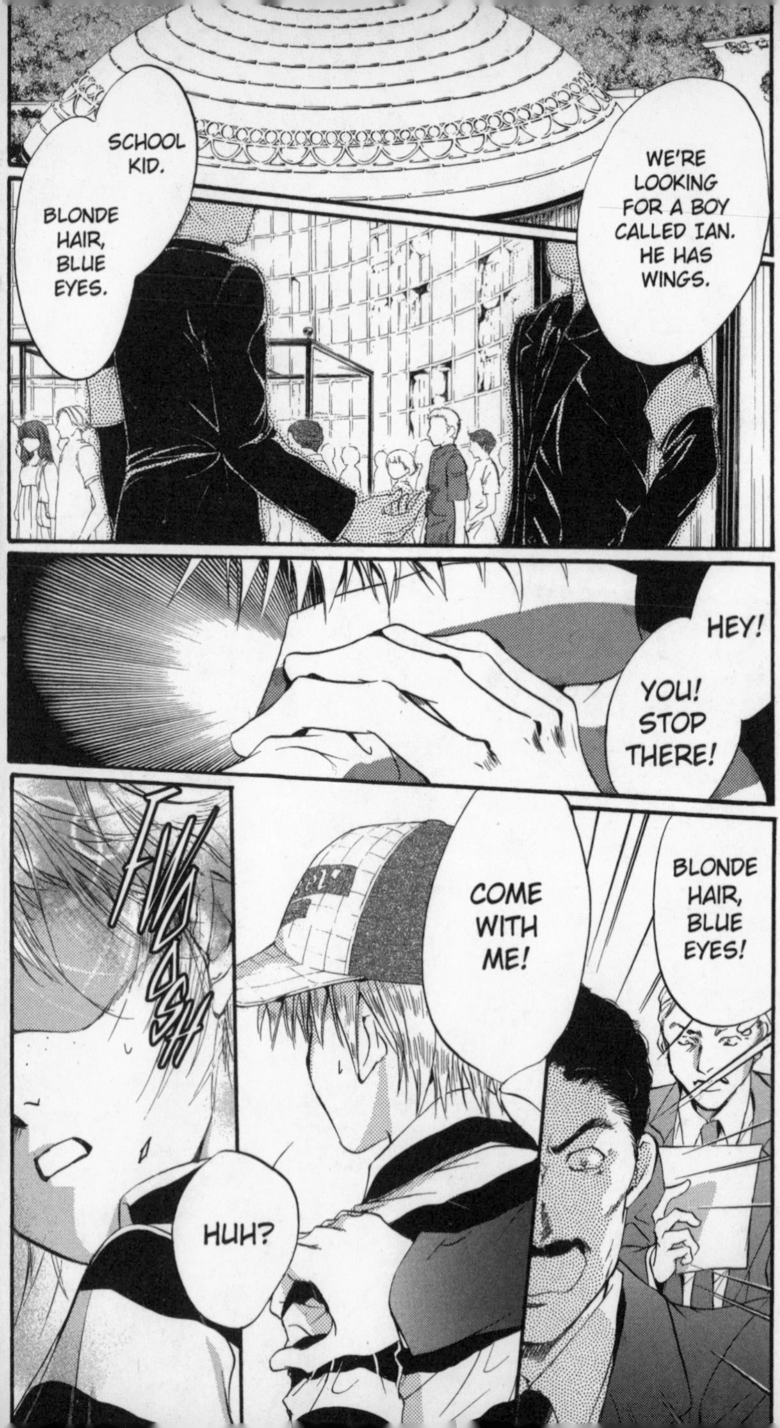
WE'RE LOOKING FOR A BOY CALLED IAN. HE HAS WINGS.
SCHOOL KID.
BLONDE HAIR, BLUE EYES.
HEY!
YOU! STOP THERE!
BLONDE HAIR, BLUE EYES!
COME WITH ME!
FWOOSH
HUH?

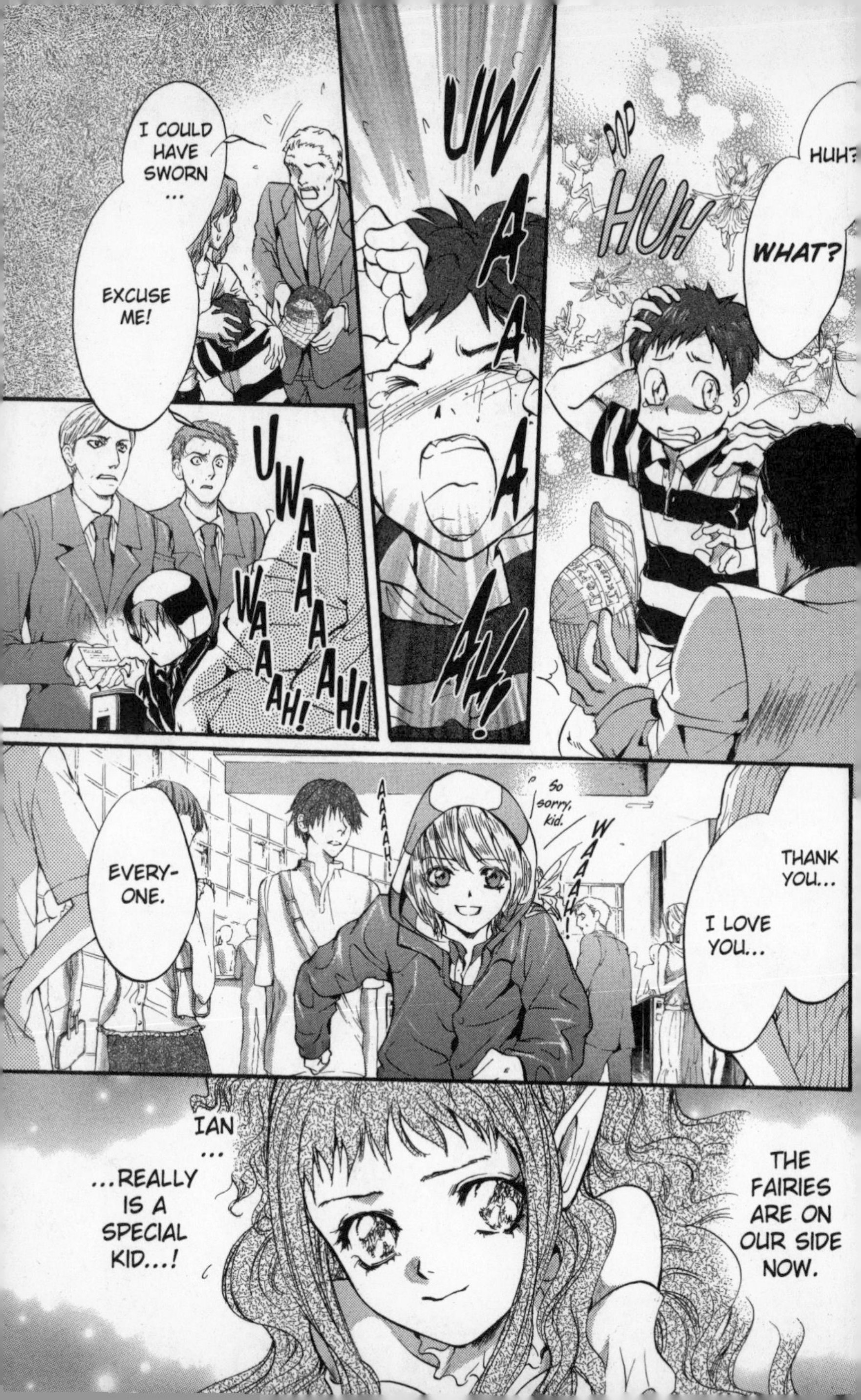
HUH?
WHAT?
POP
HUH
UWAAAAAH!
I COULD HAVE SWORN...
EXCUSE ME!
UWAAAAAH!
WAAAAH!
THANK YOU...
I LOVE YOU...
So sorry, kid.
WAAAAH!
AAAAH!
EVERY-ONE.
THE FAIRIES ARE ON OUR SIDE NOW.
IAN...
...REALLY IS A SPECIAL KID...!

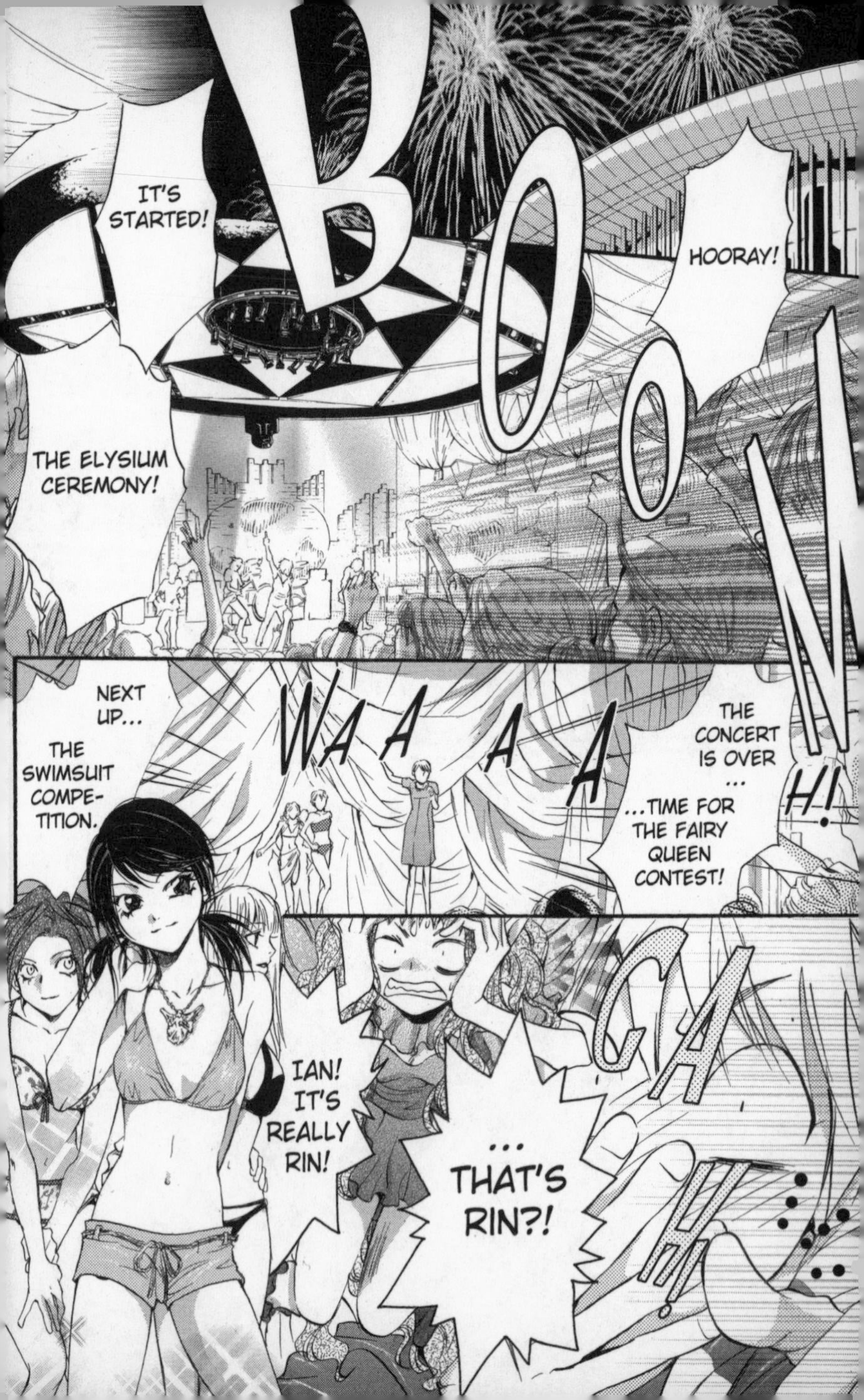
HOORAY!
IT'S STARTED!
THE ELYSIUM CEREMONY!
WAAAAH!
THE CONCERT IS OVER ...
...TIME FOR THE FAIRY QUEEN CONTEST!
NEXT UP...
THE SWIMSUIT COMPETITION.
... THAT'S RIN?!
IAN! IT'S REALLY RIN!

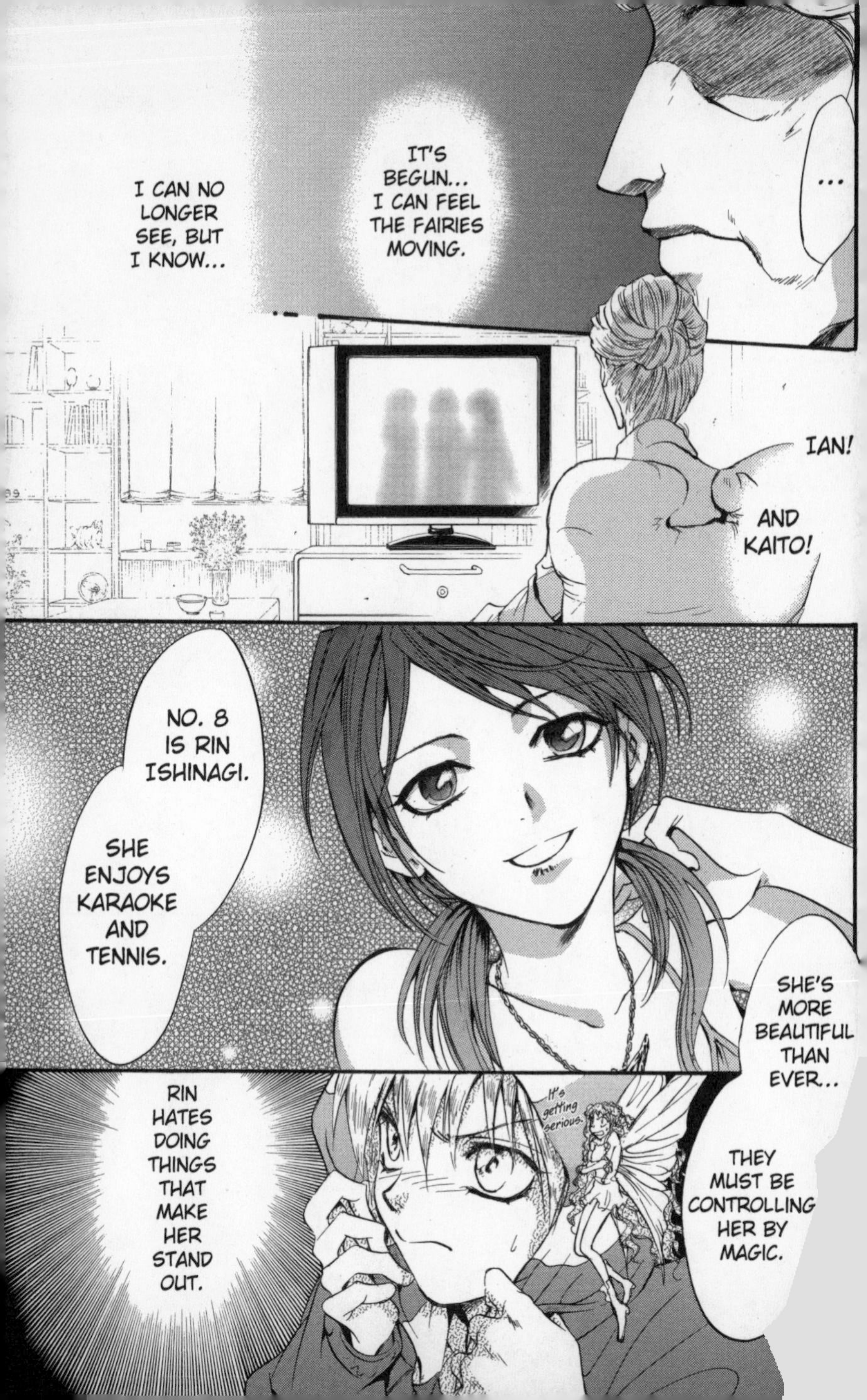
...
IT'S BEGUN... I CAN FEEL THE FAIRIES MOVING.
I CAN NO LONGER SEE, BUT I KNOW...
IAN!
AND KAITO!
NO. 8 IS RIN ISHINAGI.
SHE ENJOYS KARAOKE AND TENNIS.
SHE'S MORE BEAUTIFUL THAN EVER...
THEY MUST BE CONTROLLING HER BY MAGIC.
It's getting serious.
RIN HATES DOING THINGS THAT MAKE HER STAND OUT.

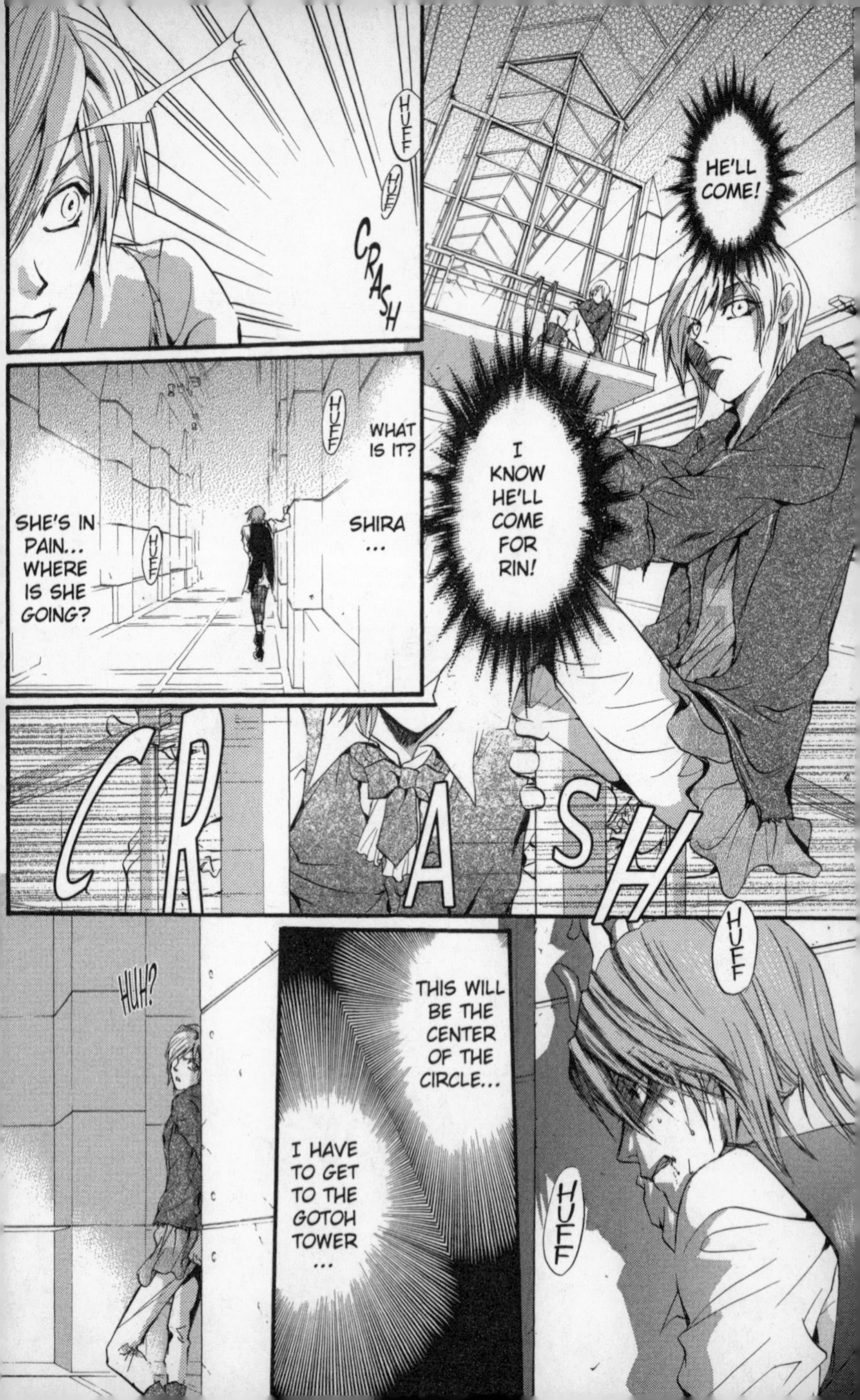
HE'LL COME!
I KNOW HE'LL COME FOR RIN!
HUFF
HUFF
CRASH
HUFF
WHAT IS IT?
SHIRA...
HUFF
SHE'S IN PAIN... WHERE IS SHE GOING?
CRASH
HUFF
HUFF
THIS WILL BE THE CENTER OF THE CIRCLE...
I HAVE TO GET TO THE GOTOH TOWER...
HUH?

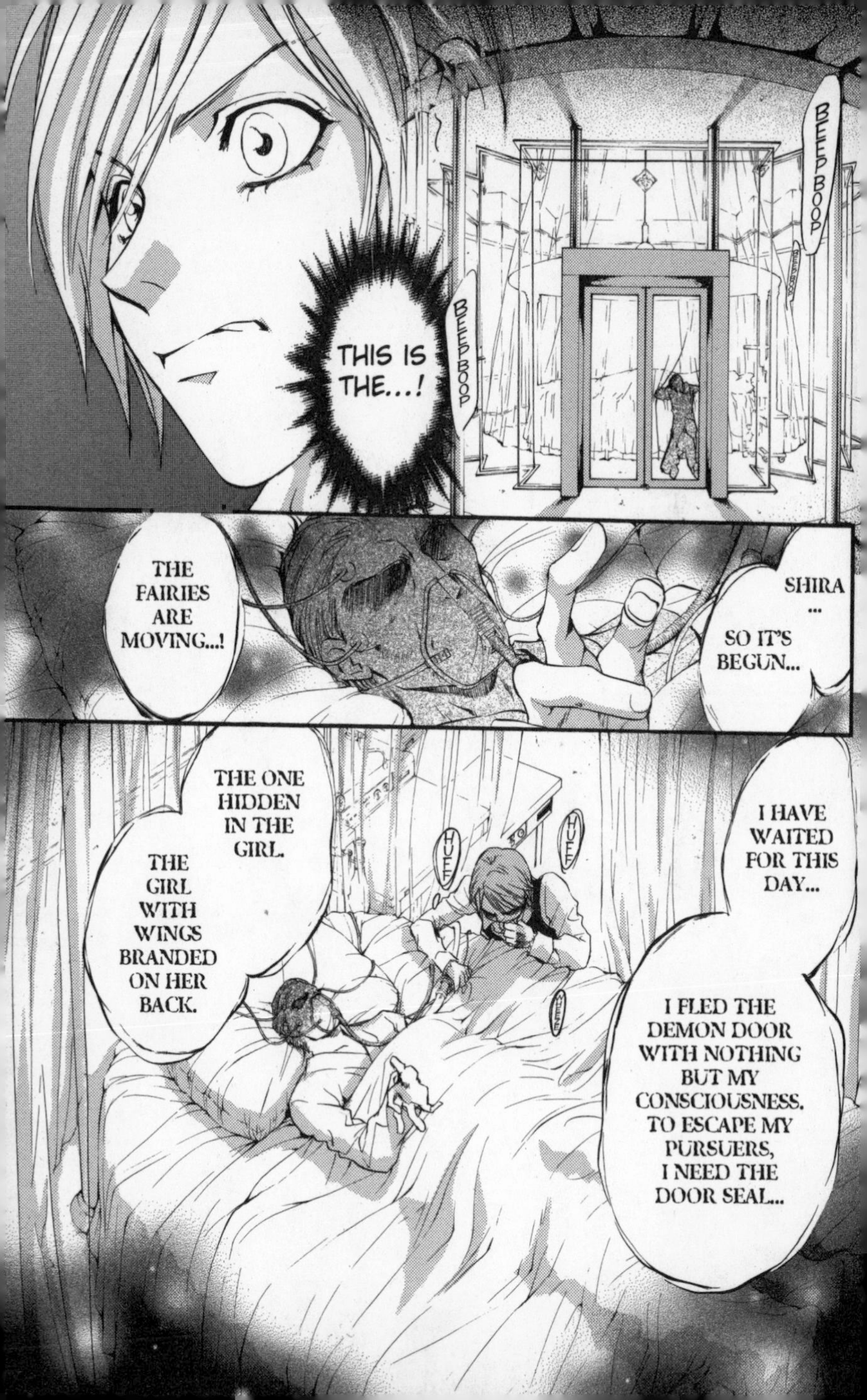
BEEP BOOP
BEEP BOOP
THIS IS THE...!
SHIRA ... SO IT'S BEGUN...
THE FAIRIES ARE MOVING...!
I HAVE WAITED FOR THIS DAY...
I FLED THE DEMON DOOR WITH NOTHING BUT MY CONSCIOUSNESS. TO ESCAPE MY PURSUERS, I NEED THE DOOR SEAL...
HUFF
HUFF
THE ONE HIDDEN IN THE GIRL.
THE GIRL WITH WINGS BRANDED ON HER BACK.

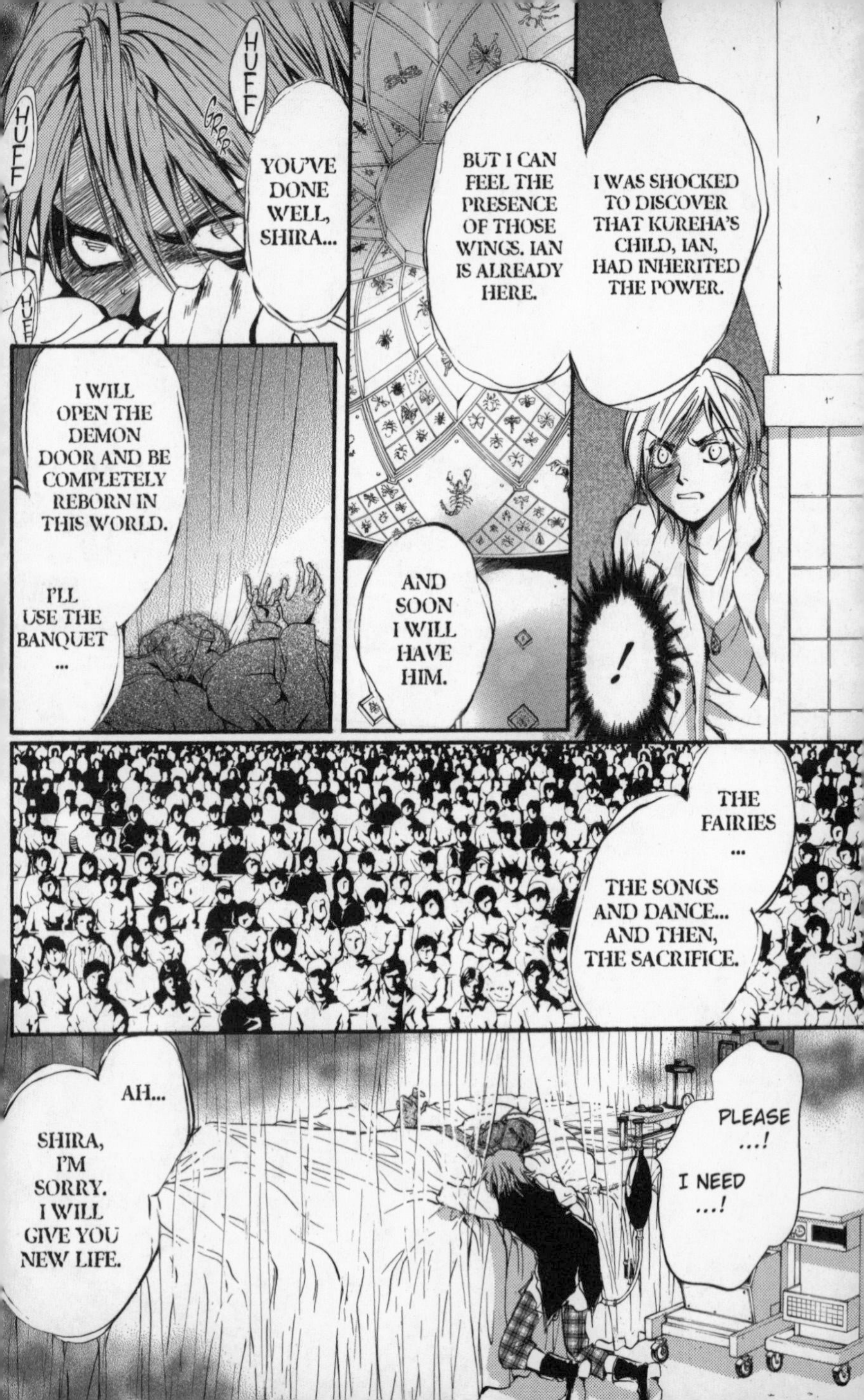
I WAS SHOCKED TO DISCOVER THAT KUREHA'S CHILD, IAN, HAD INHERITED THE POWER.
BUT I CAN FEEL THE PRESENCE OF THOSE WINGS. IAN IS ALREADY HERE.
AND SOON I WILL HAVE HIM.
!
HUFF HUFF
GRRR
HUFF HUFF
HUFF
YOU'VE DONE WELL, SHIRA...
I WILL OPEN THE DEMON DOOR AND BE COMPLETELY REBORN IN THIS WORLD.
I'LL USE THE BANQUET ...
THE FAIRIES ...
THE SONGS AND DANCE... AND THEN, THE SACRIFICE.
PLEASE ...!
I NEED ...!
AH...
SHIRA, I'M SORRY. I WILL GIVE YOU NEW LIFE.

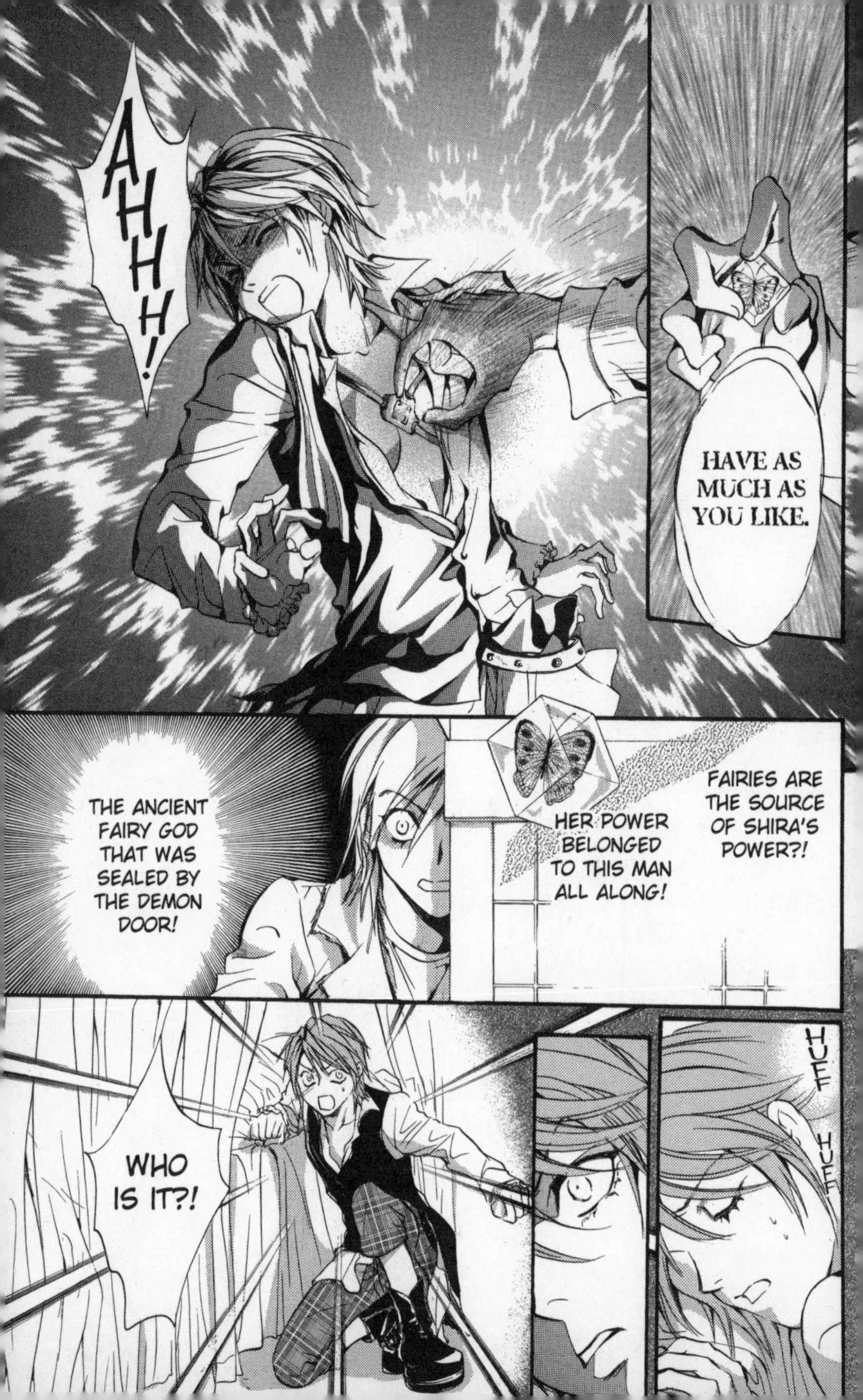
HAVE AS MUCH AS YOU LIKE.
AHHH!
FAIRIES ARE THE SOURCE OF SHIRA'S POWER?!
HER POWER BELONGED TO THIS MAN ALL ALONG!
THE ANCIENT FAIRY GOD THAT WAS SEALED BY THE DEMON DOOR!
HUFF
HUFF
WHO IS IT?!

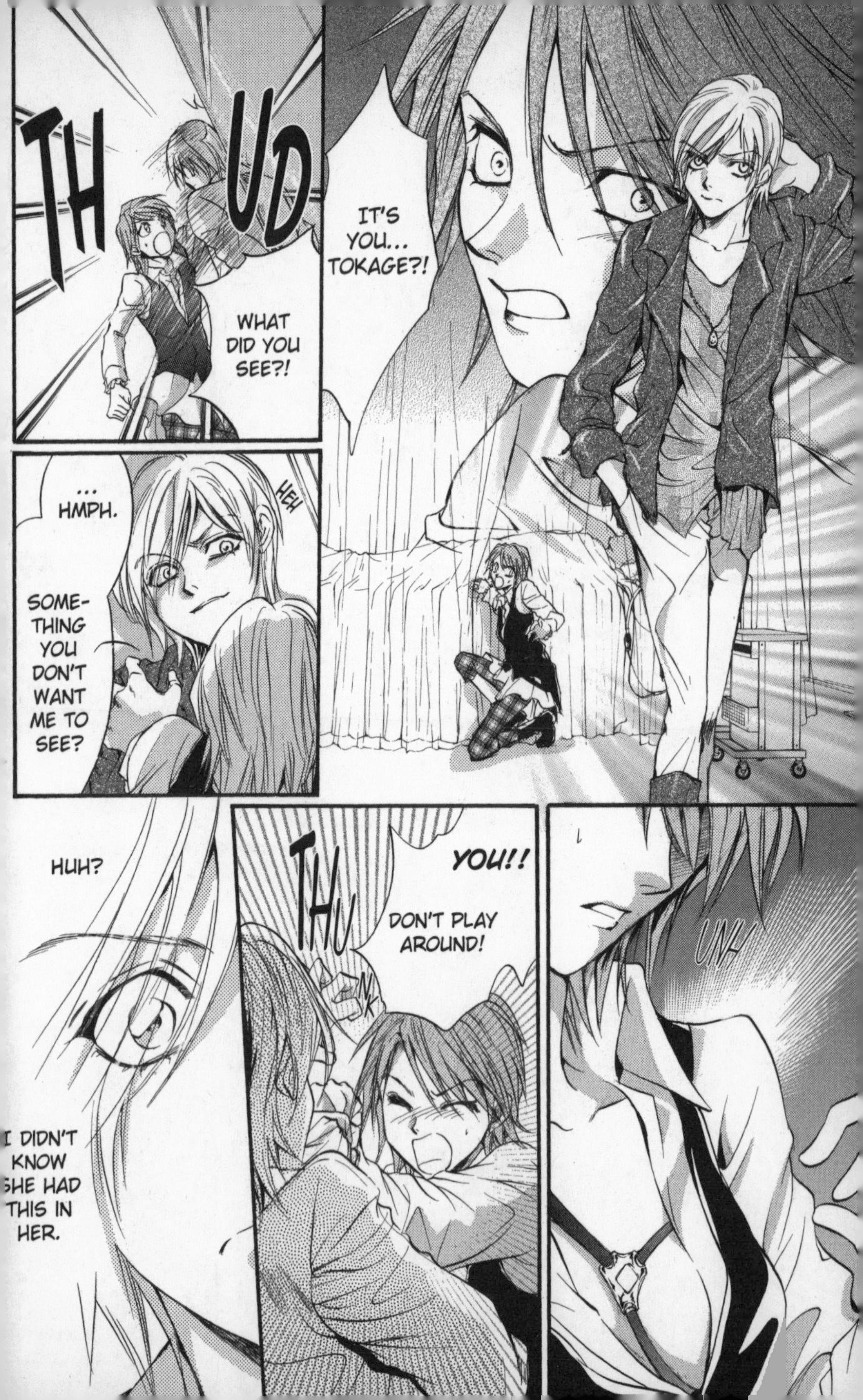
IT'S YOU... TOKAGE?!
THUD
WHAT DID YOU SEE?!
... HMPH.
HEH
SOME-THING YOU DON'T WANT ME TO SEE?
UNH
YOU!!
THUNK
DON'T PLAY AROUND!
HUH?
I DIDN'T KNOW SHE HAD THIS IN HER.

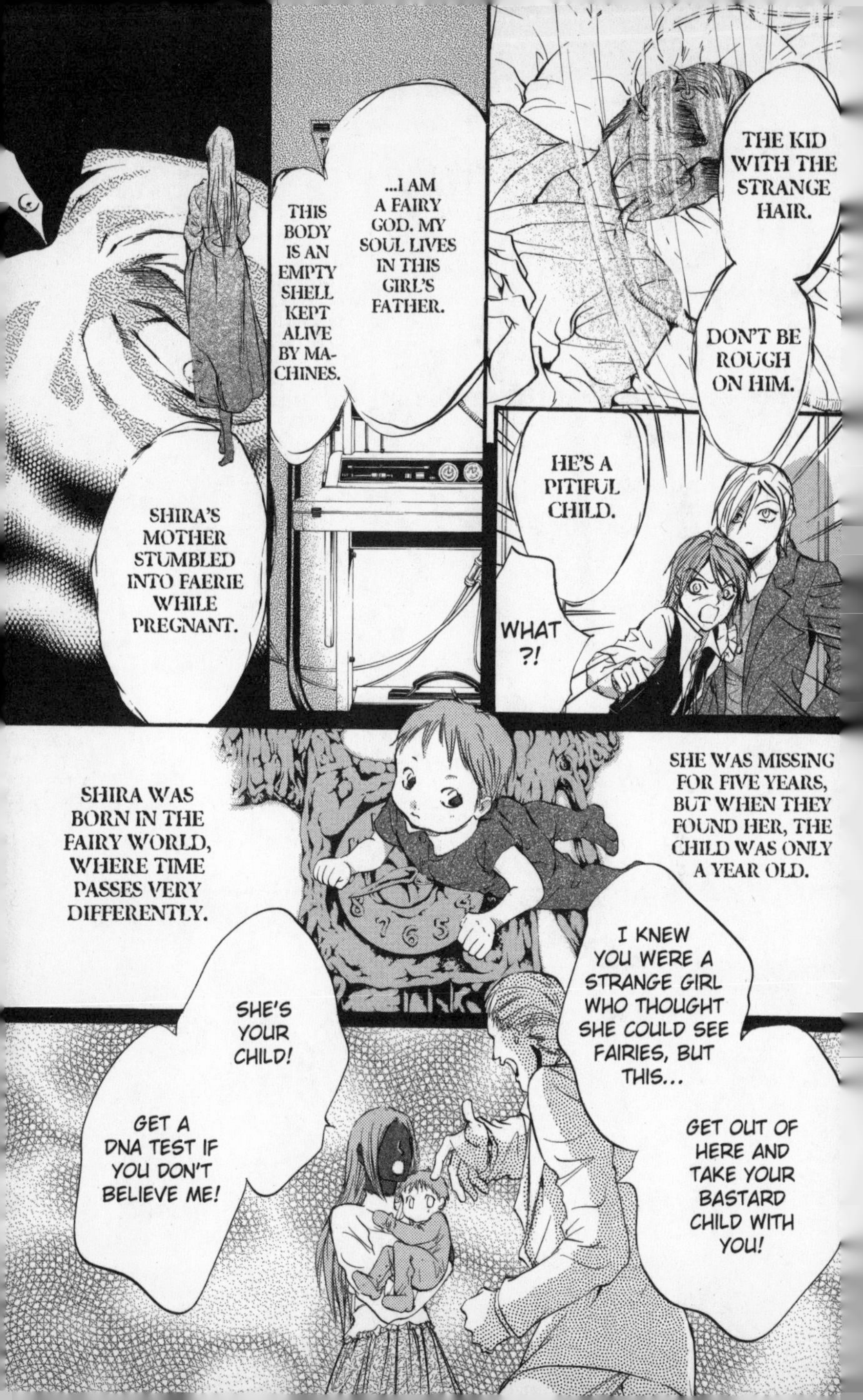
THE KID WITH THE STRANGE HAIR.
DON'T BE ROUGH ON HIM.
HE'S A PITIFUL CHILD.
WHAT?!
...I AM A FAIRY GOD. MY SOUL LIVES IN THIS GIRL'S FATHER.
THIS BODY IS AN EMPTY SHELL KEPT ALIVE BY MA-CHINES.
SHIRA'S MOTHER STUMBLED INTO FAERIE WHILE PREGNANT.
SHE WAS MISSING FOR FIVE YEARS, BUT WHEN THEY FOUND HER, THE CHILD WAS ONLY A YEAR OLD.
SHIRA WAS BORN IN THE FAIRY WORLD, WHERE TIME PASSES VERY DIFFERENTLY.
I KNEW YOU WERE A STRANGE GIRL WHO THOUGHT SHE COULD SEE FAIRIES, BUT THIS...
GET OUT OF HERE AND TAKE YOUR BASTARD CHILD WITH YOU!
SHE'S YOUR CHILD!
GET A DNA TEST IF YOU DON'T BELIEVE ME!

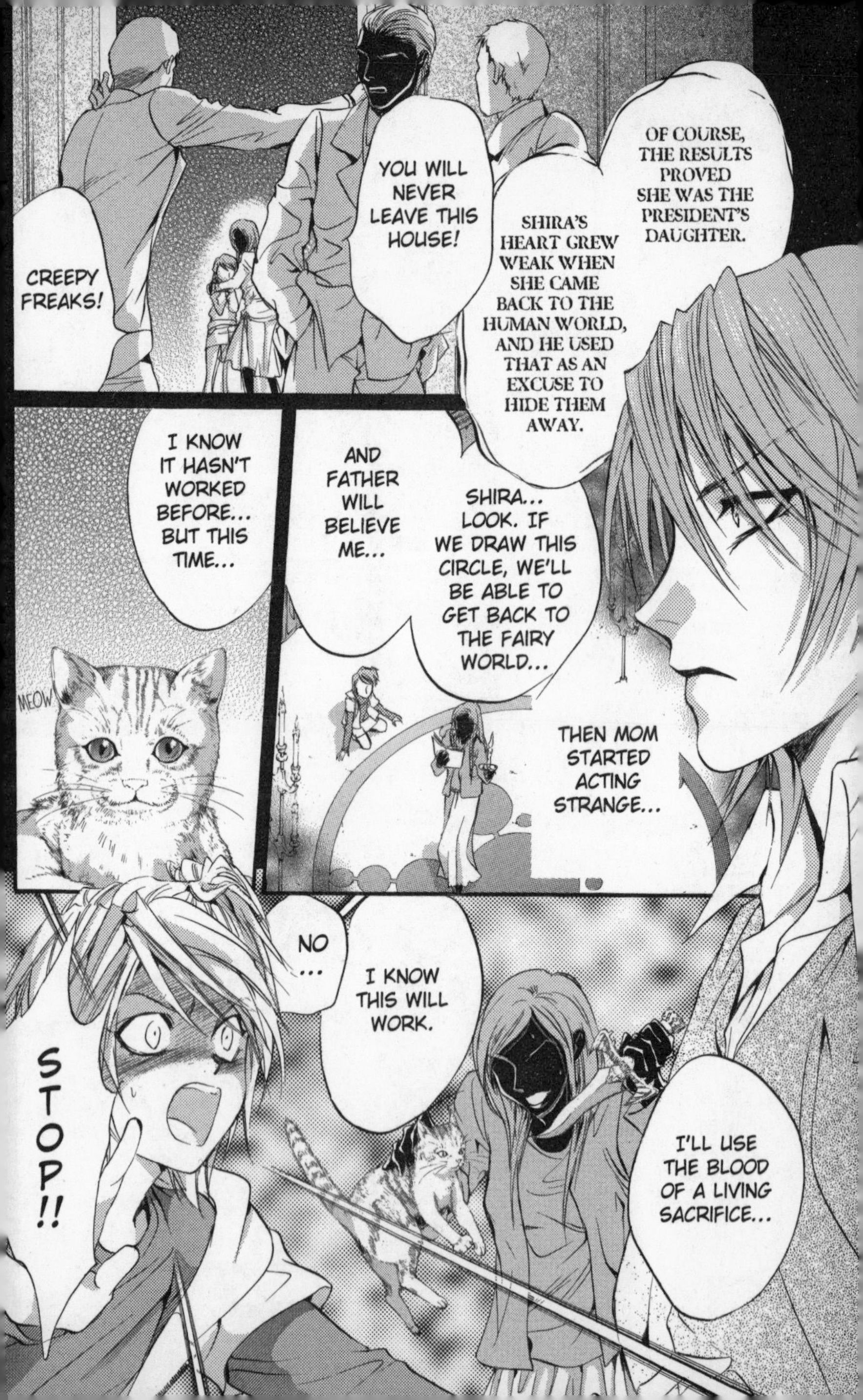
OF COURSE, THE RESULTS PROVED SHE WAS THE PRESIDENT'S DAUGHTER.
SHIRA'S HEART GREW WEAK WHEN SHE CAME BACK TO THE HUMAN WORLD, AND HE USED THAT AS AN EXCUSE TO HIDE THEM AWAY.
YOU WILL NEVER LEAVE THIS HOUSE!
CREEPY FREAKS!
THEN MOM STARTED ACTING STRANGE...
SHIRA... LOOK. IF WE DRAW THIS CIRCLE, WE'LL BE ABLE TO GET BACK TO THE FAIRY WORLD...
AND FATHER WILL BELIEVE ME...
I KNOW IT HASN'T WORKED BEFORE... BUT THIS TIME...
MEOW
I'LL USE THE BLOOD OF A LIVING SACRIFICE...
I KNOW THIS WILL WORK.
NO...
STOP!!

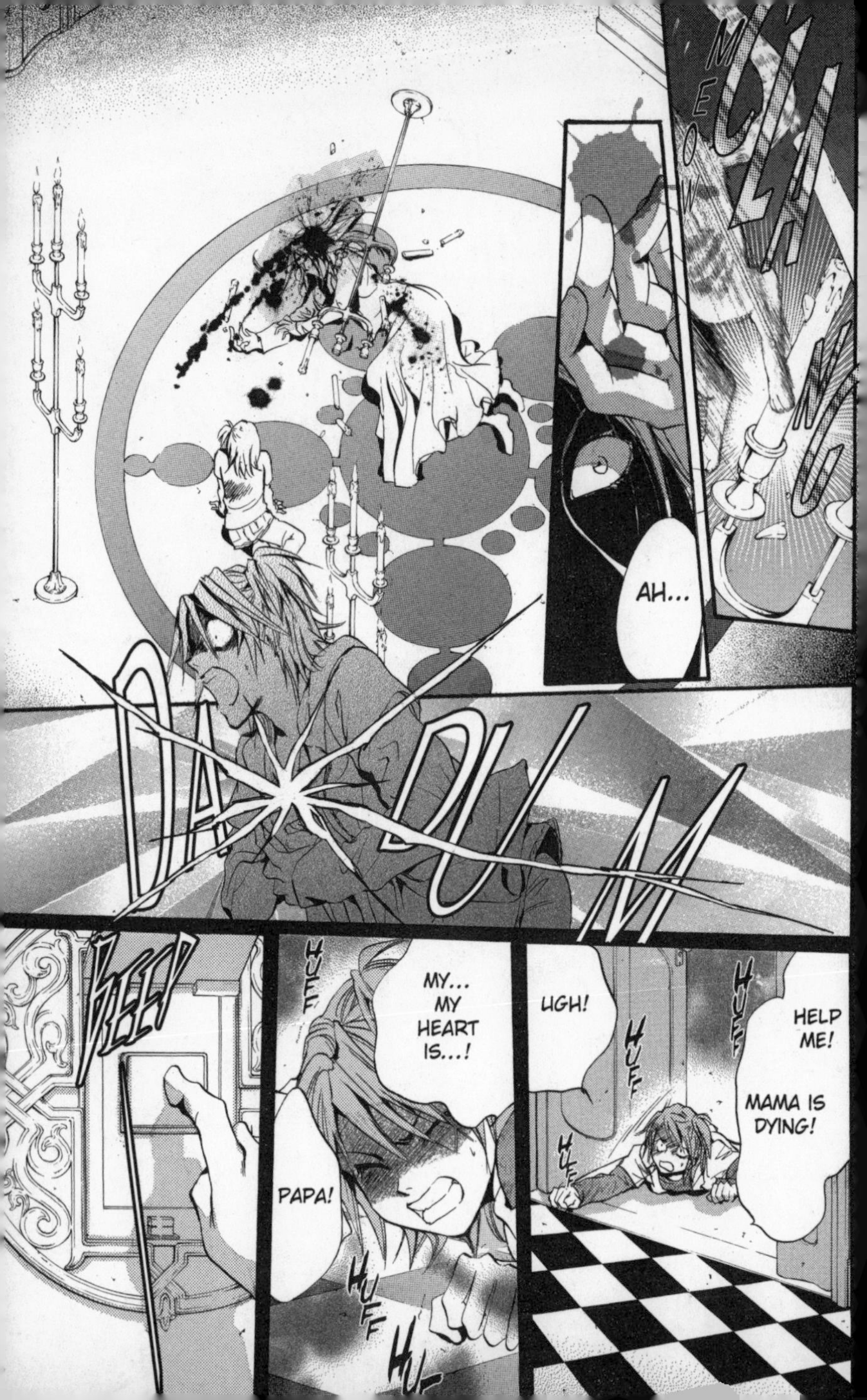
CLANG
MEOW
AH...
DA-DUM
HUFF
HELP ME!
MAMA IS DYING!
UGH!
HUFF
HUFF
MY... MY HEART IS...!
HUFF
PAPA!
HUFF
HU-
BEEP

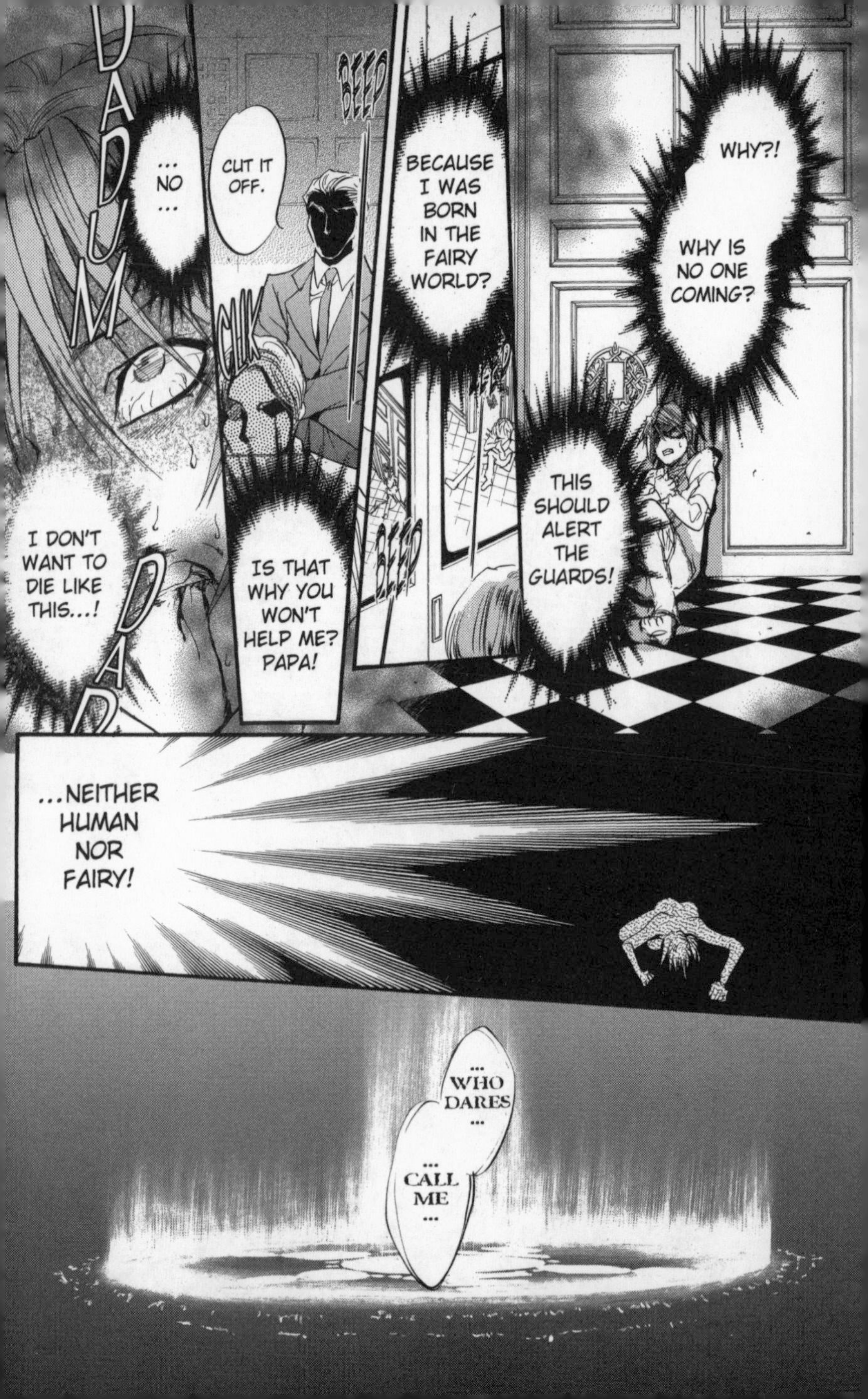
WHY?!
WHY IS NO ONE COMING?
THIS SHOULD ALERT THE GUARDS!
BEEP
BECAUSE I WAS BORN IN THE FAIRY WORLD?
BEEP
CUT IT OFF.
CLIK
IS THAT WHY YOU WON'T HELP ME? PAPA!
DADUM
... NO ...
I DON'T WANT TO DIE LIKE THIS...!
...NEITHER HUMAN NOR FAIRY!
... WHO DARES ...
... CALL ME ...

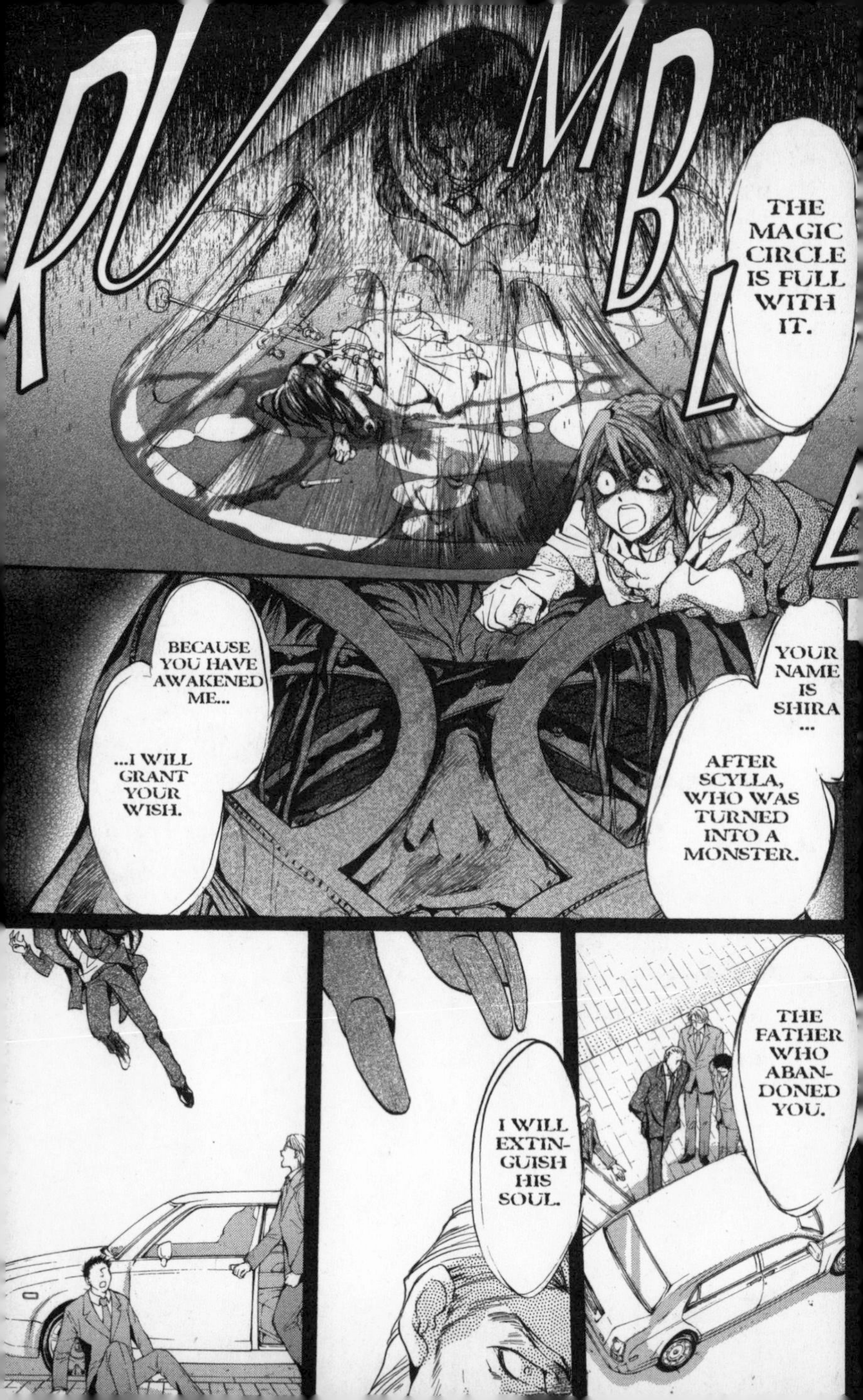
RUMBLE
THE MAGIC CIRCLE IS FULL WITH IT.
YOUR NAME IS SHIRA...
AFTER SCYLLA, WHO WAS TURNED INTO A MONSTER.
BECAUSE YOU HAVE AWAKENED ME...
...I WILL GRANT YOUR WISH.
THE FATHER WHO ABANDONED YOU.
I WILL EXTINGUISH HIS SOUL.

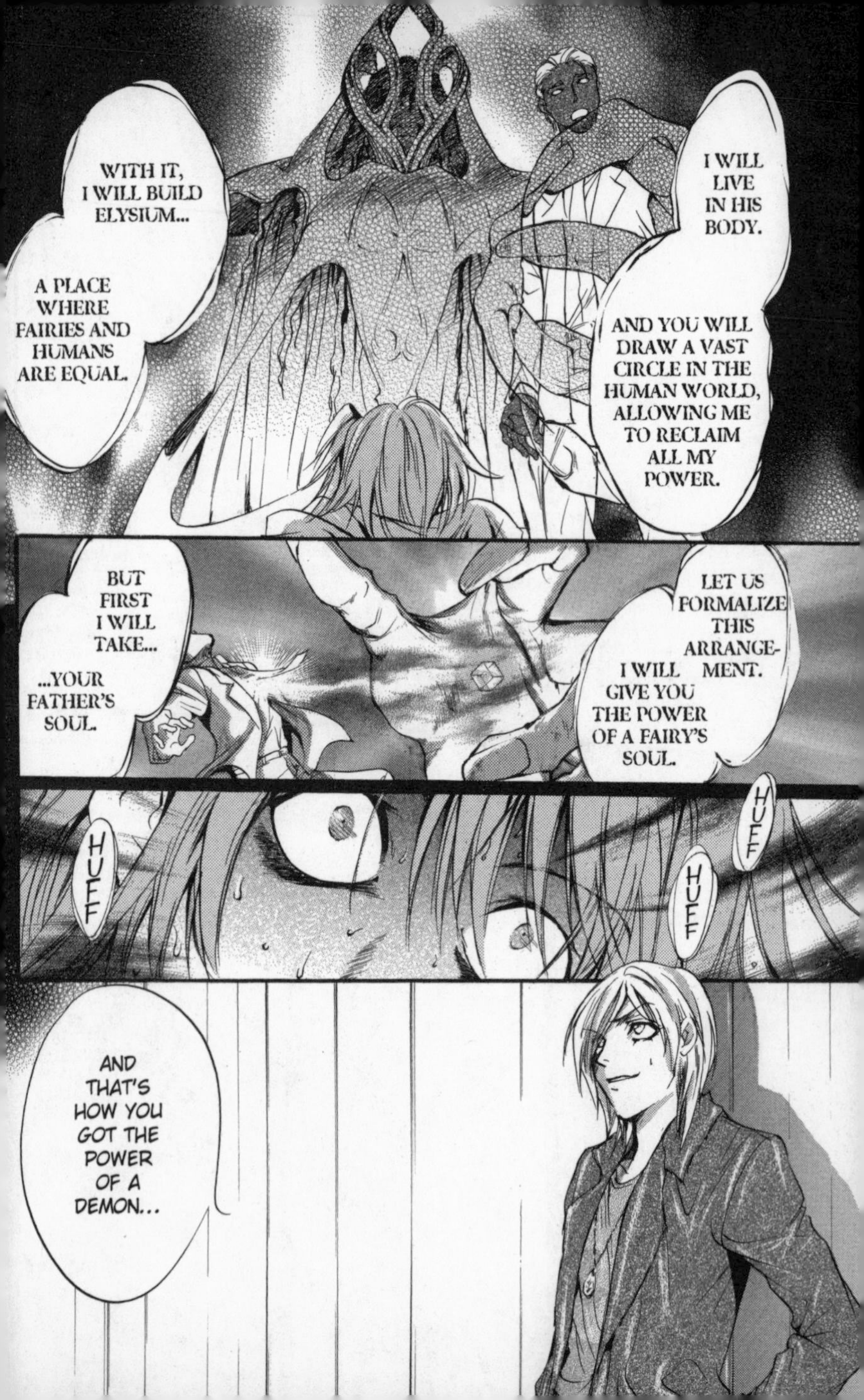
I WILL LIVE IN HIS BODY.
AND YOU WILL DRAW A VAST CIRCLE IN THE HUMAN WORLD, ALLOWING ME TO RECLAIM ALL MY POWER.
WITH IT, I WILL BUILD ELYSIUM...
A PLACE WHERE FAIRIES AND HUMANS ARE EQUAL.
LET US FORMALIZE THIS ARRANGE-MENT.
I WILL GIVE YOU THE POWER OF A FAIRY'S SOUL.
BUT FIRST I WILL TAKE...
...YOUR FATHER'S SOUL.
HUFF
HUFF
HUFF
AND THAT'S HOW YOU GOT THE POWER OF A DEMON...

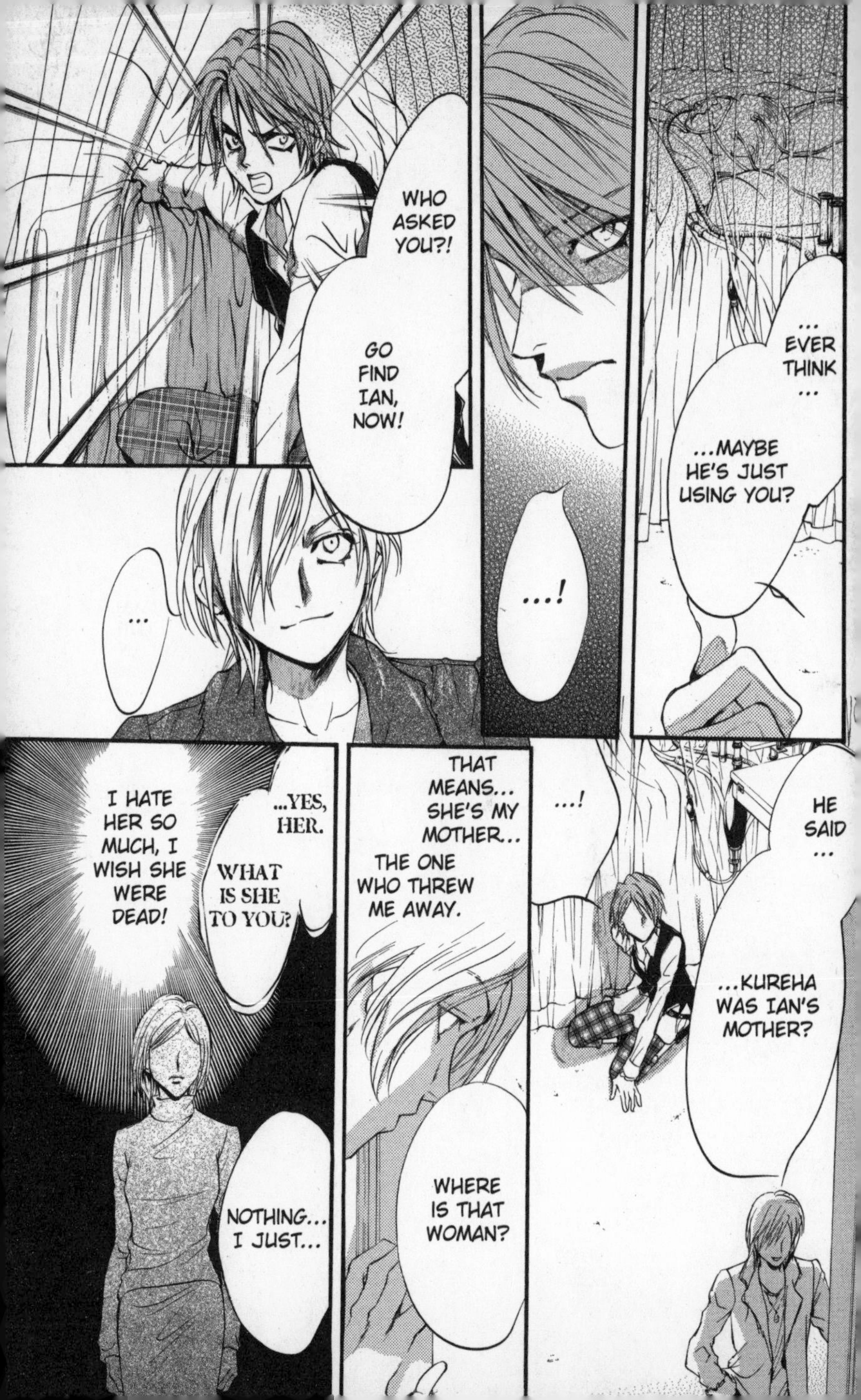
... EVER THINK ...
...MAYBE HE'S JUST USING YOU?
...!
WHO ASKED YOU?!
GO FIND IAN, NOW!
...
HE SAID ...
...!
...KUREHA WAS IAN'S MOTHER?
THAT MEANS... SHE'S MY MOTHER...
THE ONE WHO THREW ME AWAY.
WHERE IS THAT WOMAN?
...YES, HER.
WHAT IS SHE TO YOU?
I HATE HER SO MUCH, I WISH SHE WERE DEAD!
NOTHING... I JUST...

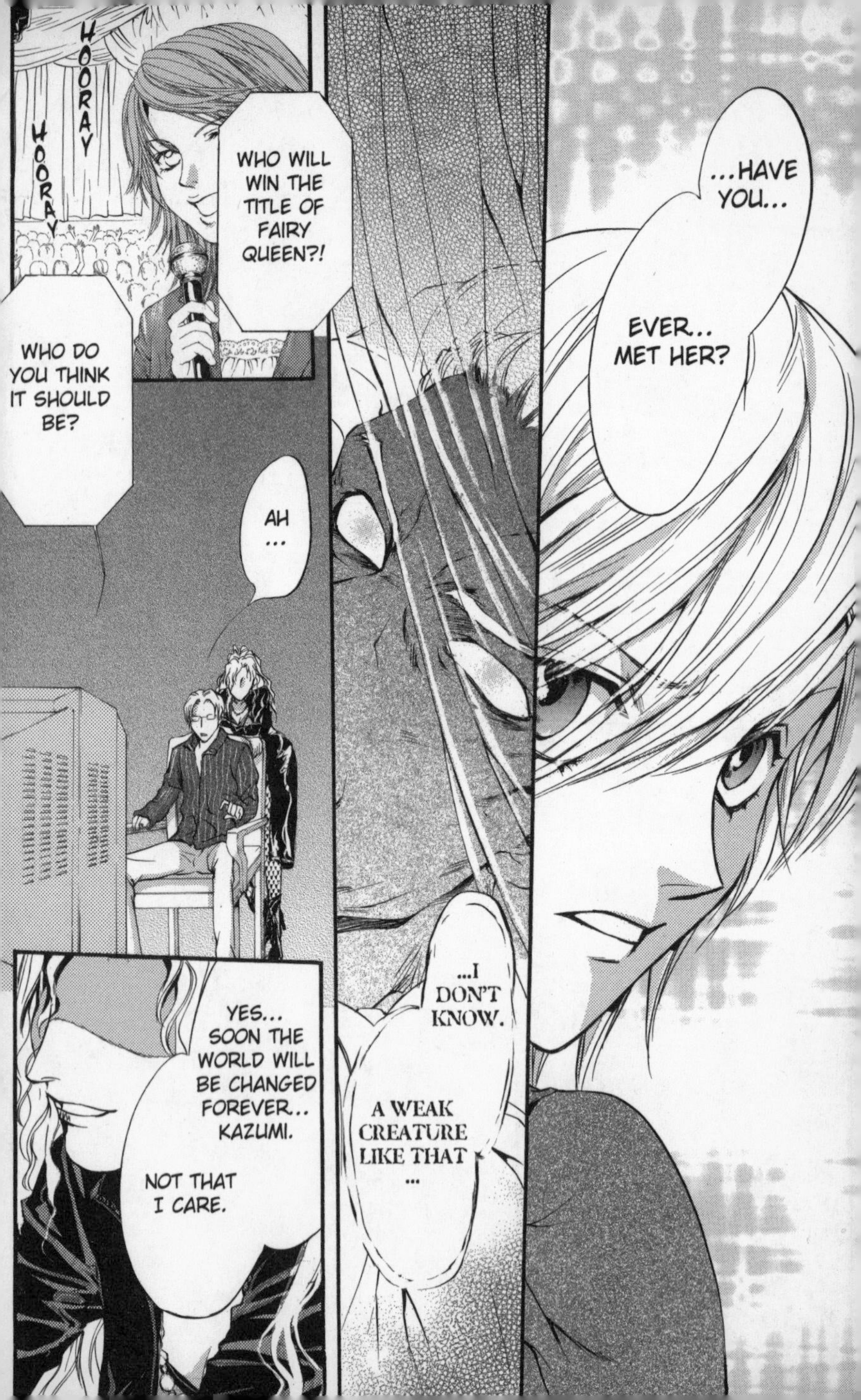
...HAVE YOU...
EVER... MET HER?
...I DON'T KNOW.
A WEAK CREATURE LIKE THAT ...
HOORAY
HOORAY
WHO WILL WIN THE TITLE OF FAIRY QUEEN?!
WHO DO YOU THINK IT SHOULD BE?
AH ...
YES... SOON THE WORLD WILL BE CHANGED FOREVER... KAZUMI.
NOT THAT I CARE.

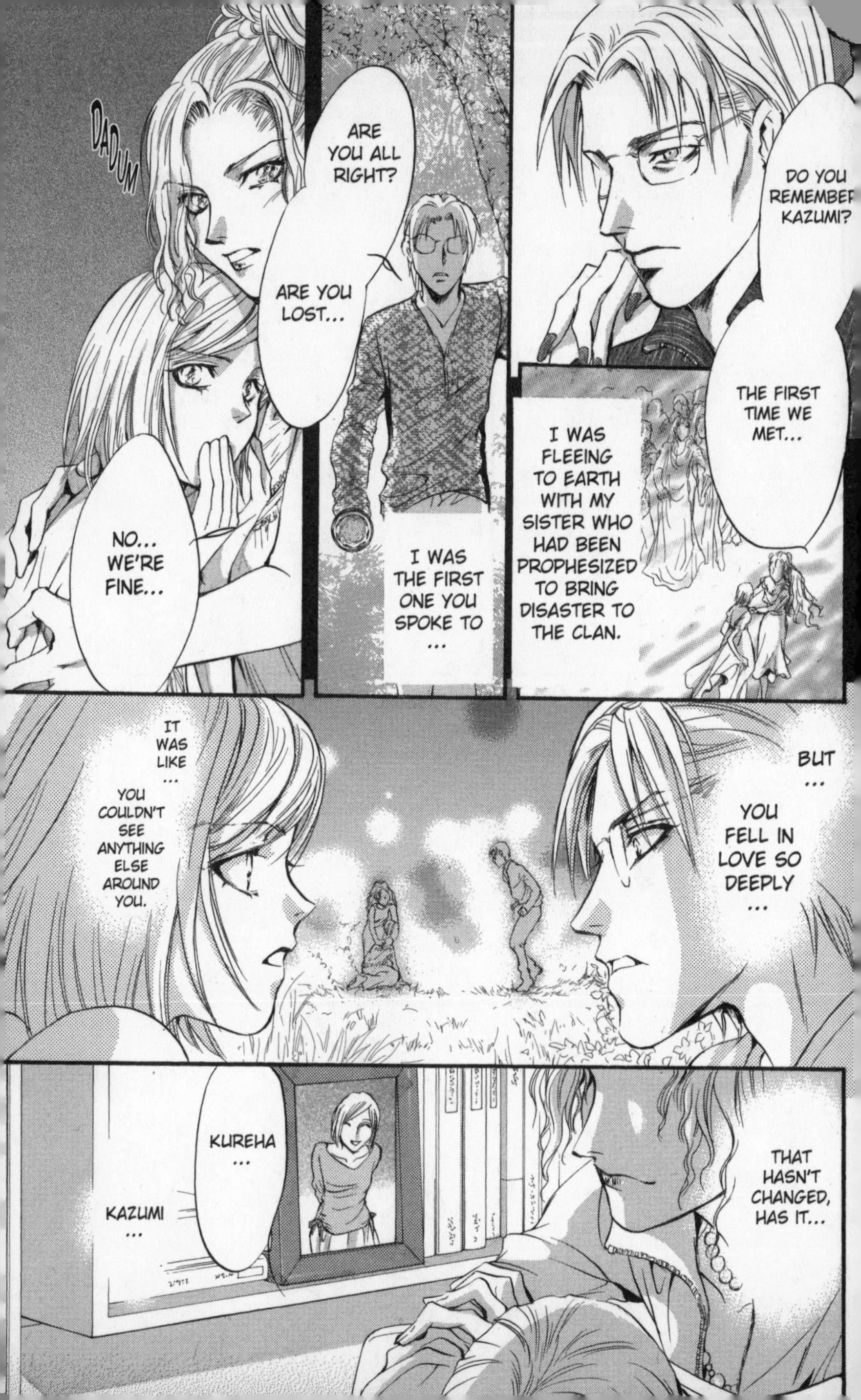
DO YOU REMEMBER KAZUMI?
THE FIRST TIME WE MET...
I WAS FLEEING TO EARTH WITH MY SISTER WHO HAD BEEN PROPHESIZED TO BRING DISASTER TO THE CLAN.
ARE YOU ALL RIGHT?
ARE YOU LOST...
I WAS THE FIRST ONE YOU SPOKE TO ...
DADUM
NO... WE'RE FINE...
BUT ...
YOU FELL IN LOVE SO DEEPLY ...
IT WAS LIKE ...
YOU COULDN'T SEE ANYTHING ELSE AROUND YOU.
THAT HASN'T CHANGED, HAS IT...
KUREHA ...
KAZUMI ...

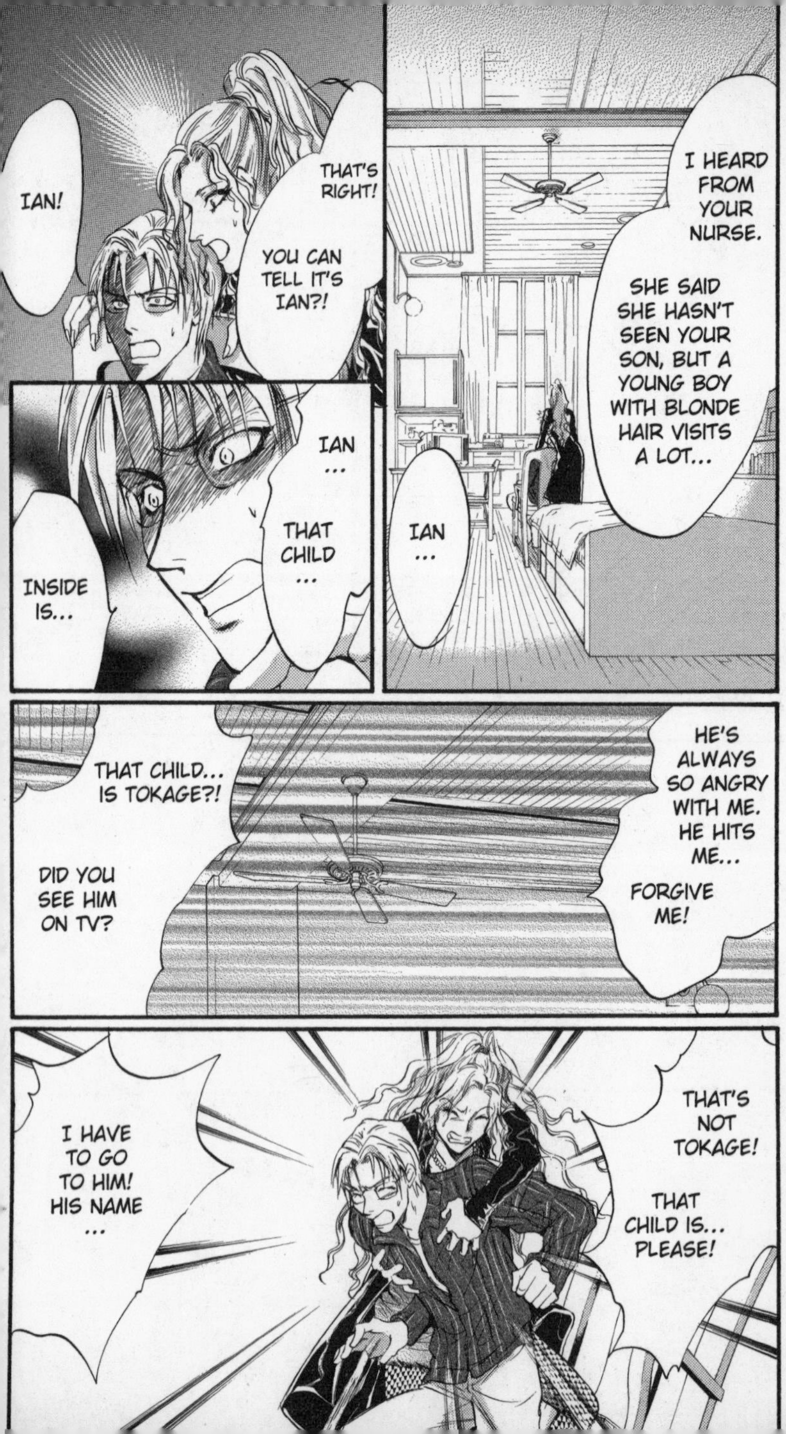
I HEARD FROM YOUR NURSE.
SHE SAID SHE HASN'T SEEN YOUR SON, BUT A YOUNG BOY WITH BLONDE HAIR VISITS A LOT...
IAN ...
THAT'S RIGHT!
YOU CAN TELL IT'S IAN?!
IAN!
IAN ...
THAT CHILD ...
INSIDE IS...
HE'S ALWAYS SO ANGRY WITH ME. HE HITS ME...
FORGIVE ME!
THAT CHILD... IS TOKAGE?!
DID YOU SEE HIM ON TV?
THAT'S NOT TOKAGE!
THAT CHILD IS... PLEASE!
I HAVE TO GO TO HIM! HIS NAME ...

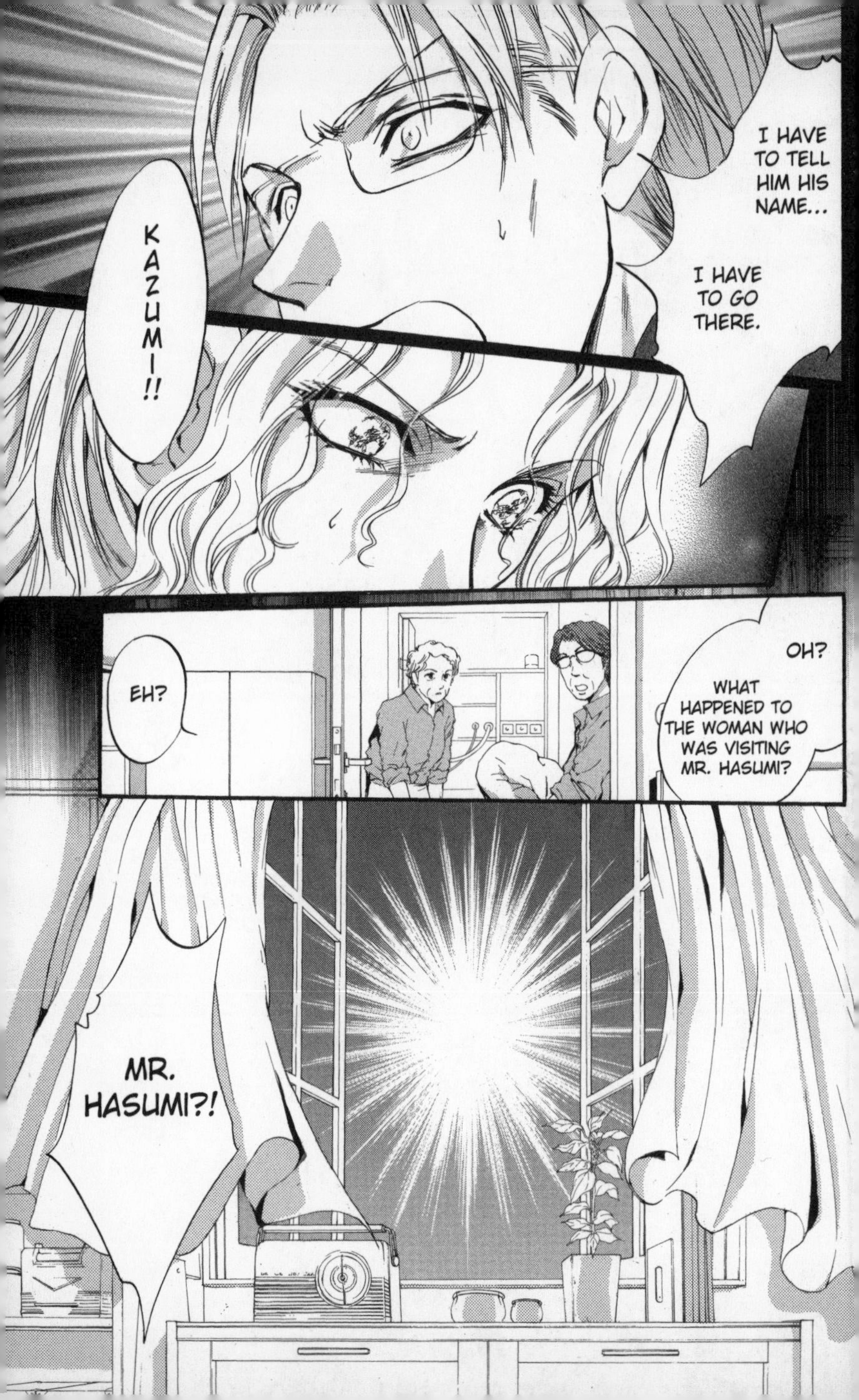
I HAVE TO TELL HIM HIS NAME...
I HAVE TO GO THERE.
KAZUMI!!
OH?
WHAT HAPPENED TO THE WOMAN WHO WAS VISITING MR. HASUMI?
EH?
MR. HASUMI?!

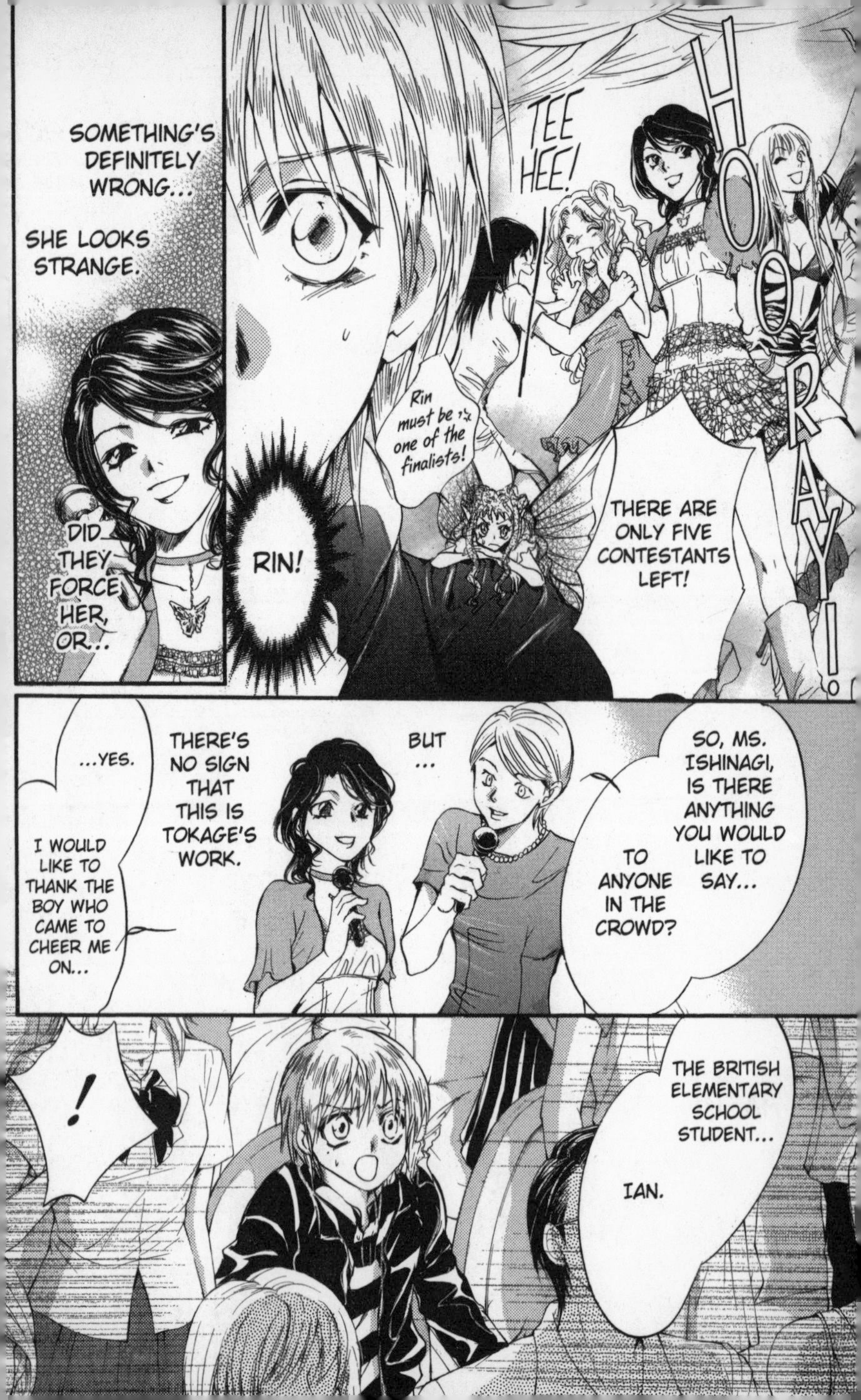
HOORAY!
TEE HEE!
THERE ARE ONLY FIVE CONTESTANTS LEFT!
Rin must be one of the finalists!
RIN!
SOMETHING'S DEFINITELY WRONG...
SHE LOOKS STRANGE.
DID THEY FORCE HER, OR...
SO, MS. ISHINAGI, IS THERE ANYTHING YOU WOULD LIKE TO SAY...
TO ANYONE IN THE CROWD?
BUT...
THERE'S NO SIGN THAT THIS IS TOKAGE'S WORK.
...YES.
I WOULD LIKE TO THANK THE BOY WHO CAME TO CHEER ME ON...
THE BRITISH ELEMENTARY SCHOOL STUDENT...
IAN.
!

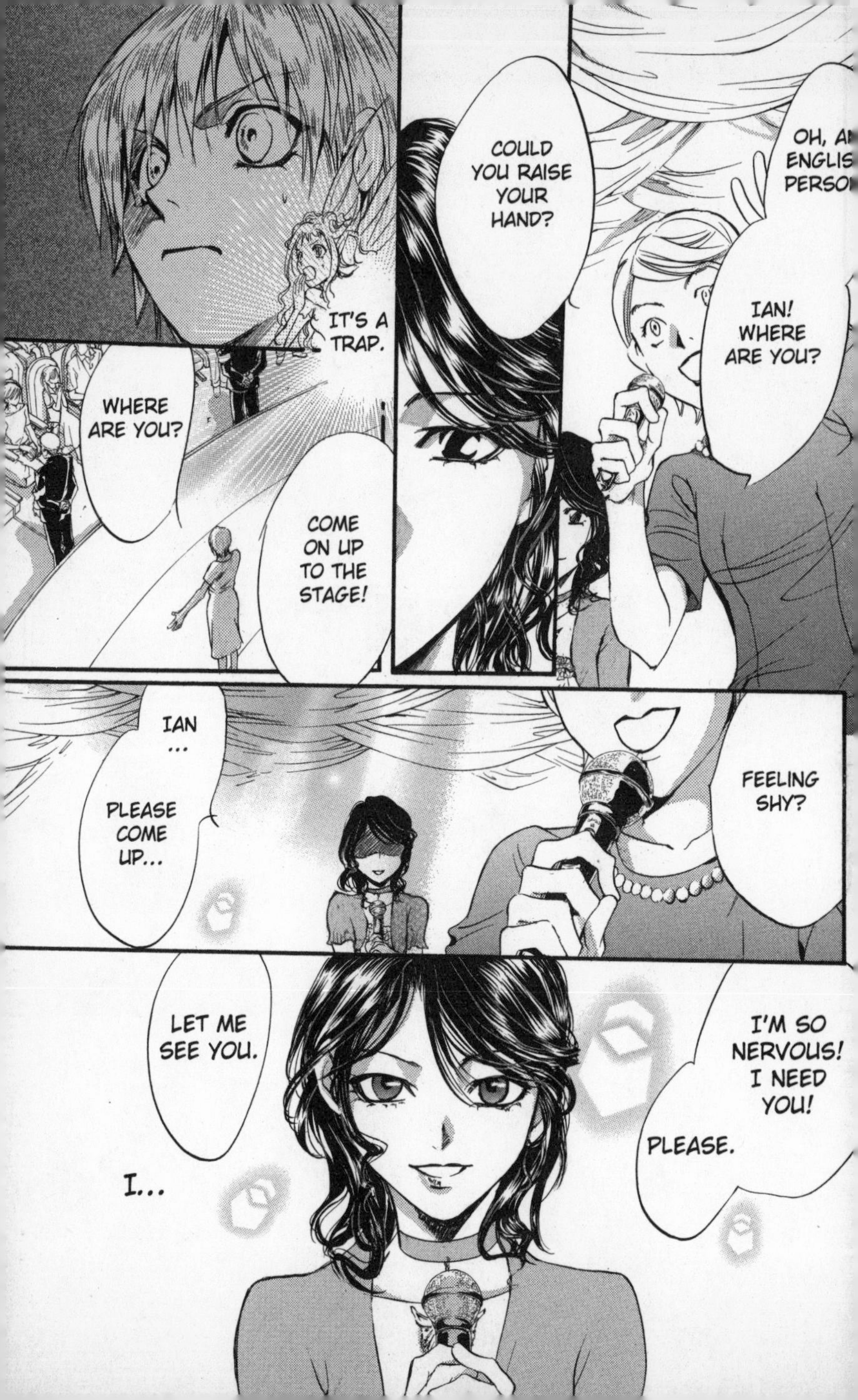

OH, A ENGLIS PERSO
IAN! WHERE ARE YOU?
COULD YOU RAISE YOUR HAND?
IT'S A TRAP.
WHERE ARE YOU?
COME ON UP TO THE STAGE!
FEELING SHY?
IAN ...
PLEASE COME UP...
I'M SO NERVOUS! I NEED YOU!
PLEASE.
LET ME SEE YOU.
I...

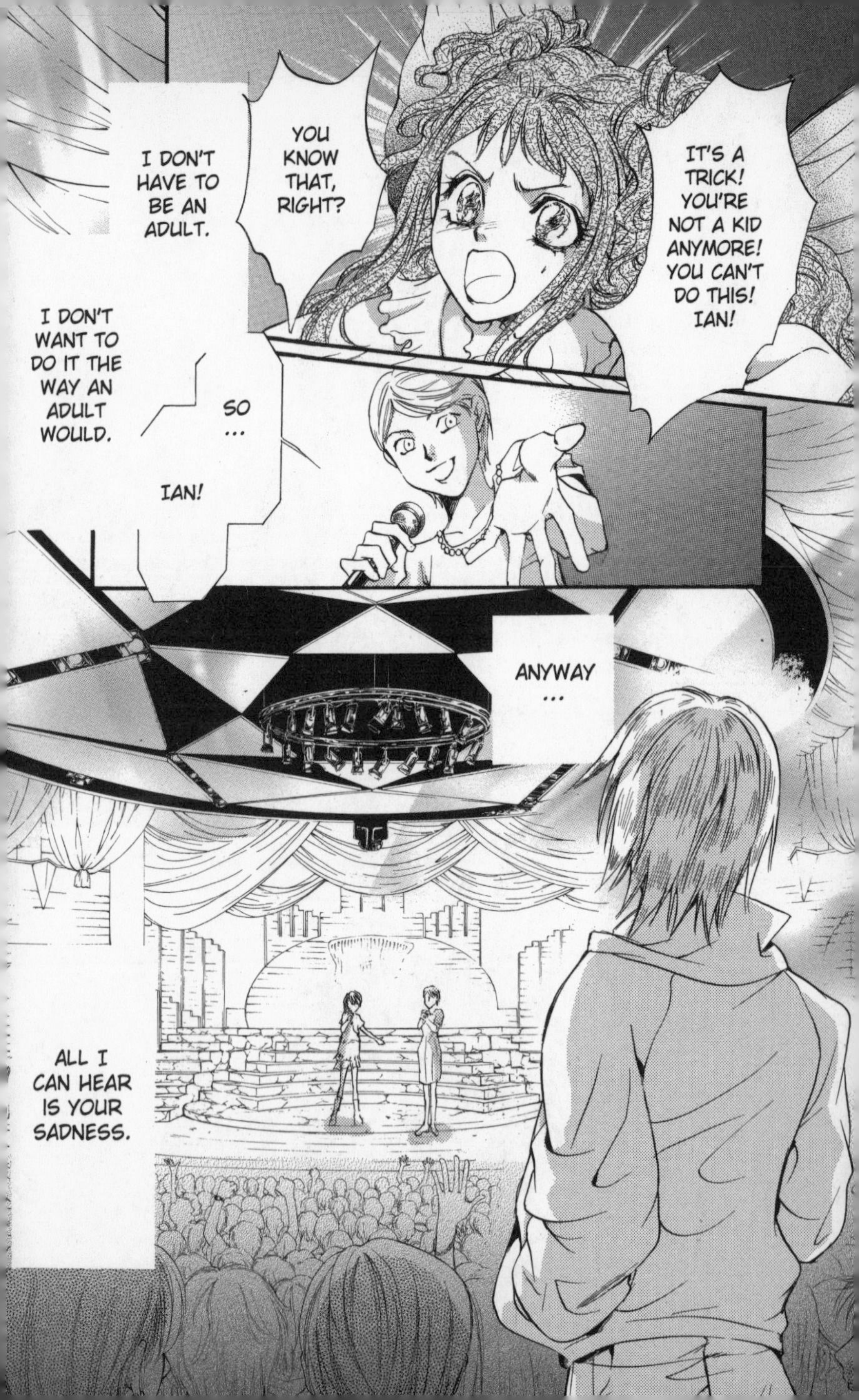
IT'S A TRICK! YOU'RE NOT A KID ANYMORE! YOU CAN'T DO THIS! IAN!
YOU KNOW THAT, RIGHT?
I DON'T HAVE TO BE AN ADULT.
SO ... IAN!
I DON'T WANT TO DO IT THE WAY AN ADULT WOULD.
ANYWAY ...
ALL I CAN HEAR IS YOUR SADNESS.

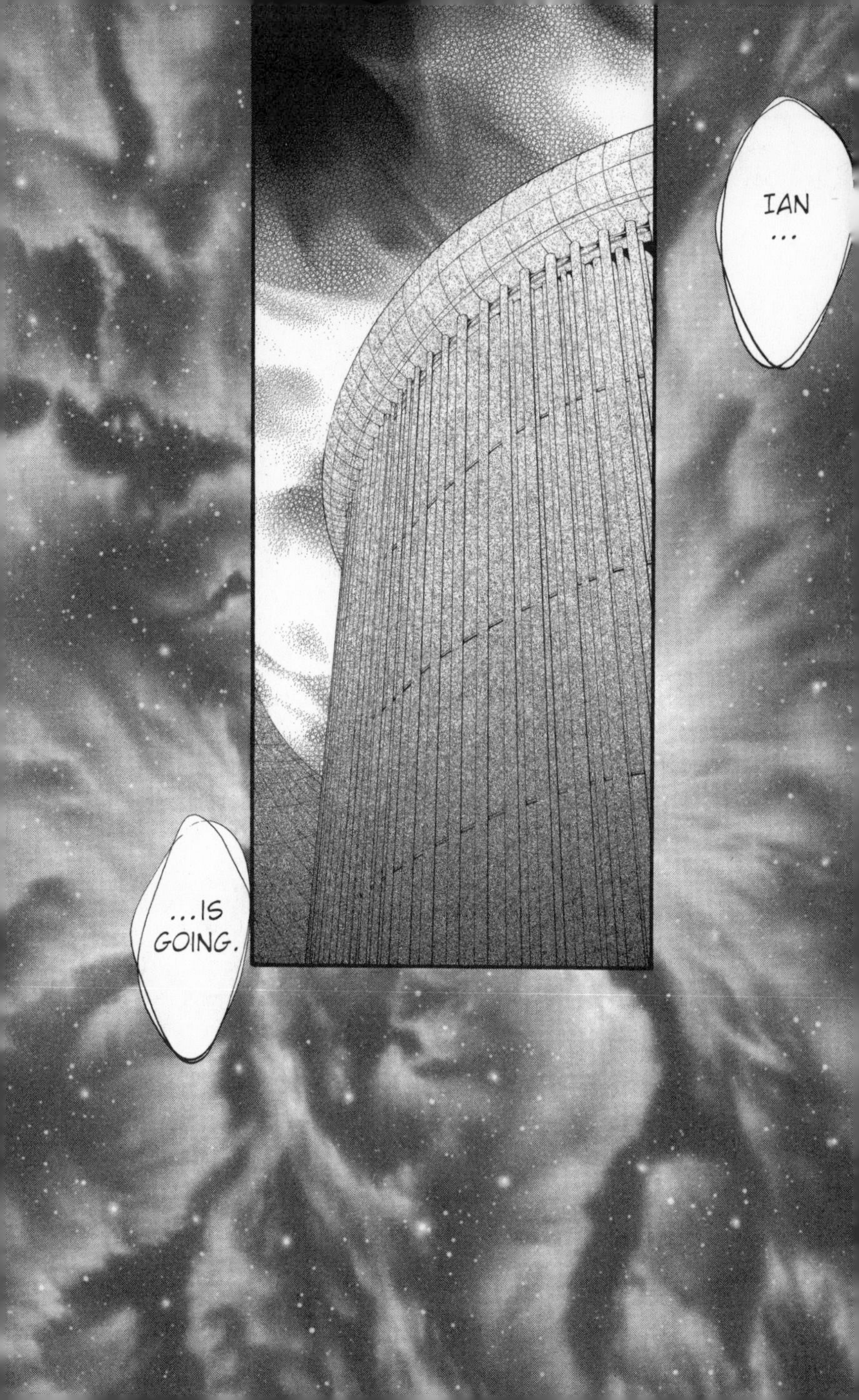
IAN ...
...IS GOING.

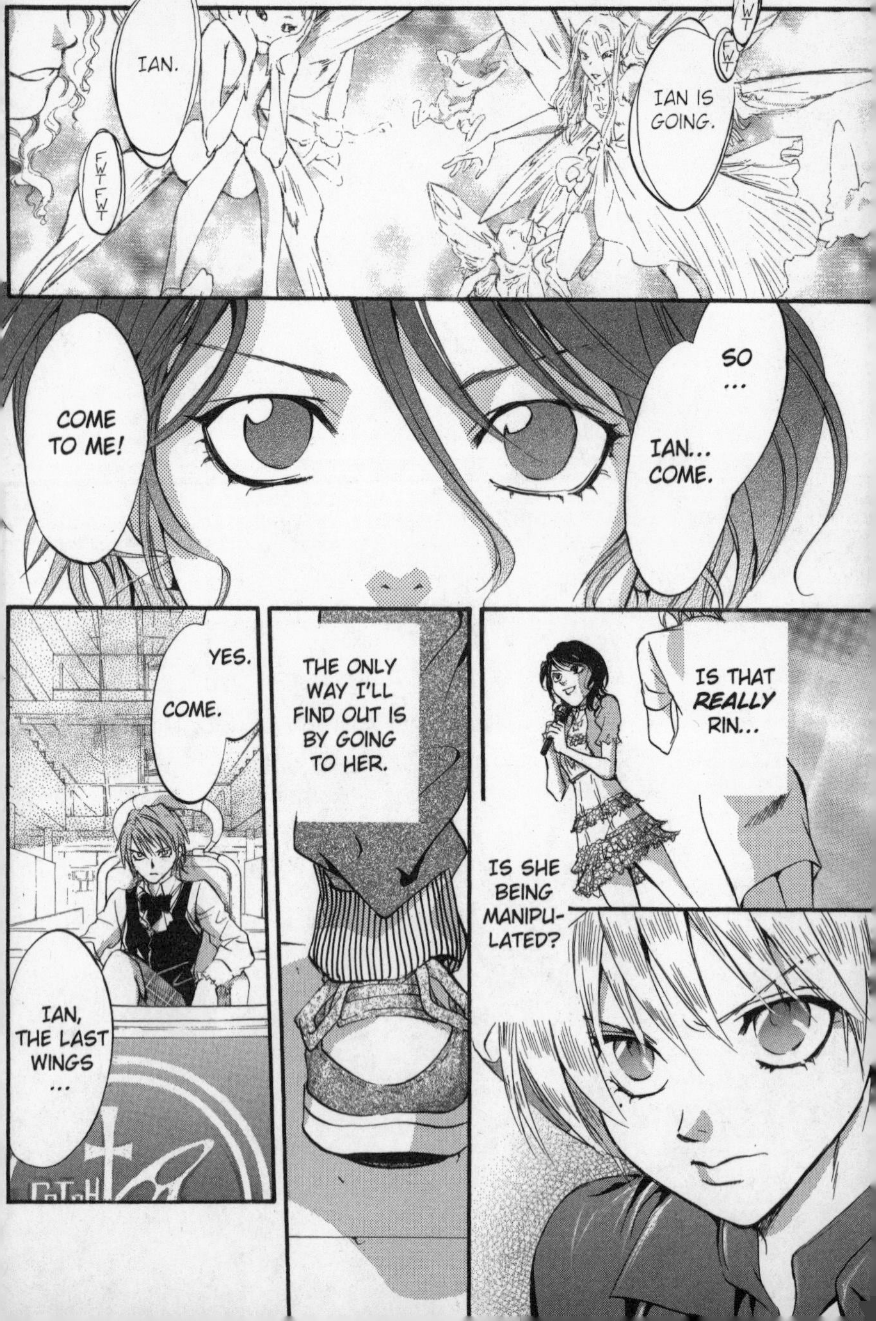
FWT
FWT
IAN IS GOING.
IAN.
FWT FWT
SO ... IAN... COME.
COME TO ME!
IS THAT *REALLY* RIN...
IS SHE BEING MANIPULATED?
THE ONLY WAY I'LL FIND OUT IS BY GOING TO HER.
YES. COME.
IAN, THE LAST WINGS ...

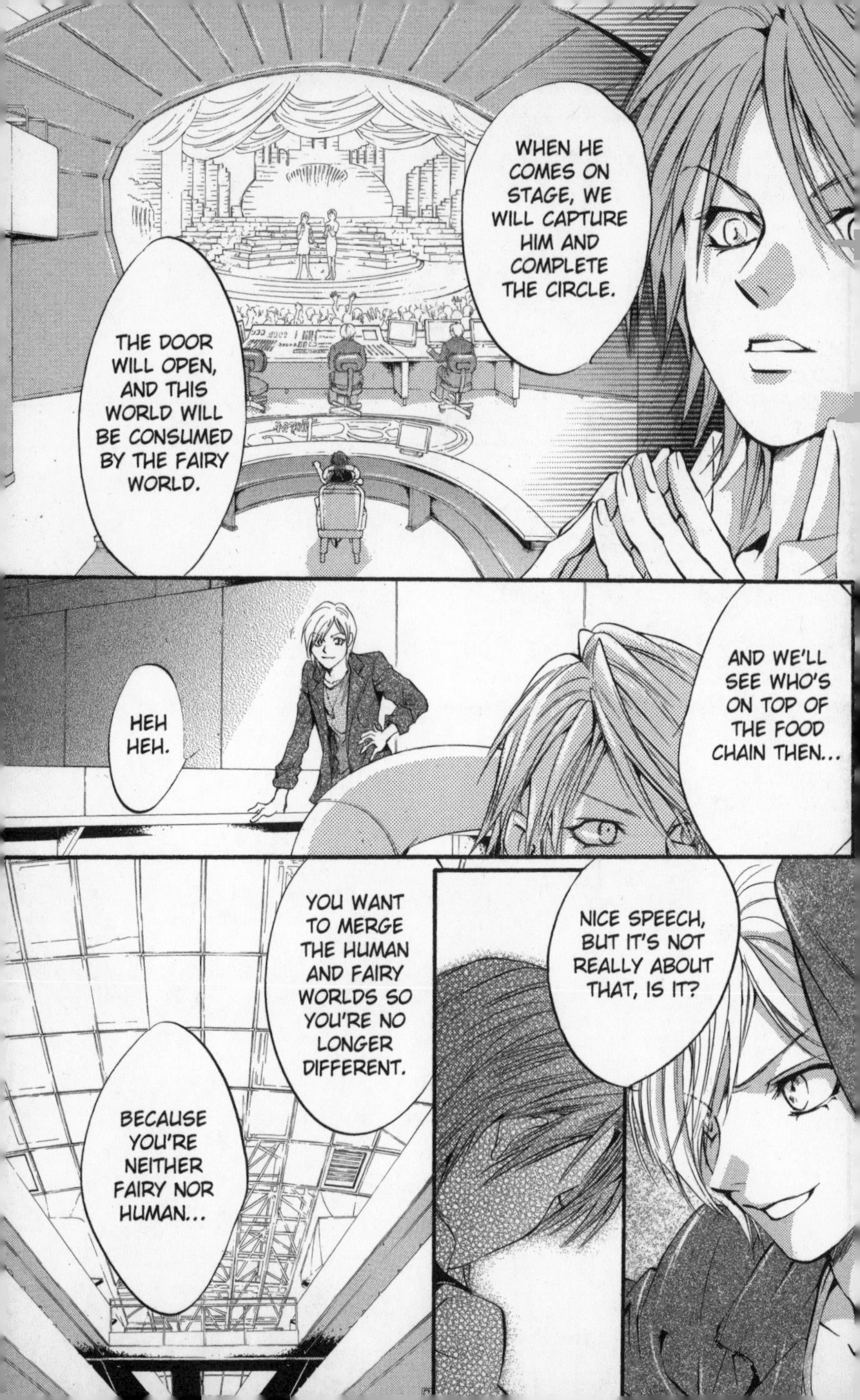
WHEN HE COMES ON STAGE, WE WILL CAPTURE HIM AND COMPLETE THE CIRCLE.
THE DOOR WILL OPEN, AND THIS WORLD WILL BE CONSUMED BY THE FAIRY WORLD.
AND WE'LL SEE WHO'S ON TOP OF THE FOOD CHAIN THEN...
HEH HEH.
NICE SPEECH, BUT IT'S NOT REALLY ABOUT THAT, IS IT?
YOU WANT TO MERGE THE HUMAN AND FAIRY WORLDS SO YOU'RE NO LONGER DIFFERENT.
BECAUSE YOU'RE NEITHER FAIRY NOR HUMAN...

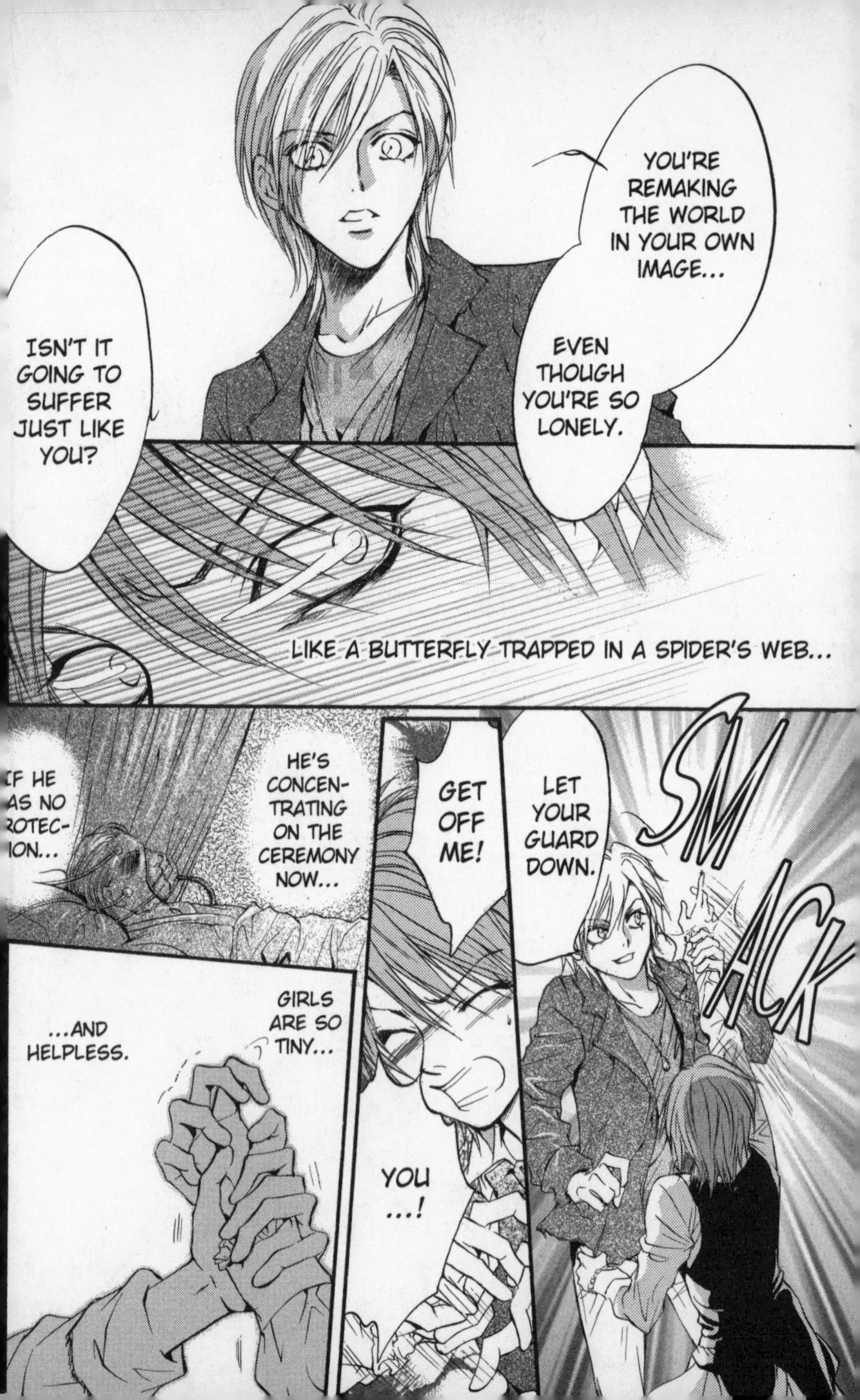
YOU'RE REMAKING THE WORLD IN YOUR OWN IMAGE...
EVEN THOUGH YOU'RE SO LONELY.
ISN'T IT GOING TO SUFFER JUST LIKE YOU?
LIKE A BUTTERFLY TRAPPED IN A SPIDER'S WEB...
SMACK
LET YOUR GUARD DOWN.
GET OFF ME!
YOU ...!
HE'S CONCEN-TRATING ON THE CEREMONY NOW...
F HE AS NO ROTEC- ION...
GIRLS ARE SO TINY...
...AND HELPLESS.

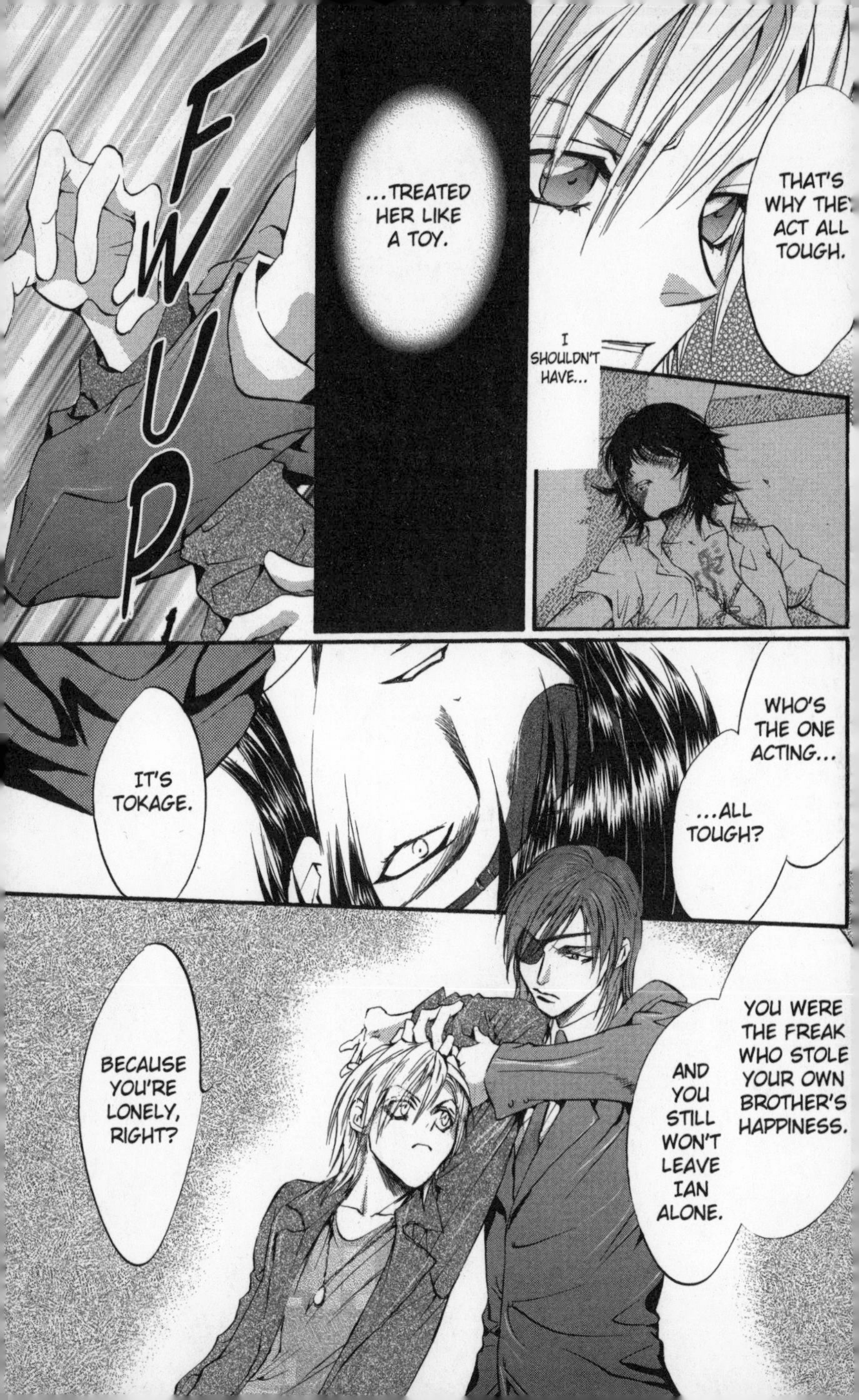
THAT'S WHY THEY ACT ALL TOUGH.
I SHOULDN'T HAVE...
...TREATED HER LIKE A TOY.
FWUP
WHO'S THE ONE ACTING...
...ALL TOUGH?
IT'S TOKAGE.
YOU WERE THE FREAK WHO STOLE YOUR OWN BROTHER'S HAPPINESS.
AND YOU STILL WON'T LEAVE IAN ALONE.
BECAUSE YOU'RE LONELY, RIGHT?

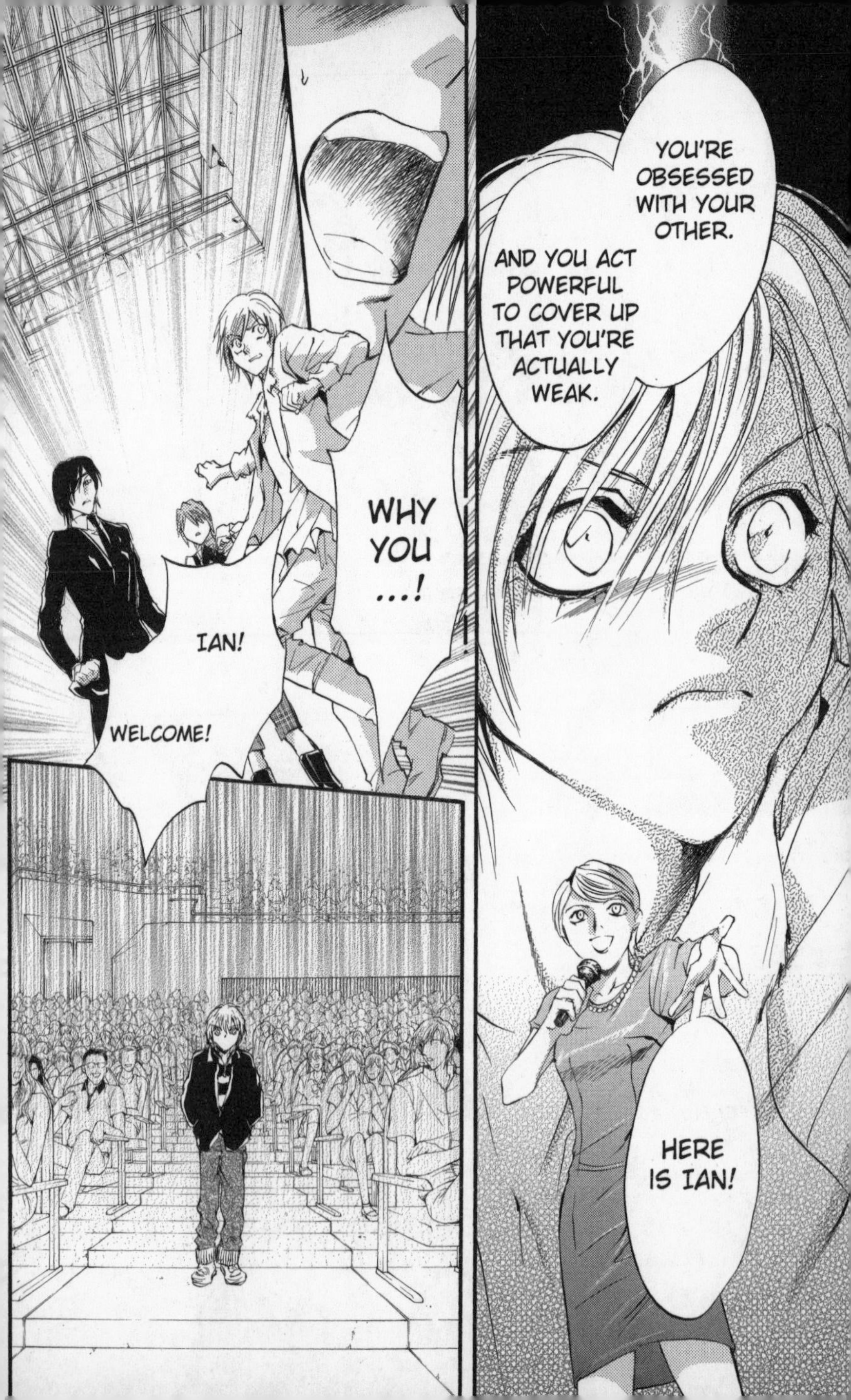
YOU'RE OBSESSED WITH YOUR OTHER.
AND YOU ACT POWERFUL TO COVER UP THAT YOU'RE ACTUALLY WEAK.
HERE IS IAN!
WHY YOU ...!
IAN!
WELCOME!

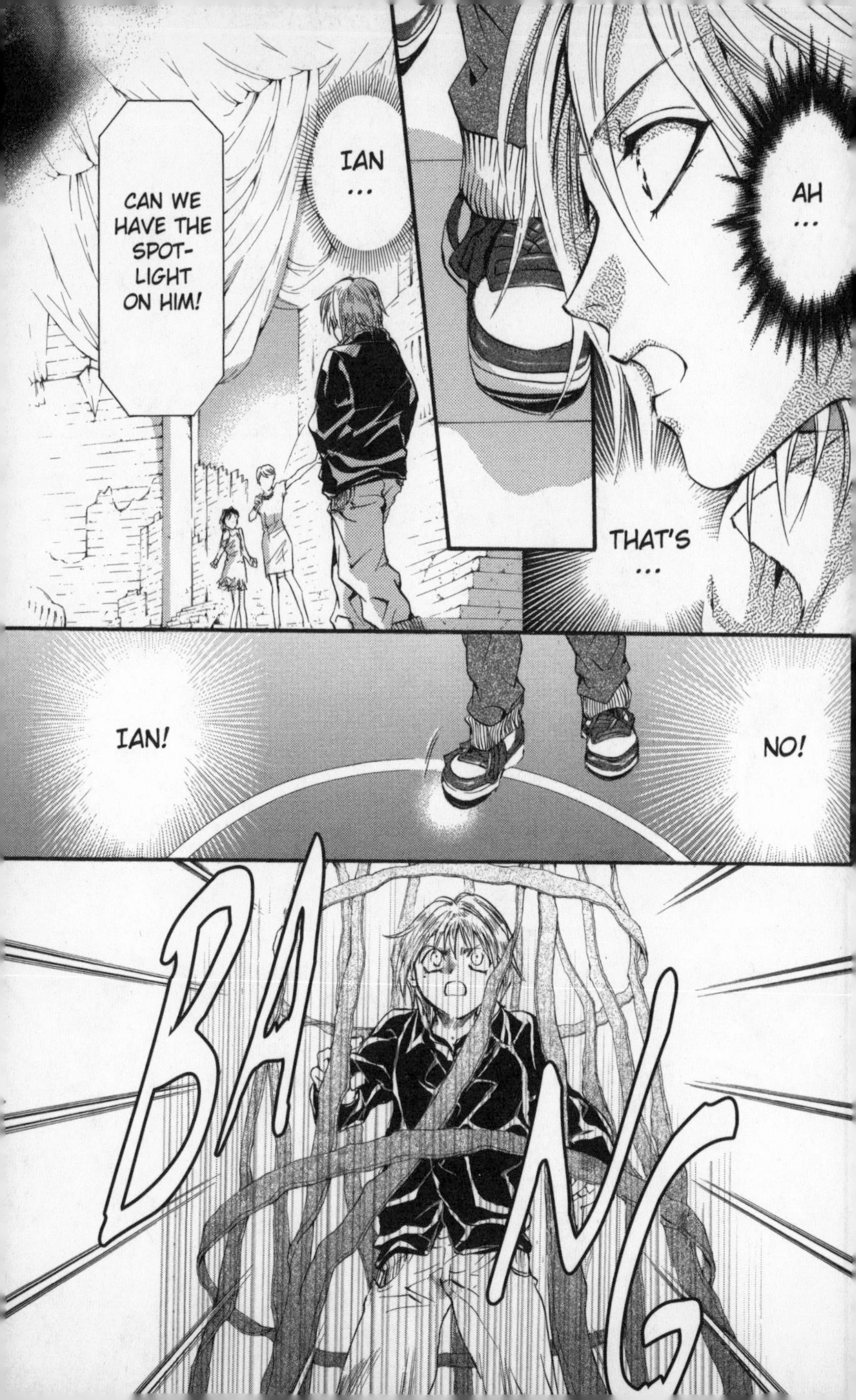
AH ...
THAT'S ...
IAN ...
CAN WE HAVE THE SPOT-LIGHT ON HIM!
NO!
IAN!
BANG

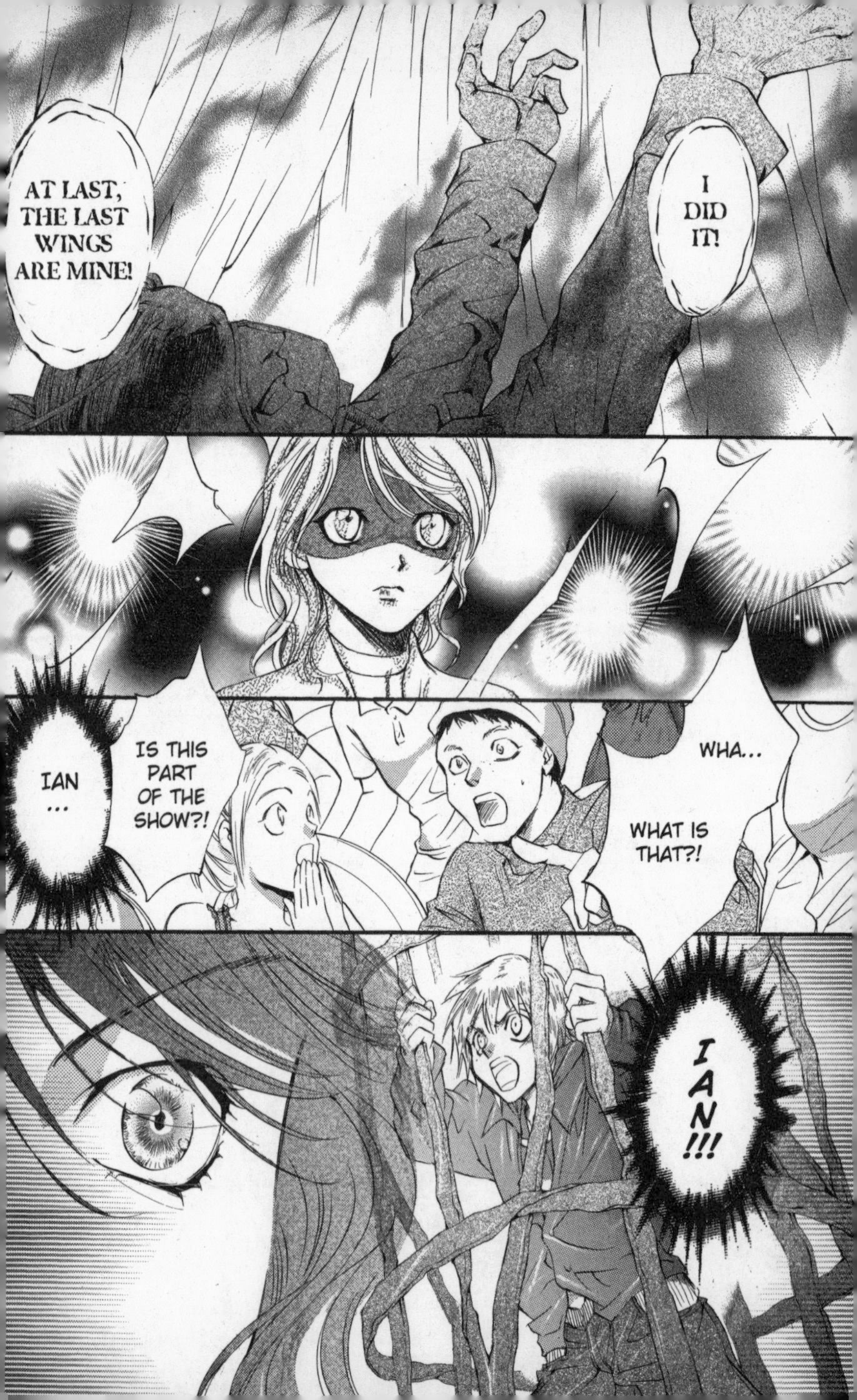
I DID IT!
AT LAST, THE LAST WINGS ARE MINE!
WHA...
WHAT IS THAT?!
IS THIS PART OF THE SHOW?!
IAN ...
IAN!!!

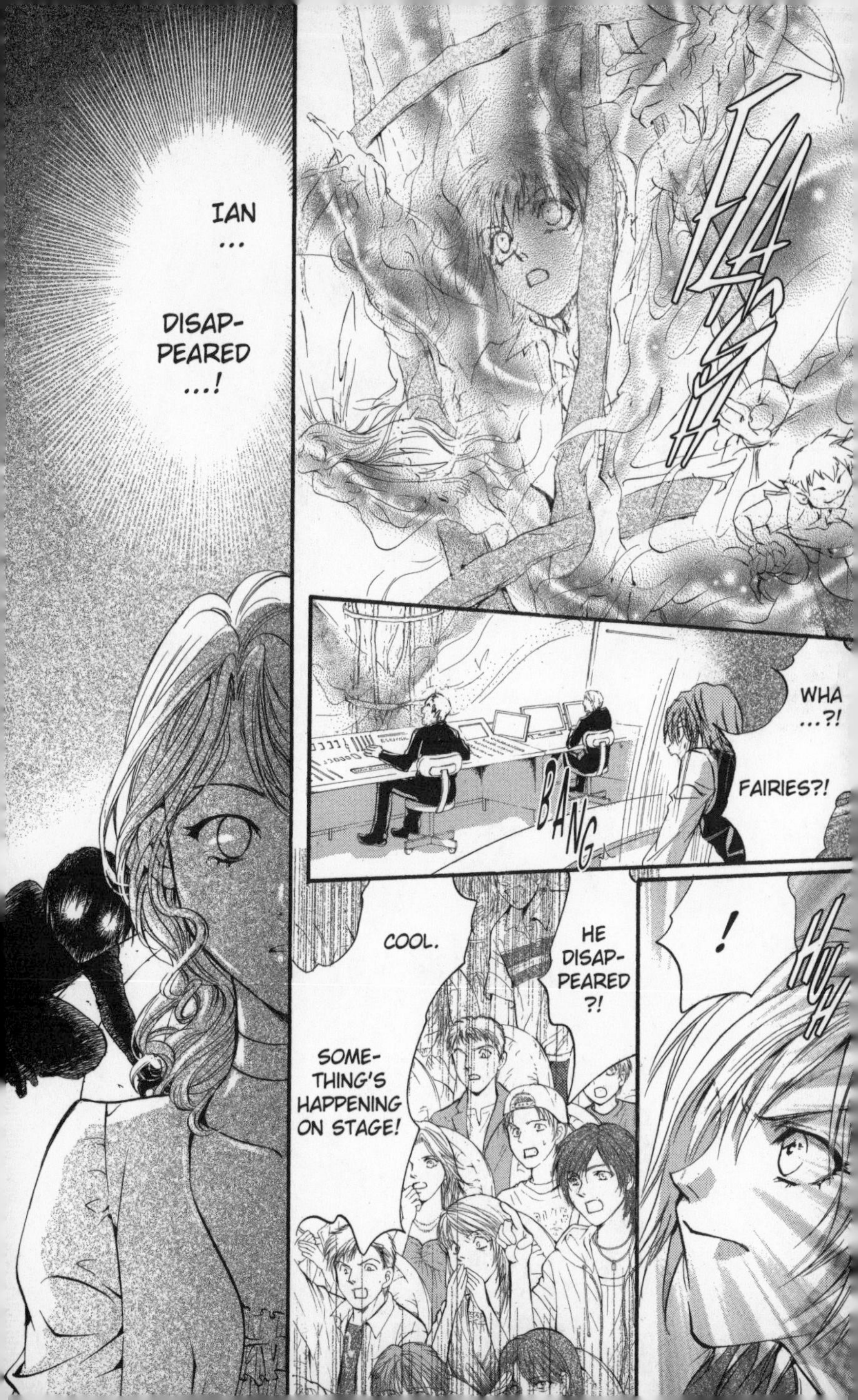
FLASH
WHA ...?!
FAIRIES?!
BANG
!
HUH
HE DISAP-PEARED?!
COOL.
SOME-THING'S HAPPENING ON STAGE!
IAN ...
DISAP-PEARED ...!

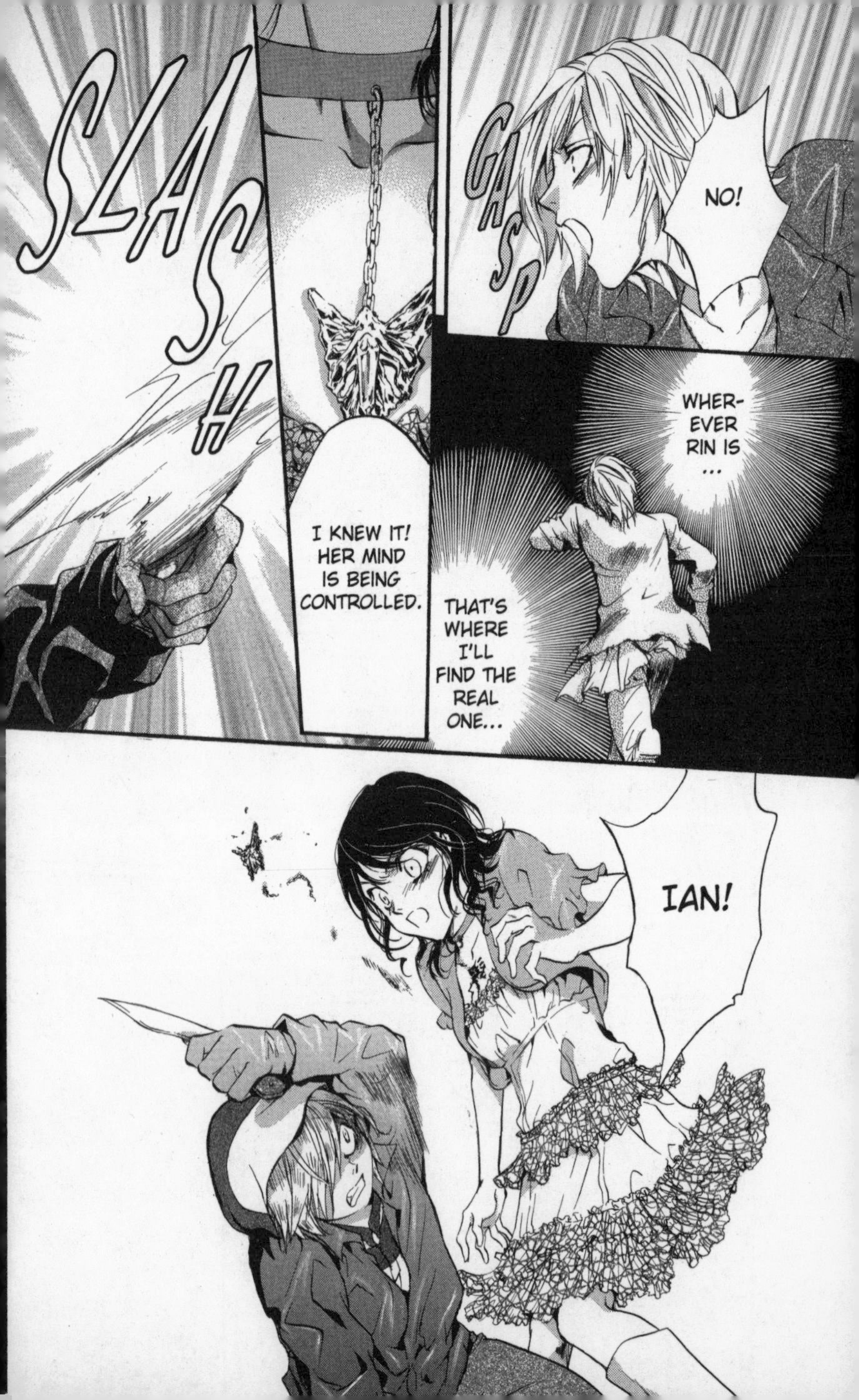
NO!
GASP
WHER-EVER RIN IS ...
THAT'S WHERE I'LL FIND THE REAL ONE...
I KNEW IT! HER MIND IS BEING CONTROLLED.
SLASH
IAN!

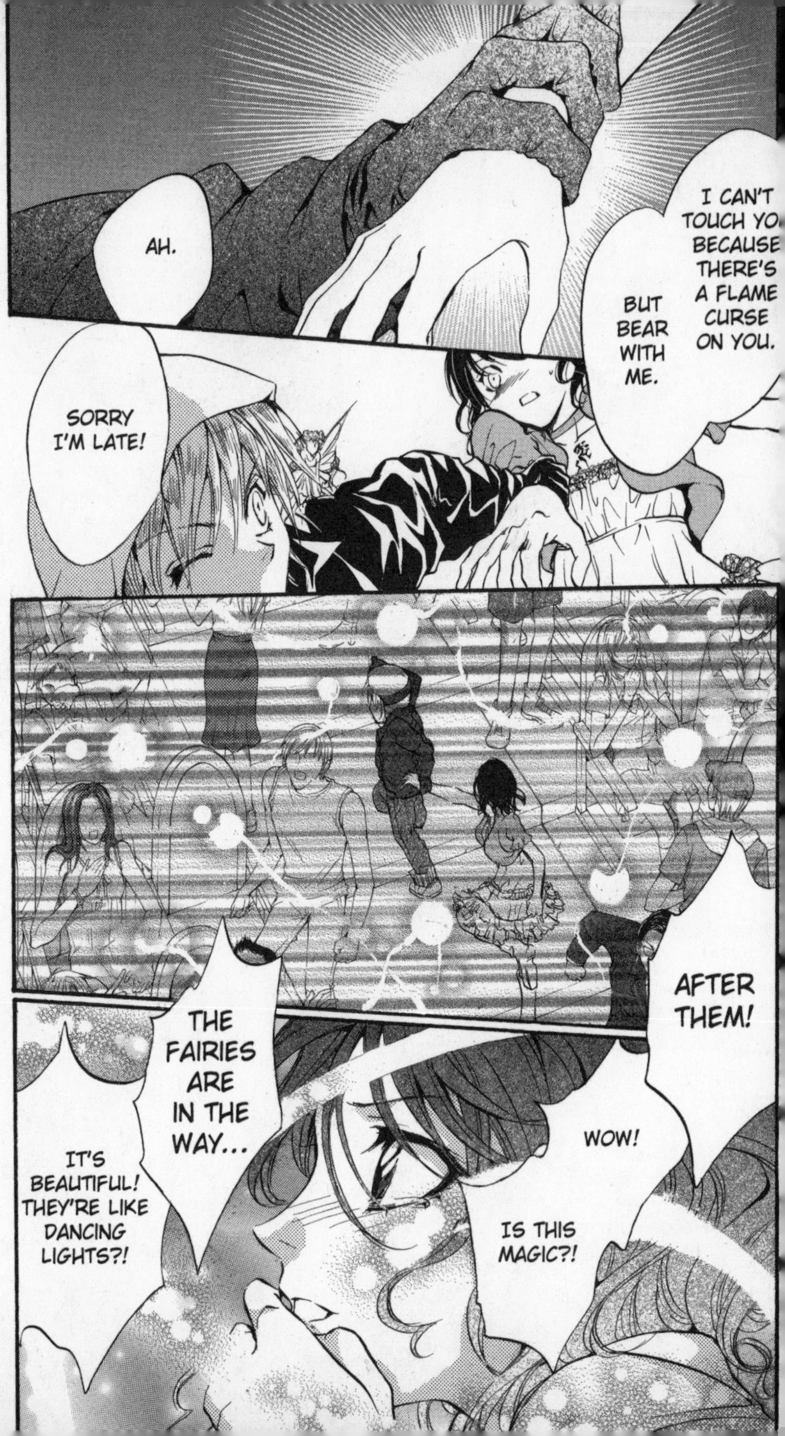
AH.
I CAN'T TOUCH YO BECAUSE THERE'S A FLAME CURSE ON YOU.
BUT BEAR WITH ME.
SORRY I'M LATE!
AFTER THEM!
THE FAIRIES ARE IN THE WAY...
WOW!
IS THIS MAGIC?!
IT'S BEAUTIFUL! THEY'RE LIKE DANCING LIGHTS?!

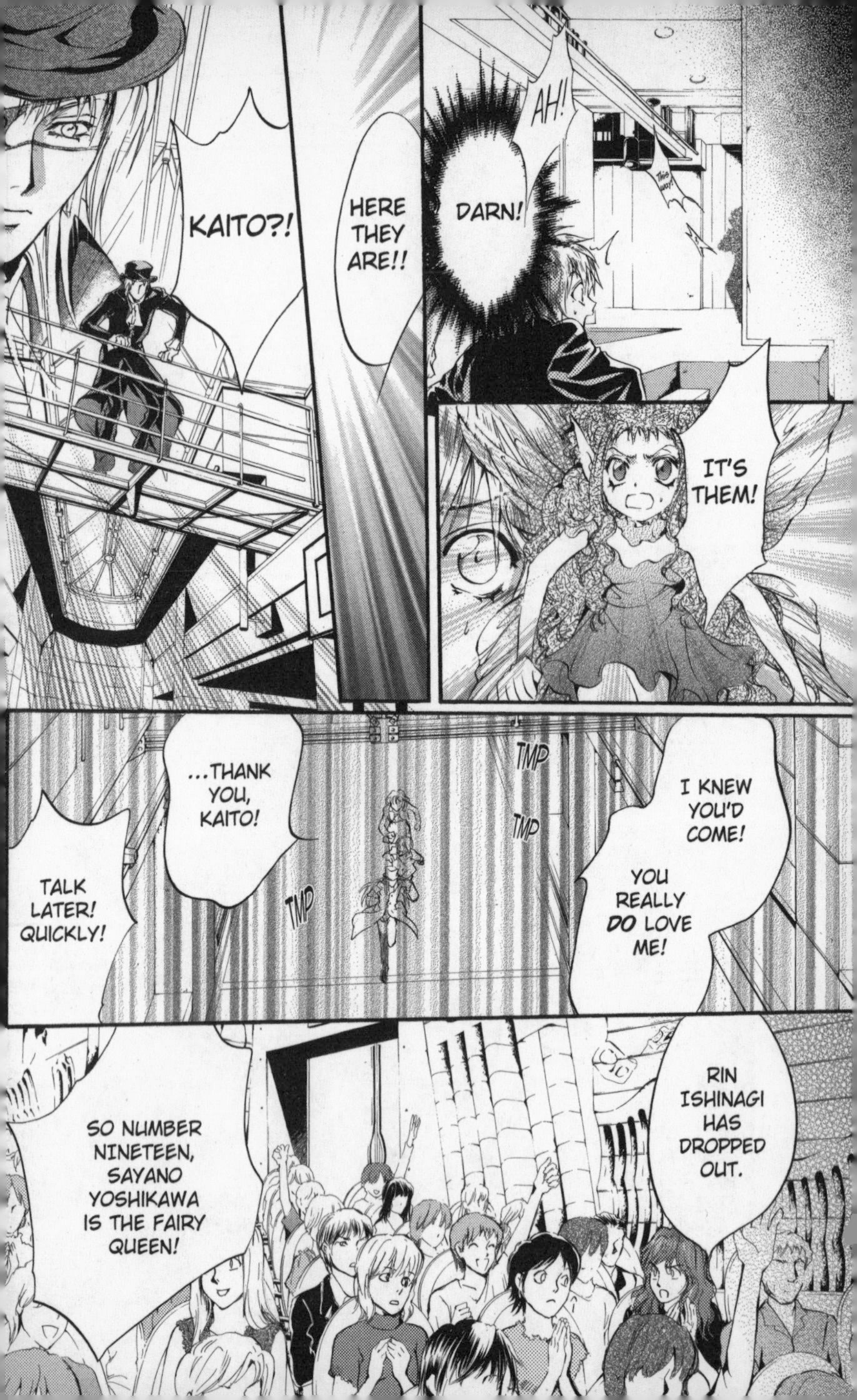
AH!
This way!
DARN!
IT'S THEM!
HERE THEY ARE!!
KAITO?!
I KNEW YOU'D COME!
YOU REALLY *DO* LOVE ME!
TMP
TMP
TMP
...THANK YOU, KAITO!
TALK LATER! QUICKLY!
RIN ISHINAGI HAS DROPPED OUT.
SO NUMBER NINETEEN, SAYANO YOSHIKAWA IS THE FAIRY QUEEN!

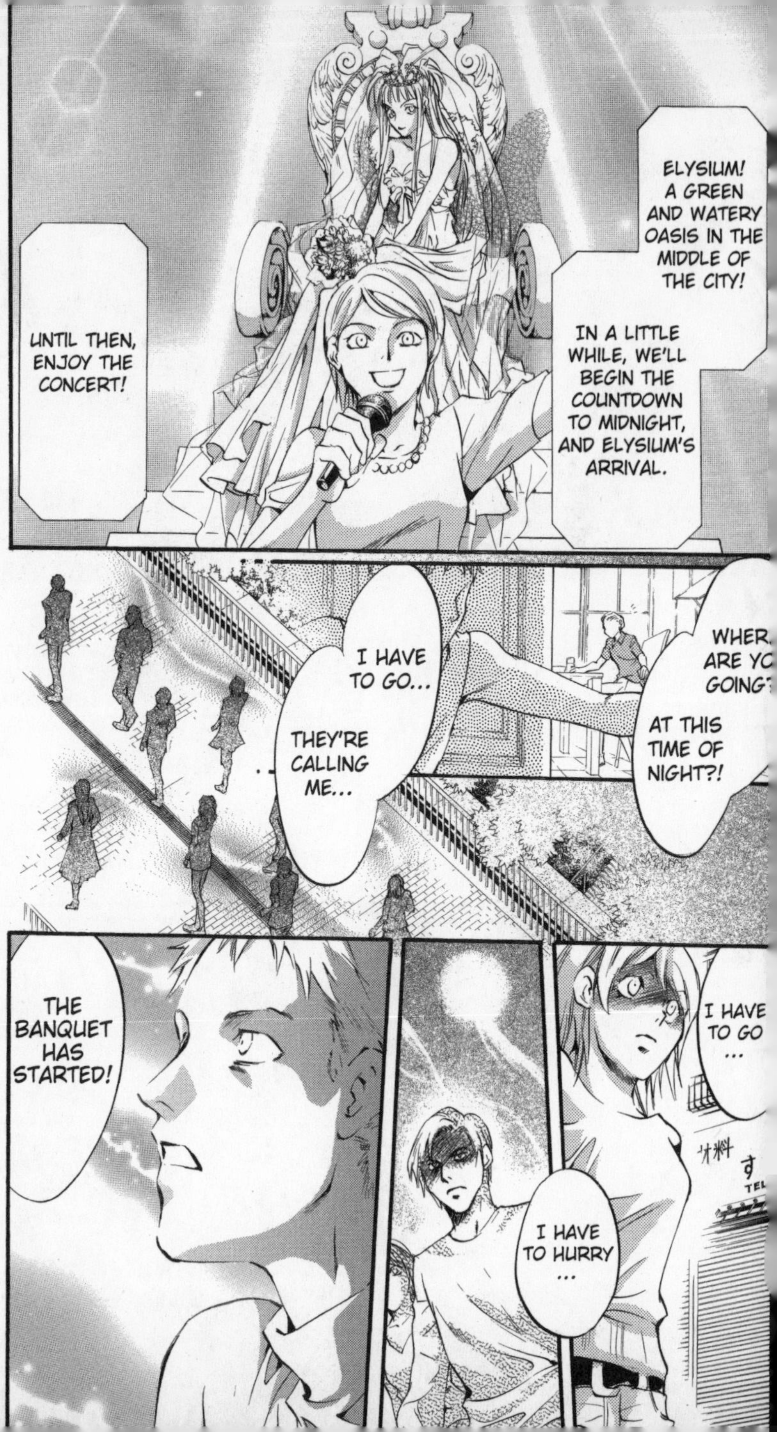
ELYSIUM! A GREEN AND WATERY OASIS IN THE MIDDLE OF THE CITY!
IN A LITTLE WHILE, WE'LL BEGIN THE COUNTDOWN TO MIDNIGHT, AND ELYSIUM'S ARRIVAL.
UNTIL THEN, ENJOY THE CONCERT!
WHER ARE YO GOING
AT THIS TIME OF NIGHT?!
I HAVE TO GO...
THEY'RE CALLING ME...
I HAVE TO GO ...
I HAVE TO HURRY ...
THE BANQUET HAS STARTED!

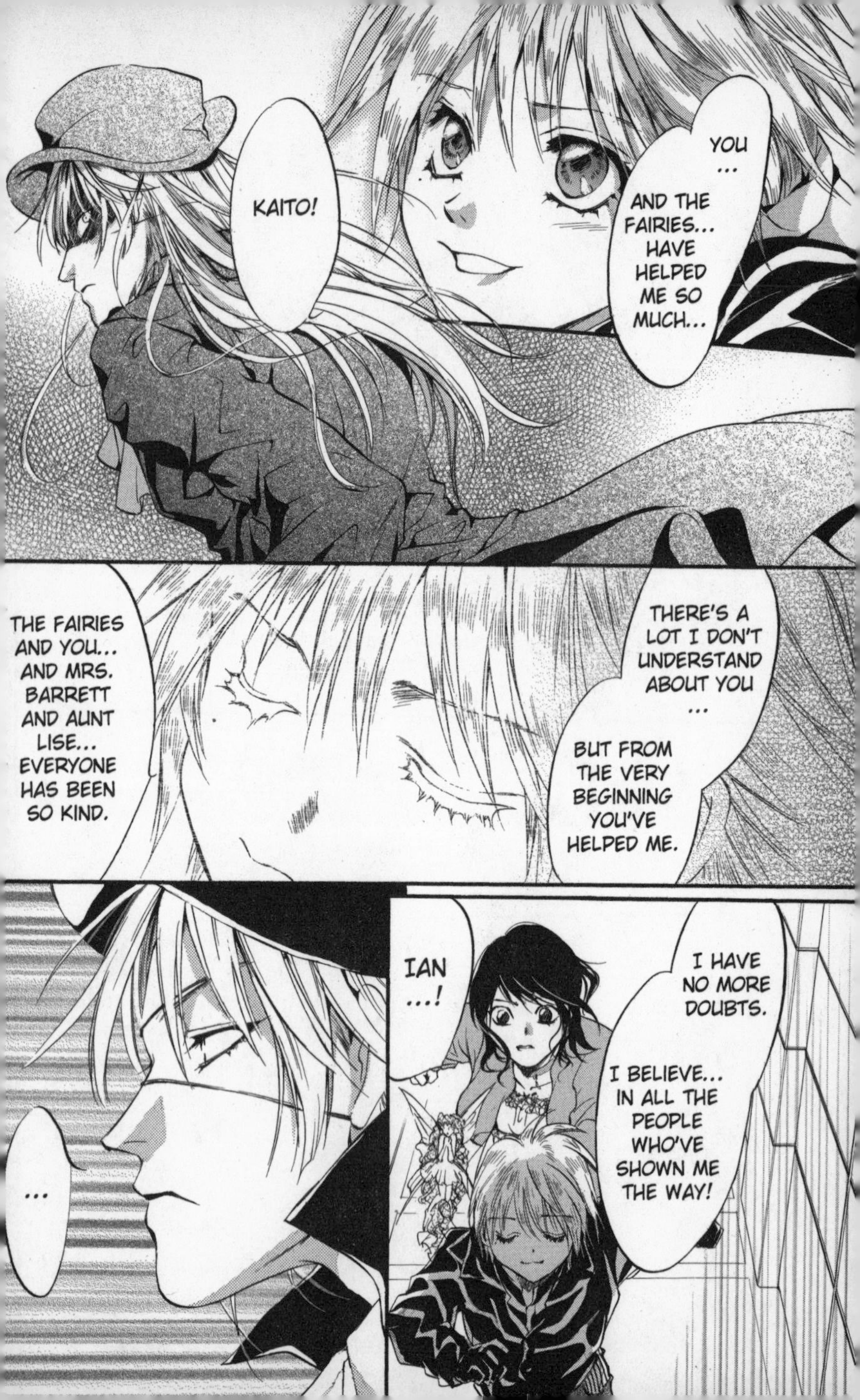
YOU ... AND THE FAIRIES... HAVE HELPED ME SO MUCH...
KAITO!
THERE'S A LOT I DON'T UNDERSTAND ABOUT YOU ...
BUT FROM THE VERY BEGINNING YOU'VE HELPED ME.
THE FAIRIES AND YOU... AND MRS. BARRETT AND AUNT LISE... EVERYONE HAS BEEN SO KIND.
I HAVE NO MORE DOUBTS.
IAN ...!
I BELIEVE... IN ALL THE PEOPLE WHO'VE SHOWN ME THE WAY!
...

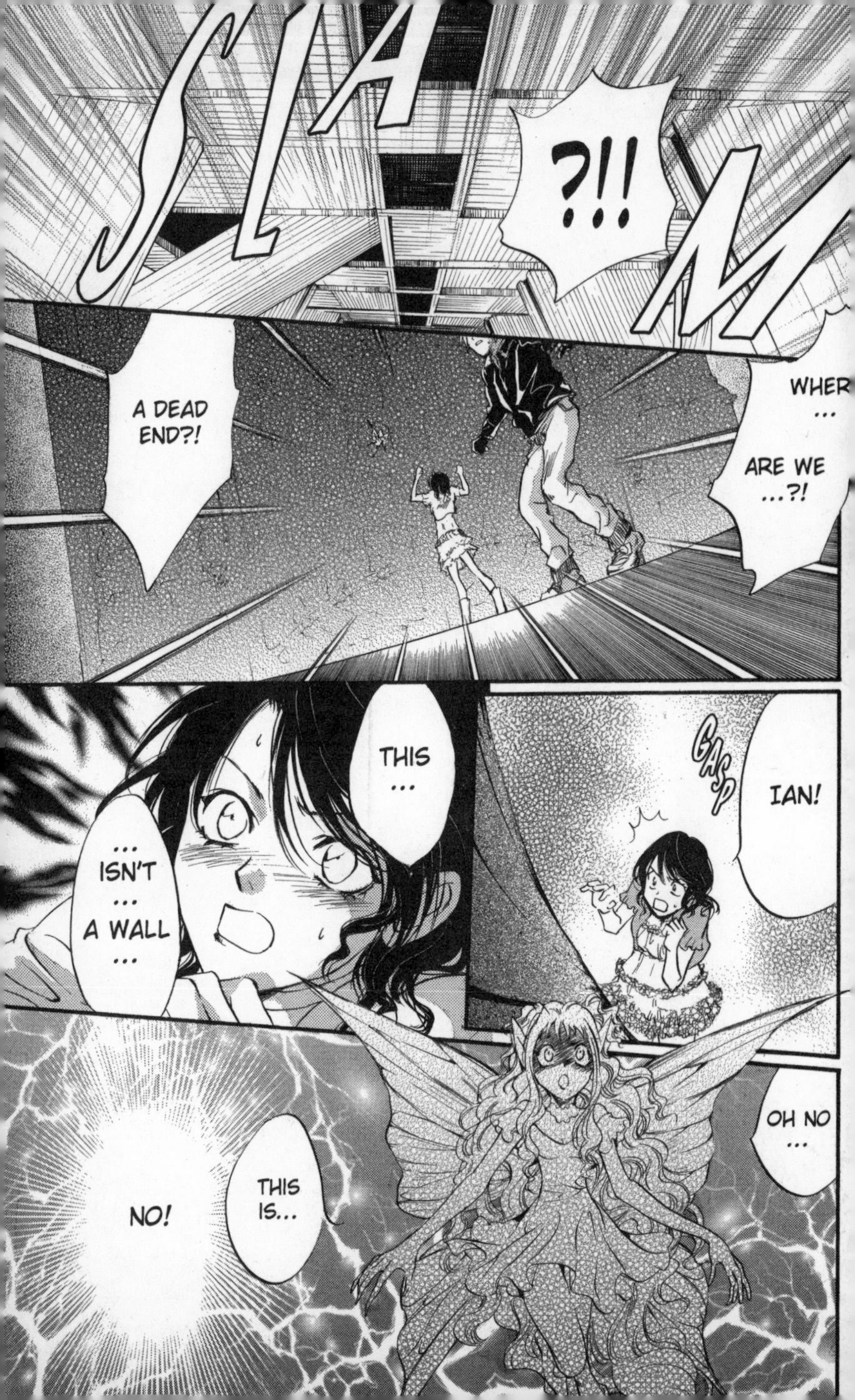
?!!
SLAM
WHER ... ARE WE ...?!
A DEAD END?!
GASP
IAN!
THIS ...
... ISN'T ... A WALL ...
OH NO ...
THIS IS...
NO!

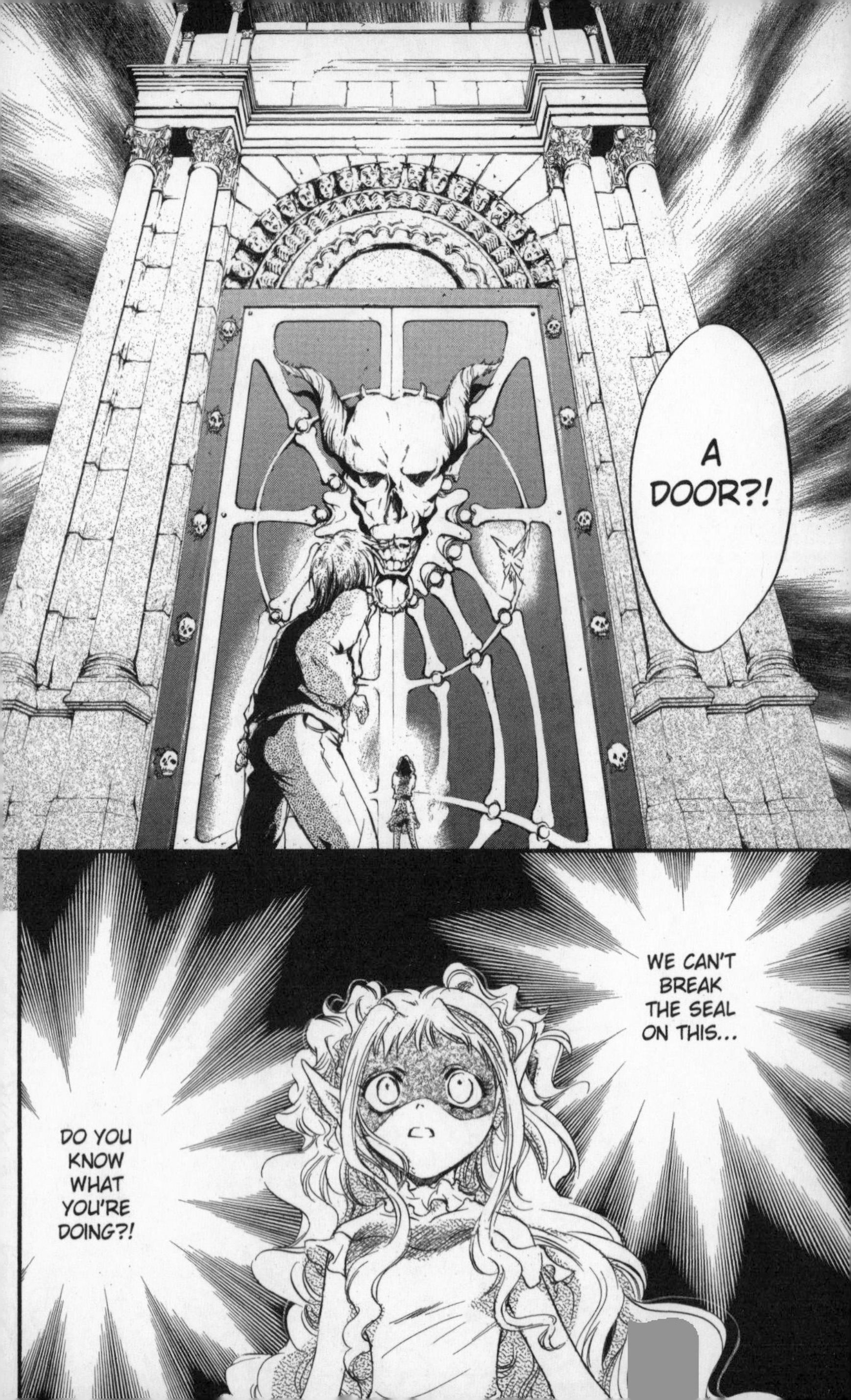
A DOOR?!
WE CAN'T BREAK THE SEAL ON THIS...
DO YOU KNOW WHAT YOU'RE DOING?!

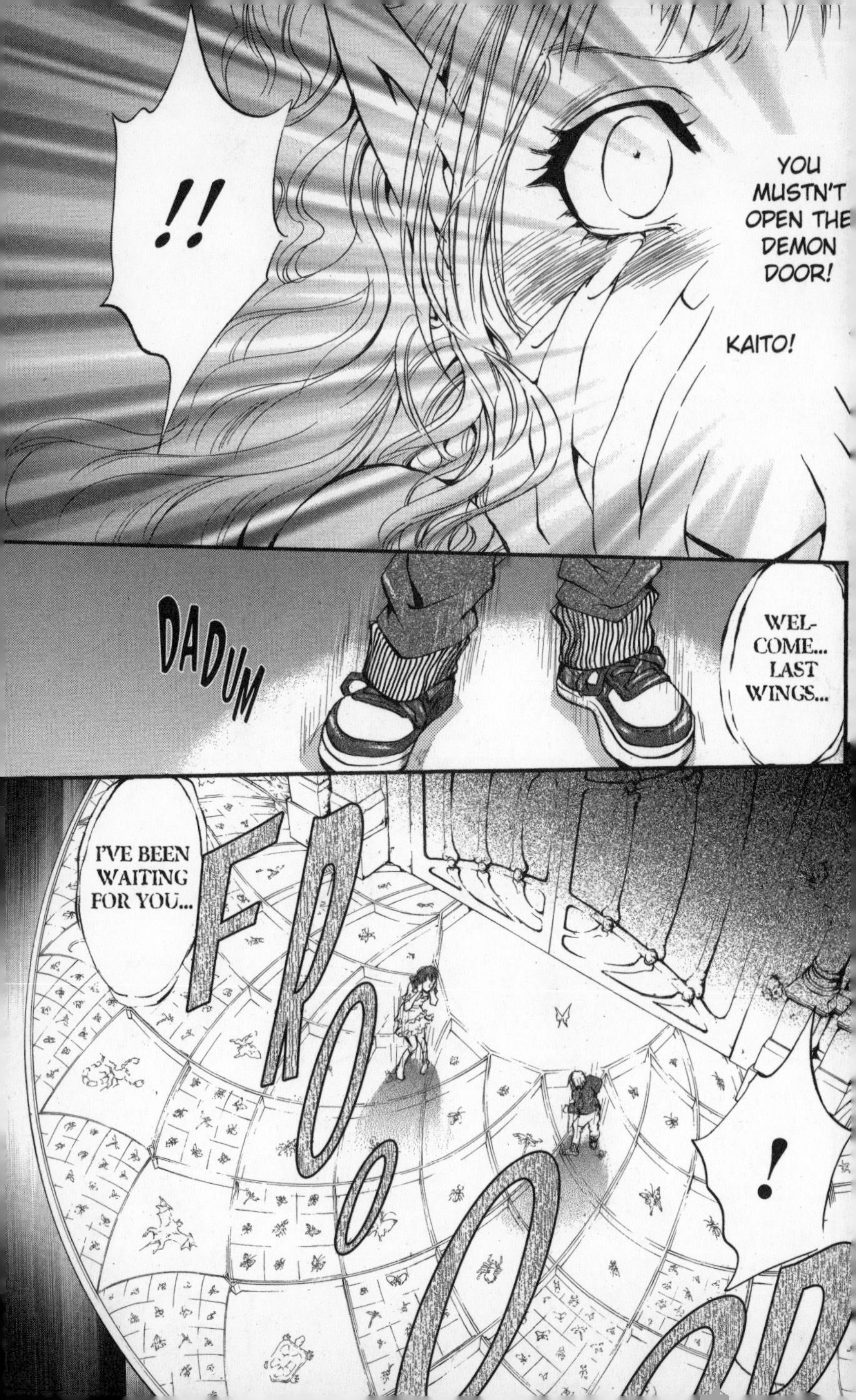
YOU MUSTN'T OPEN THE DEMON DOOR!
KAITO!
!!
WEL-COME... LAST WINGS...
DADUM
I'VE BEEN WAITING FOR YOU...
FROOOO
!

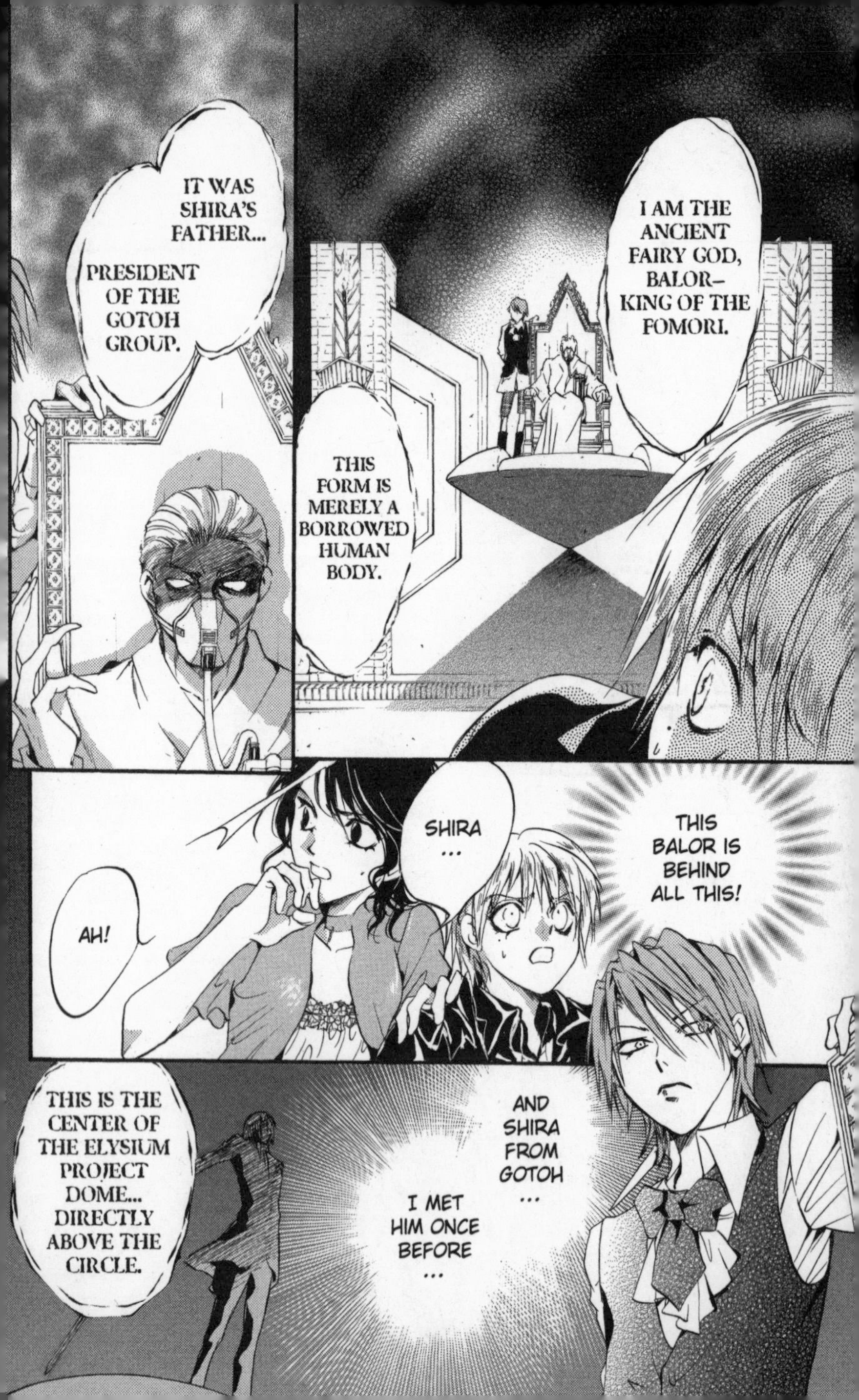
I AM THE ANCIENT FAIRY GOD, BALOR— KING OF THE FOMORI.
THIS FORM IS MERELY A BORROWED HUMAN BODY.
IT WAS SHIRA'S FATHER...
PRESIDENT OF THE GOTOH GROUP.
THIS BALOR IS BEHIND ALL THIS!
SHIRA ...
AH!
AND SHIRA FROM GOTOH ...
I MET HIM ONCE BEFORE ...
THIS IS THE CENTER OF THE ELYSIUM PROJECT DOME... DIRECTLY ABOVE THE CIRCLE.

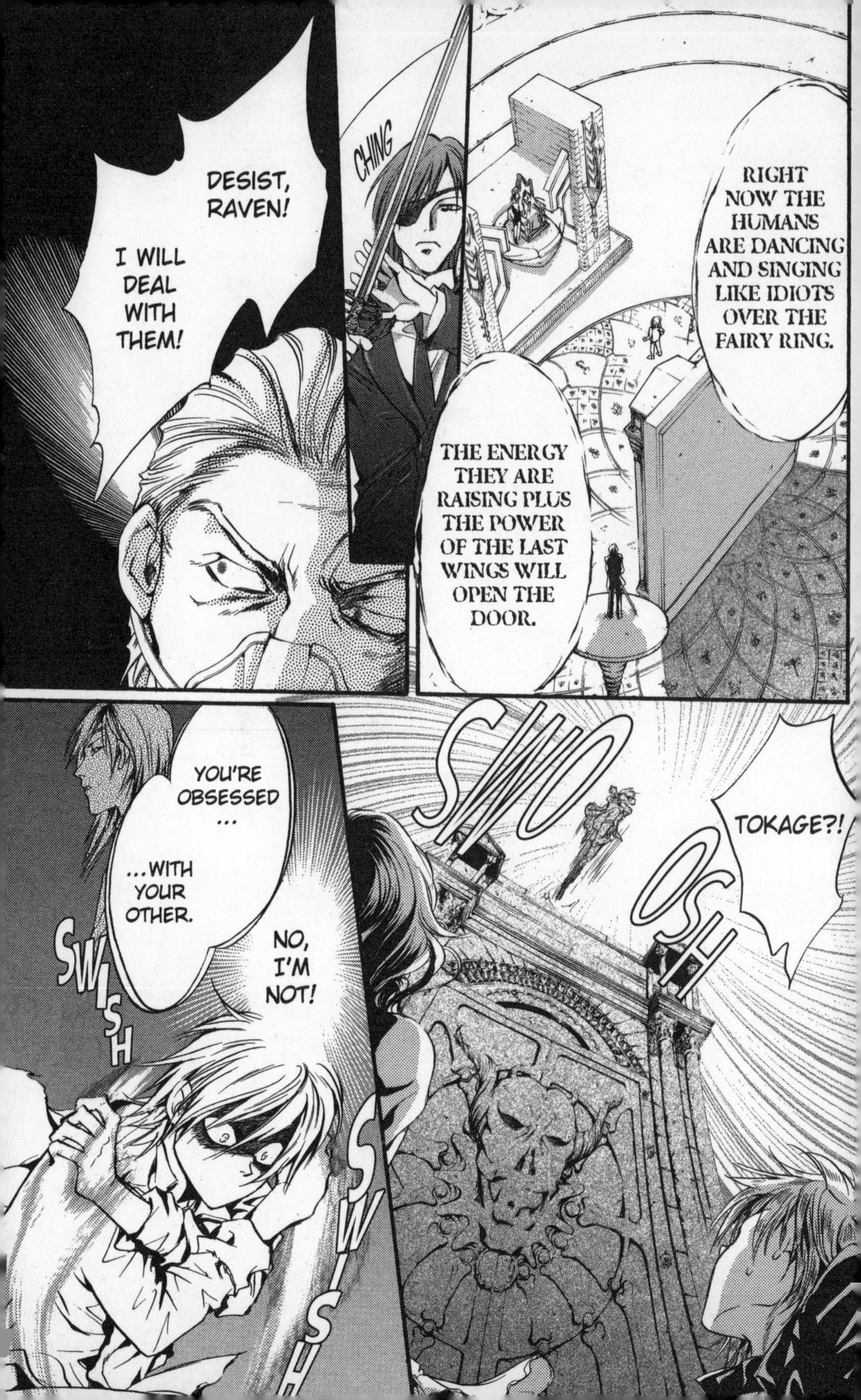

RIGHT NOW THE HUMANS ARE DANCING AND SINGING LIKE IDIOTS OVER THE FAIRY RING.
THE ENERGY THEY ARE RAISING PLUS THE POWER OF THE LAST WINGS WILL OPEN THE DOOR.
CHING
DESIST, RAVEN!
I WILL DEAL WITH THEM!
TOKAGE?!
SWOOSH
YOU'RE OBSESSED ...
...WITH YOUR OTHER.
SWISH
NO, I'M NOT!
SWISH

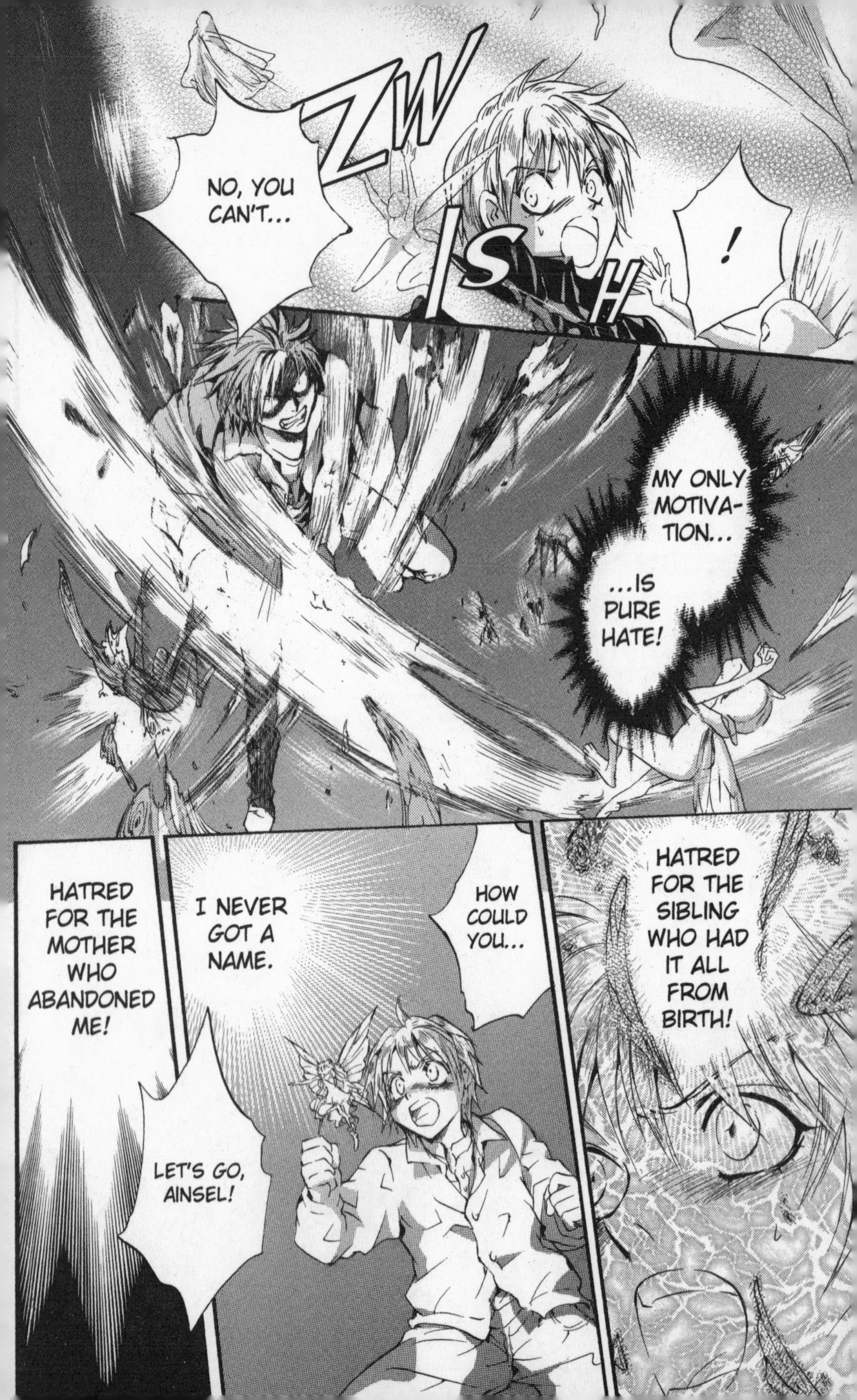
!
ZWISH
NO, YOU CAN'T...
MY ONLY MOTIVATION...
...IS PURE HATE!
HATRED FOR THE SIBLING WHO HAD IT ALL FROM BIRTH!
HOW COULD YOU...
I NEVER GOT A NAME.
HATRED FOR THE MOTHER WHO ABANDONED ME!
LET'S GO, AINSEL!

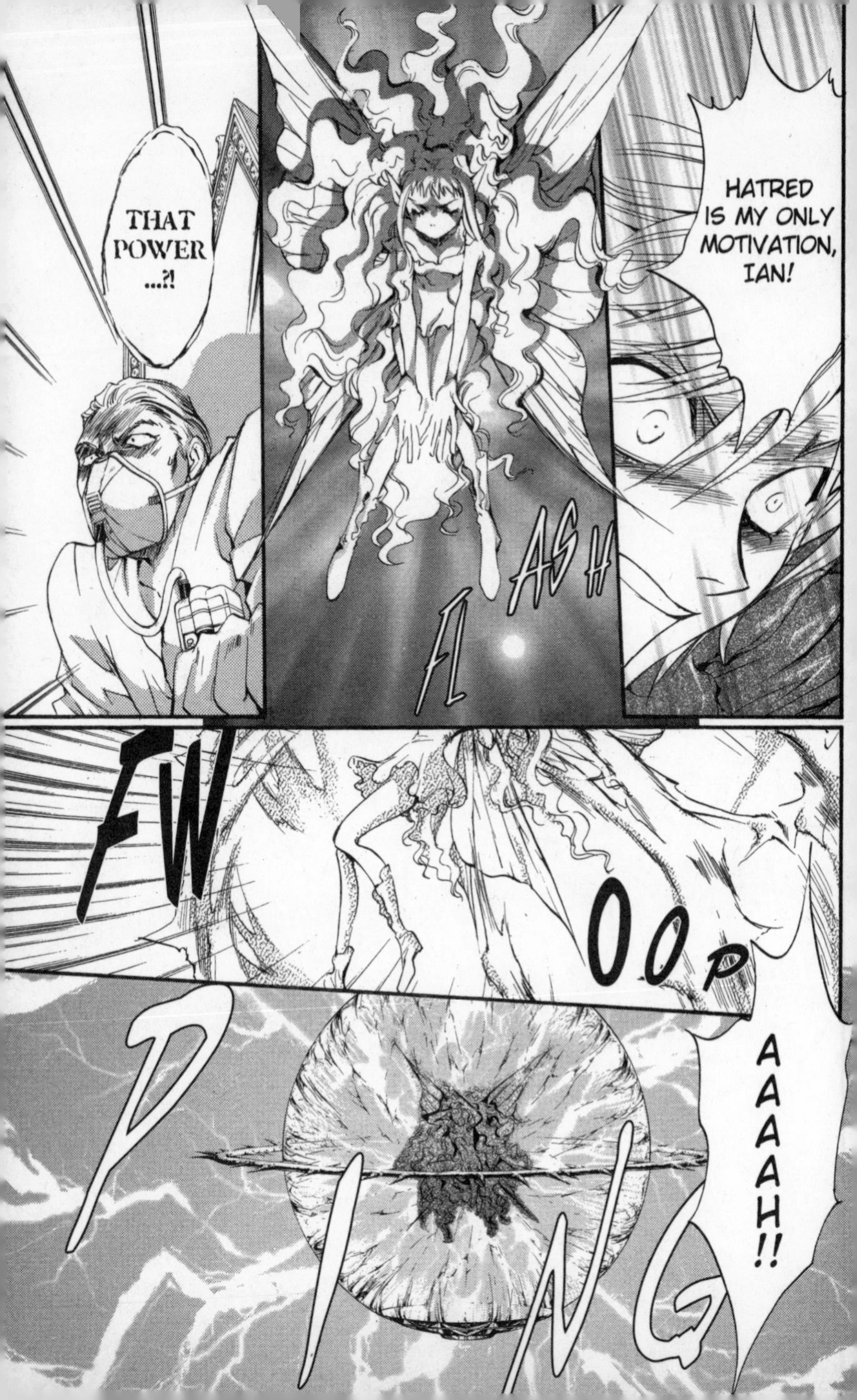
HATRED IS MY ONLY MOTIVATION, IAN!
FLASH
THAT POWER ...?!
FWOOP
AAAAAH!!
DING

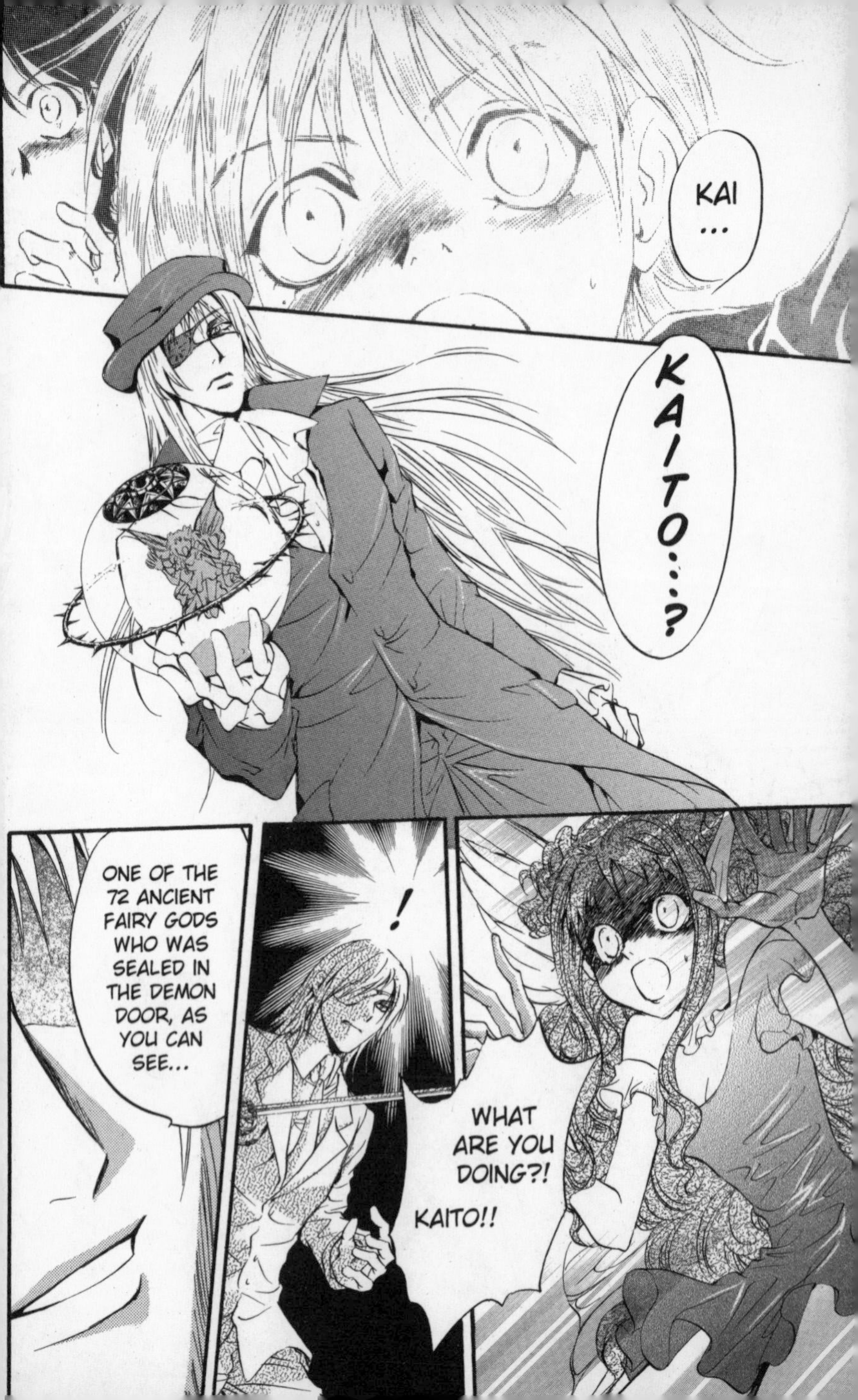
KAI ...
KAITO...?
WHAT ARE YOU DOING?!
KAITO!!
!
ONE OF THE 72 ANCIENT FAIRY GODS WHO WAS SEALED IN THE DEMON DOOR, AS YOU CAN SEE...

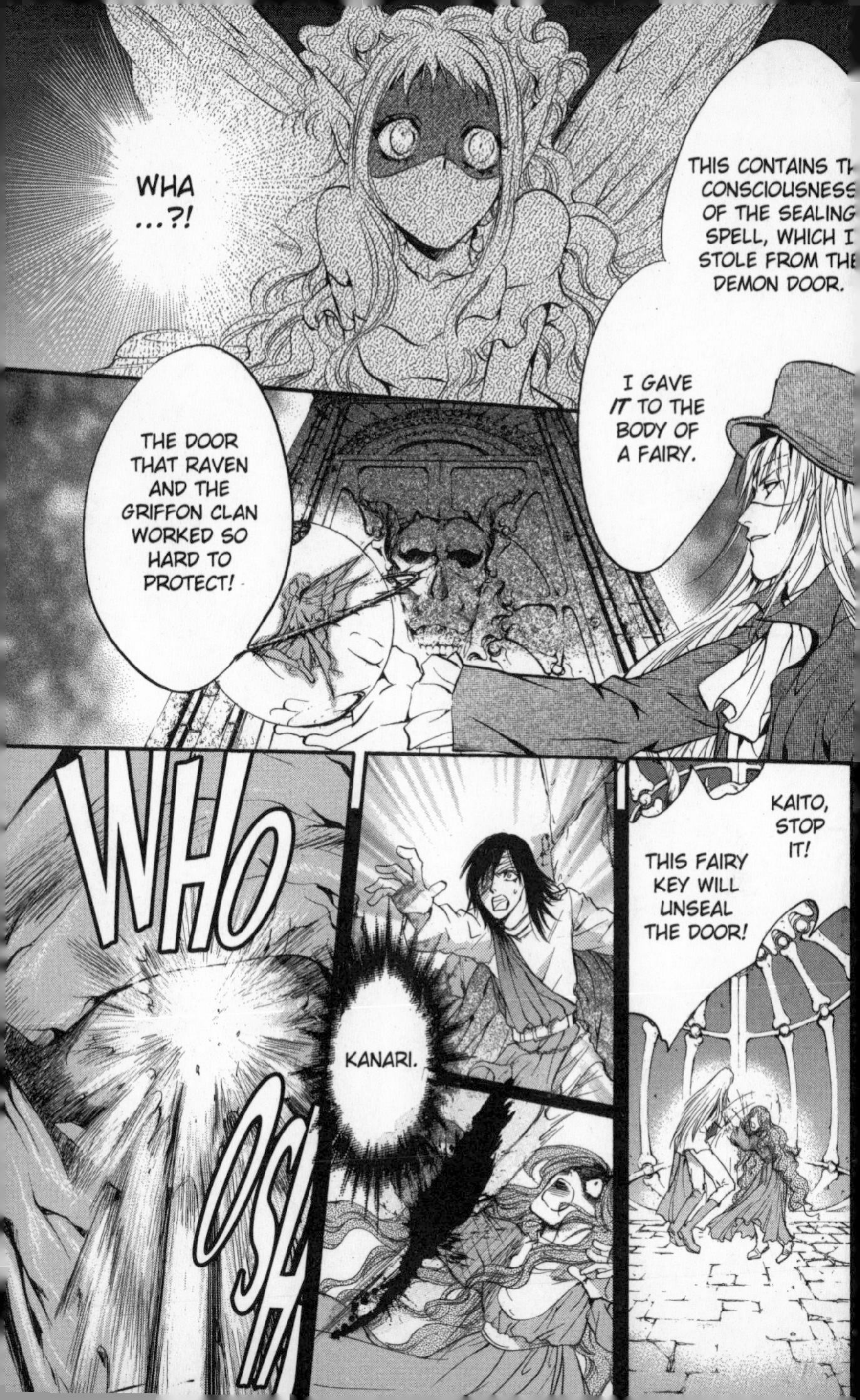
THIS CONTAINS TH CONSCIOUSNESS OF THE SEALING SPELL, WHICH I STOLE FROM THE DEMON DOOR.
WHA ...?!
I GAVE *IT* TO THE BODY OF A FAIRY.
THE DOOR THAT RAVEN AND THE GRIFFON CLAN WORKED SO HARD TO PROTECT!
KAITO, STOP IT!
THIS FAIRY KEY WILL UNSEAL THE DOOR!
KANARI.
WHO
OSH

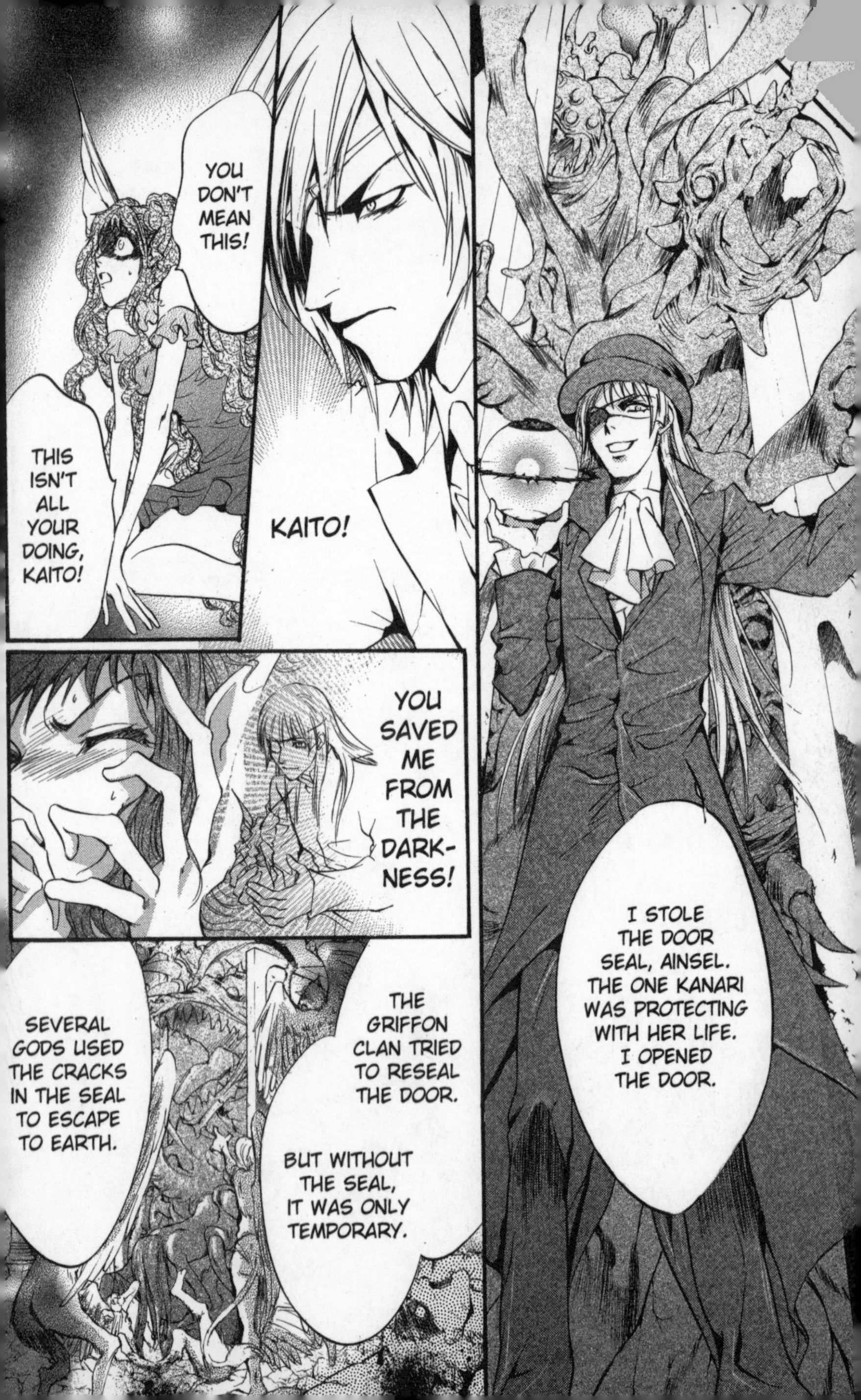
I STOLE THE DOOR SEAL, AINSEL. THE ONE KANARI WAS PROTECTING WITH HER LIFE. I OPENED THE DOOR.
YOU DON'T MEAN THIS!
KAITO!
THIS ISN'T ALL YOUR DOING, KAITO!
YOU SAVED ME FROM THE DARK-NESS!
THE GRIFFON CLAN TRIED TO RESEAL THE DOOR.
BUT WITHOUT THE SEAL, IT WAS ONLY TEMPORARY.
SEVERAL GODS USED THE CRACKS IN THE SEAL TO ESCAPE TO EARTH.

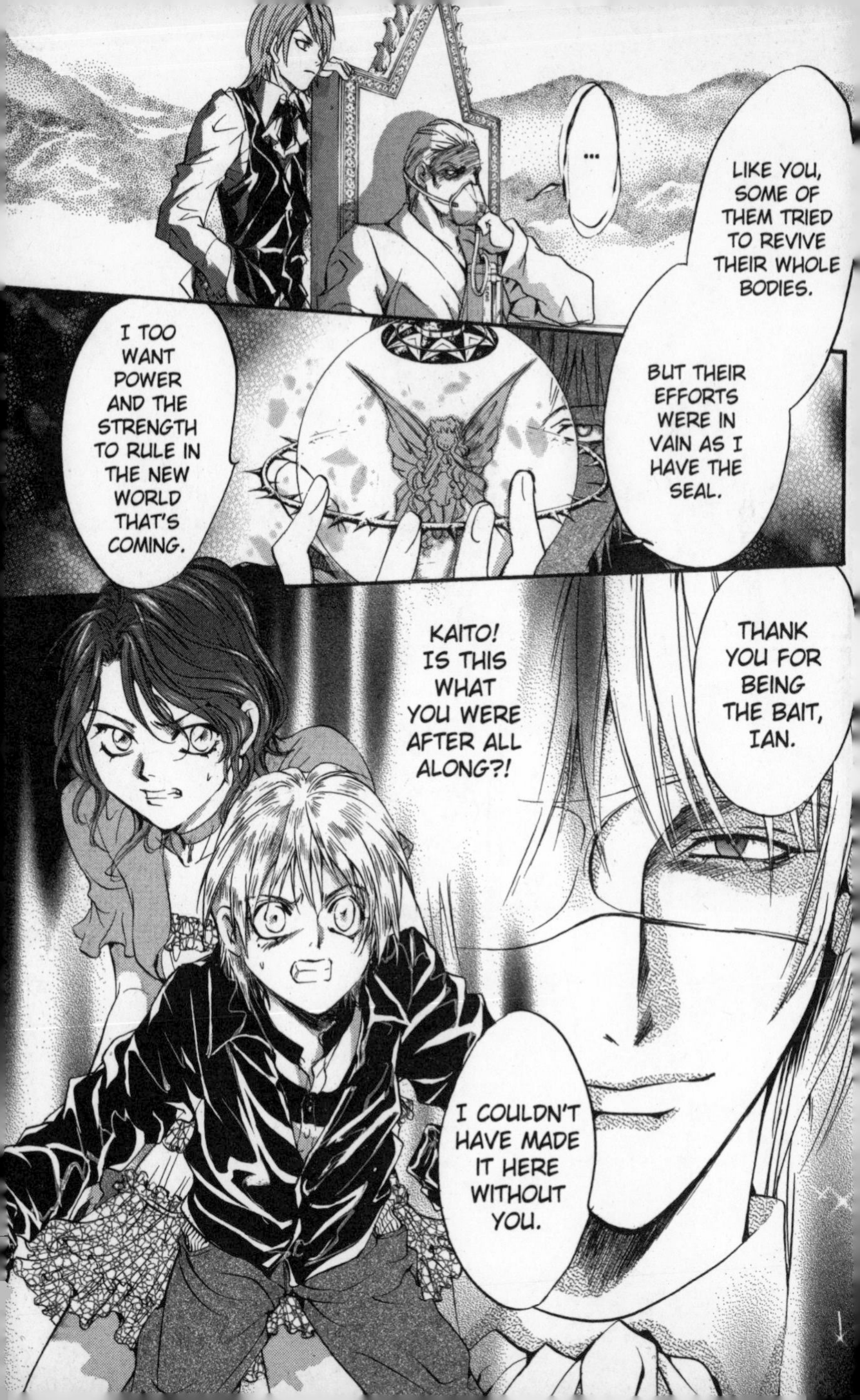
LIKE YOU, SOME OF THEM TRIED TO REVIVE THEIR WHOLE BODIES.
...
BUT THEIR EFFORTS WERE IN VAIN AS I HAVE THE SEAL.
I TOO WANT POWER AND THE STRENGTH TO RULE IN THE NEW WORLD THAT'S COMING.
THANK YOU FOR BEING THE BAIT, IAN.
KAITO! IS THIS WHAT YOU WERE AFTER ALL ALONG?!
I COULDN'T HAVE MADE IT HERE WITHOUT YOU.

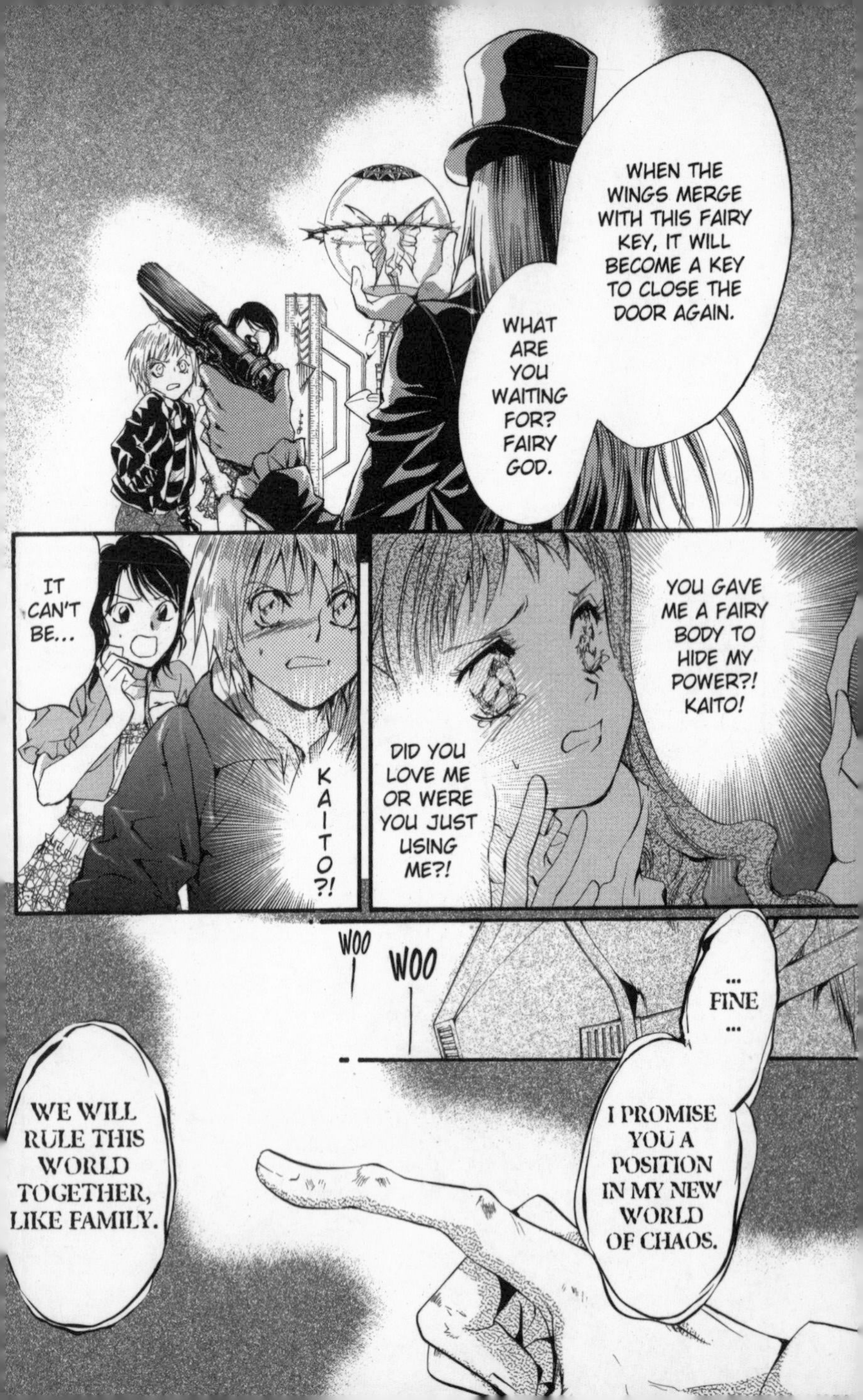
WHEN THE WINGS MERGE WITH THIS FAIRY KEY, IT WILL BECOME A KEY TO CLOSE THE DOOR AGAIN.
WHAT ARE YOU WAITING FOR? FAIRY GOD.
YOU GAVE ME A FAIRY BODY TO HIDE MY POWER?! KAITO!
DID YOU LOVE ME OR WERE YOU JUST USING ME?!
IT CAN'T BE...
KAITO?!
WOO
WOO
...FINE...
I PROMISE YOU A POSITION IN MY NEW WORLD OF CHAOS.
WE WILL RULE THIS WORLD TOGETHER, LIKE FAMILY.

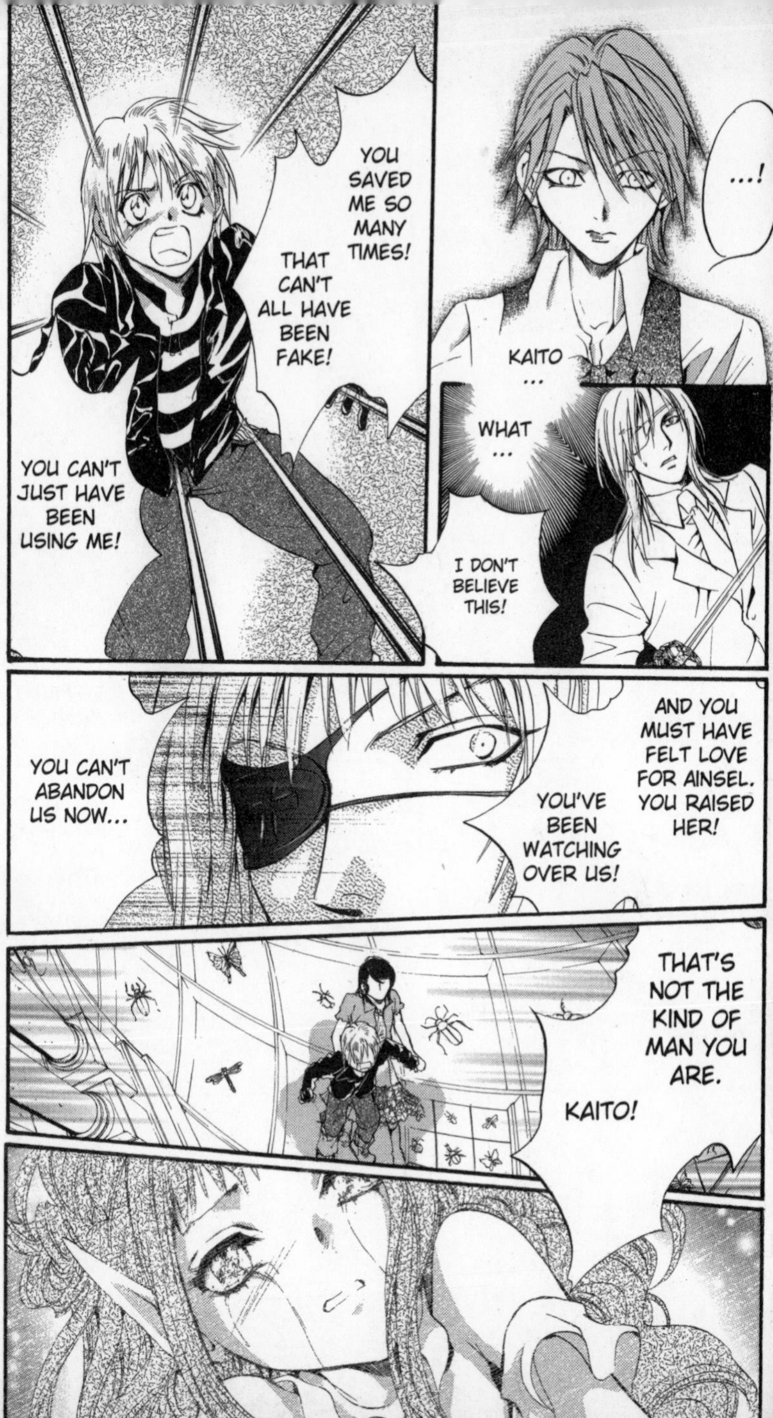
...!
KAITO ...
WHAT ...
I DON'T BELIEVE THIS!
YOU SAVED ME SO MANY TIMES!
THAT CAN'T ALL HAVE BEEN FAKE!
YOU CAN'T JUST HAVE BEEN USING ME!
AND YOU MUST HAVE FELT LOVE FOR AINSEL. YOU RAISED HER!
YOU'VE BEEN WATCHING OVER US!
YOU CAN'T ABANDON US NOW...
THAT'S NOT THE KIND OF MAN YOU ARE.
KAITO!

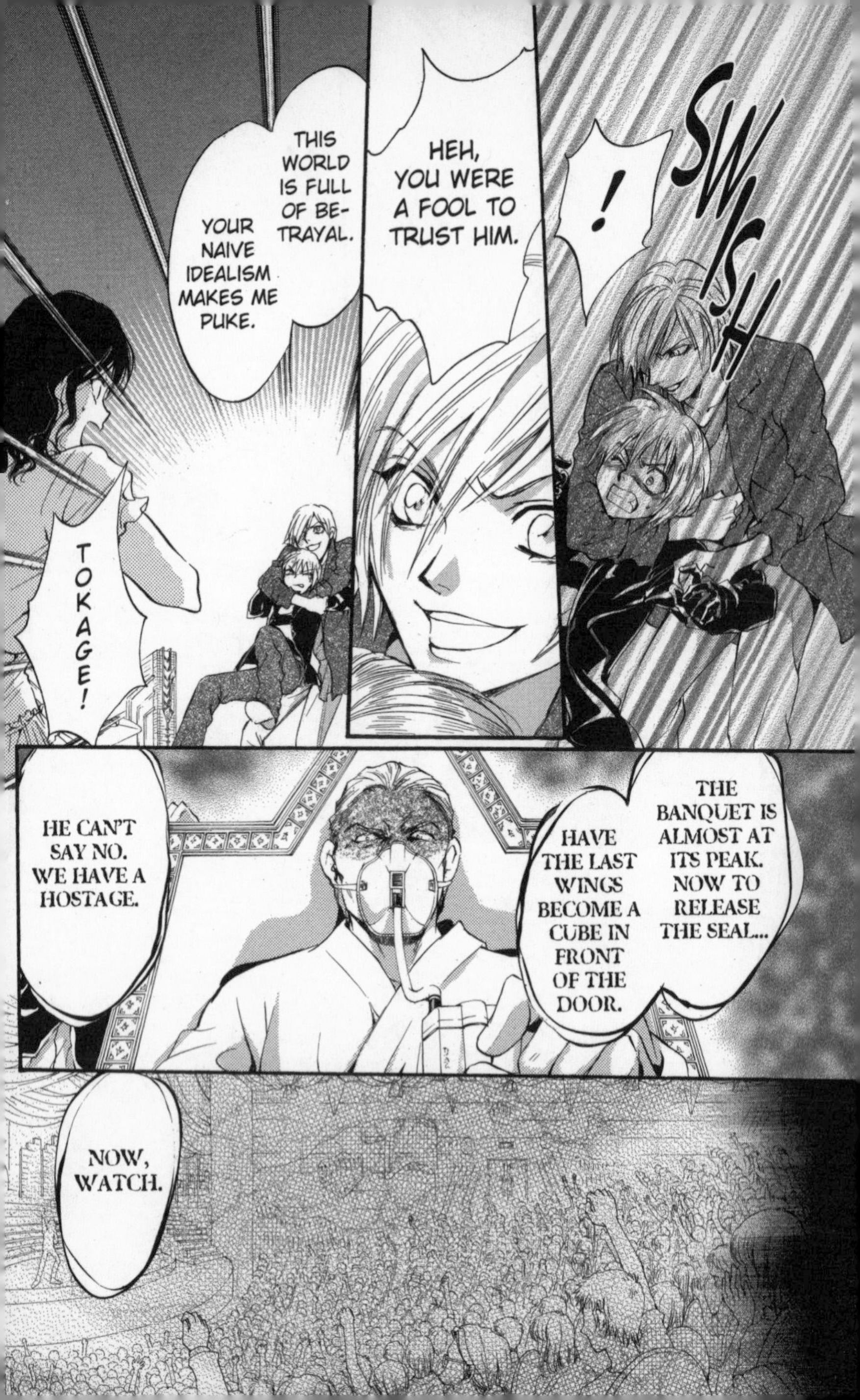
SWISH
!
HEH, YOU WERE A FOOL TO TRUST HIM.
THIS WORLD IS FULL OF BE-TRAYAL.
YOUR NAIVE IDEALISM MAKES ME PUKE.
TOKAGE!
THE BANQUET IS ALMOST AT ITS PEAK. NOW TO RELEASE THE SEAL...
HAVE THE LAST WINGS BECOME A CUBE IN FRONT OF THE DOOR.
HE CAN'T SAY NO. WE HAVE A HOSTAGE.
NOW, WATCH.

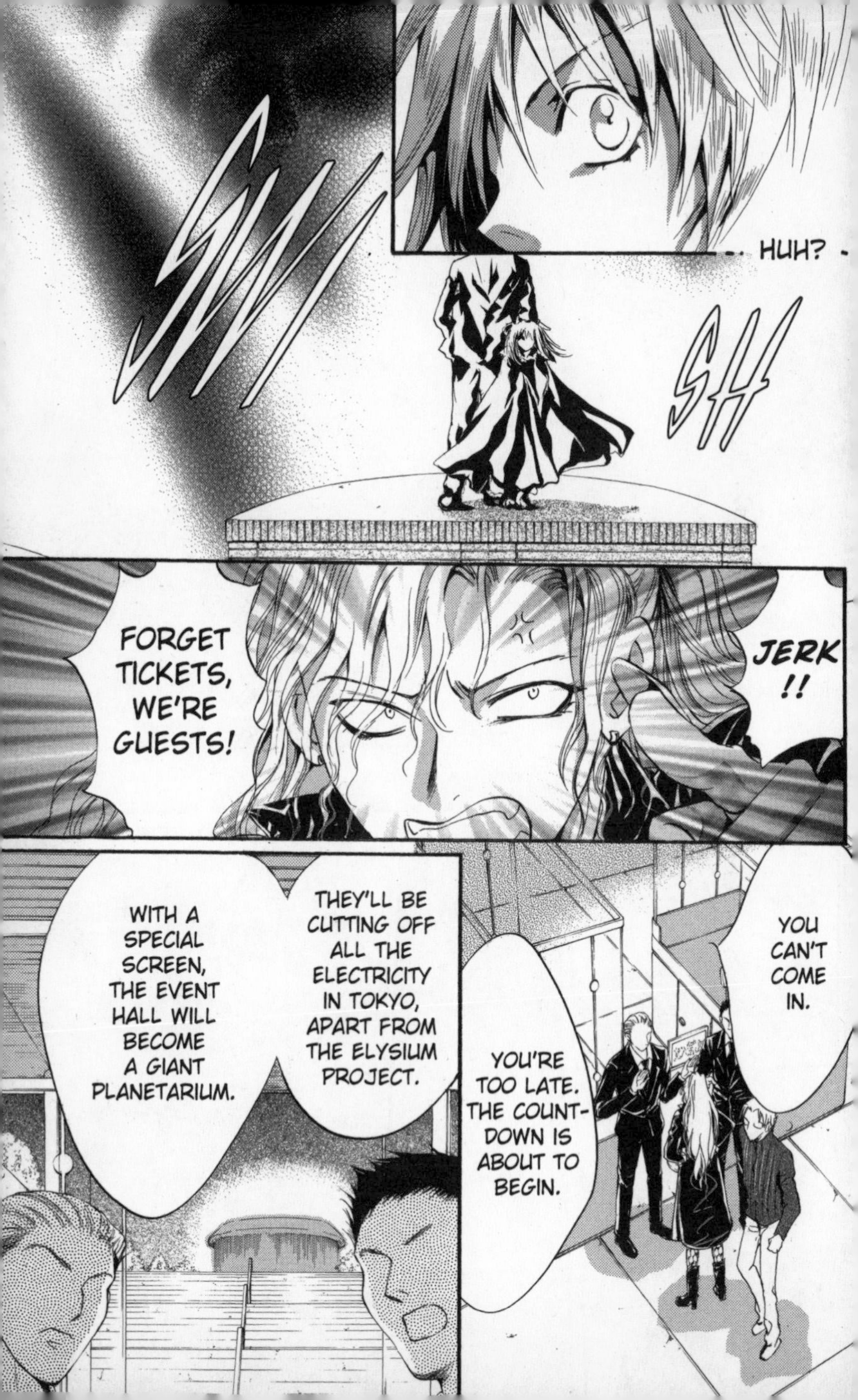

...HUH?...
SWI
SH
JERK!!
FORGET TICKETS, WE'RE GUESTS!
YOU CAN'T COME IN.
YOU'RE TOO LATE. THE COUNT-DOWN IS ABOUT TO BEGIN.
THEY'LL BE CUTTING OFF ALL THE ELECTRICITY IN TOKYO, APART FROM THE ELYSIUM PROJECT.
WITH A SPECIAL SCREEN, THE EVENT HALL WILL BECOME A GIANT PLANETARIUM.

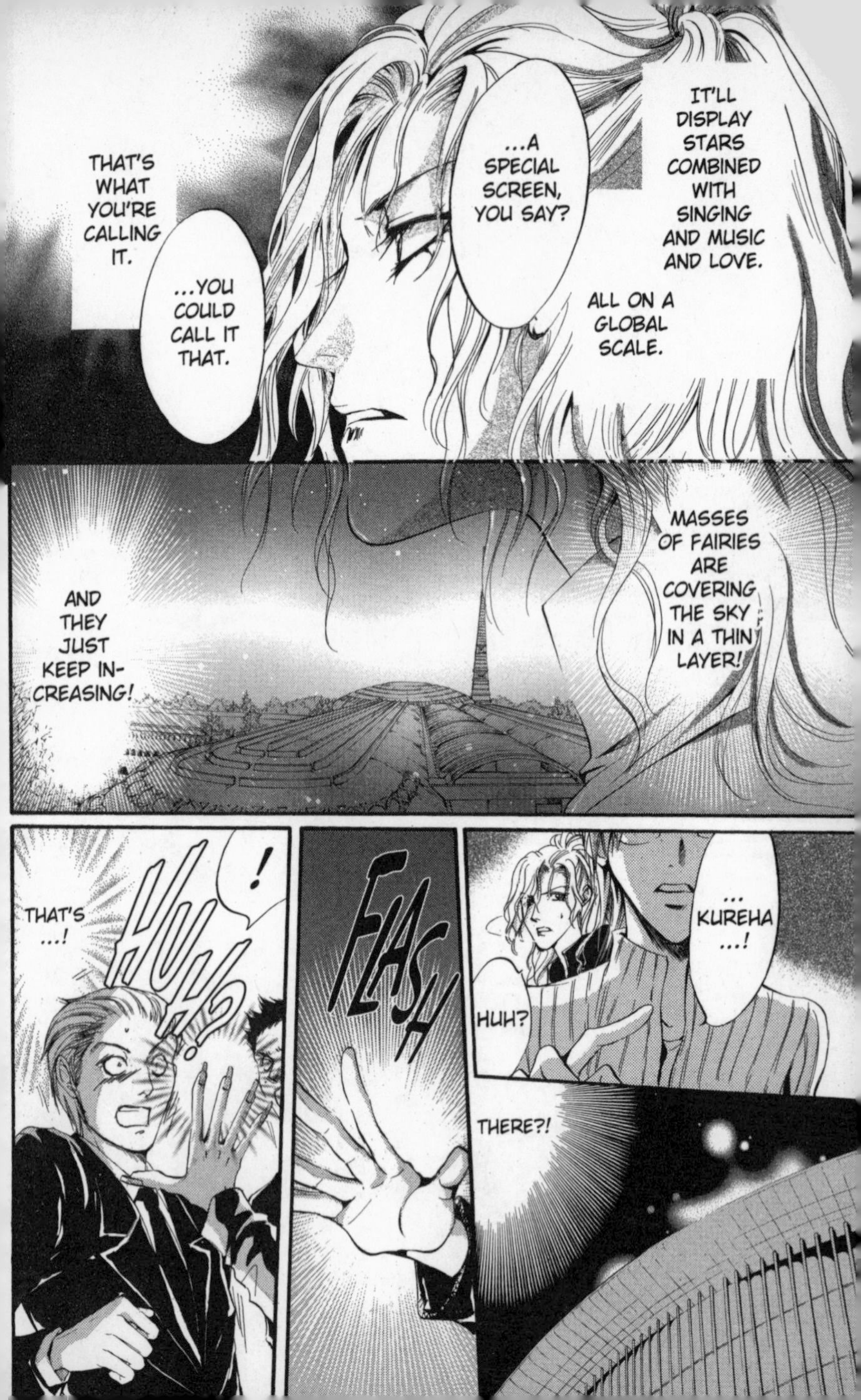

IT'LL DISPLAY STARS COMBINED WITH SINGING AND MUSIC AND LOVE.
ALL ON A GLOBAL SCALE.
...A SPECIAL SCREEN, YOU SAY?
THAT'S WHAT YOU'RE CALLING IT.
...YOU COULD CALL IT THAT.
MASSES OF FAIRIES ARE COVERING THE SKY IN A THIN LAYER!
AND THEY JUST KEEP IN-CREASING!
...KUREHA ...!
HUH?
THERE?!
FLASH
!
HUH!?
THAT'S ...!

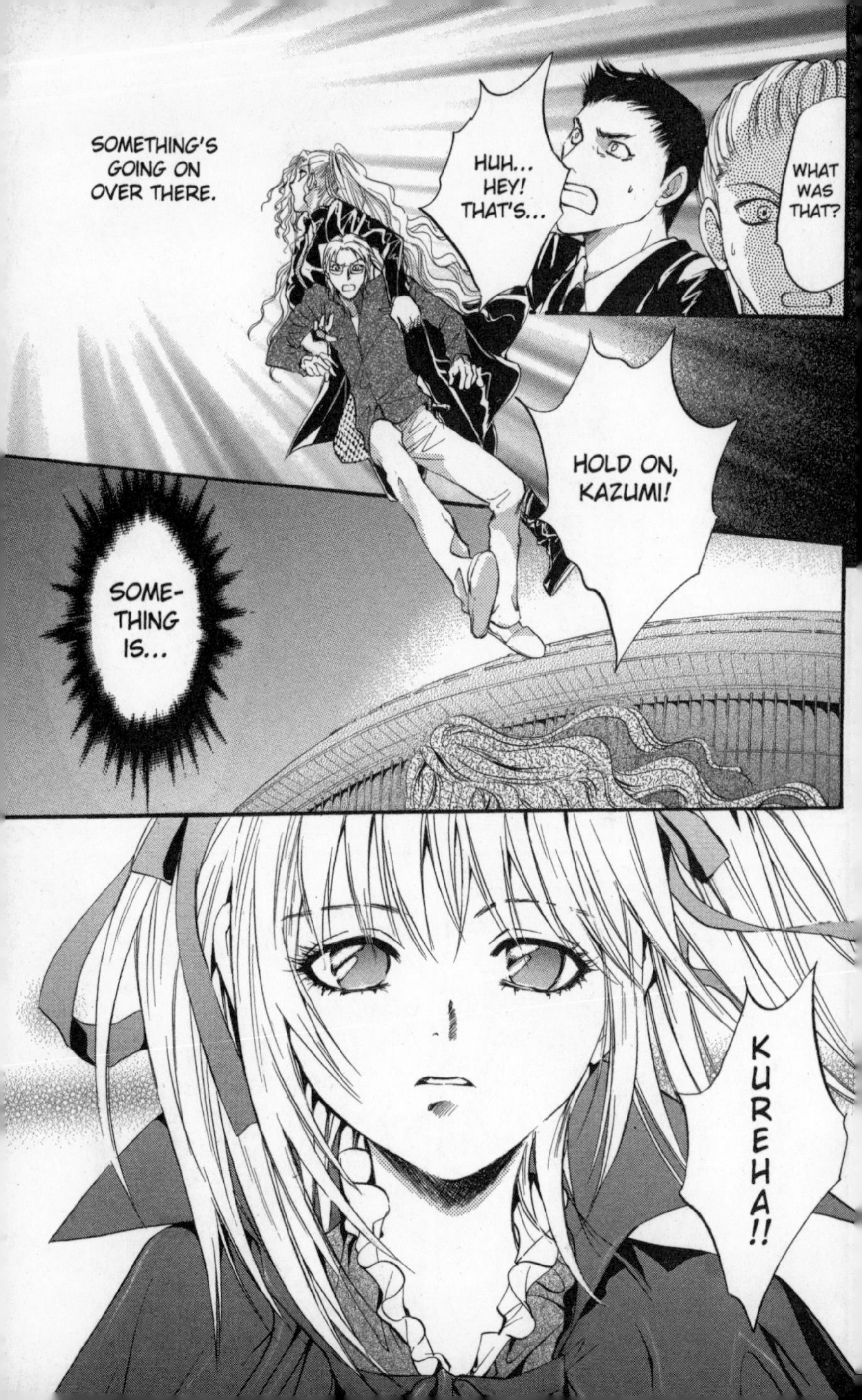
WHAT WAS THAT?
HUH... HEY! THAT'S...
SOMETHING'S GOING ON OVER THERE.
HOLD ON, KAZUMI!
SOME-THING IS...
KUREHA!!

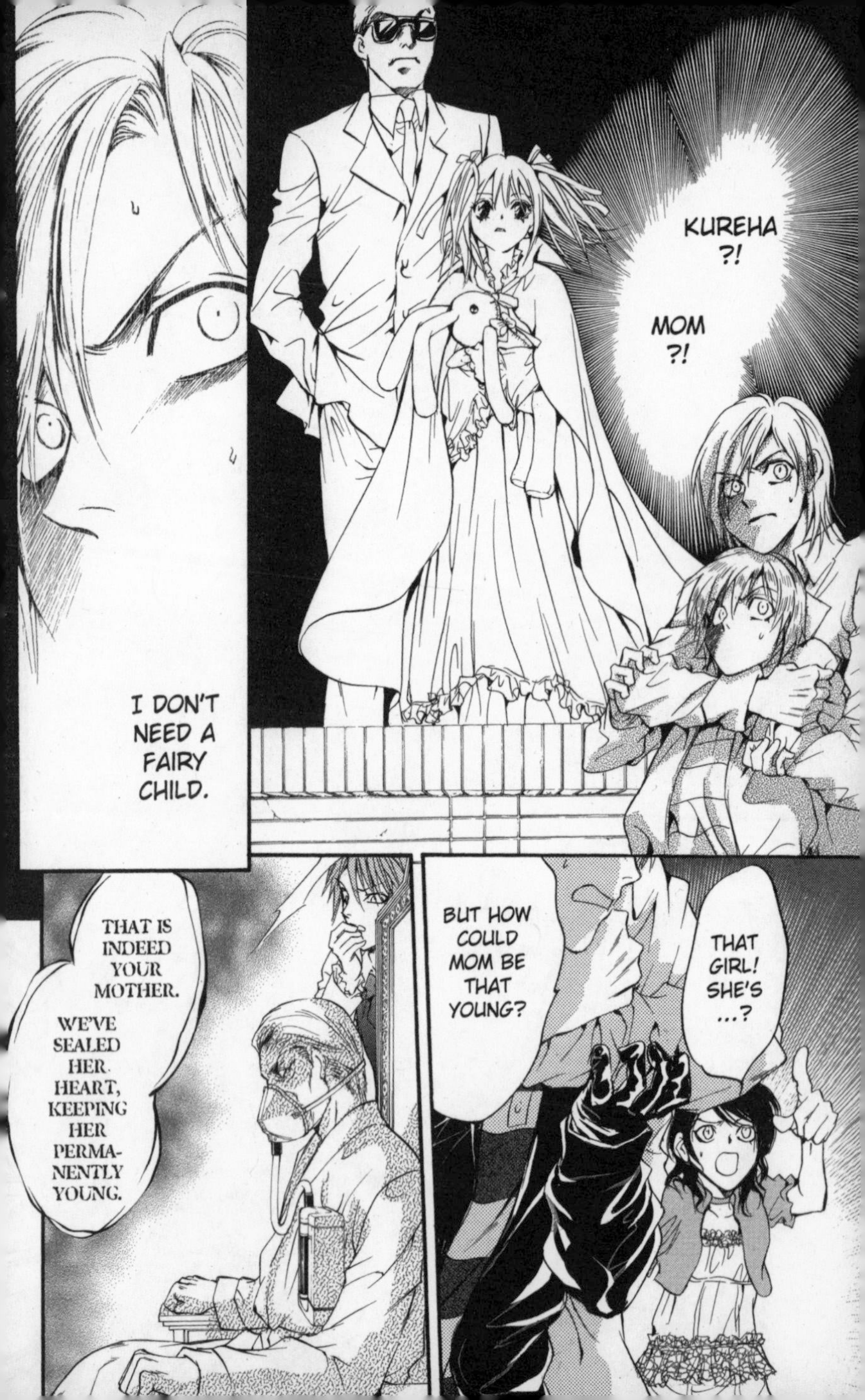
KUREHA ?!
MOM ?!
I DON'T NEED A FAIRY CHILD.
THAT GIRL! SHE'S ...?
BUT HOW COULD MOM BE THAT YOUNG?
THAT IS INDEED YOUR MOTHER.
WE'VE SEALED HER HEART, KEEPING HER PERMANENTLY YOUNG.

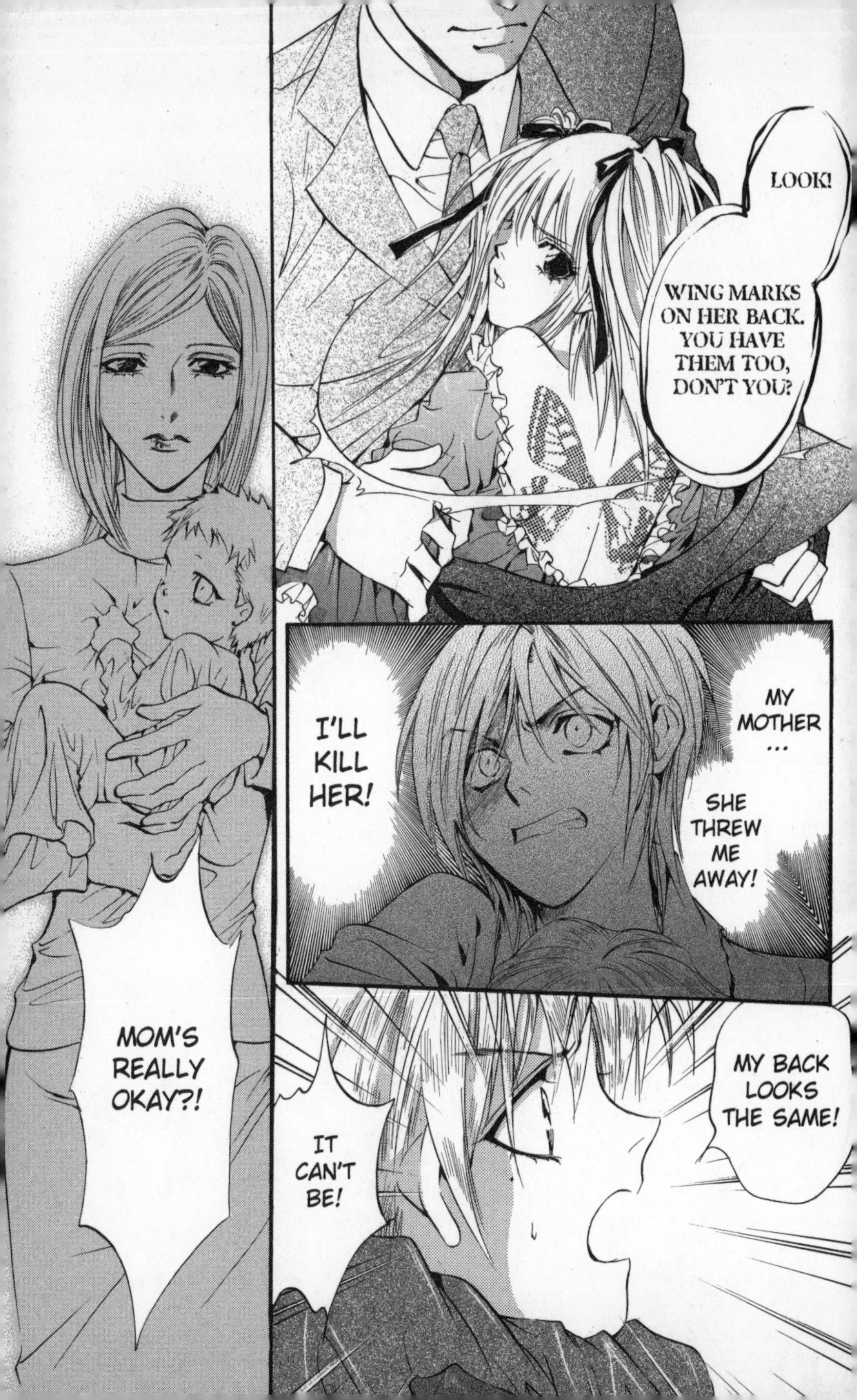
LOOK!
WING MARKS ON HER BACK. YOU HAVE THEM TOO, DON'T YOU?
MY MOTHER...
SHE THREW ME AWAY!
I'LL KILL HER!
MY BACK LOOKS THE SAME!
IT CAN'T BE!
MOM'S REALLY OKAY?!

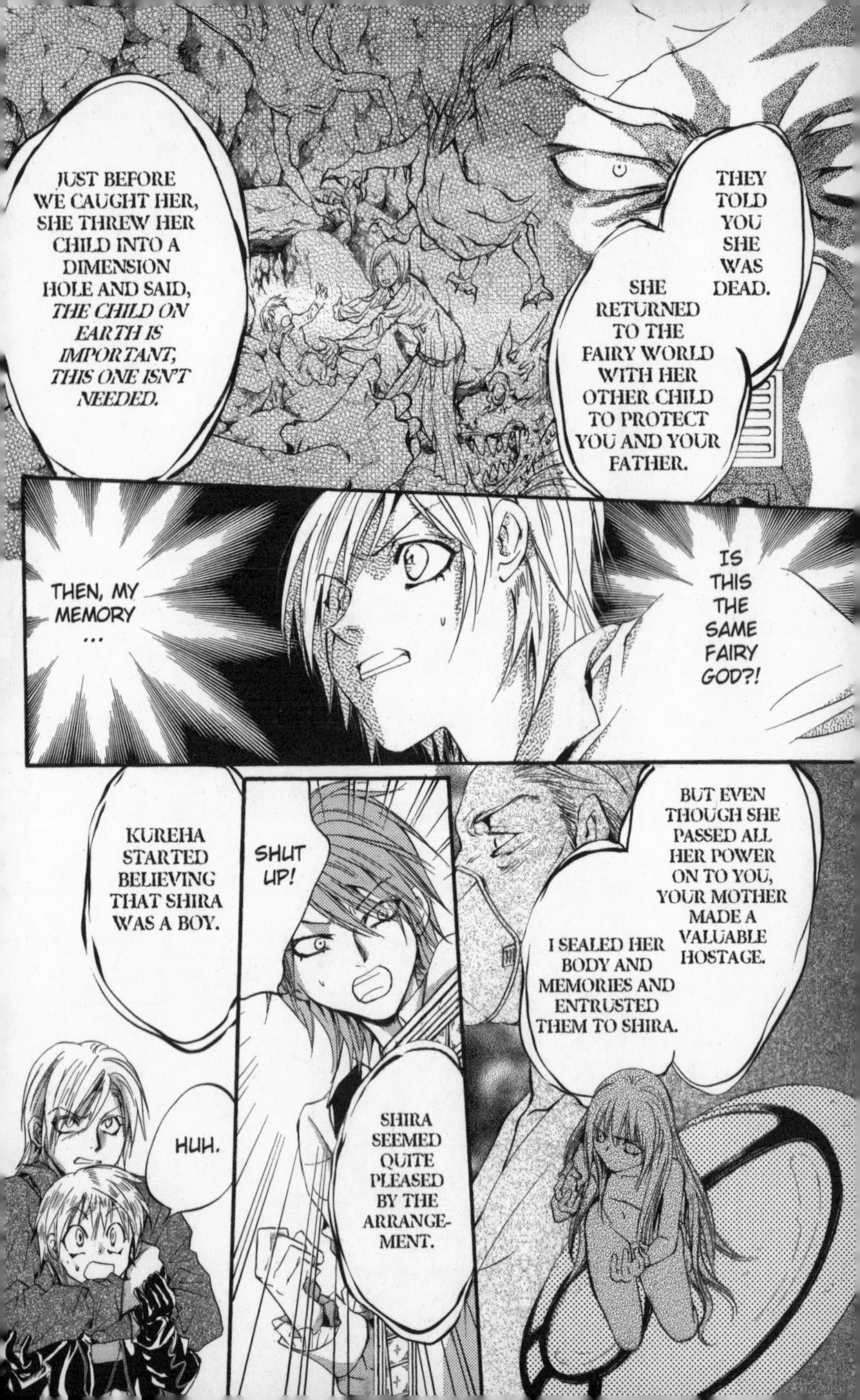
THEY TOLD YOU SHE WAS DEAD.
SHE RETURNED TO THE FAIRY WORLD WITH HER OTHER CHILD TO PROTECT YOU AND YOUR FATHER.
JUST BEFORE WE CAUGHT HER, SHE THREW HER CHILD INTO A DIMENSION HOLE AND SAID, *THE CHILD ON EARTH IS IMPORTANT, THIS ONE ISN'T NEEDED.*
IS THIS THE SAME FAIRY GOD?!
THEN, MY MEMORY ...
BUT EVEN THOUGH SHE PASSED ALL HER POWER ON TO YOU, YOUR MOTHER MADE A VALUABLE HOSTAGE.
I SEALED HER BODY AND MEMORIES AND ENTRUSTED THEM TO SHIRA.
SHIRA SEEMED QUITE PLEASED BY THE ARRANGEMENT.
SHUT UP!
KUREHA STARTED BELIEVING THAT SHIRA WAS A BOY.
HUH.

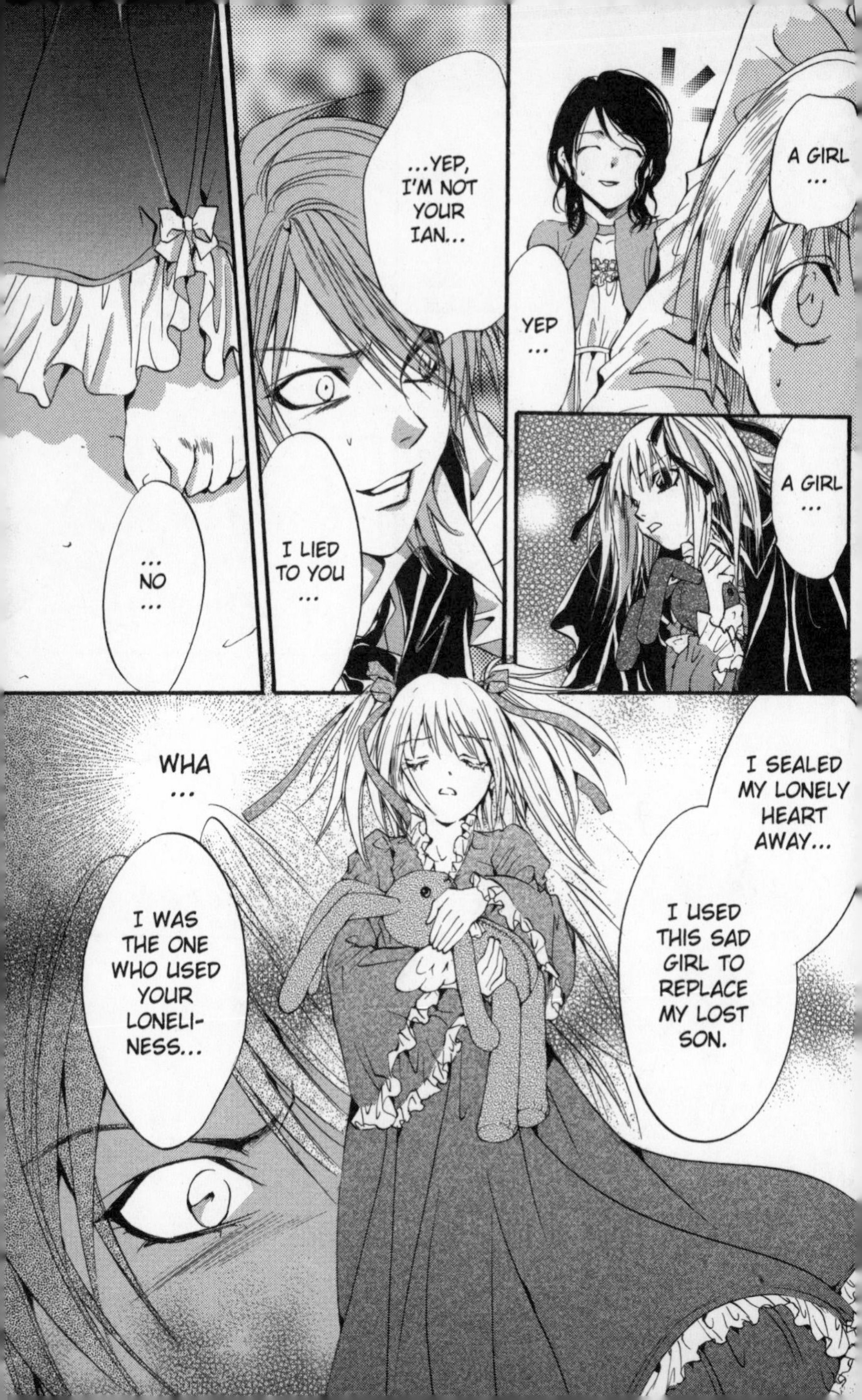
A GIRL ...
YEP ...
A GIRL ...
...YEP, I'M NOT YOUR IAN...
I LIED TO YOU ...
... NO ...
I SEALED MY LONELY HEART AWAY...
I USED THIS SAD GIRL TO REPLACE MY LOST SON.
WHA ...
I WAS THE ONE WHO USED YOUR LONELINESS...

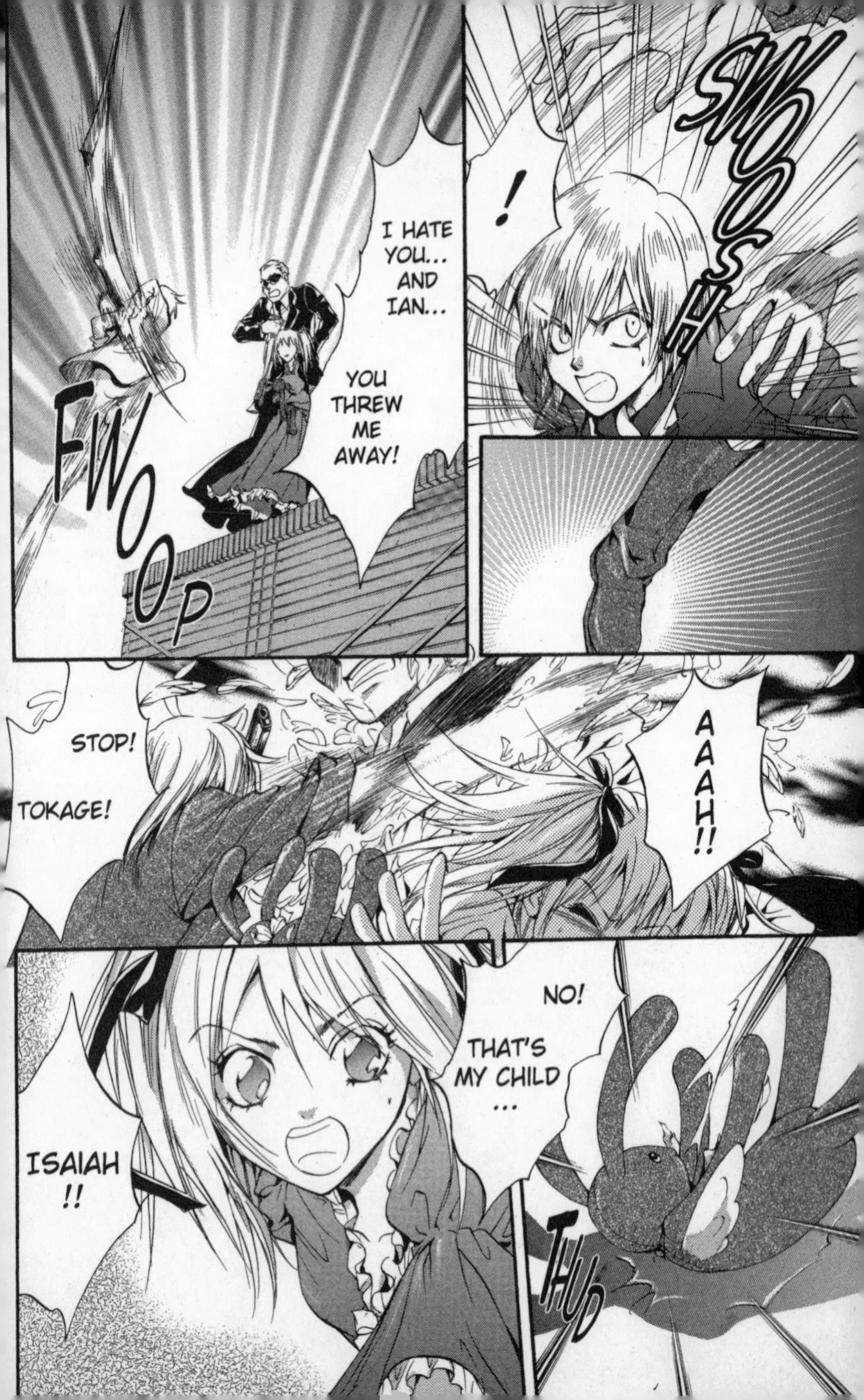
SWOOOSH
!
I HATE YOU... AND IAN...
YOU THREW ME AWAY!
FWOOP
AAAH!!
STOP! TOKAGE!
NO! THAT'S MY CHILD...
THUD
ISAIAH!!

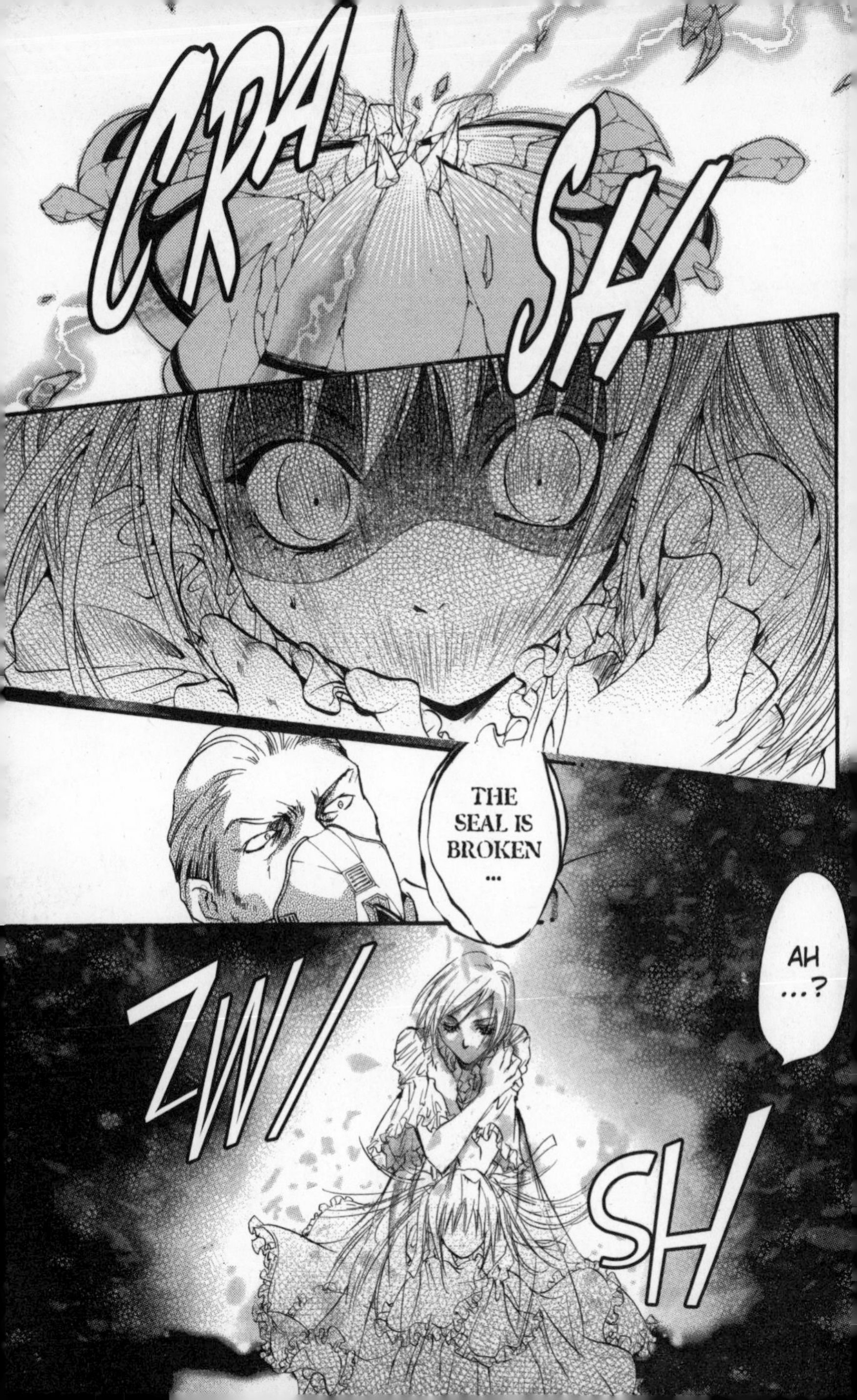
CRASH
THE SEAL IS BROKEN ...
AH ...?
ZWISH

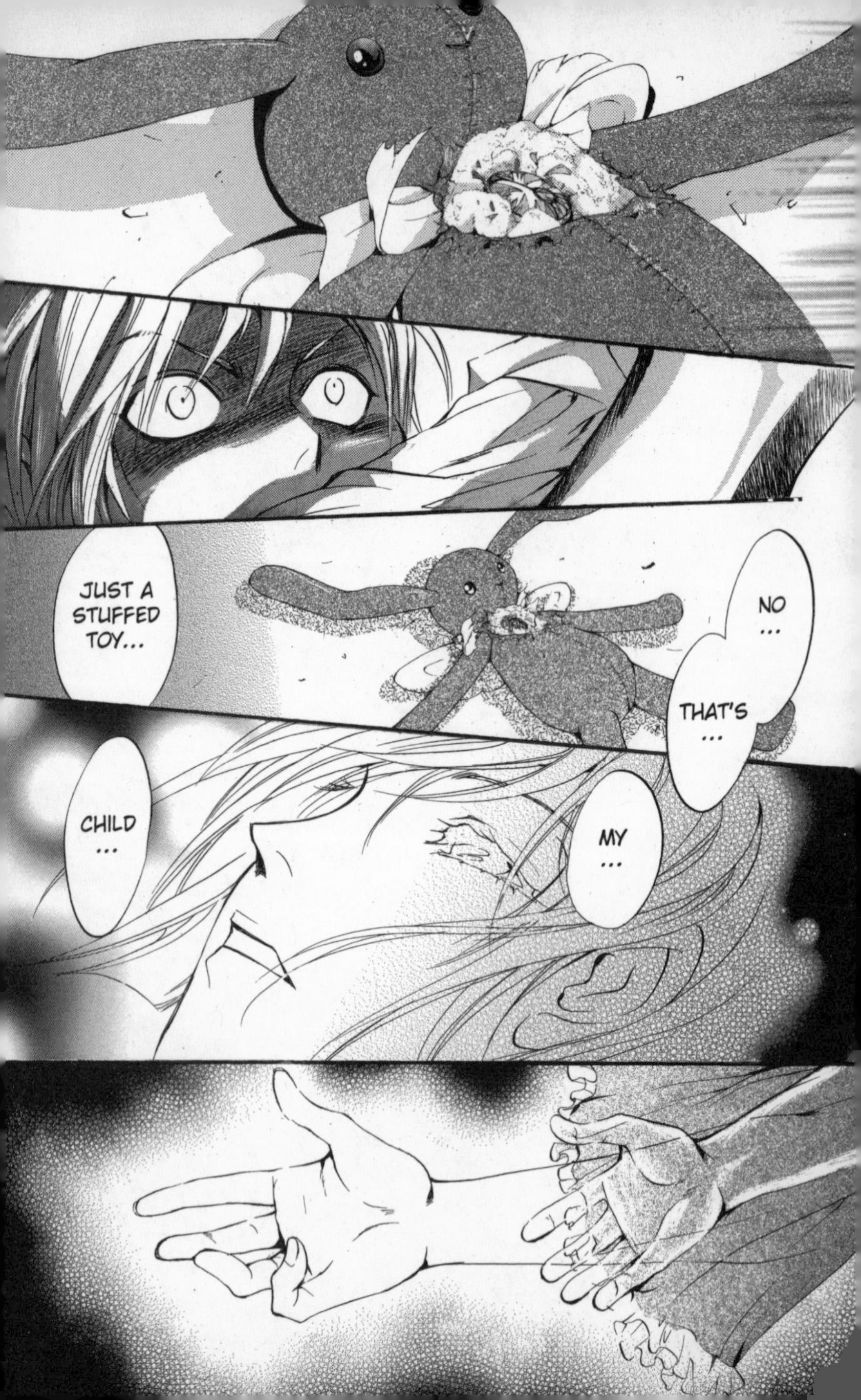
JUST A STUFFED TOY...
NO ...
THAT'S ...
MY ...
CHILD ...

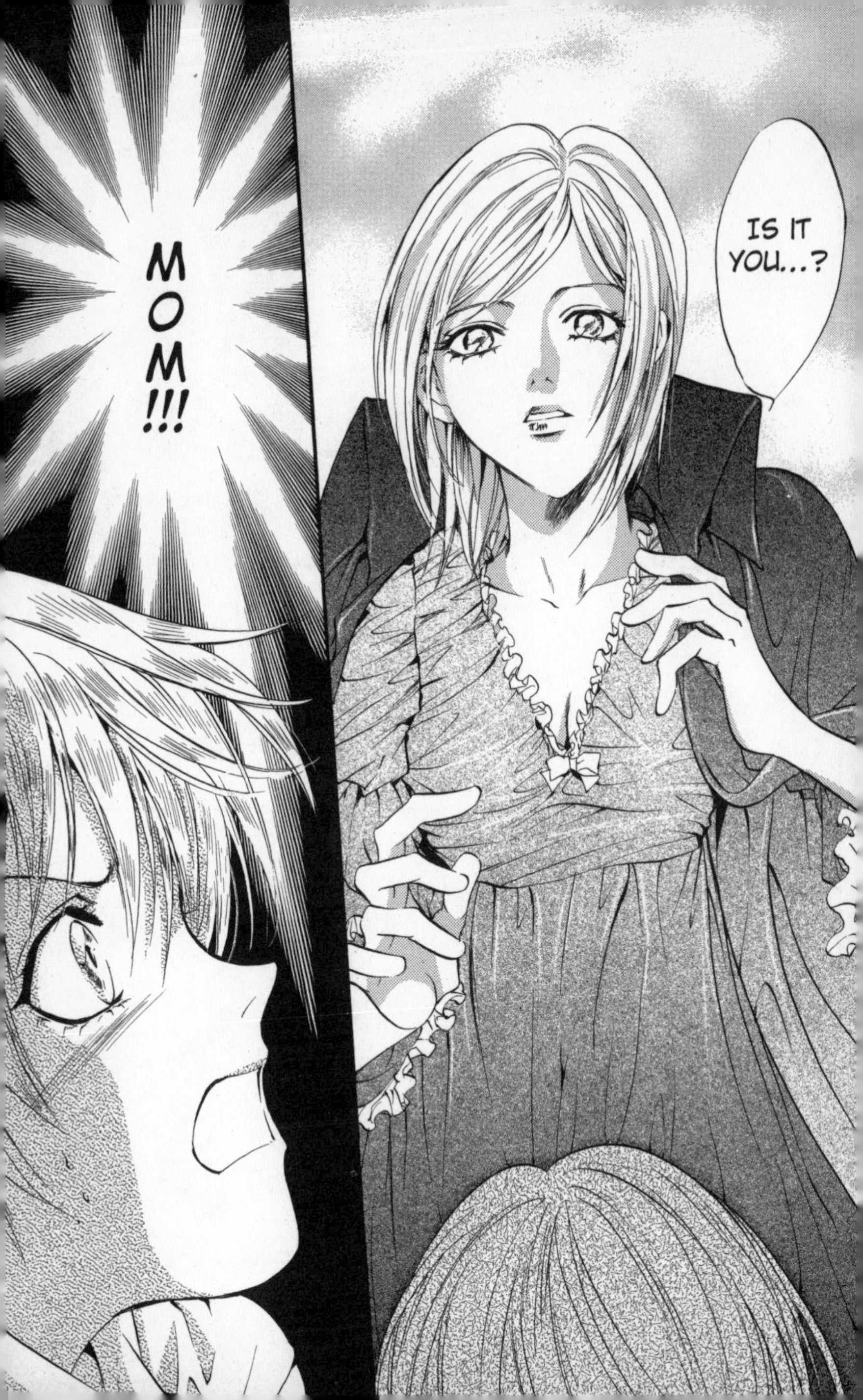
IS IT YOU...?
MOM!!!

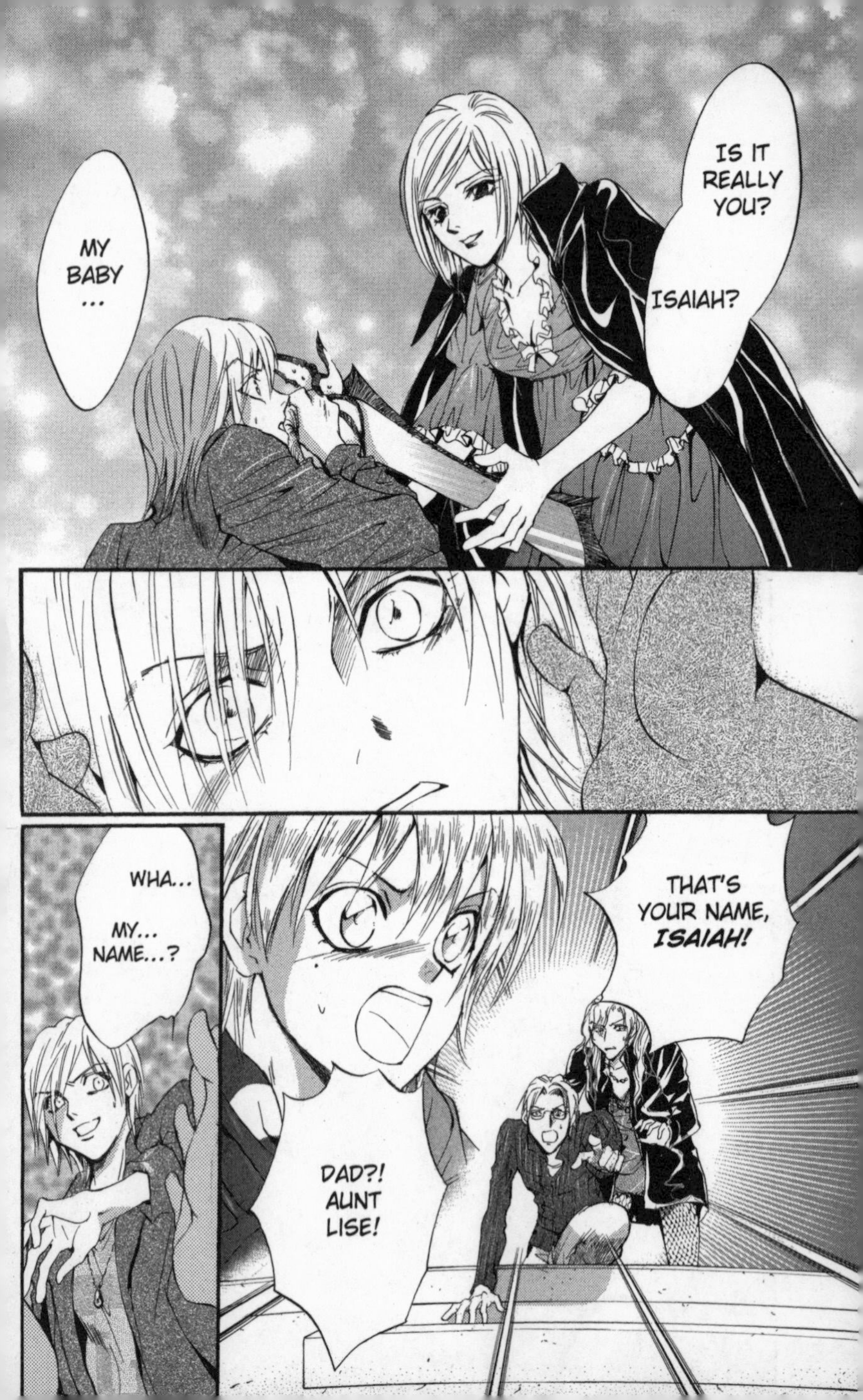
IS IT REALLY YOU?
ISAIAH?
MY BABY...
THAT'S YOUR NAME, *ISAIAH!*
DAD?! AUNT LISE!
WHA...
MY... NAME...?

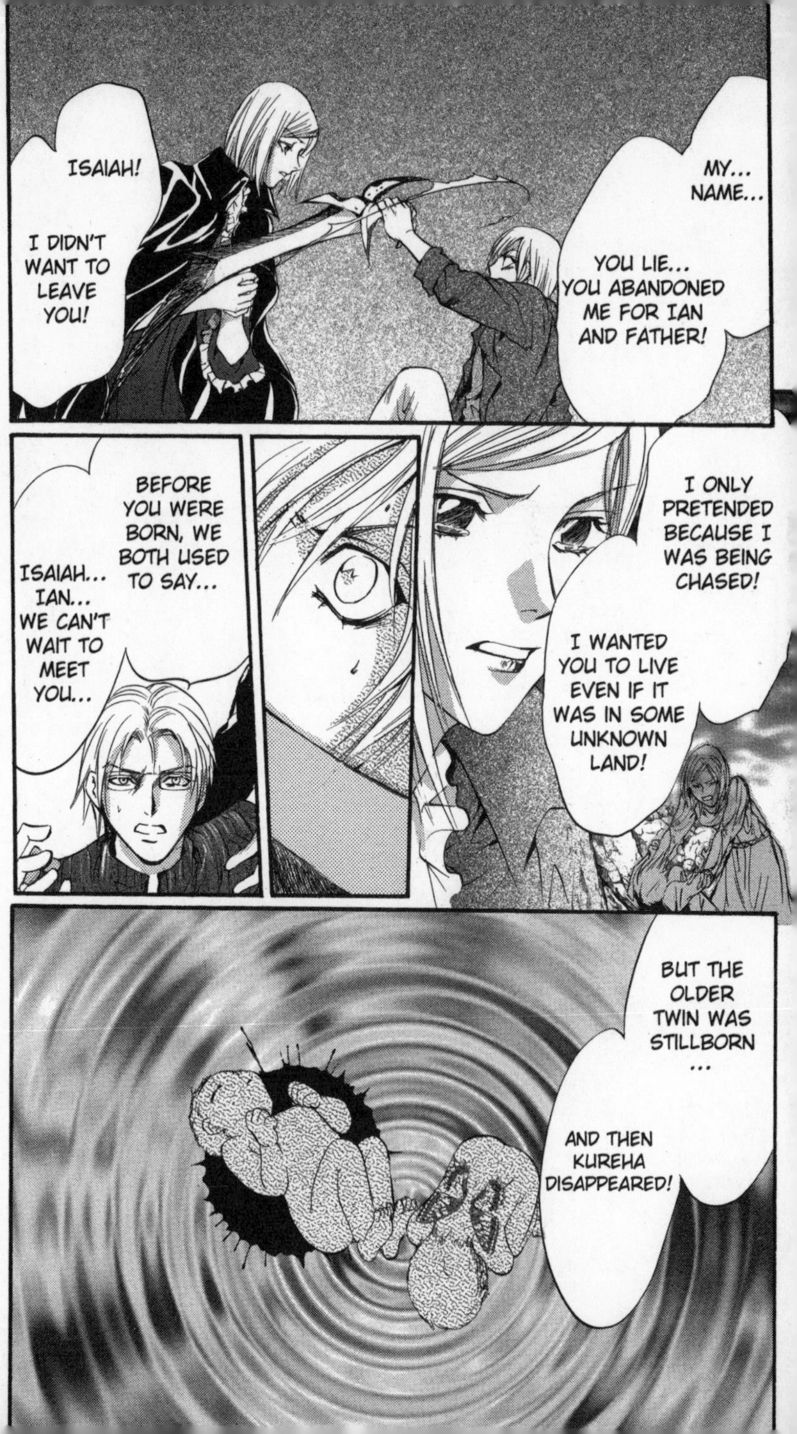
MY... NAME...
YOU LIE... YOU ABANDONED ME FOR IAN AND FATHER!
ISAIAH!
I DIDN'T WANT TO LEAVE YOU!
I ONLY PRETENDED BECAUSE I WAS BEING CHASED!
I WANTED YOU TO LIVE EVEN IF IT WAS IN SOME UNKNOWN LAND!
BEFORE YOU WERE BORN, WE BOTH USED TO SAY...
ISAIAH... IAN... WE CAN'T WAIT TO MEET YOU...
BUT THE OLDER TWIN WAS STILLBORN ...
AND THEN KUREHA DISAPPEARED!

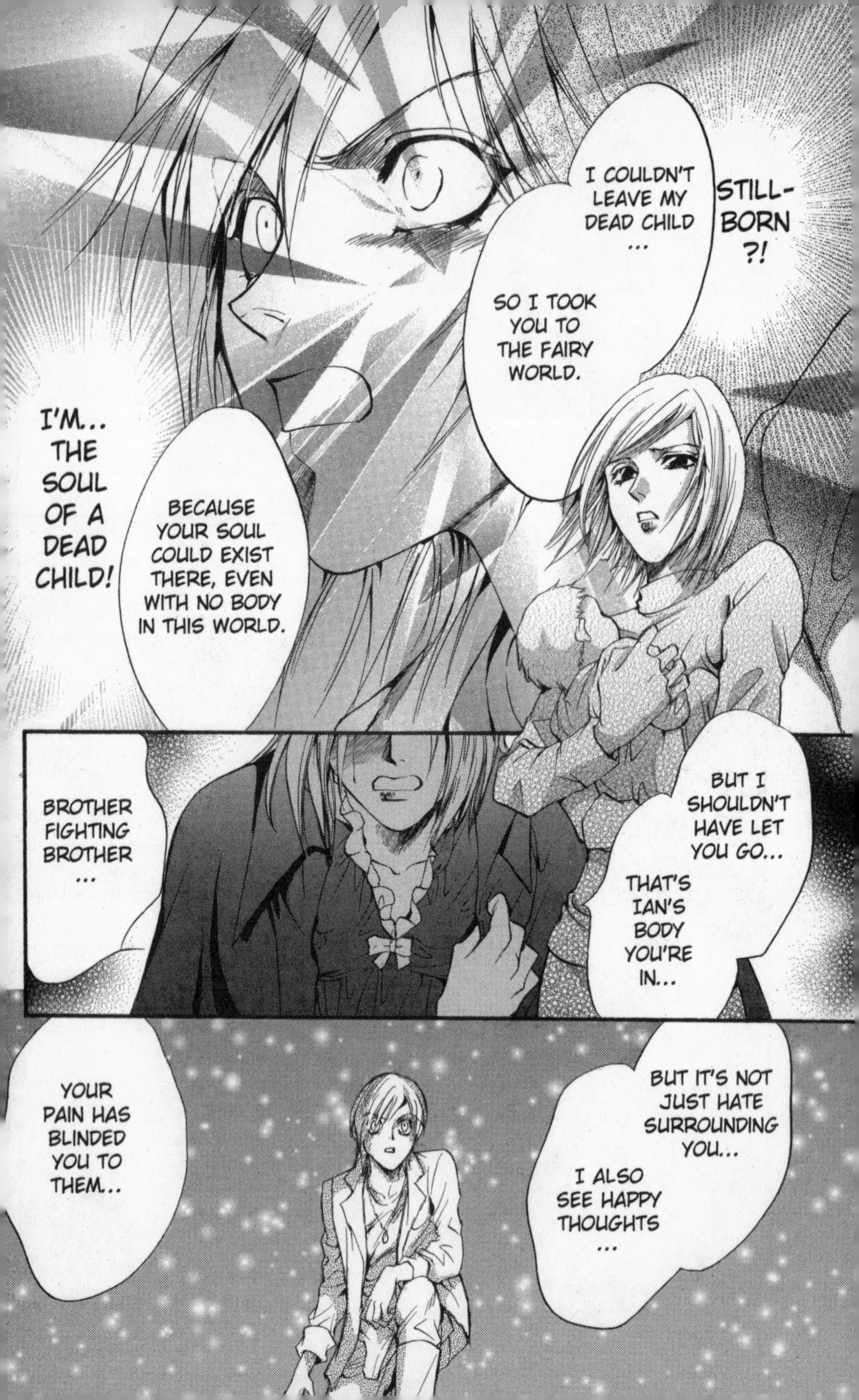
STILL-BORN?!
I COULDN'T LEAVE MY DEAD CHILD...
SO I TOOK YOU TO THE FAIRY WORLD.
BECAUSE YOUR SOUL COULD EXIST THERE, EVEN WITH NO BODY IN THIS WORLD.
I'M... THE SOUL OF A DEAD CHILD!
BUT I SHOULDN'T HAVE LET YOU GO...
THAT'S IAN'S BODY YOU'RE IN...
BROTHER FIGHTING BROTHER...
BUT IT'S NOT JUST HATE SURROUNDING YOU...
I ALSO SEE HAPPY THOUGHTS...
YOUR PAIN HAS BLINDED YOU TO THEM...

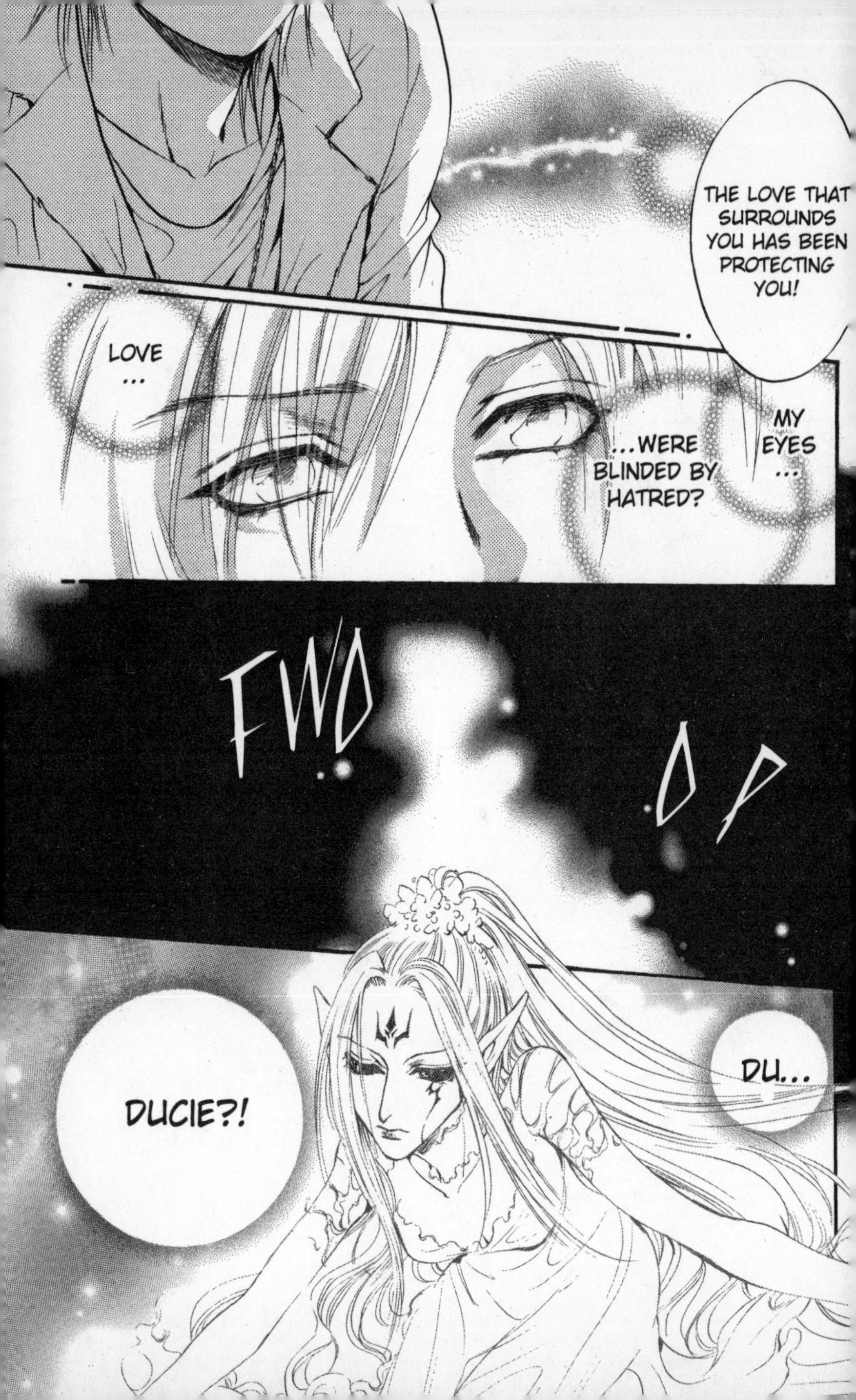
THE LOVE THAT SURROUNDS YOU HAS BEEN PROTECTING YOU!
MY EYES ...
...WERE BLINDED BY HATRED?
LOVE ...
FWO
OP
DU...
DUCIE?!

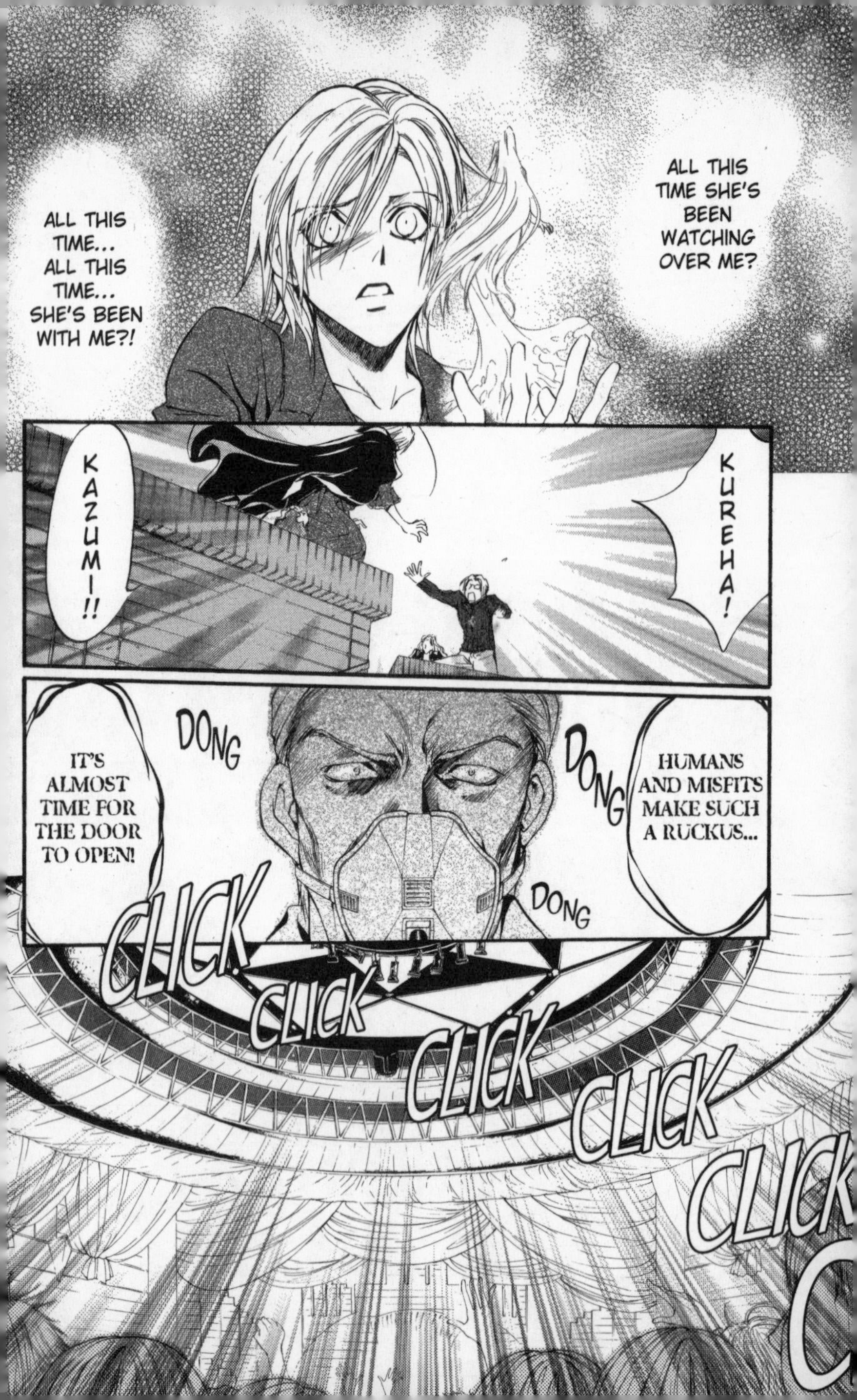
ALL THIS TIME SHE'S BEEN WATCHING OVER ME?
ALL THIS TIME... ALL THIS TIME... SHE'S BEEN WITH ME?!
KUREHA!
KAZUMI!!
HUMANS AND MISFITS MAKE SUCH A RUCKUS...
DONG
DONG
DONG
IT'S ALMOST TIME FOR THE DOOR TO OPEN!
CLICK
CLICK
CLICK
CLICK
CLICK

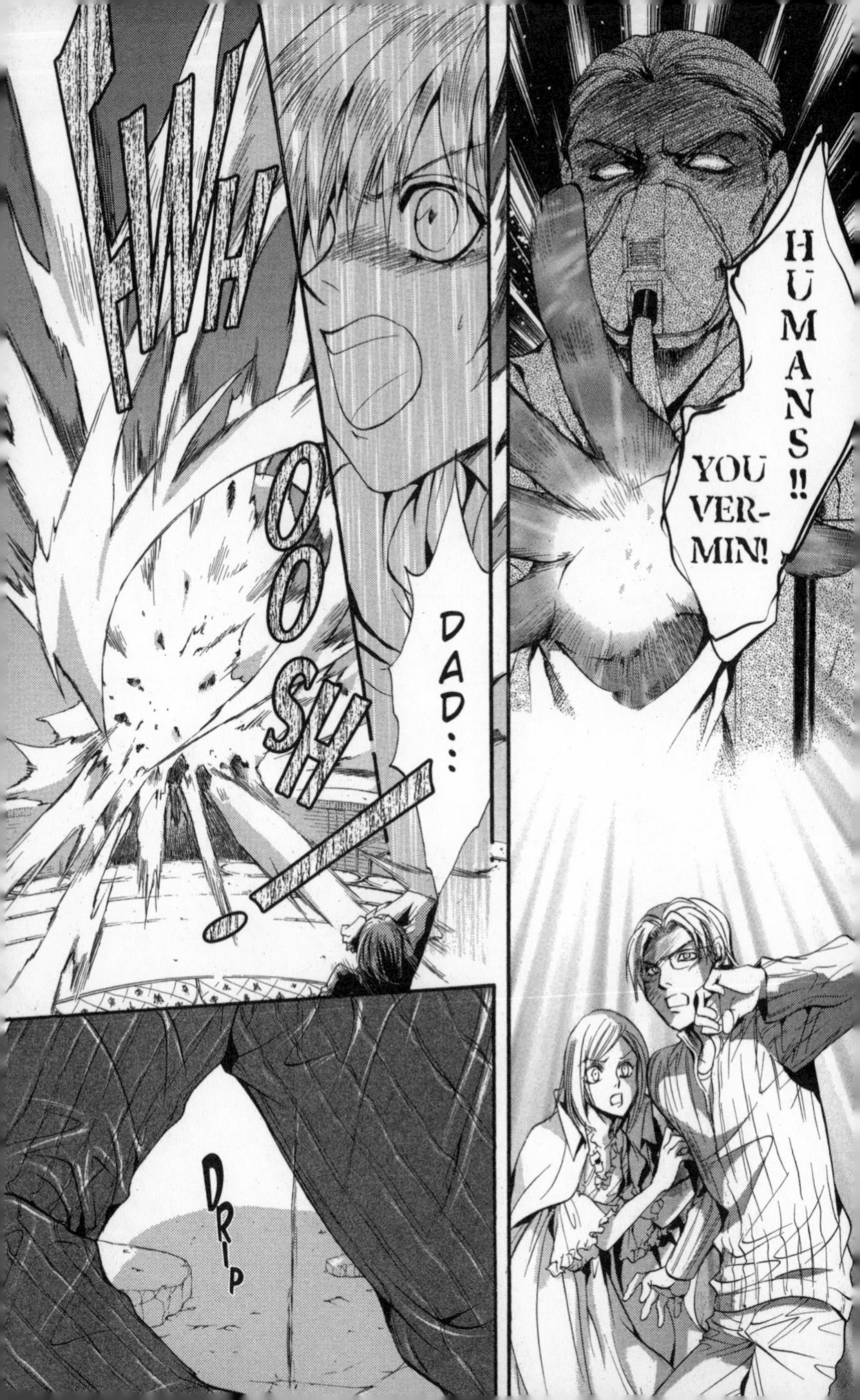

HUMANS!!
YOU VERMIN!
FWHOOOSH
DAD...
DRIP

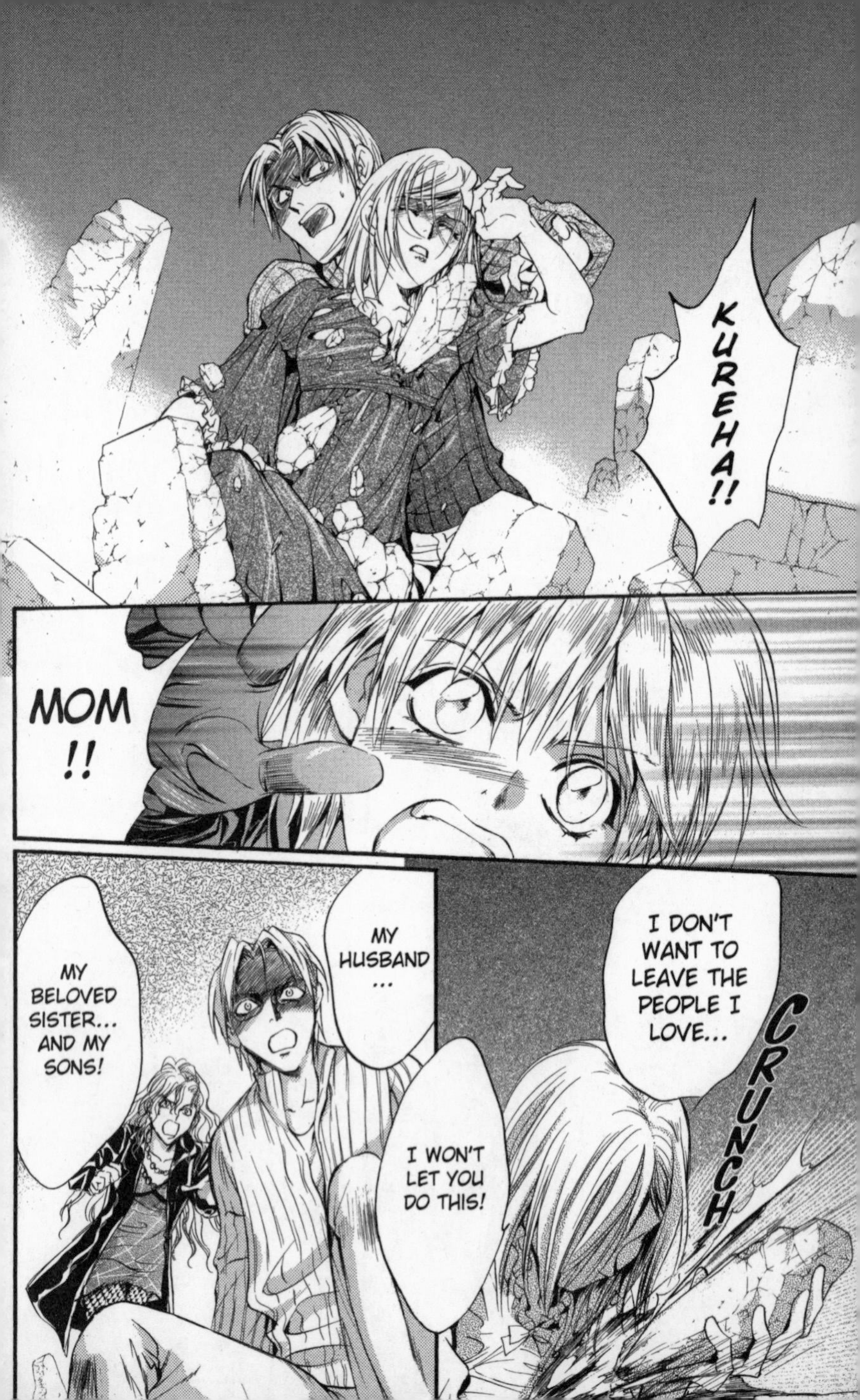
KUREHA!!
MOM !!
I DON'T WANT TO LEAVE THE PEOPLE I LOVE...
MY HUSBAND...
MY BELOVED SISTER... AND MY SONS!
CRUNCH
I WON'T LET YOU DO THIS!

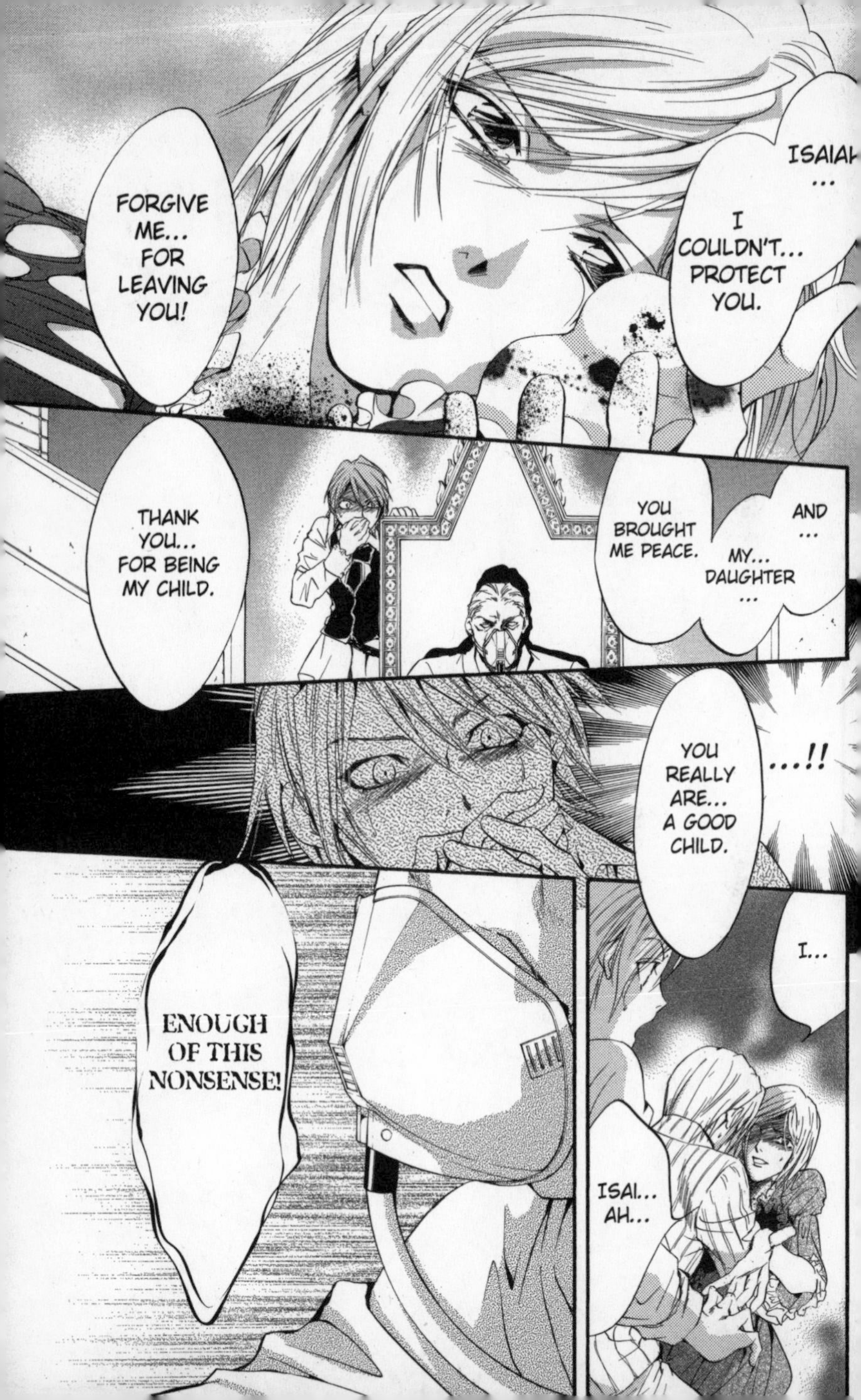
ISAIAH... I COULDN'T... PROTECT YOU.
FORGIVE ME... FOR LEAVING YOU!
AND... MY... DAUGHTER...
YOU BROUGHT ME PEACE.
THANK YOU... FOR BEING MY CHILD.
...!!
YOU REALLY ARE... A GOOD CHILD.
I...
ISAI... AH...
ENOUGH OF THIS NONSENSE!

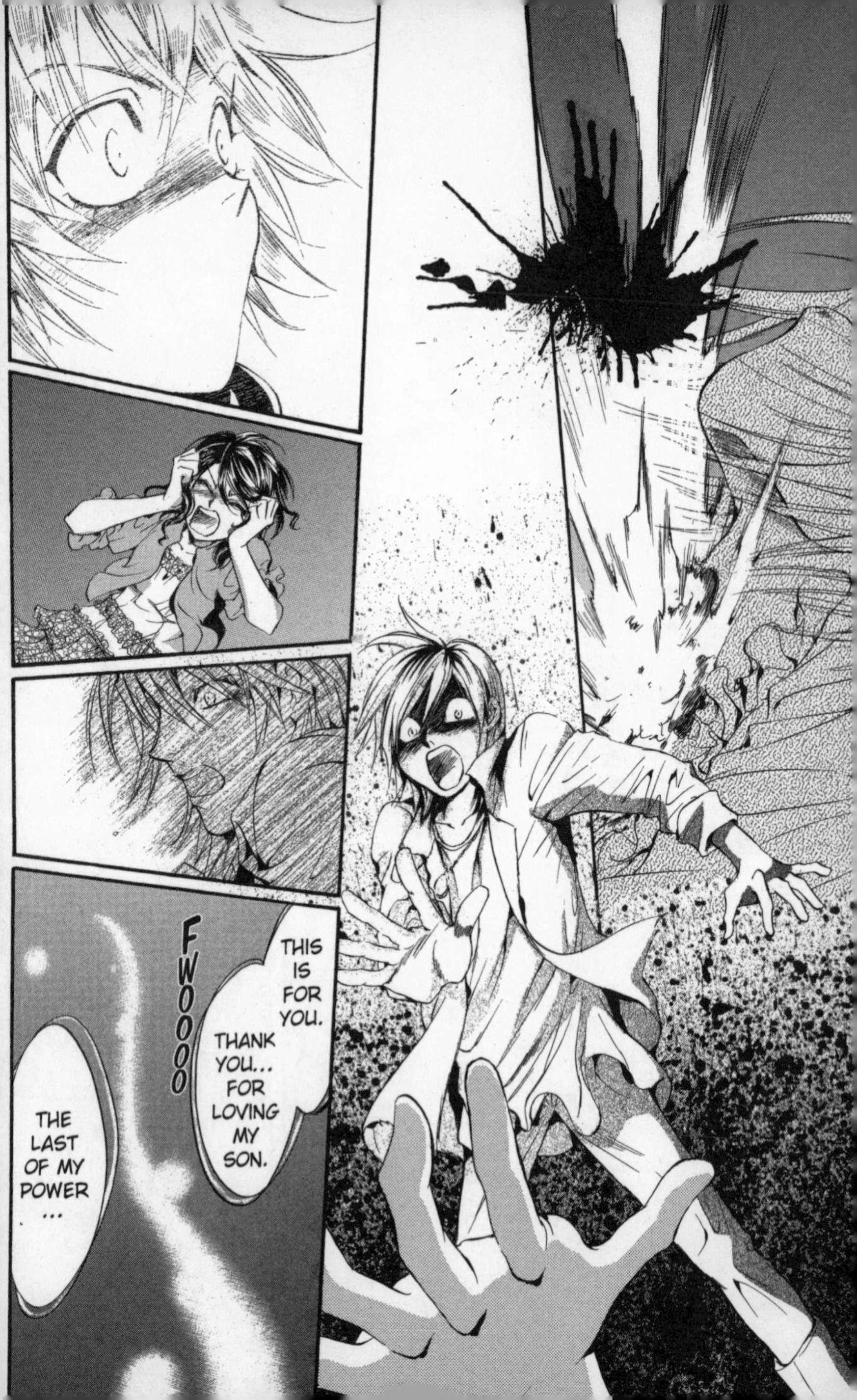
THIS IS FOR YOU.
THANK YOU... FOR LOVING MY SON.
FWOOOOO
THE LAST OF MY POWER...

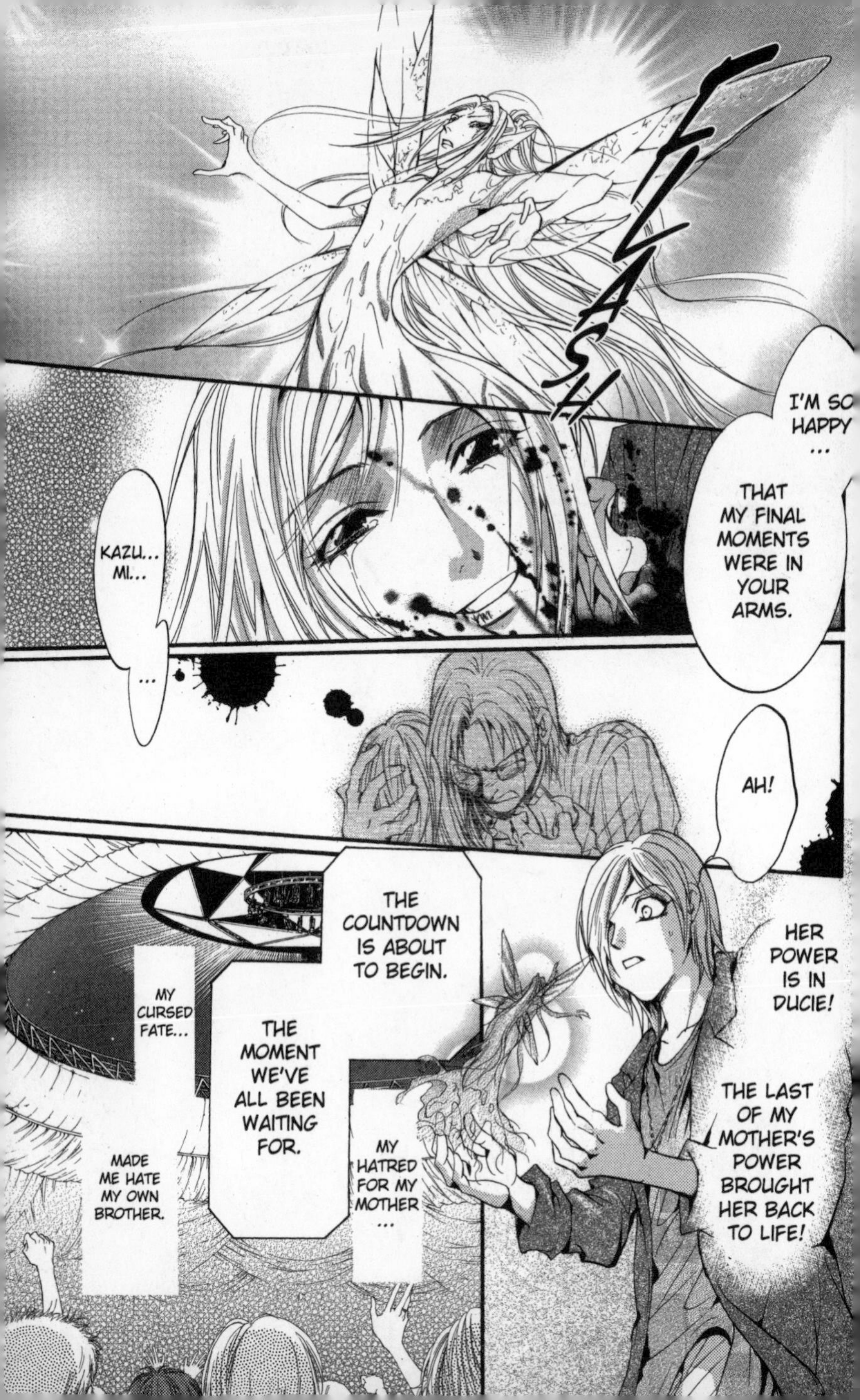
FLASH
I'M SO HAPPY... THAT MY FINAL MOMENTS WERE IN YOUR ARMS.
KAZU... MI...
AH!
...
HER POWER IS IN DUCIE!
THE LAST OF MY MOTHER'S POWER BROUGHT HER BACK TO LIFE!
THE COUNTDOWN IS ABOUT TO BEGIN.
THE MOMENT WE'VE ALL BEEN WAITING FOR.
MY HATRED FOR MY MOTHER...
MY CURSED FATE...
MADE ME HATE MY OWN BROTHER.

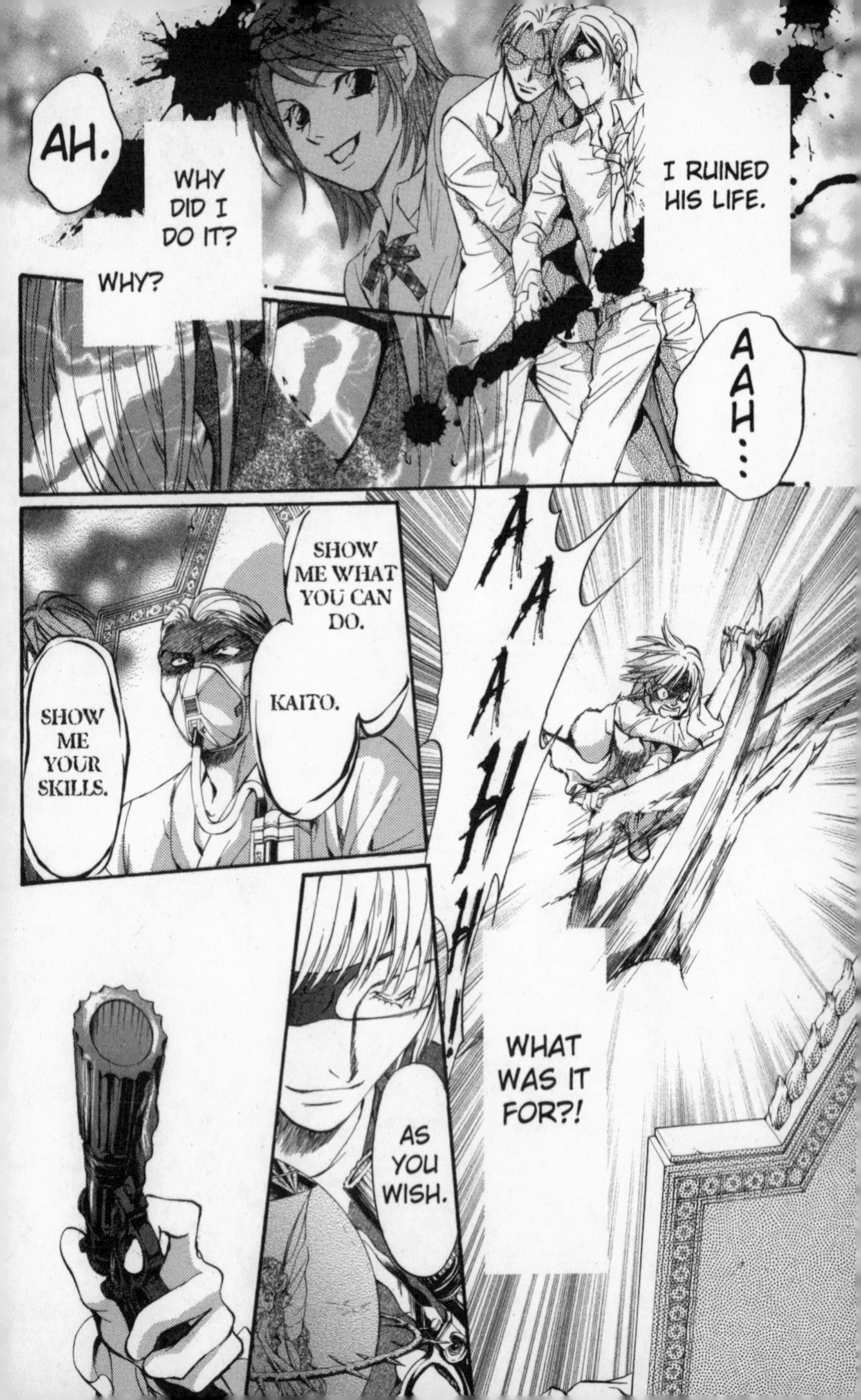
I RUINED HIS LIFE.
AAH...
AH.
WHY DID I DO IT?
WHY?
AAAAHHH!!
SHOW ME WHAT YOU CAN DO.
KAITO.
SHOW ME YOUR SKILLS.
WHAT WAS IT FOR?!
AS YOU WISH.

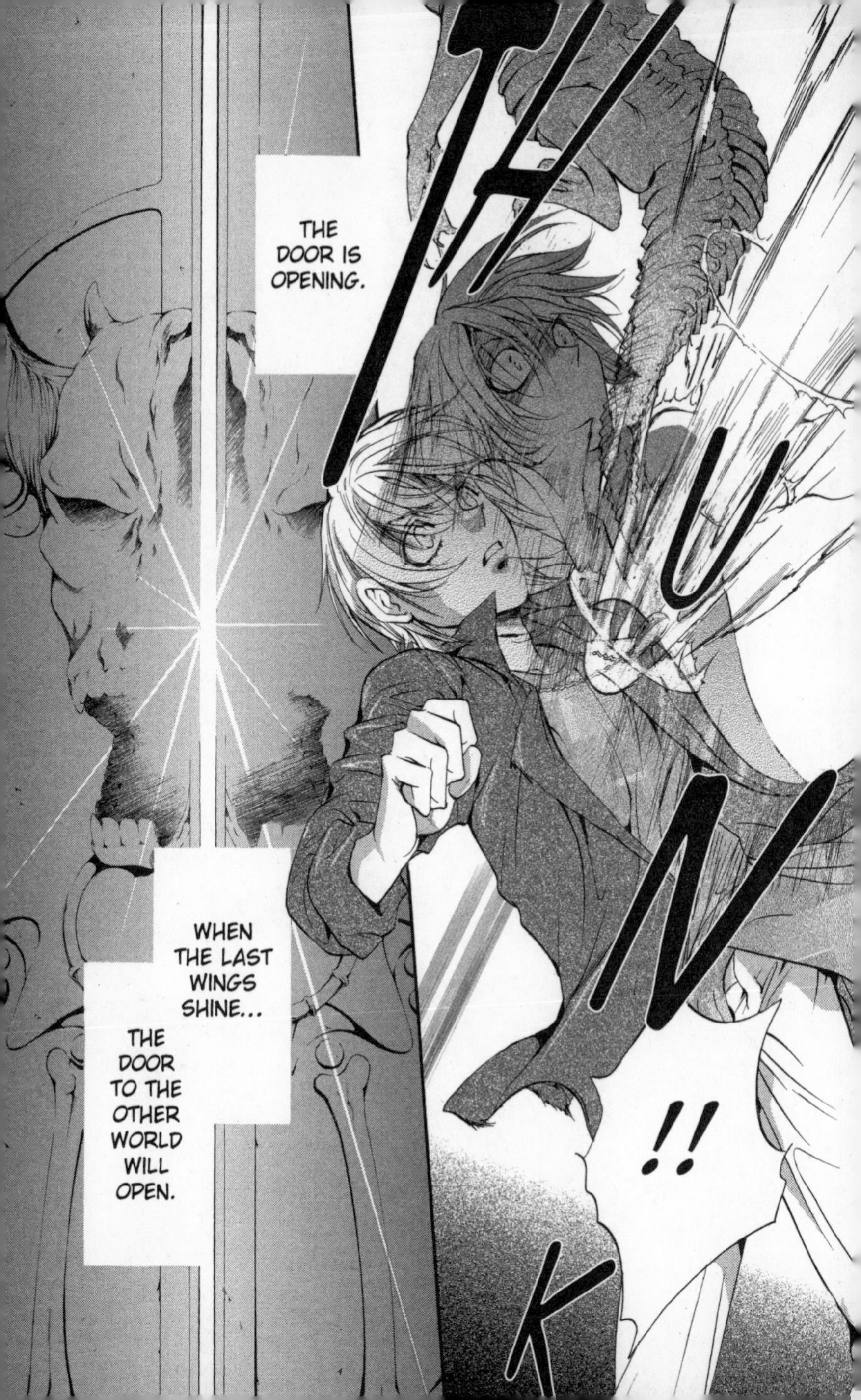
THUNK
THE DOOR IS OPENING.
!!
WHEN THE LAST WINGS SHINE...
THE DOOR TO THE OTHER WORLD WILL OPEN.

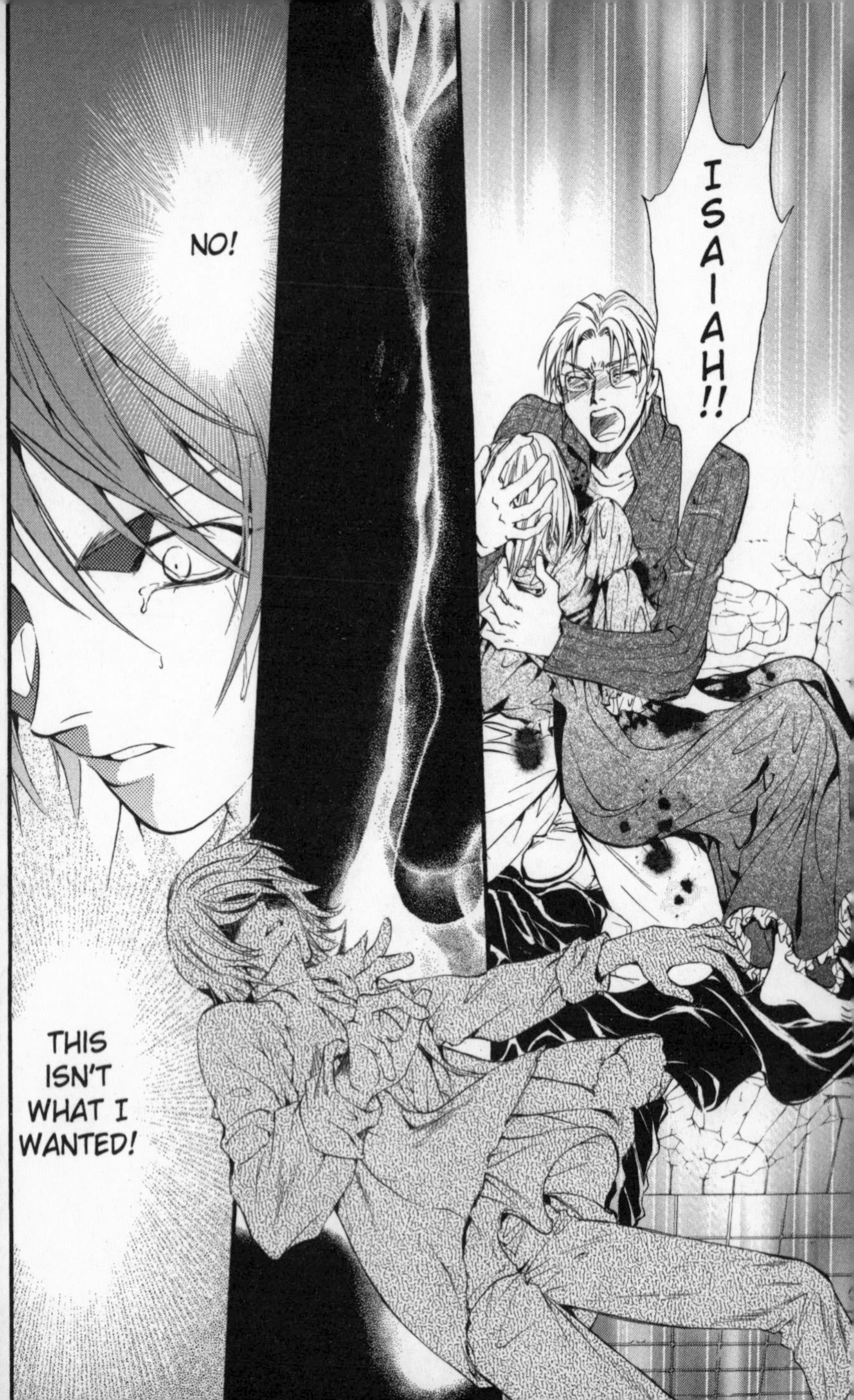
ISAIAH!!
NO!
THIS ISN'T WHAT I WANTED!

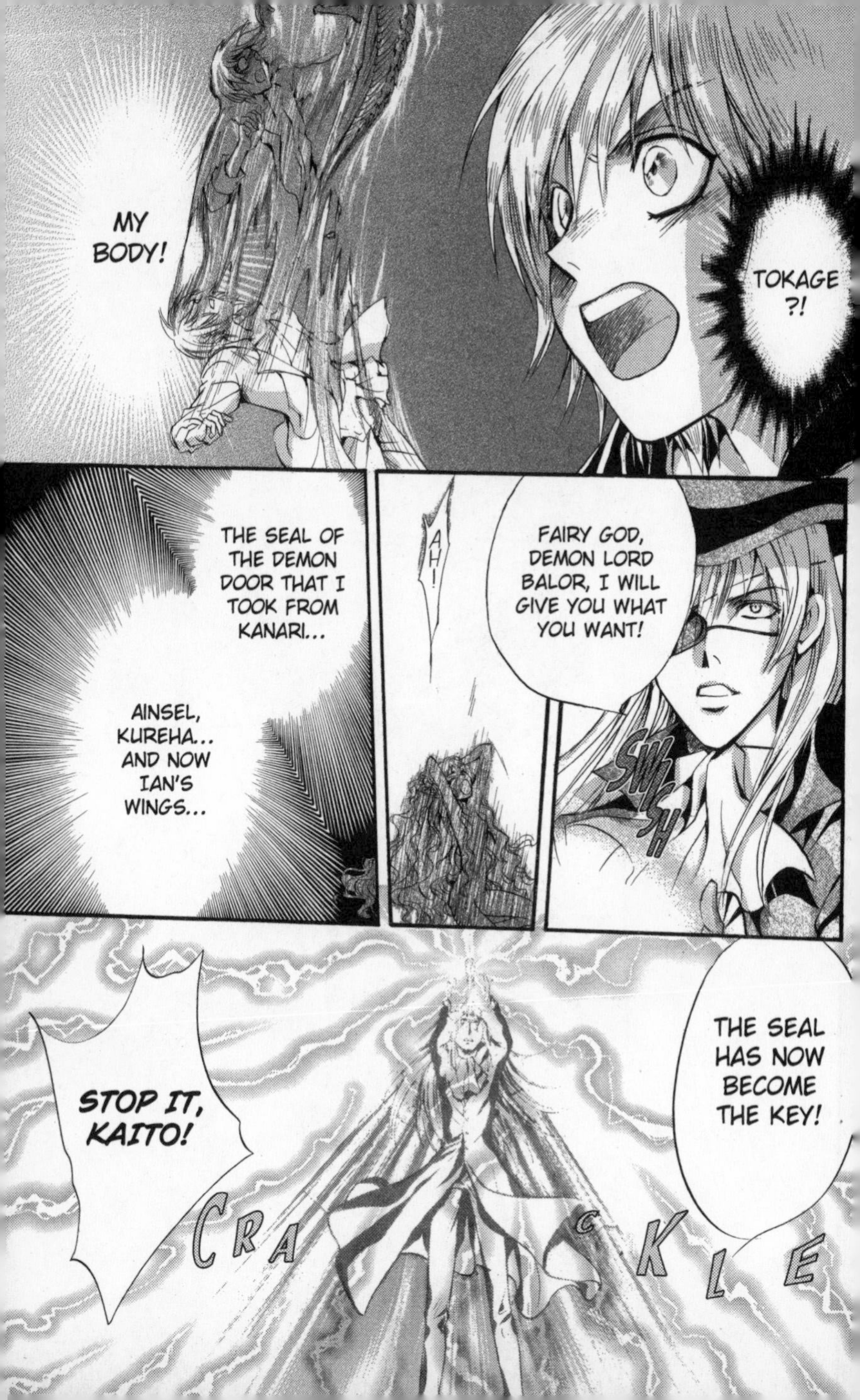
TOKAGE ?!
MY BODY!
FAIRY GOD, DEMON LORD BALOR, I WILL GIVE YOU WHAT YOU WANT!
SWISH
AH!
THE SEAL OF THE DEMON DOOR THAT I TOOK FROM KANARI...
AINSEL, KUREHA... AND NOW IAN'S WINGS...
THE SEAL HAS NOW BECOME THE KEY!
STOP IT, KAITO!
CRACKLE

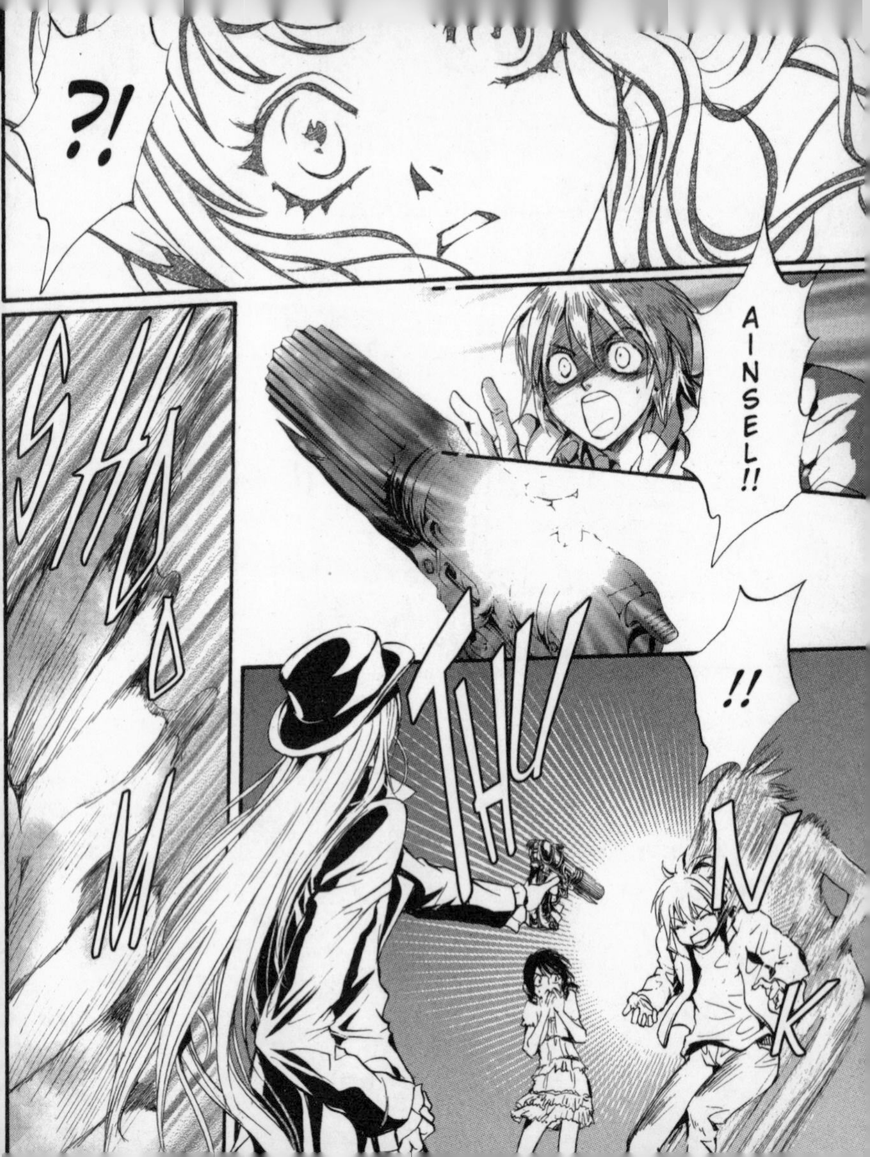
?!
AINSEL!!
!!
THUNK
SHOOM

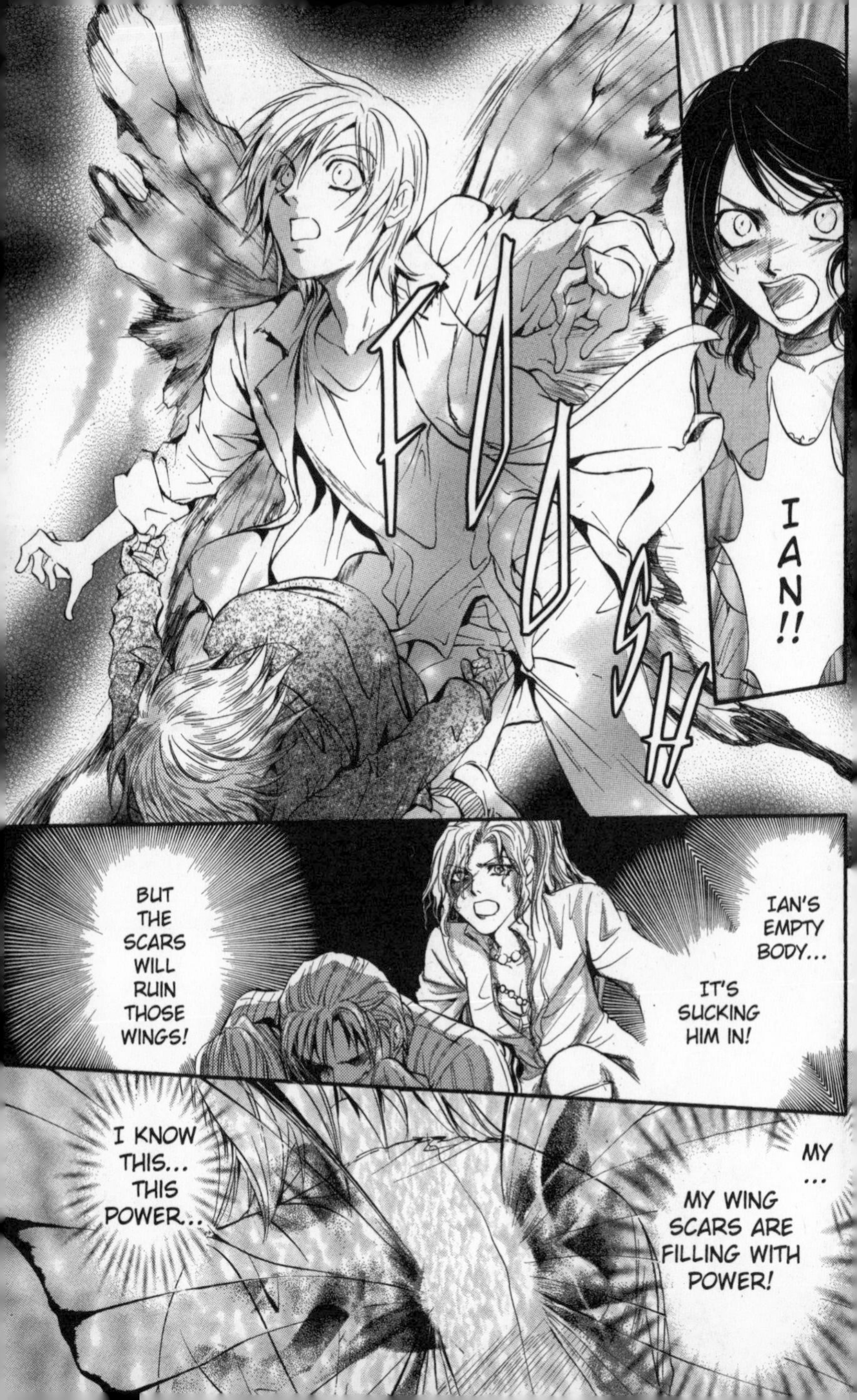
IAN!!
FLASH
IAN'S EMPTY BODY...
IT'S SUCKING HIM IN!
BUT THE SCARS WILL RUIN THOSE WINGS!
MY ...
MY WING SCARS ARE FILLING WITH POWER!
I KNOW THIS... THIS POWER..

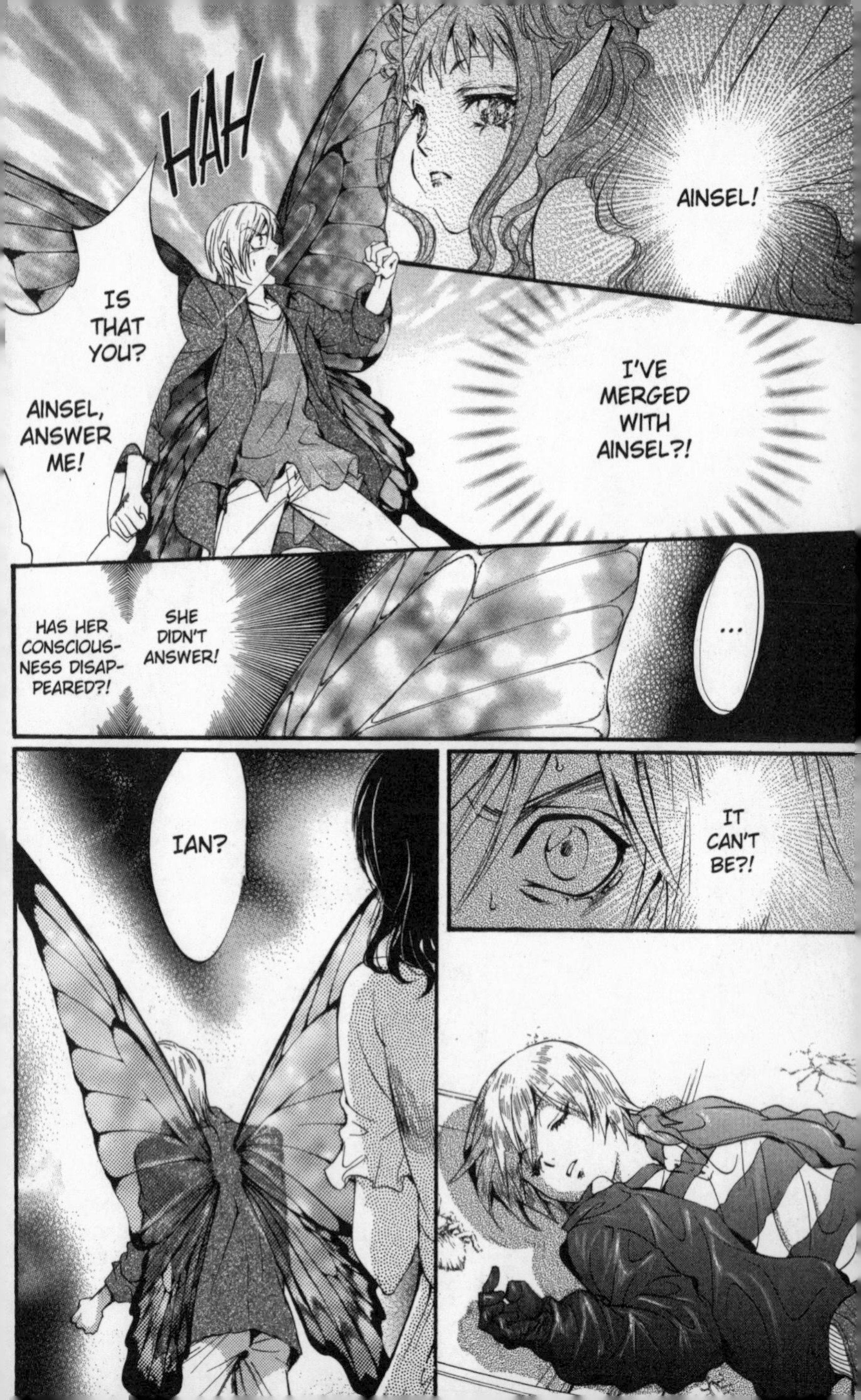
AINSEL!
I'VE MERGED WITH AINSEL?!
HAH
IS THAT YOU?
AINSEL, ANSWER ME!
...
SHE DIDN'T ANSWER!
HAS HER CONSCIOUS-NESS DISAP-PEARED?!
IT CAN'T BE?!
IAN?

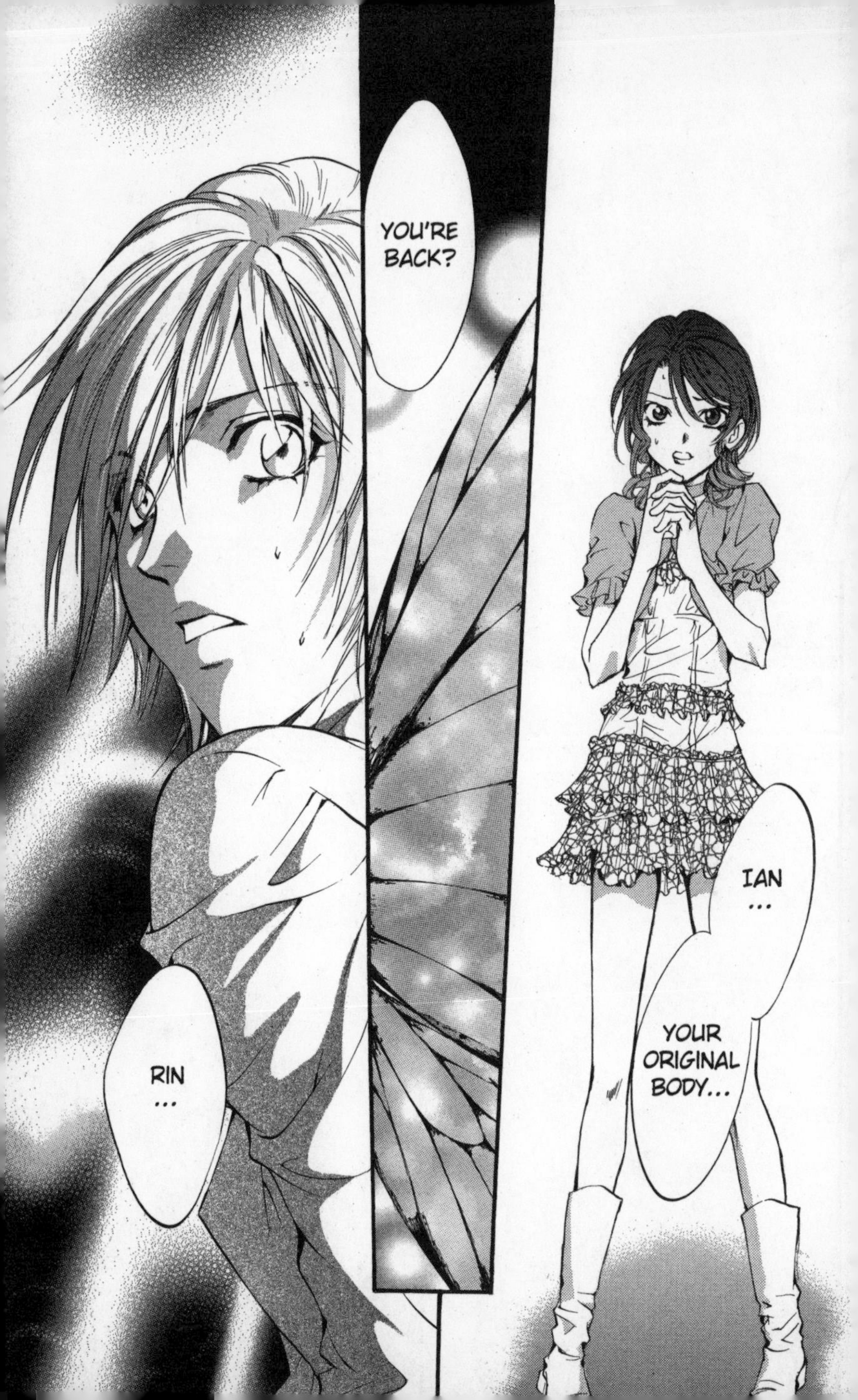
IAN ...
YOUR ORIGINAL BODY...
YOU'RE BACK?
RIN ...

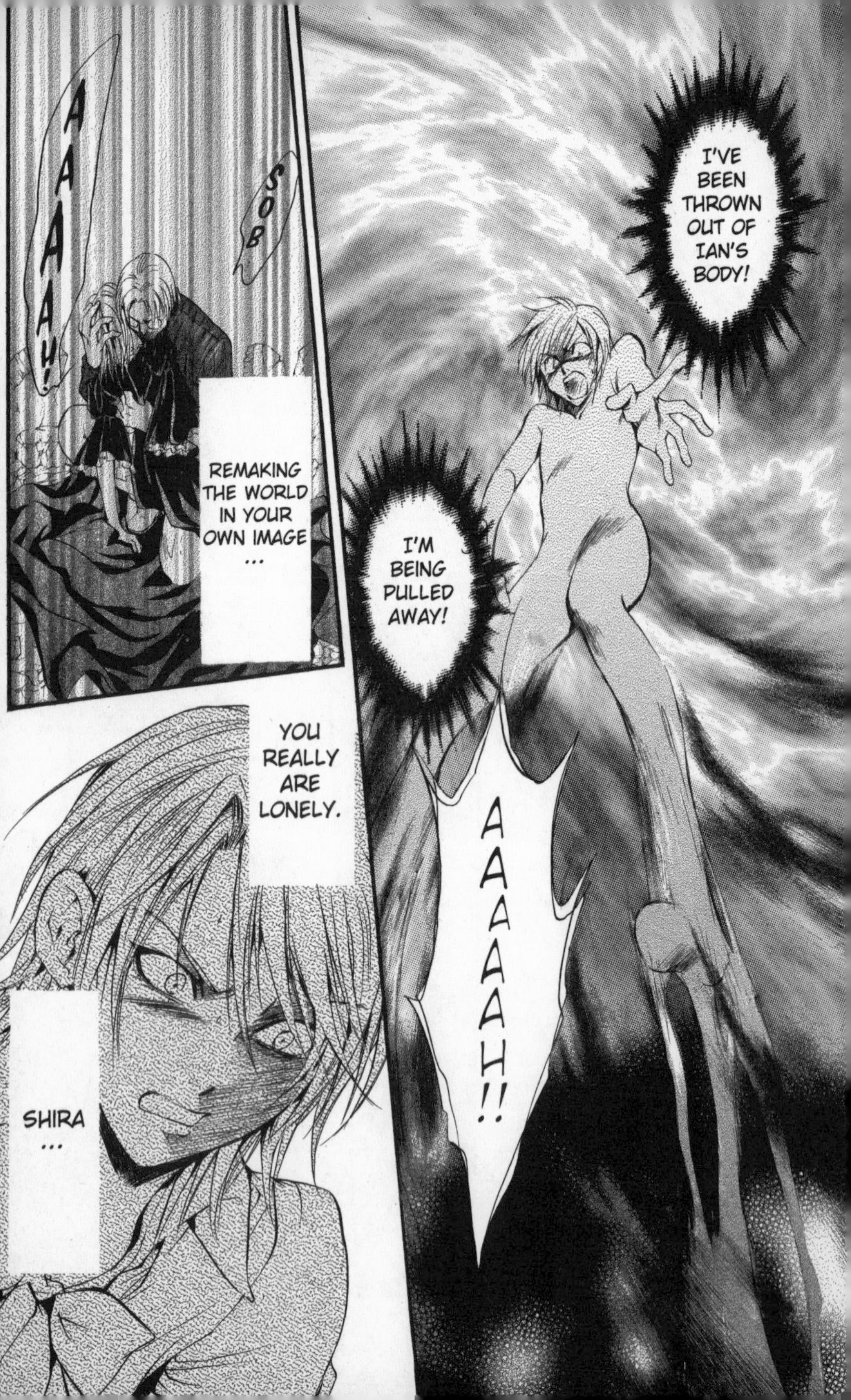
I'VE BEEN THROWN OUT OF IAN'S BODY!
I'M BEING PULLED AWAY!
AAAAAH!!
SOB
AAAAH!
REMAKING THE WORLD IN YOUR OWN IMAGE ...
YOU REALLY ARE LONELY.
SHIRA ...

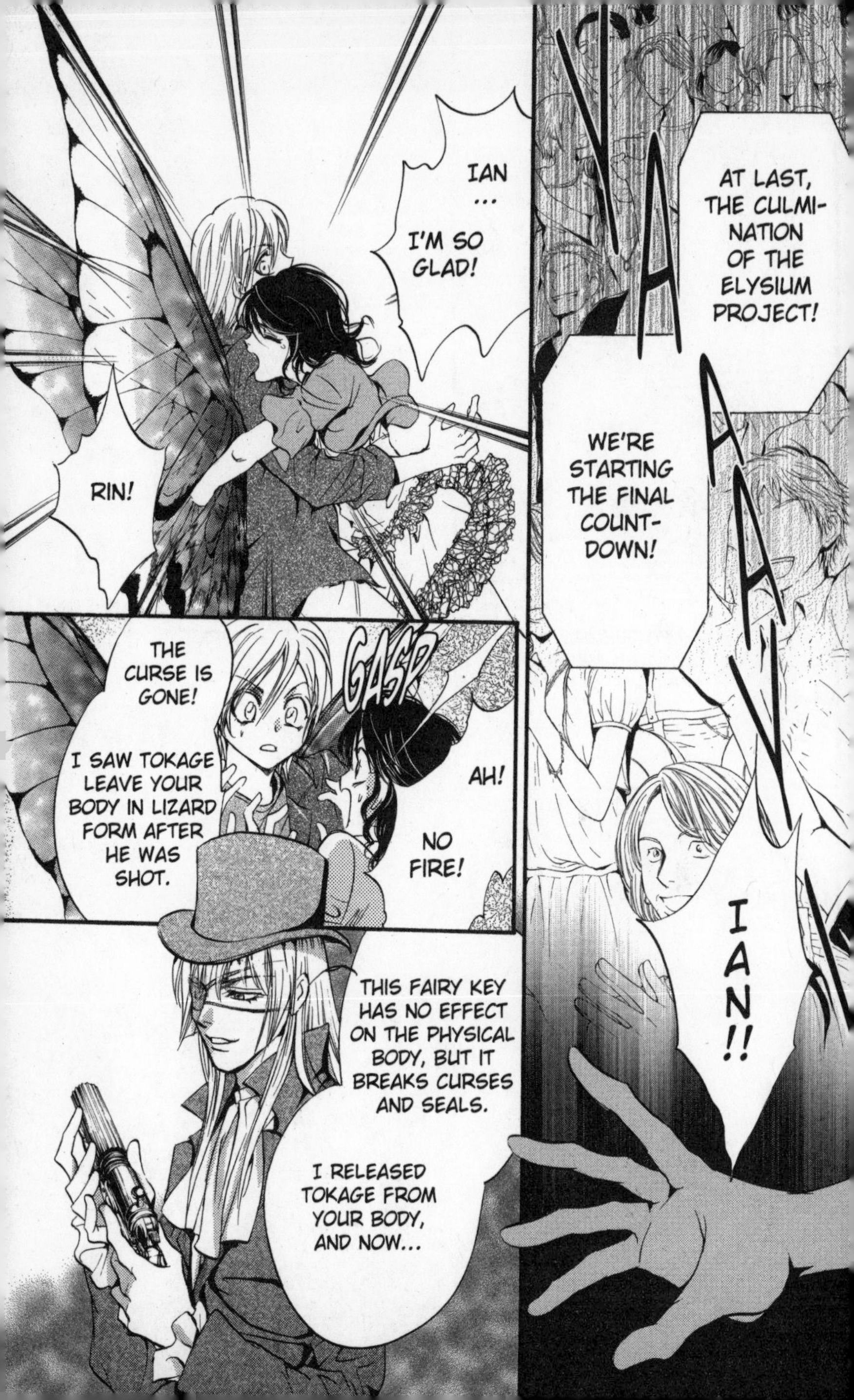
AT LAST, THE CULMINATION OF THE ELYSIUM PROJECT!
WE'RE STARTING THE FINAL COUNTDOWN!
IAN!!
IAN ... I'M SO GLAD!
RIN!
GASP
THE CURSE IS GONE!
AH!
NO FIRE!
I SAW TOKAGE LEAVE YOUR BODY IN LIZARD FORM AFTER HE WAS SHOT.
THIS FAIRY KEY HAS NO EFFECT ON THE PHYSICAL BODY, BUT IT BREAKS CURSES AND SEALS.
I RELEASED TOKAGE FROM YOUR BODY, AND NOW...

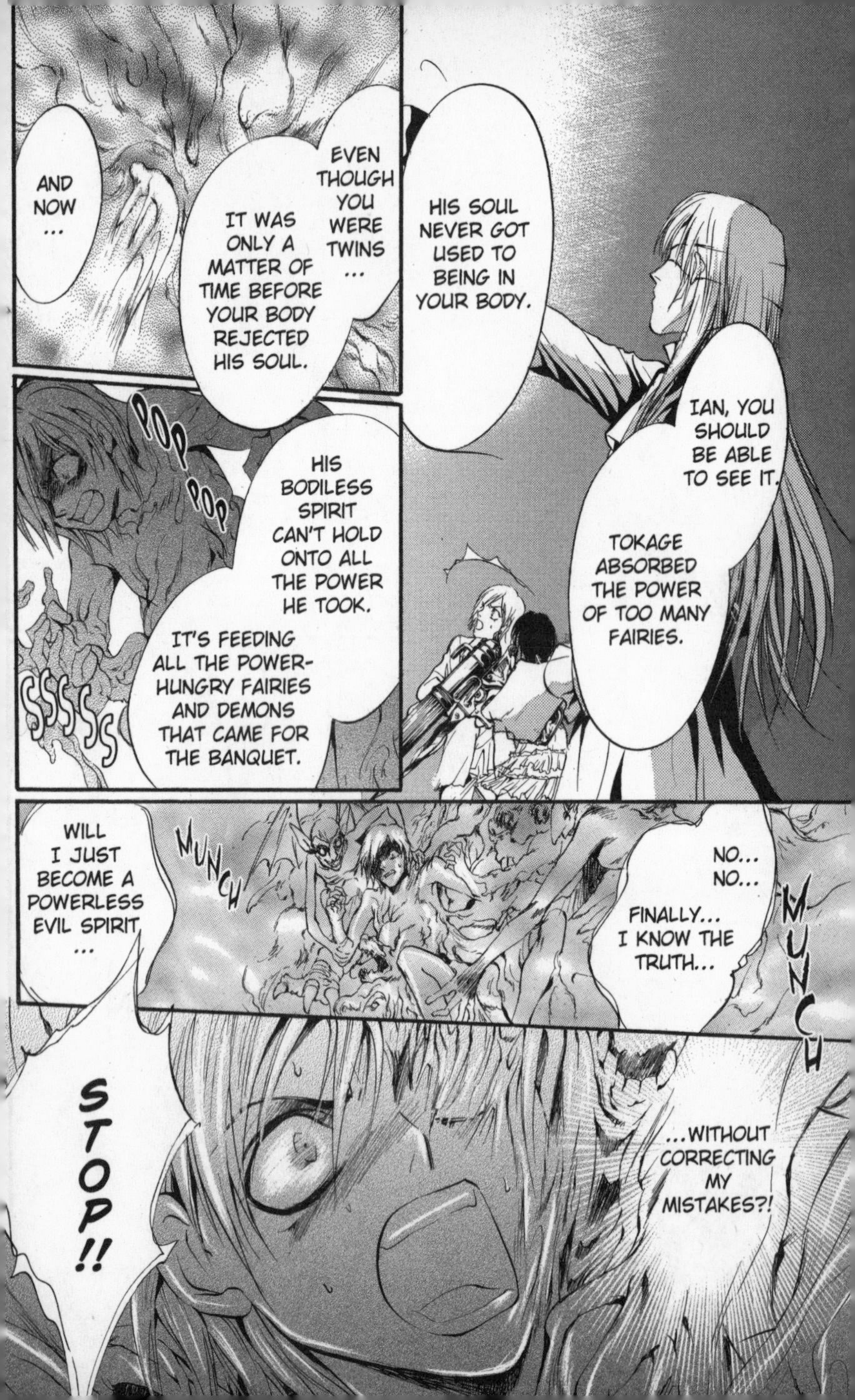
HIS SOUL NEVER GOT USED TO BEING IN YOUR BODY.
IAN, YOU SHOULD BE ABLE TO SEE IT.
TOKAGE ABSORBED THE POWER OF TOO MANY FAIRIES.
EVEN THOUGH YOU WERE TWINS...
IT WAS ONLY A MATTER OF TIME BEFORE YOUR BODY REJECTED HIS SOUL.
AND NOW...
POP POP
HIS BODILESS SPIRIT CAN'T HOLD ONTO ALL THE POWER HE TOOK.
IT'S FEEDING ALL THE POWER-HUNGRY FAIRIES AND DEMONS THAT CAME FOR THE BANQUET.
SSSSS
MUNCH
NO... NO...
FINALLY... I KNOW THE TRUTH...
MUNCH
WILL I JUST BECOME A POWERLESS EVIL SPIRIT...
...WITHOUT CORRECTING MY MISTAKES?!
STOP!!

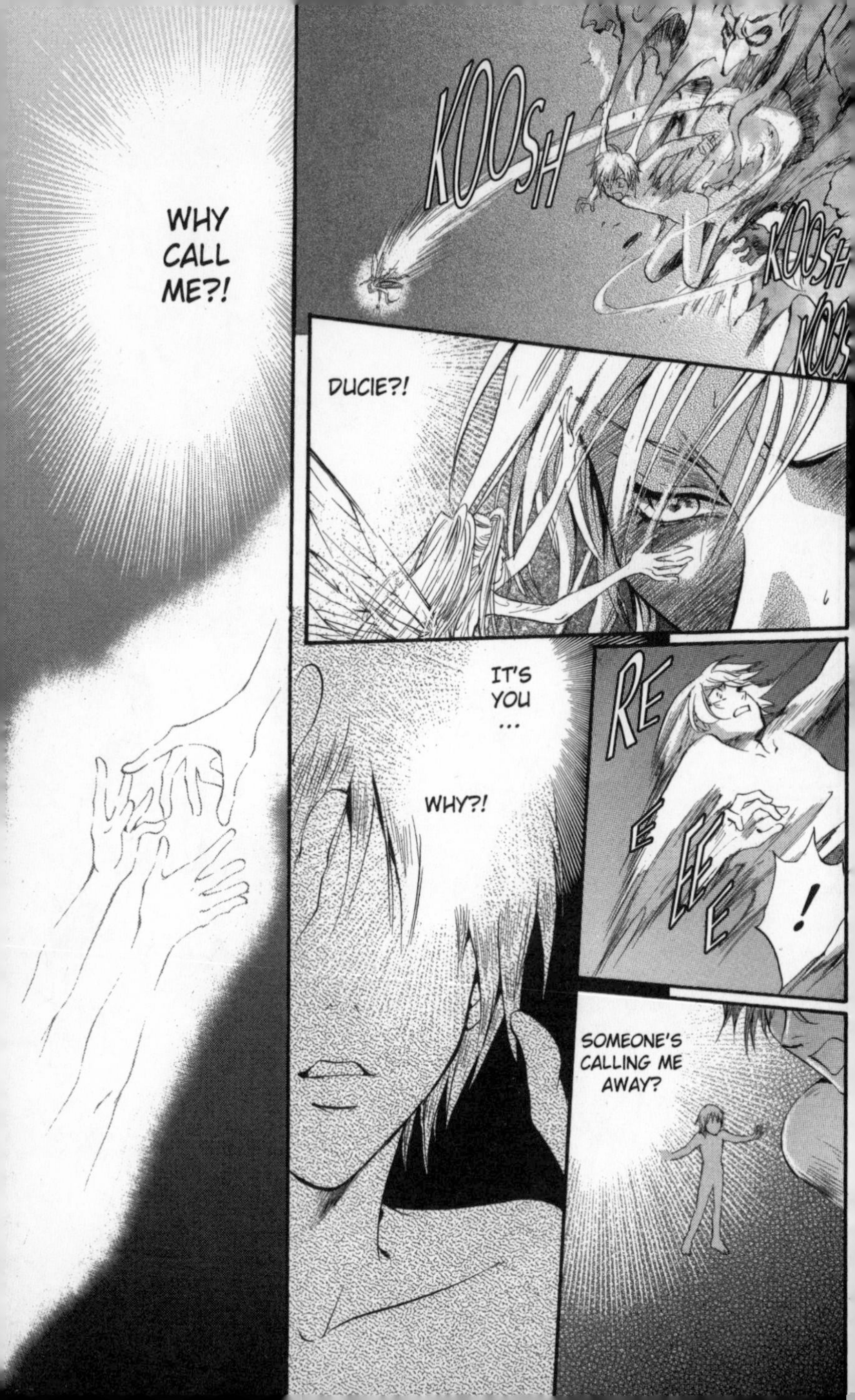
KOOSH
KOOSH
DUCIE?!
REEEEE
!
IT'S YOU...
WHY?!
SOMEONE'S CALLING ME AWAY?
WHY CALL ME?!

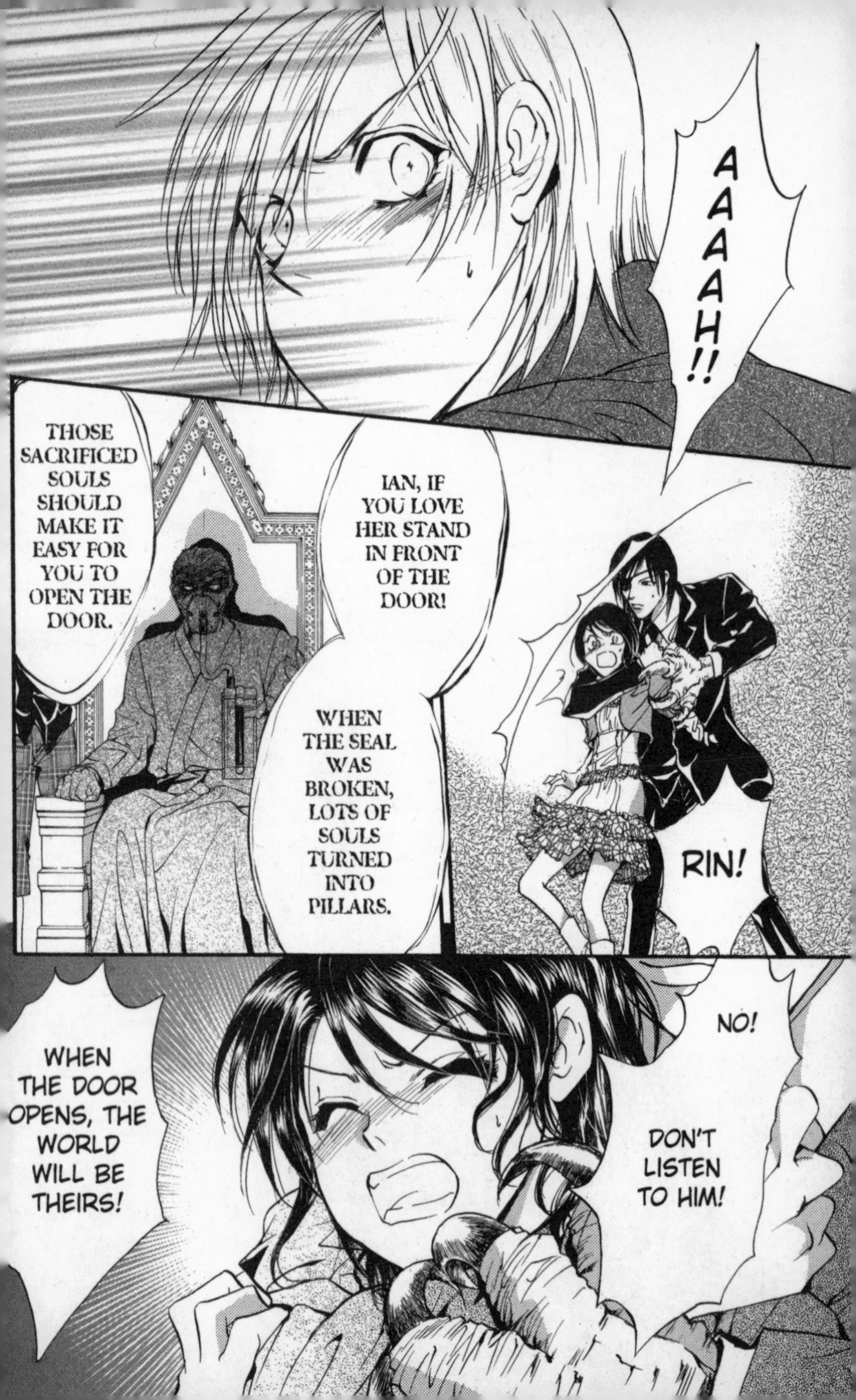
AAAAH!!
RIN!
IAN, IF YOU LOVE HER STAND IN FRONT OF THE DOOR!
WHEN THE SEAL WAS BROKEN, LOTS OF SOULS TURNED INTO PILLARS.
THOSE SACRIFICED SOULS SHOULD MAKE IT EASY FOR YOU TO OPEN THE DOOR.
NO!
DON'T LISTEN TO HIM!
WHEN THE DOOR OPENS, THE WORLD WILL BE THEIRS!

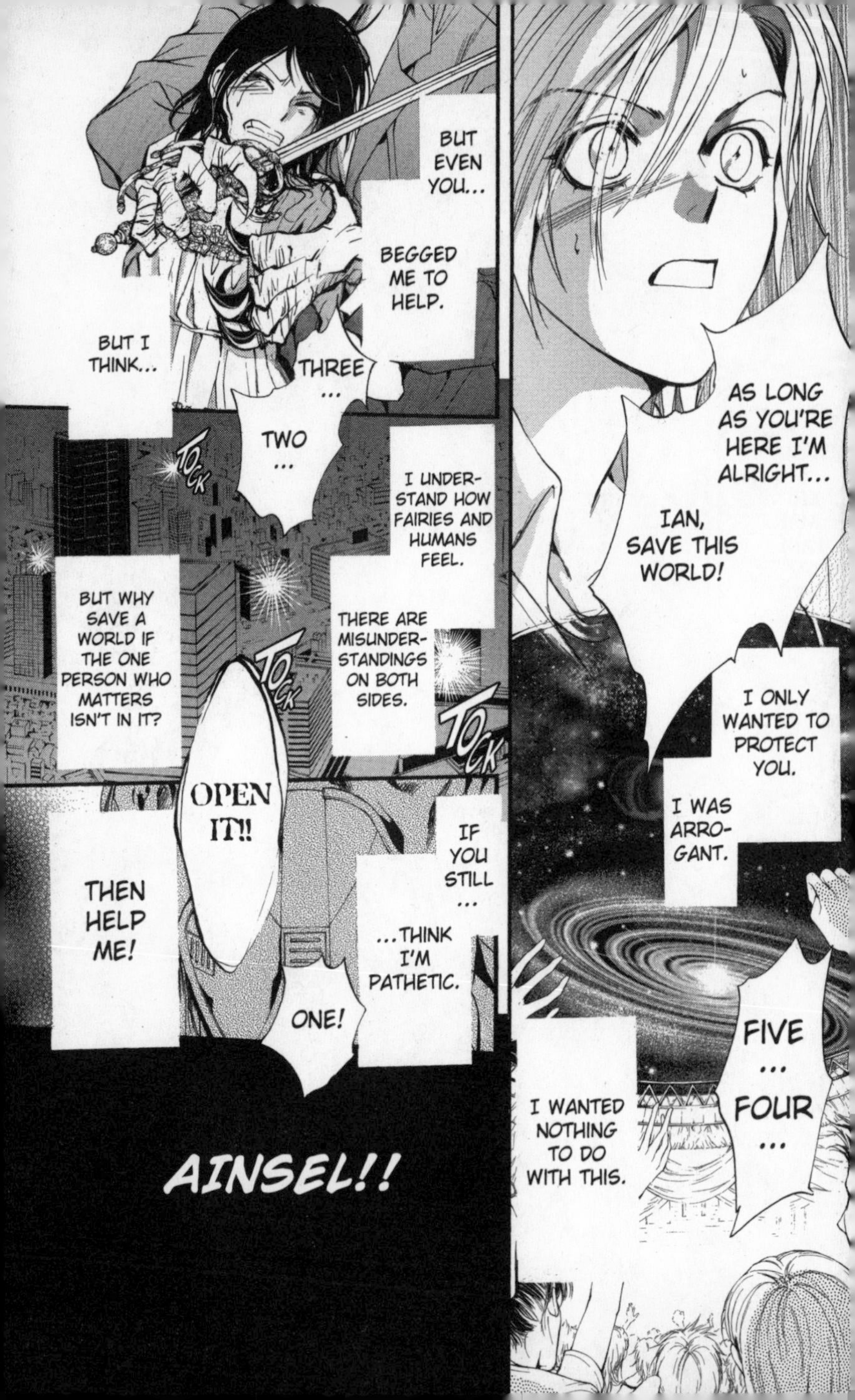

AS LONG AS YOU'RE HERE I'M ALRIGHT...
IAN, SAVE THIS WORLD!
I ONLY WANTED TO PROTECT YOU.
I WAS ARRO-GANT.
FIVE ... FOUR ...
I WANTED NOTHING TO DO WITH THIS.
BUT EVEN YOU...
BEGGED ME TO HELP.
THREE ...
BUT I THINK...
TWO ...
TOCK
I UNDER-STAND HOW FAIRIES AND HUMANS FEEL.
THERE ARE MISUNDER-STANDINGS ON BOTH SIDES.
TOCK
TOCK
BUT WHY SAVE A WORLD IF THE ONE PERSON WHO MATTERS ISN'T IN IT?
IF YOU STILL ...
...THINK I'M PATHETIC.
OPEN IT!!
ONE!
THEN HELP ME!
AINSEL!!

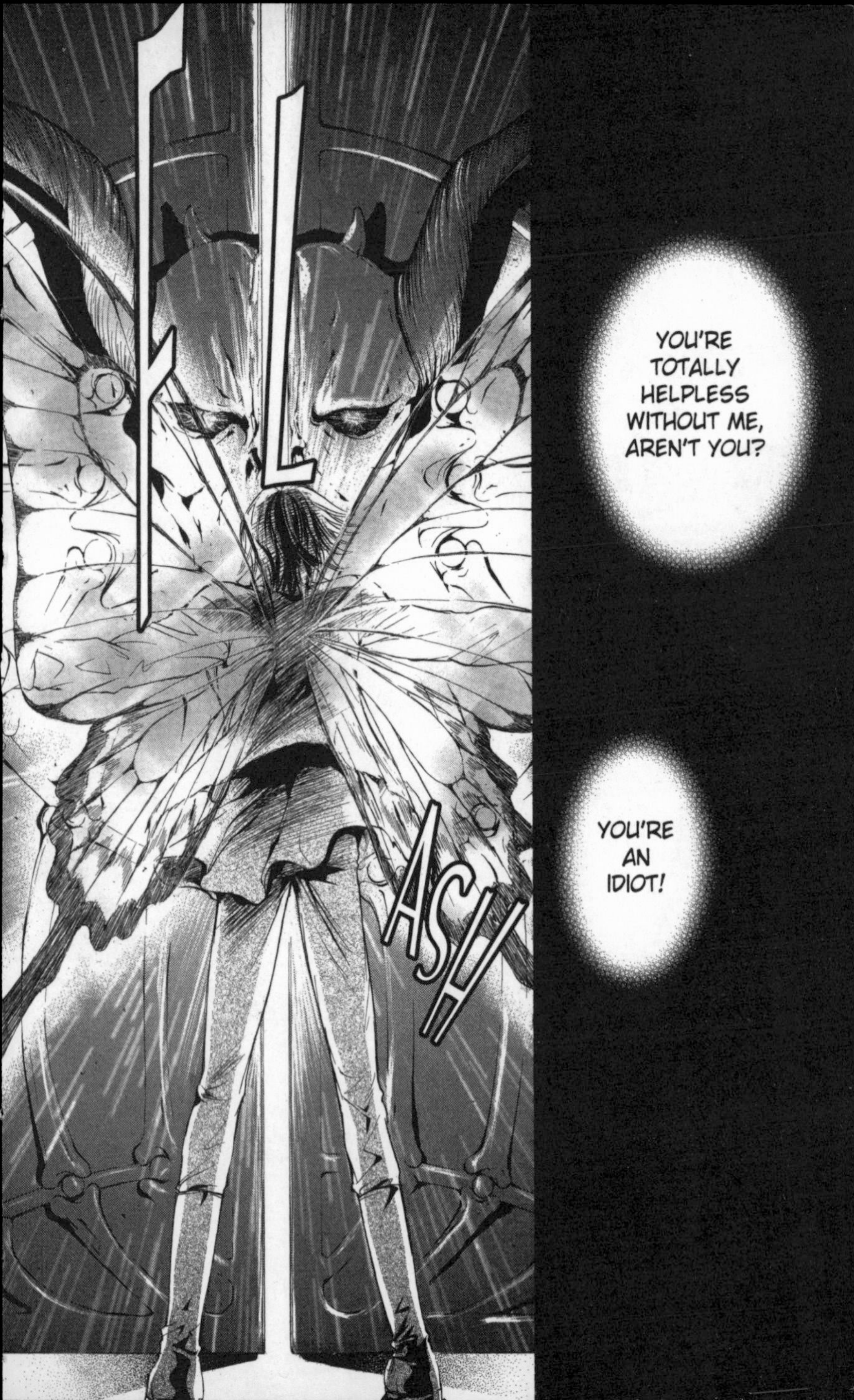
YOU'RE TOTALLY HELPLESS WITHOUT ME, AREN'T YOU?
YOU'RE AN IDIOT!

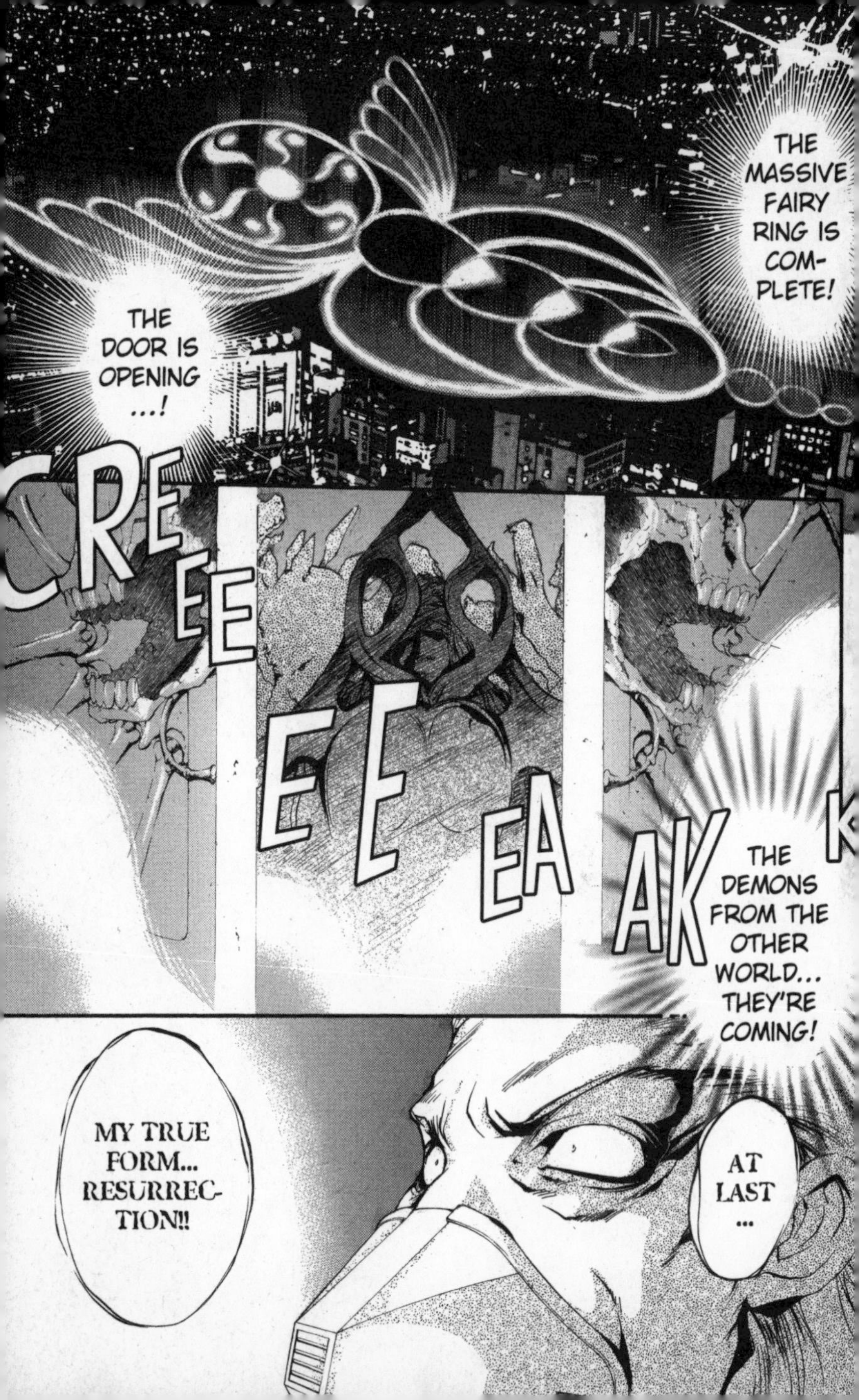
THE MASSIVE FAIRY RING IS COMPLETE!
THE DOOR IS OPENING...!
CREEEEEEAK
THE DEMONS FROM THE OTHER WORLD... THEY'RE COMING!
AT LAST...
MY TRUE FORM... RESURRECTION!!

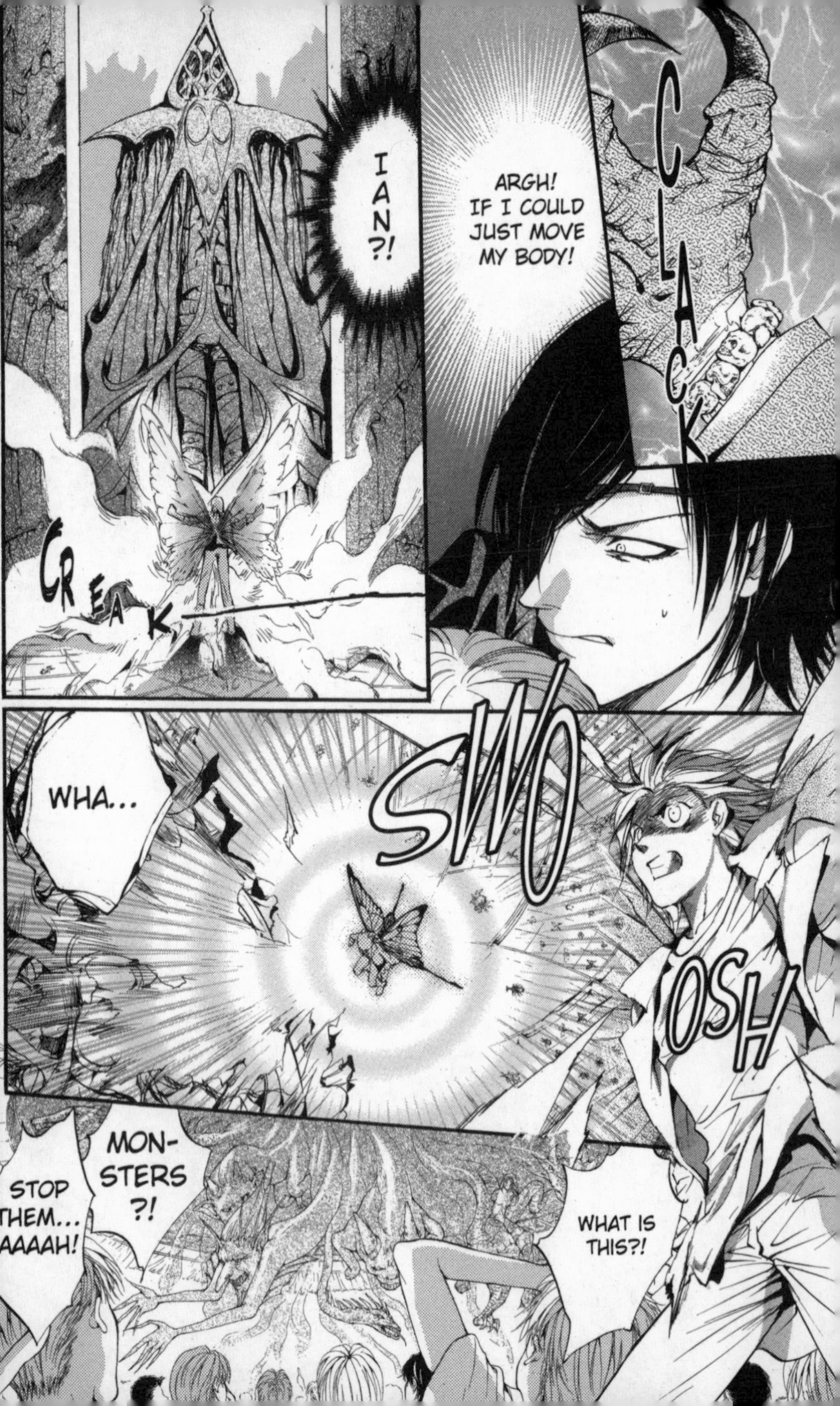
CLACK
ARGH! IF I COULD JUST MOVE MY BODY!
IAN?!
CREAK
SWOOSH
WHA...
WHAT IS THIS?!
MONSTERS?!
STOP THEM... AAAAH!

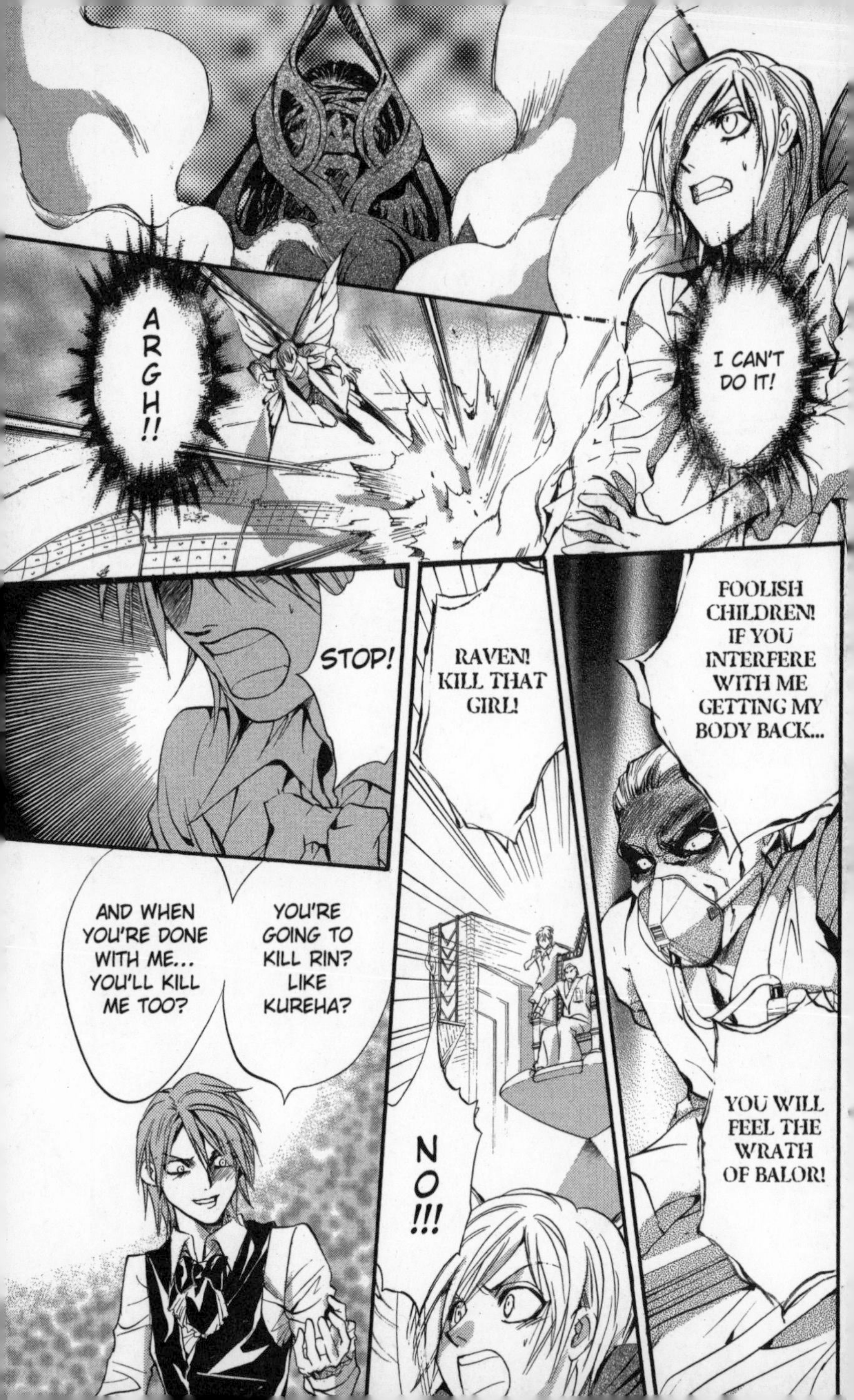
I CAN'T DO IT!
ARGH!!
FOOLISH CHILDREN! IF YOU INTERFERE WITH ME GETTING MY BODY BACK...
YOU WILL FEEL THE WRATH OF BALOR!
RAVEN! KILL THAT GIRL!
NO!!!
STOP!
YOU'RE GOING TO KILL RIN? LIKE KUREHA?
AND WHEN YOU'RE DONE WITH ME... YOU'LL KILL ME TOO?

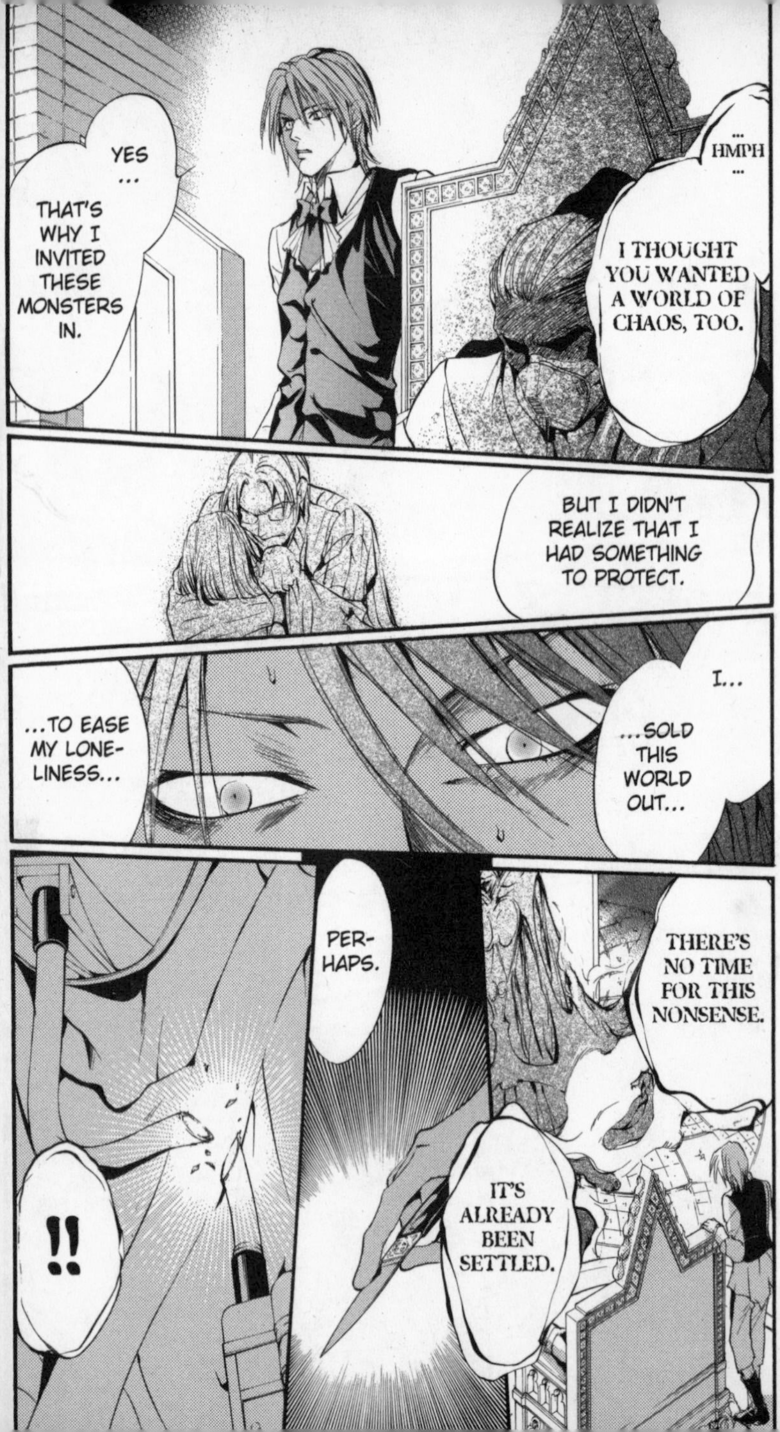

...HMPH...
I THOUGHT YOU WANTED A WORLD OF CHAOS, TOO.
YES... THAT'S WHY I INVITED THESE MONSTERS IN.
BUT I DIDN'T REALIZE THAT I HAD SOMETHING TO PROTECT.
I...
...SOLD THIS WORLD OUT...
...TO EASE MY LONE-LINESS...
THERE'S NO TIME FOR THIS NONSENSE.
IT'S ALREADY BEEN SETTLED.
PER-HAPS.
!!

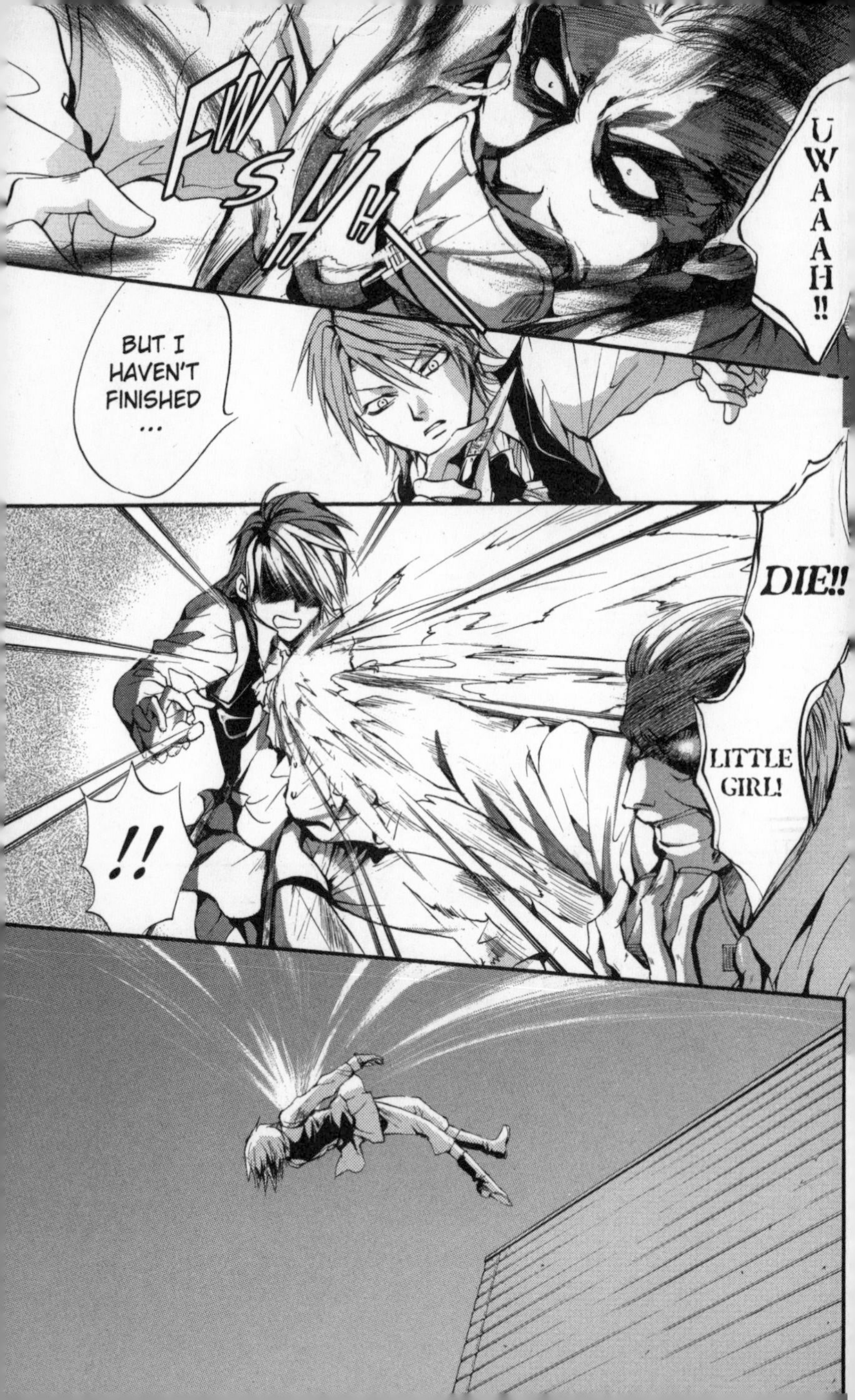
UWAAAAH!!
FWSHH
BUT I HAVEN'T FINISHED ...
DIE!!
LITTLE GIRL!
!!

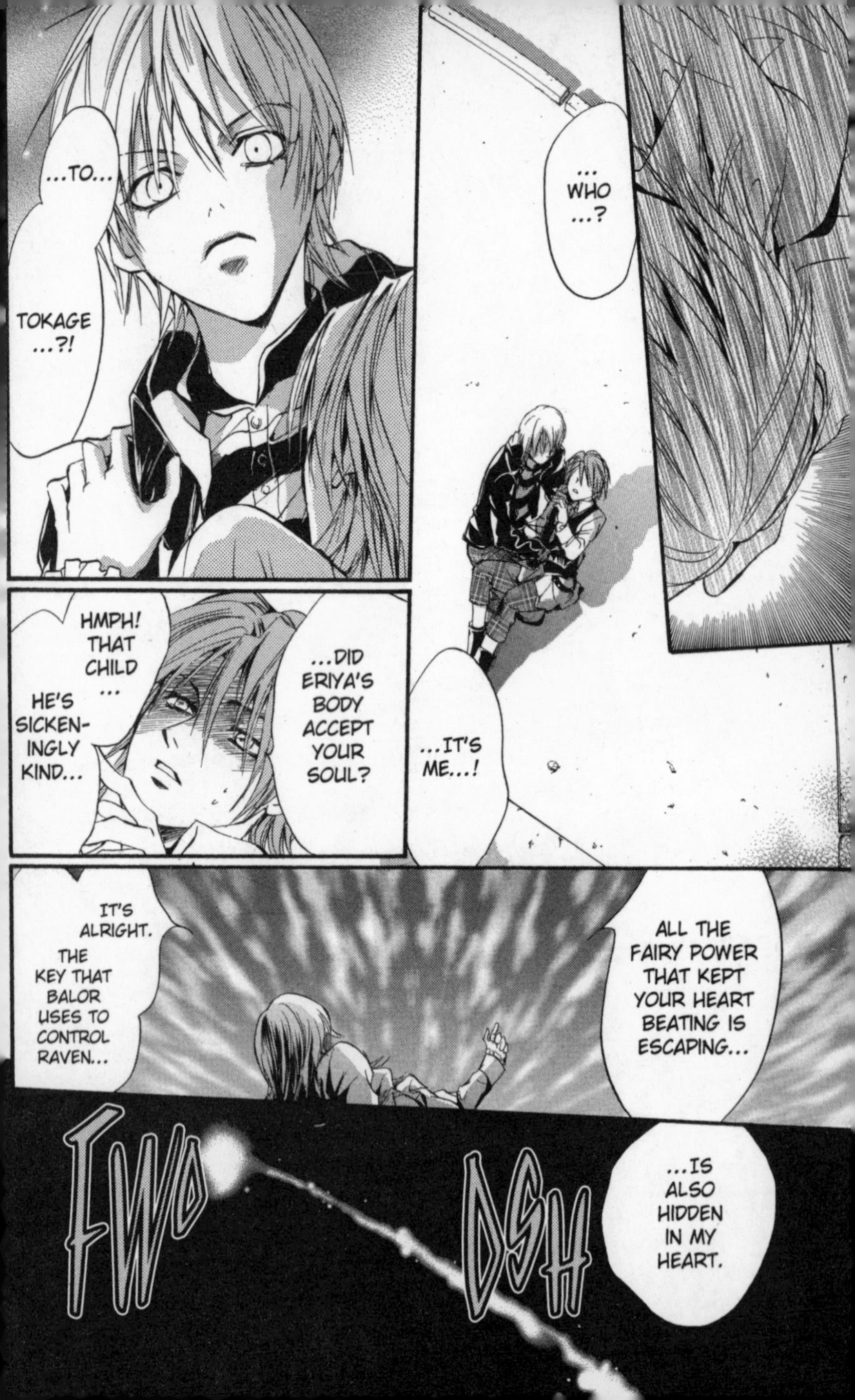
... WHO ...?
...IT'S ME...!
...TO...
TOKAGE ...?!
...DID ERIYA'S BODY ACCEPT YOUR SOUL?
HMPH! THAT CHILD ...
HE'S SICKENINGLY KIND...
ALL THE FAIRY POWER THAT KEPT YOUR HEART BEATING IS ESCAPING...
IT'S ALRIGHT.
THE KEY THAT BALOR USES TO CONTROL RAVEN...
...IS ALSO HIDDEN IN MY HEART.
DSH
FWO

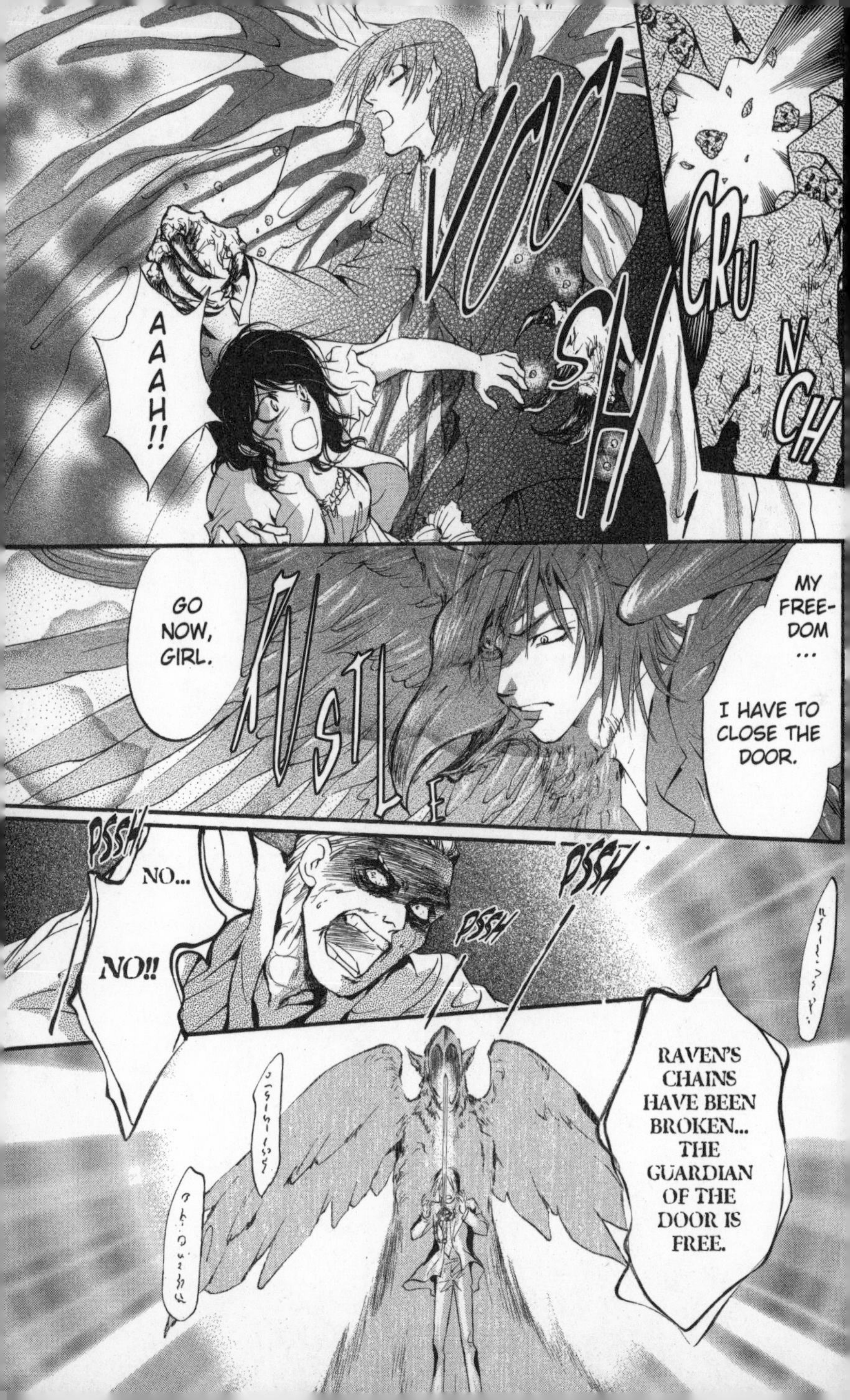
CRUNCH
VOOSH
AAAAH!!
MY FREE-DOM...
I HAVE TO CLOSE THE DOOR.
RUSTLE
GO NOW, GIRL.
PSSH
RAVEN'S CHAINS HAVE BEEN BROKEN... THE GUARDIAN OF THE DOOR IS FREE.
PSSH
NO...
NO!!
PSSH

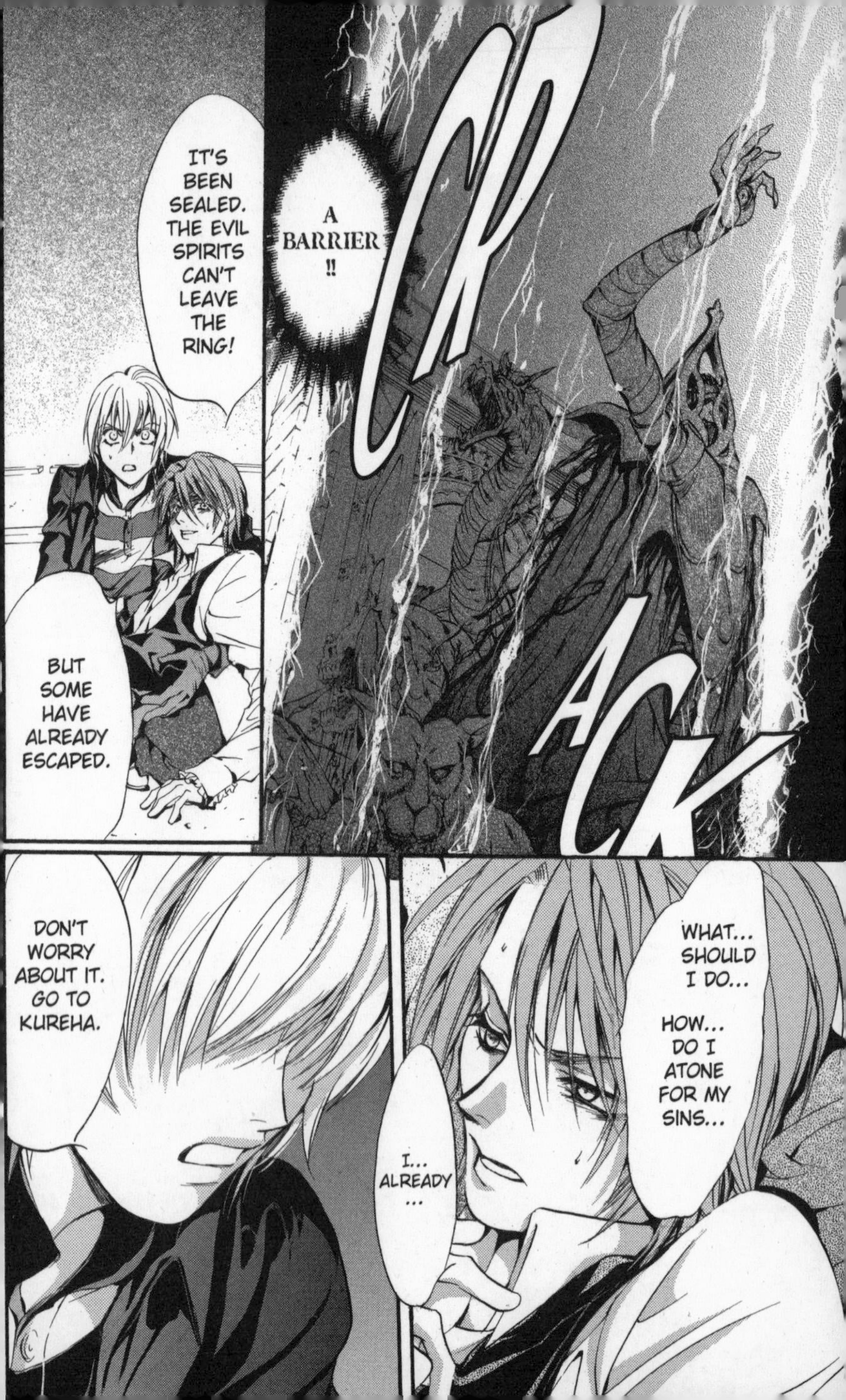
A BARRIER!!
CRACK
IT'S BEEN SEALED. THE EVIL SPIRITS CAN'T LEAVE THE RING!
BUT SOME HAVE ALREADY ESCAPED.
WHAT... SHOULD I DO...
HOW... DO I ATONE FOR MY SINS...
I... ALREADY...
DON'T WORRY ABOUT IT. GO TO KUREHA.

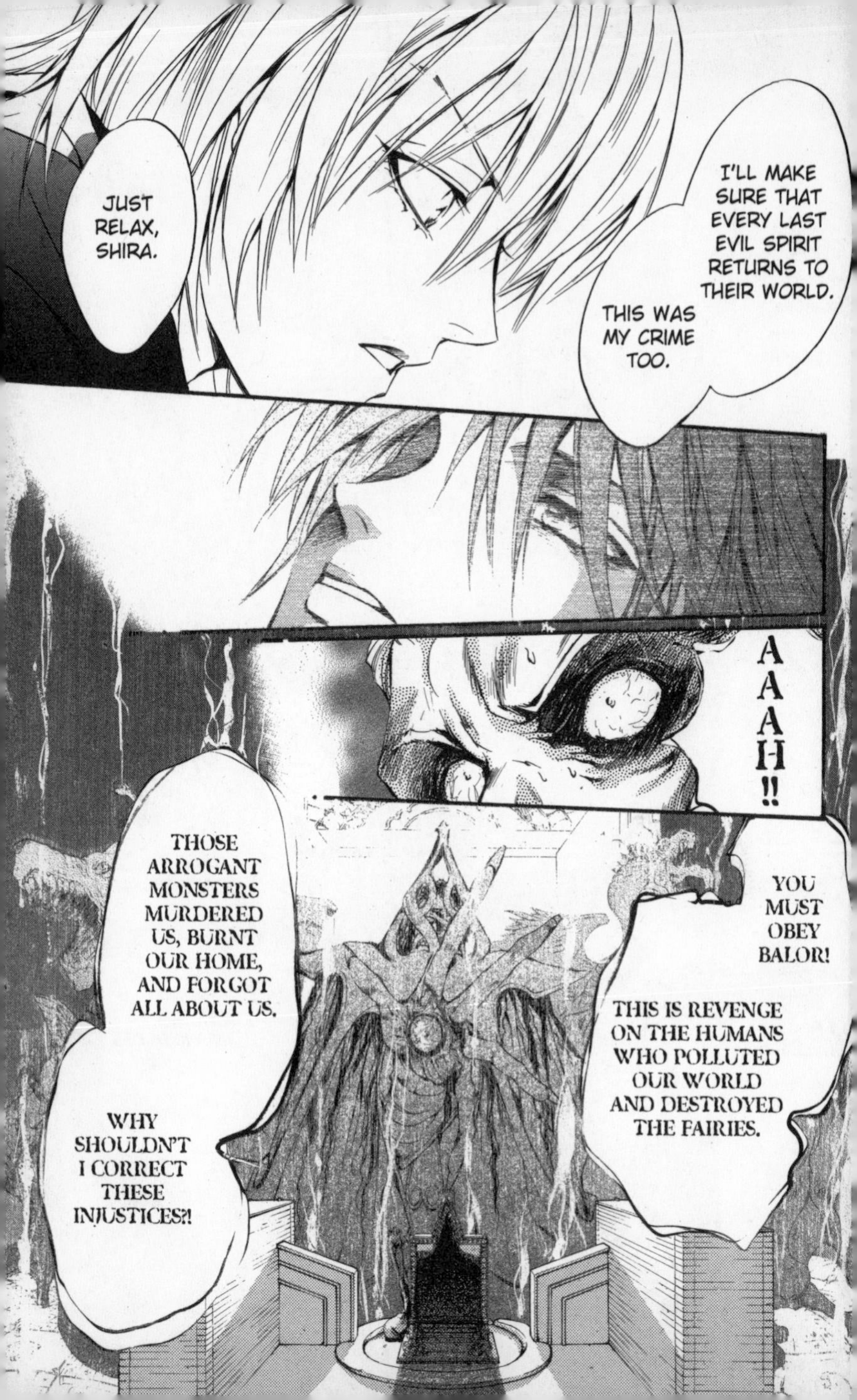
I'LL MAKE SURE THAT EVERY LAST EVIL SPIRIT RETURNS TO THEIR WORLD.
THIS WAS MY CRIME TOO.
JUST RELAX, SHIRA.
AAAAH!!
YOU MUST OBEY BALOR!
THOSE ARROGANT MONSTERS MURDERED US, BURNT OUR HOME, AND FORGOT ALL ABOUT US.
THIS IS REVENGE ON THE HUMANS WHO POLLUTED OUR WORLD AND DESTROYED THE FAIRIES.
WHY SHOULDN'T I CORRECT THESE INJUSTICES?!

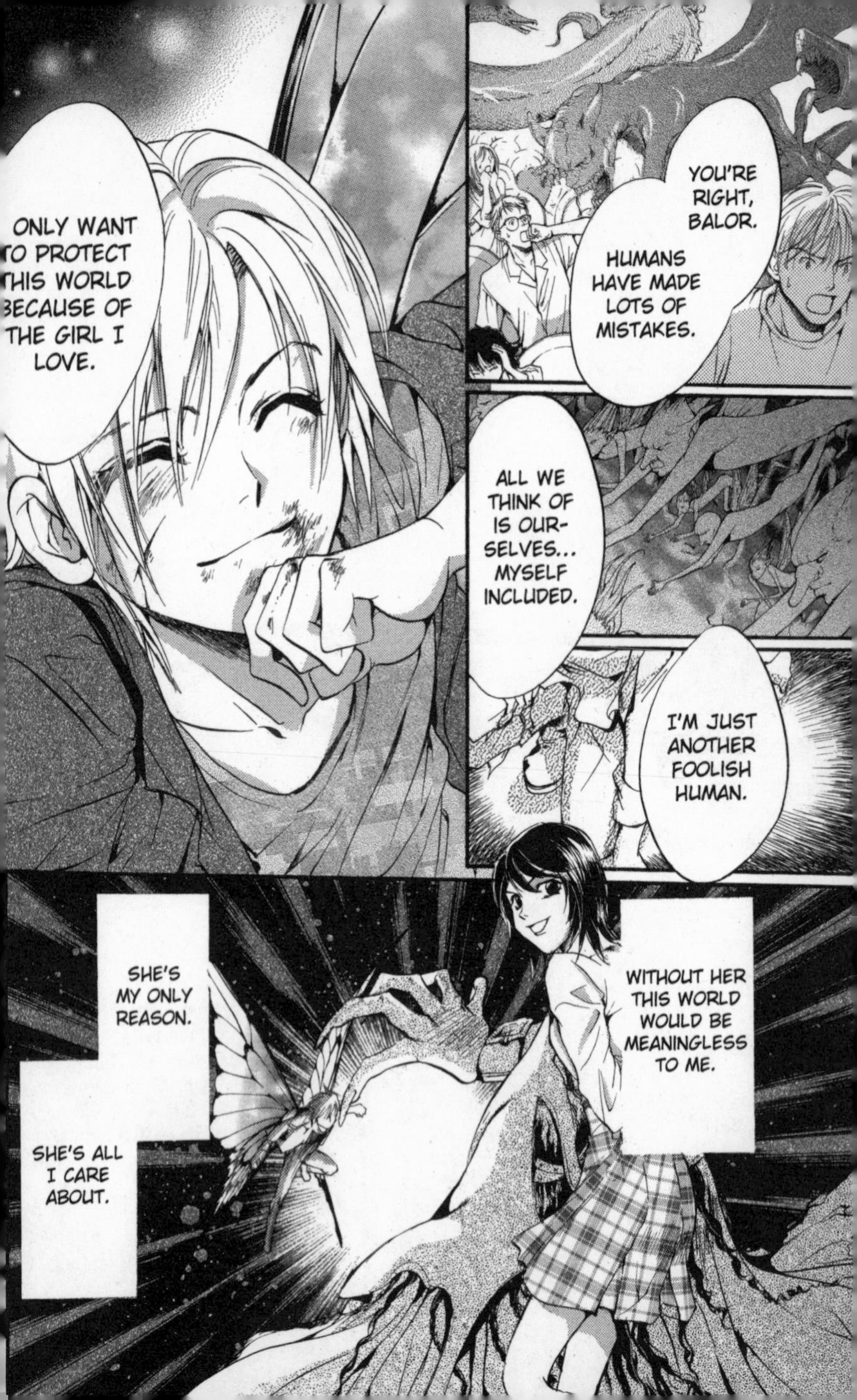
YOU'RE RIGHT, BALOR.
HUMANS HAVE MADE LOTS OF MISTAKES.
ALL WE THINK OF IS OUR-SELVES... MYSELF INCLUDED.
I'M JUST ANOTHER FOOLISH HUMAN.
ONLY WANT TO PROTECT THIS WORLD BECAUSE OF THE GIRL I LOVE.
WITHOUT HER THIS WORLD WOULD BE MEANINGLESS TO ME.
SHE'S MY ONLY REASON.
SHE'S ALL I CARE ABOUT.

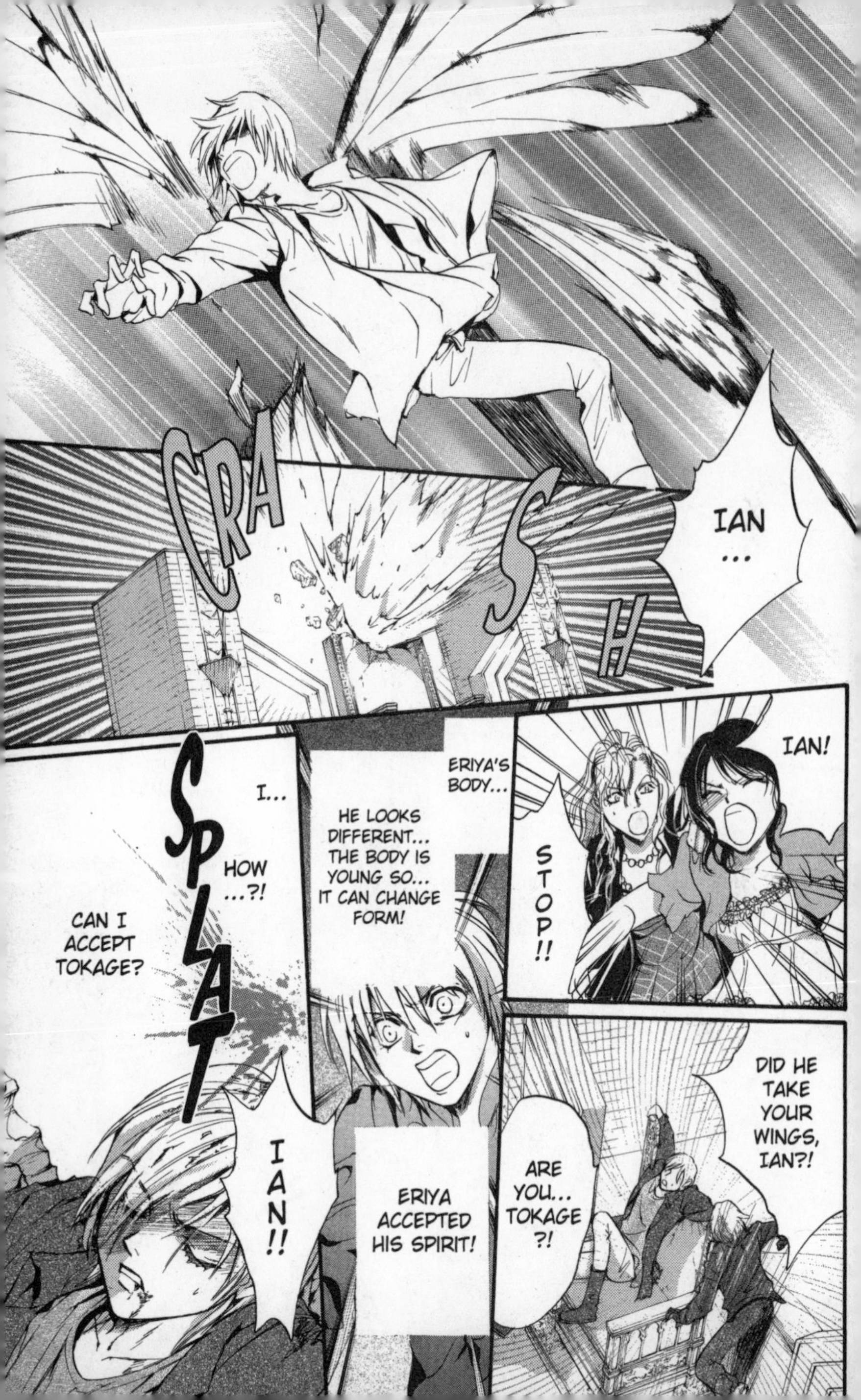
IAN ...
CRASH
IAN!
STOP!!
ERIYA'S BODY...
HE LOOKS DIFFERENT... THE BODY IS YOUNG SO... IT CAN CHANGE FORM!
I...
HOW ...?!
CAN I ACCEPT TOKAGE?
SPLAT
DID HE TAKE YOUR WINGS, IAN?!
ARE YOU... TOKAGE ?!
ERIYA ACCEPTED HIS SPIRIT!
IAN!!

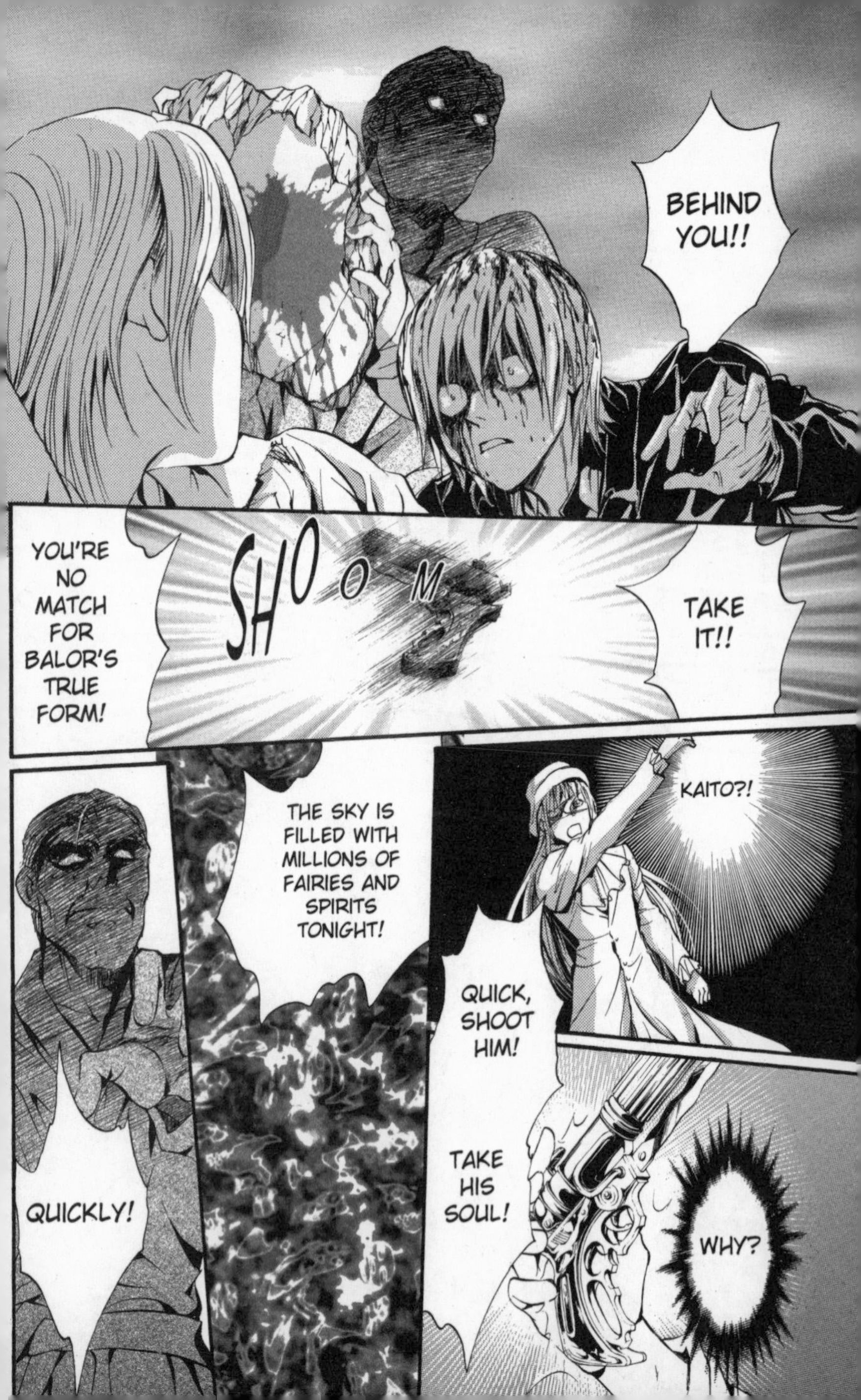
BEHIND YOU!!
TAKE IT!!
SHOOM
YOU'RE NO MATCH FOR BALOR'S TRUE FORM!
KAITO?!
QUICK, SHOOT HIM!
WHY?
TAKE HIS SOUL!
THE SKY IS FILLED WITH MILLIONS OF FAIRIES AND SPIRITS TONIGHT!
QUICKLY!

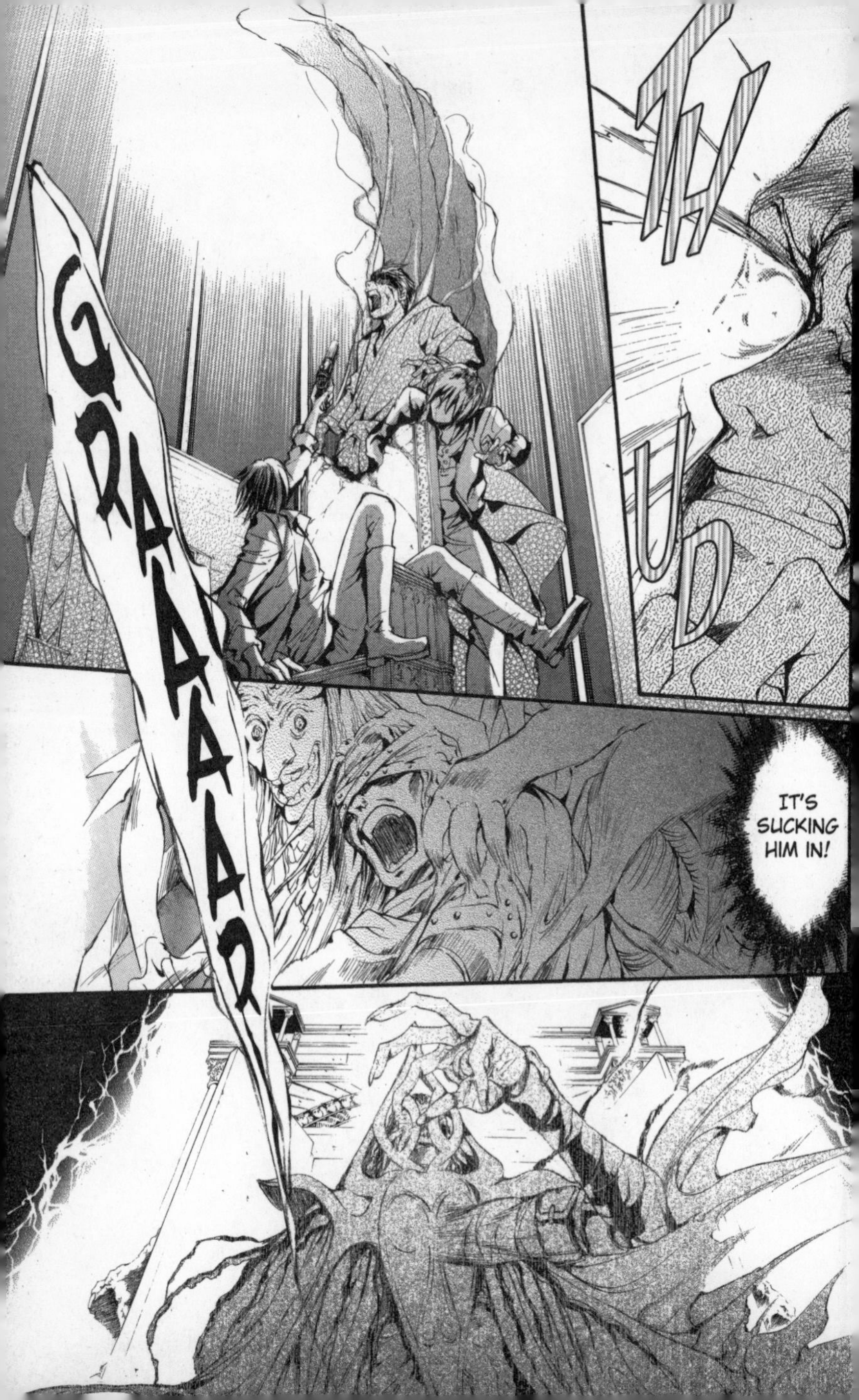
THUD
GRAAAAAR
IT'S SUCKING HIM IN!

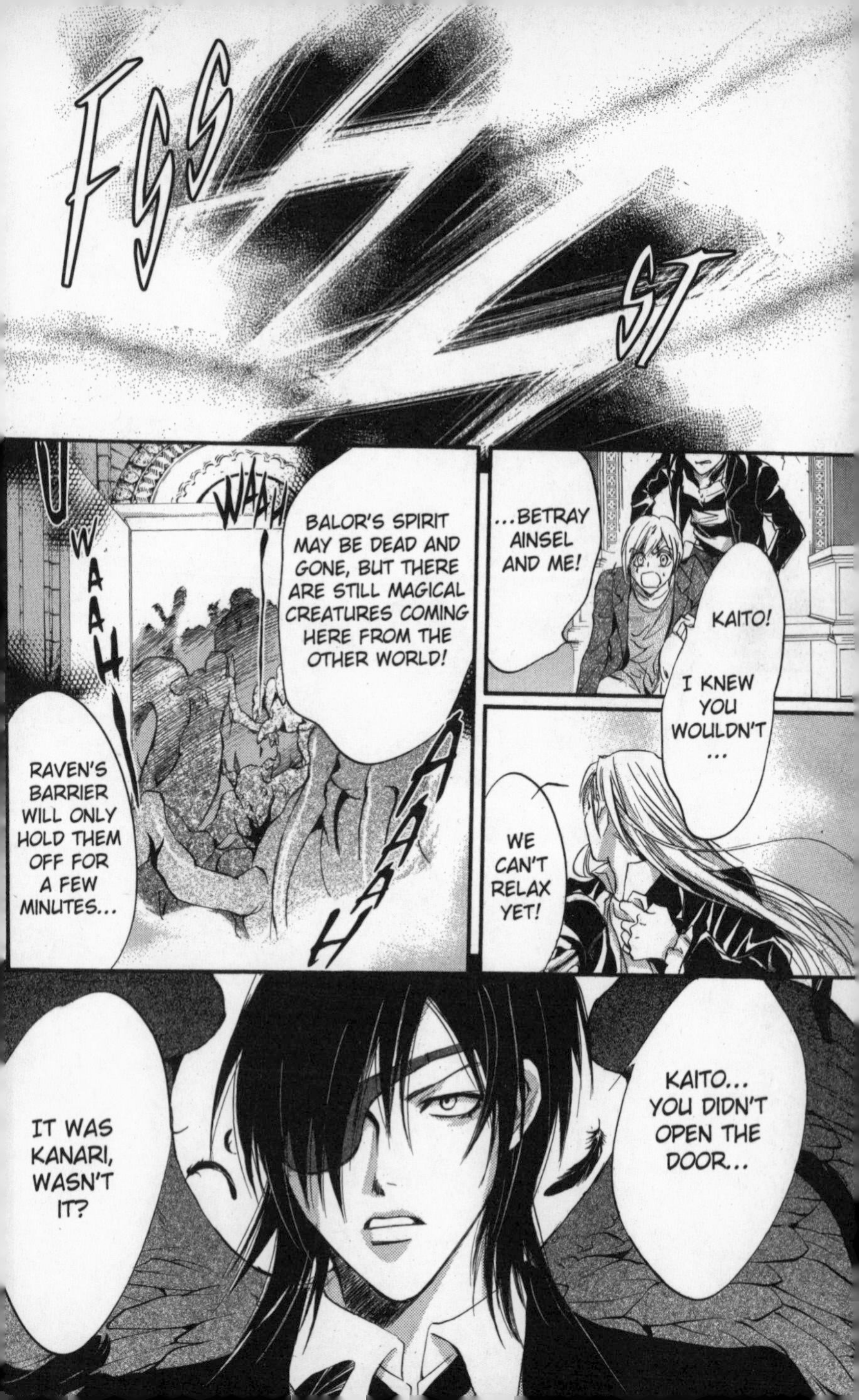
FSS
ST
KAITO!
I KNEW YOU WOULDN'T ...
...BETRAY AINSEL AND ME!
WE CAN'T RELAX YET!
WAAH
BALOR'S SPIRIT MAY BE DEAD AND GONE, BUT THERE ARE STILL MAGICAL CREATURES COMING HERE FROM THE OTHER WORLD!
WAAAH
RAVEN'S BARRIER WILL ONLY HOLD THEM OFF FOR A FEW MINUTES...
AAAAH
KAITO... YOU DIDN'T OPEN THE DOOR...
IT WAS KANARI, WASN'T IT?

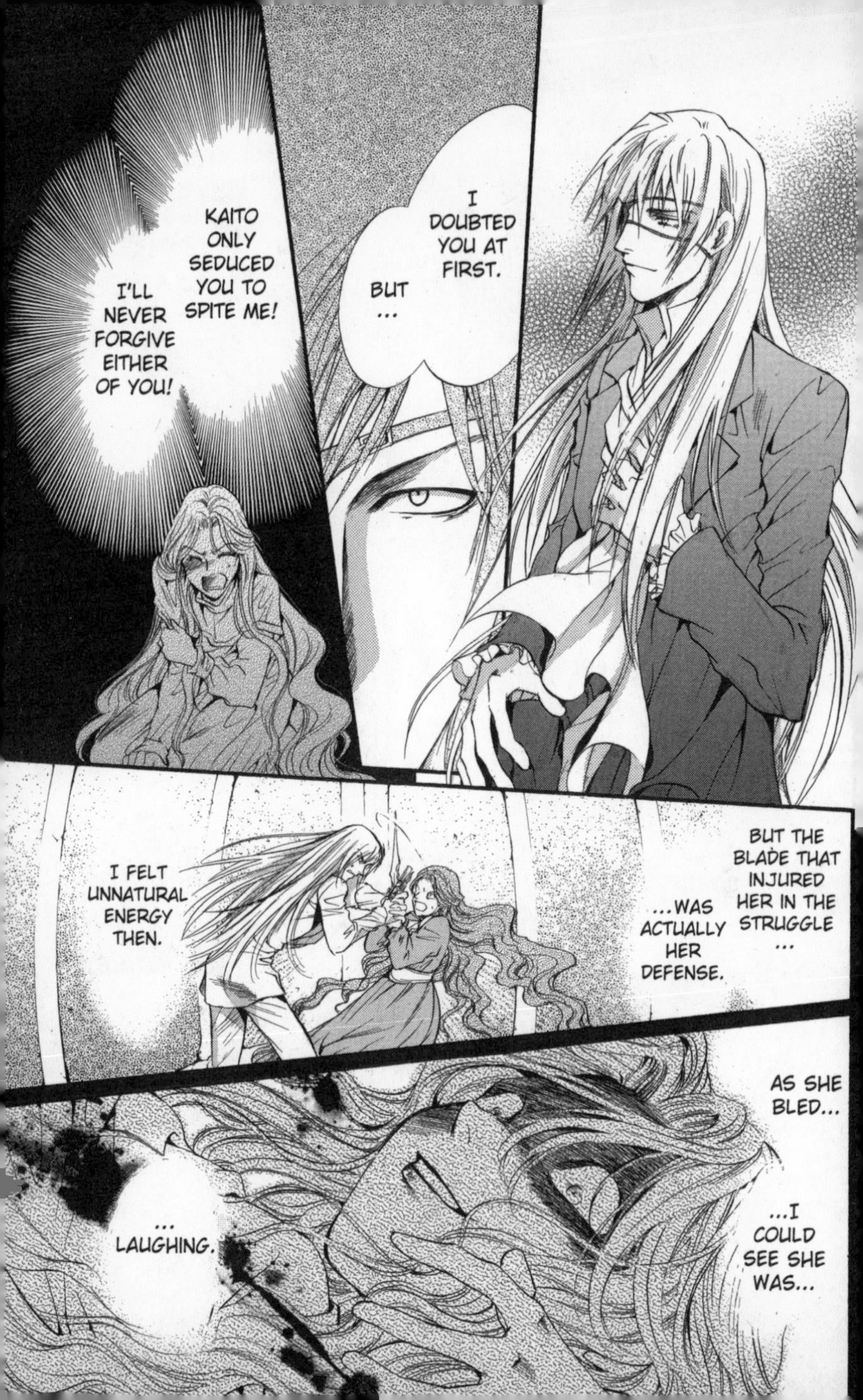
I DOUBTED YOU AT FIRST.
BUT ...
KAITO ONLY SEDUCED YOU TO SPITE ME!
I'LL NEVER FORGIVE EITHER OF YOU!
BUT THE BLADE THAT INJURED HER IN THE STRUGGLE ...
...WAS ACTUALLY HER DEFENSE.
I FELT UNNATURAL ENERGY THEN.
AS SHE BLED...
...I COULD SEE SHE WAS...
... LAUGHING.

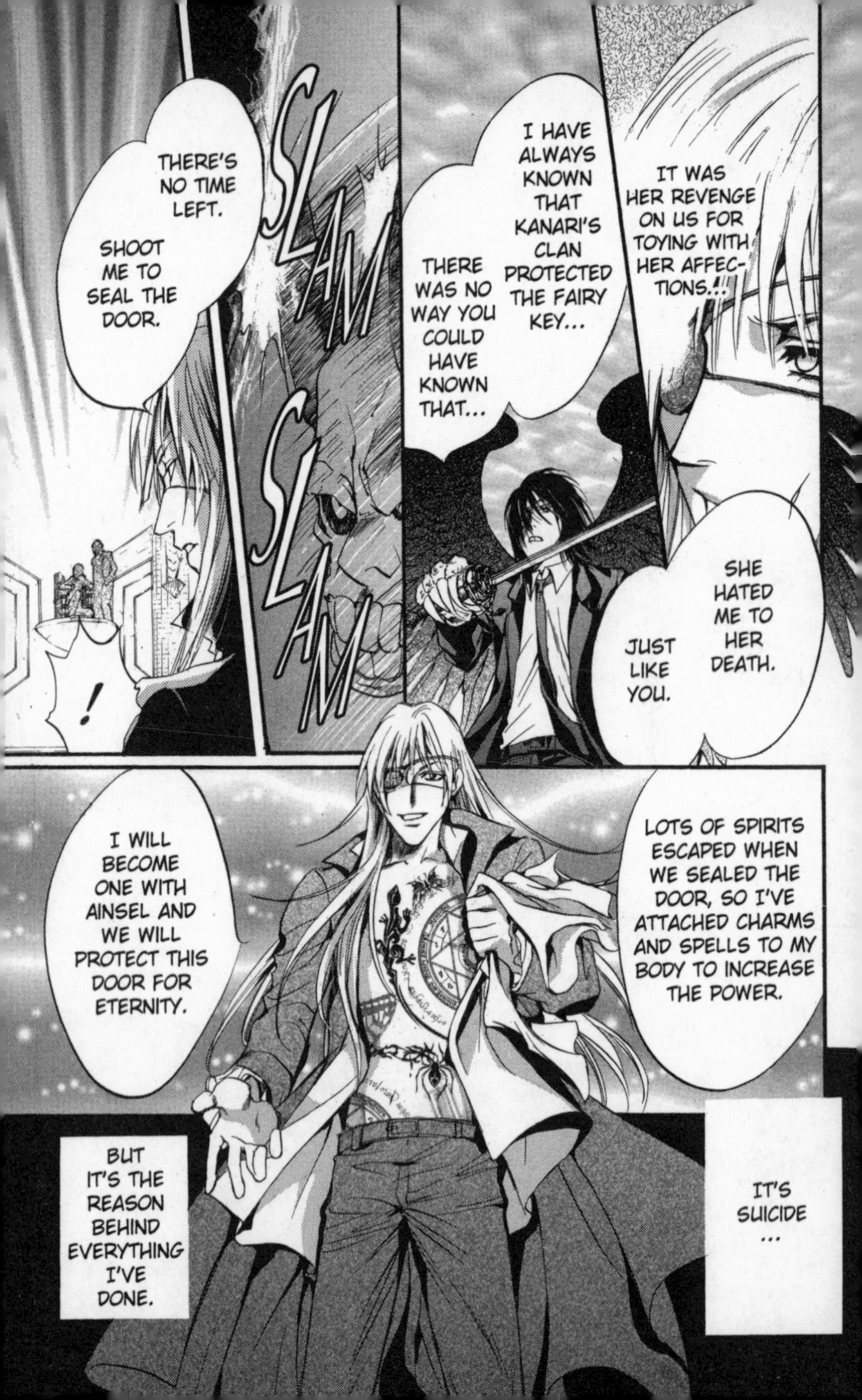
IT WAS HER REVENGE ON US FOR TOYING WITH HER AFFEC-TIONS...
SHE HATED ME TO HER DEATH.
JUST LIKE YOU.
I HAVE ALWAYS KNOWN THAT KANARI'S CLAN PROTECTED THE FAIRY KEY...
THERE WAS NO WAY YOU COULD HAVE KNOWN THAT...
SLAM
SLAM
THERE'S NO TIME LEFT.
SHOOT ME TO SEAL THE DOOR.
!
LOTS OF SPIRITS ESCAPED WHEN WE SEALED THE DOOR, SO I'VE ATTACHED CHARMS AND SPELLS TO MY BODY TO INCREASE THE POWER.
I WILL BECOME ONE WITH AINSEL AND WE WILL PROTECT THIS DOOR FOR ETERNITY.
IT'S SUICIDE...
BUT IT'S THE REASON BEHIND EVERYTHING I'VE DONE.

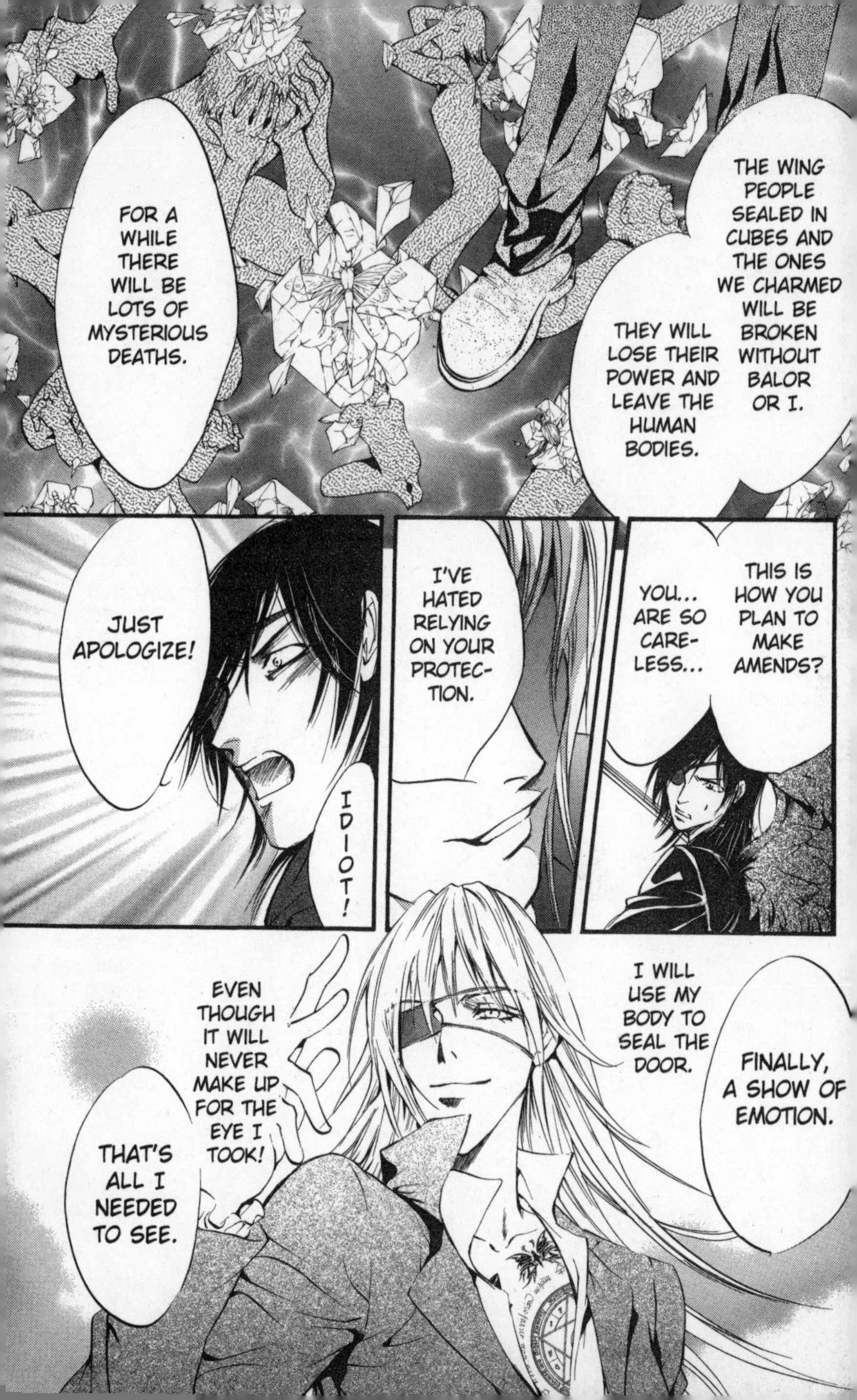
THE WING PEOPLE SEALED IN CUBES AND THE ONES WE CHARMED WILL BE BROKEN WITHOUT BALOR OR I.
THEY WILL LOSE THEIR POWER AND LEAVE THE HUMAN BODIES.
FOR A WHILE THERE WILL BE LOTS OF MYSTERIOUS DEATHS.
THIS IS HOW YOU PLAN TO MAKE AMENDS?
YOU... ARE SO CARELESS...
I'VE HATED RELYING ON YOUR PROTECTION.
JUST APOLOGIZE!
IDIOT!
FINALLY, A SHOW OF EMOTION.
I WILL USE MY BODY TO SEAL THE DOOR.
EVEN THOUGH IT WILL NEVER MAKE UP FOR THE EYE I TOOK!
THAT'S ALL I NEEDED TO SEE.

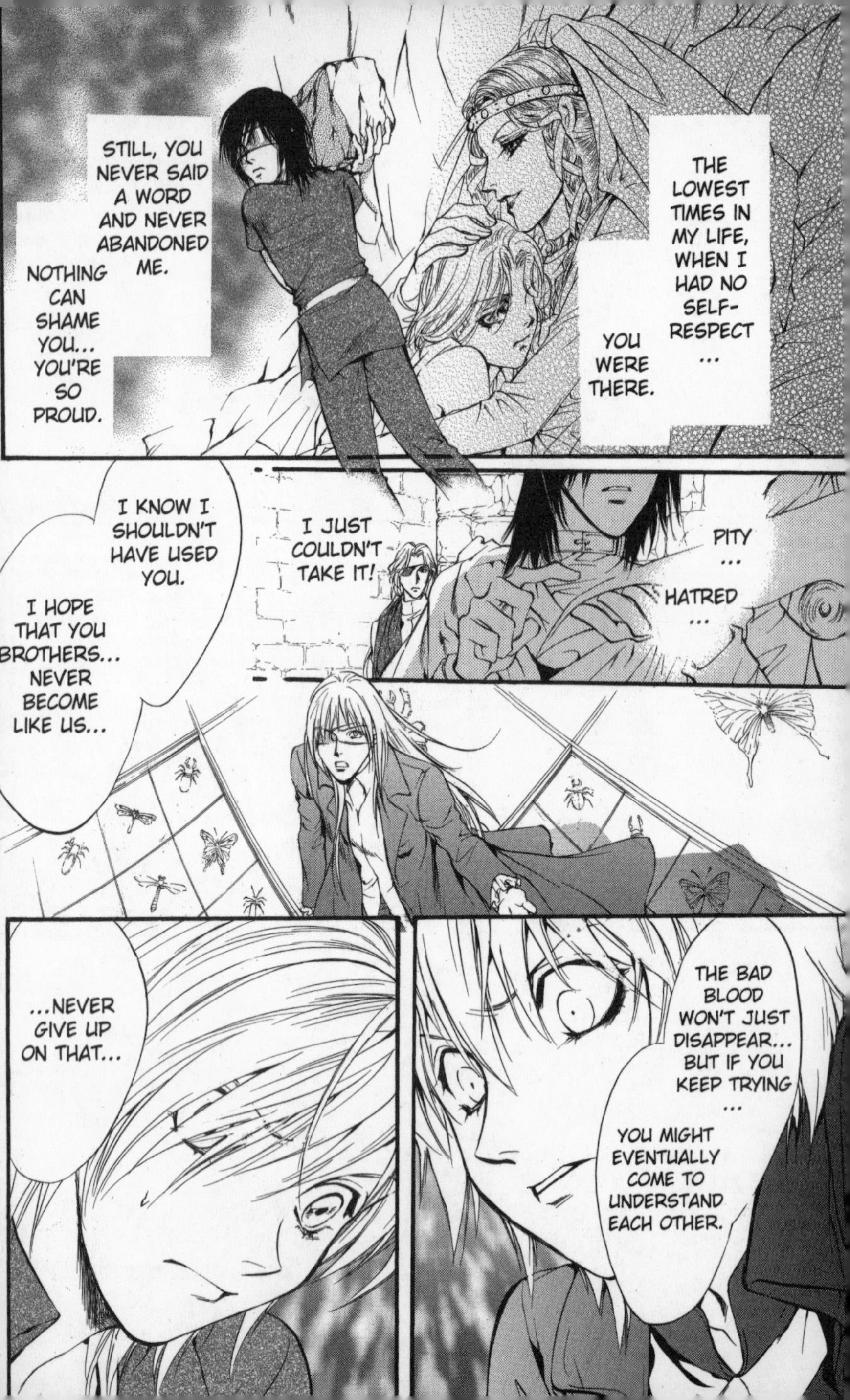
THE LOWEST TIMES IN MY LIFE, WHEN I HAD NO SELF-RESPECT...
YOU WERE THERE.
STILL, YOU NEVER SAID A WORD AND NEVER ABANDONED ME.
NOTHING CAN SHAME YOU... YOU'RE SO PROUD.
PITY... HATRED...
I JUST COULDN'T TAKE IT!
I KNOW I SHOULDN'T HAVE USED YOU.
I HOPE THAT YOU BROTHERS... NEVER BECOME LIKE US...
THE BAD BLOOD WON'T JUST DISAPPEAR... BUT IF YOU KEEP TRYING...
YOU MIGHT EVENTUALLY COME TO UNDERSTAND EACH OTHER.
...NEVER GIVE UP ON THAT...

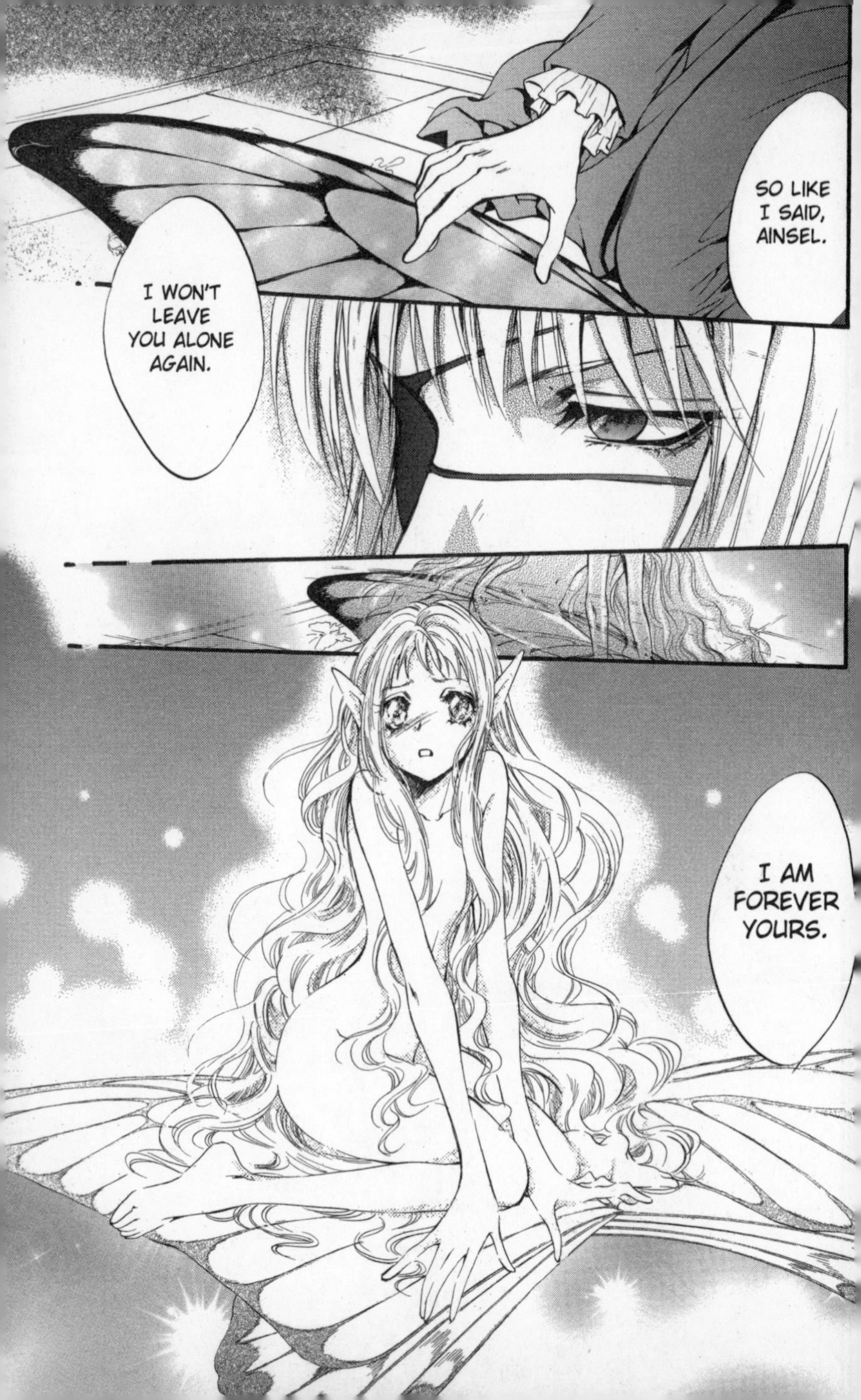
SO LIKE I SAID, AINSEL.
I WON'T LEAVE YOU ALONE AGAIN.
I AM FOREVER YOURS.

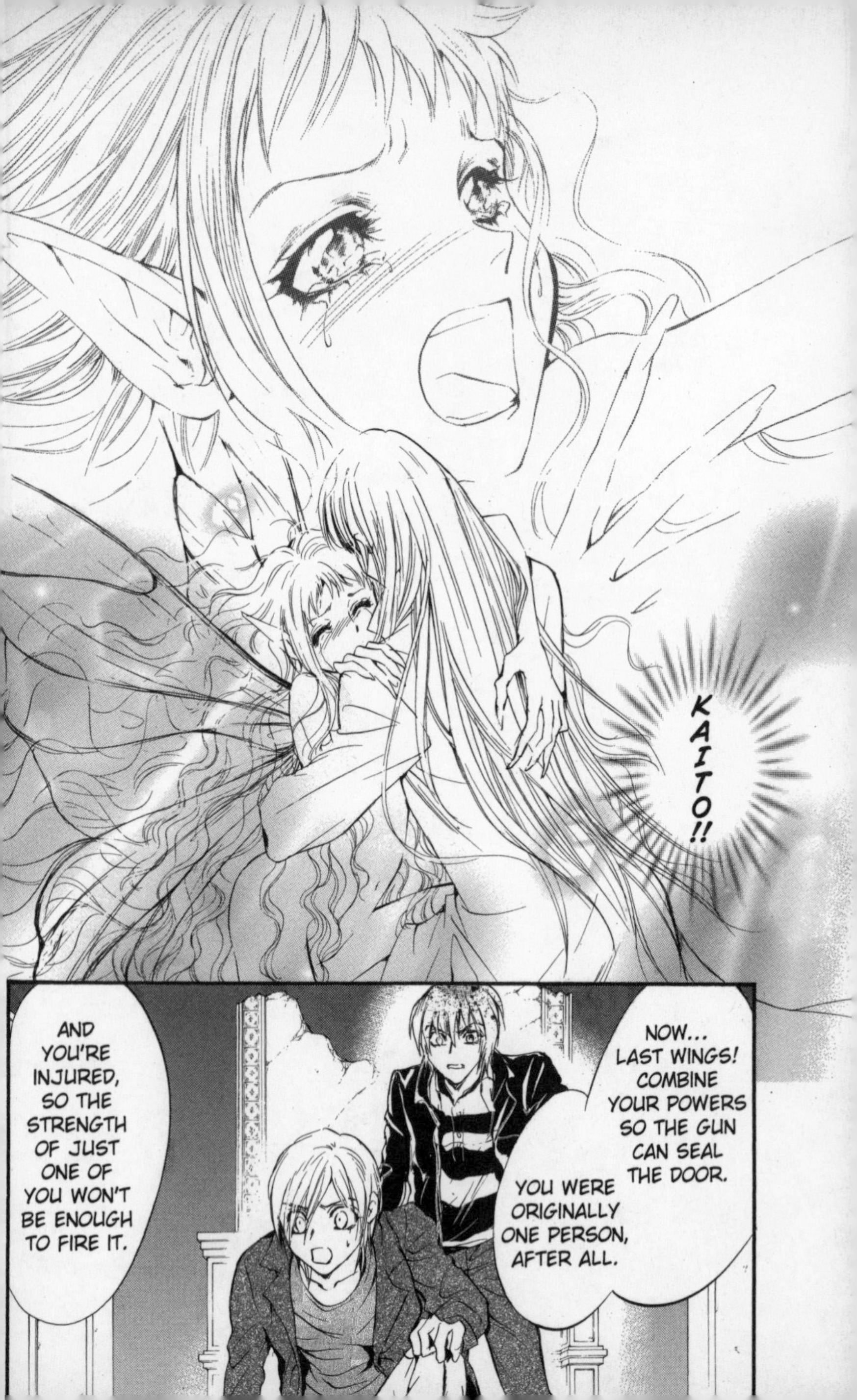
KAITO!!
NOW... LAST WINGS! COMBINE YOUR POWERS SO THE GUN CAN SEAL THE DOOR.
YOU WERE ORIGINALLY ONE PERSON, AFTER ALL.
AND YOU'RE INJURED, SO THE STRENGTH OF JUST ONE OF YOU WON'T BE ENOUGH TO FIRE IT.

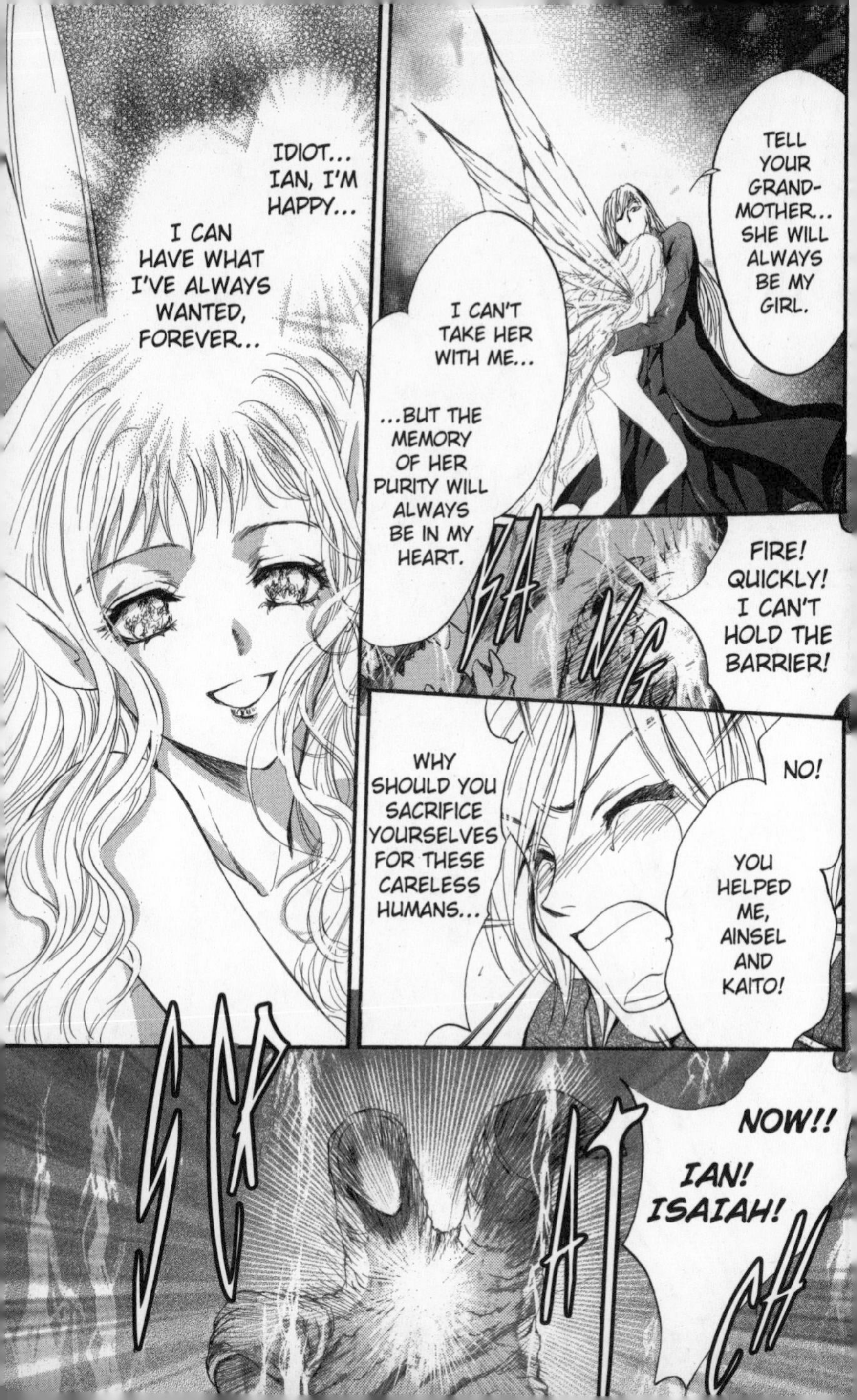
TELL YOUR GRAND-MOTHER... SHE WILL ALWAYS BE MY GIRL.
I CAN'T TAKE HER WITH ME...
...BUT THE MEMORY OF HER PURITY WILL ALWAYS BE IN MY HEART.
BANG
FIRE! QUICKLY! I CAN'T HOLD THE BARRIER!
NO!
YOU HELPED ME, AINSEL AND KAITO!
WHY SHOULD YOU SACRIFICE YOURSELVES FOR THESE CARELESS HUMANS...
IDIOT... IAN, I'M HAPPY...
I CAN HAVE WHAT I'VE ALWAYS WANTED, FOREVER...
NOW!!
IAN! ISAIAH!
SCRATCH

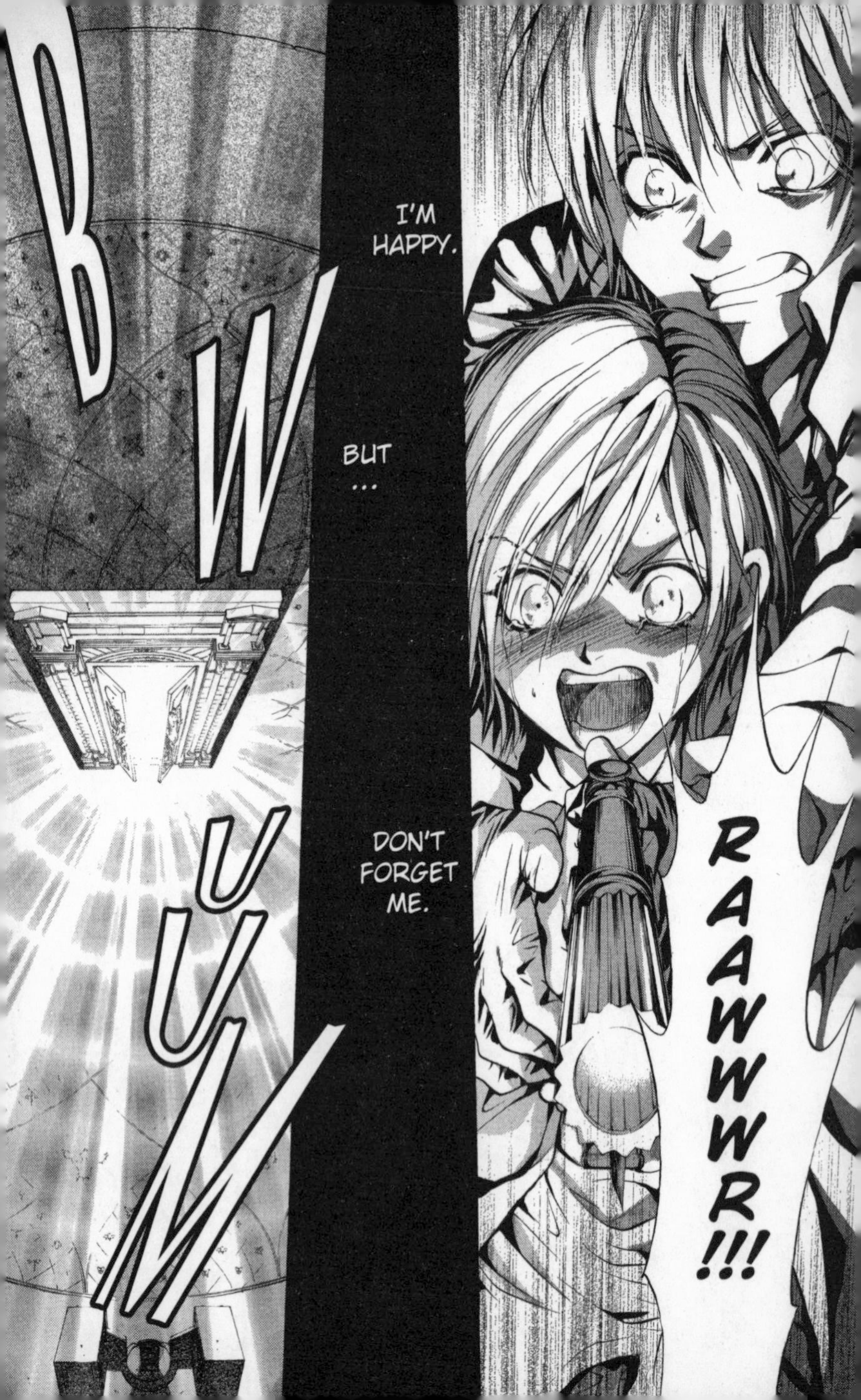
RAAWWWR!!!
I'M HAPPY.
BUT...
DON'T FORGET ME.
BWUUM

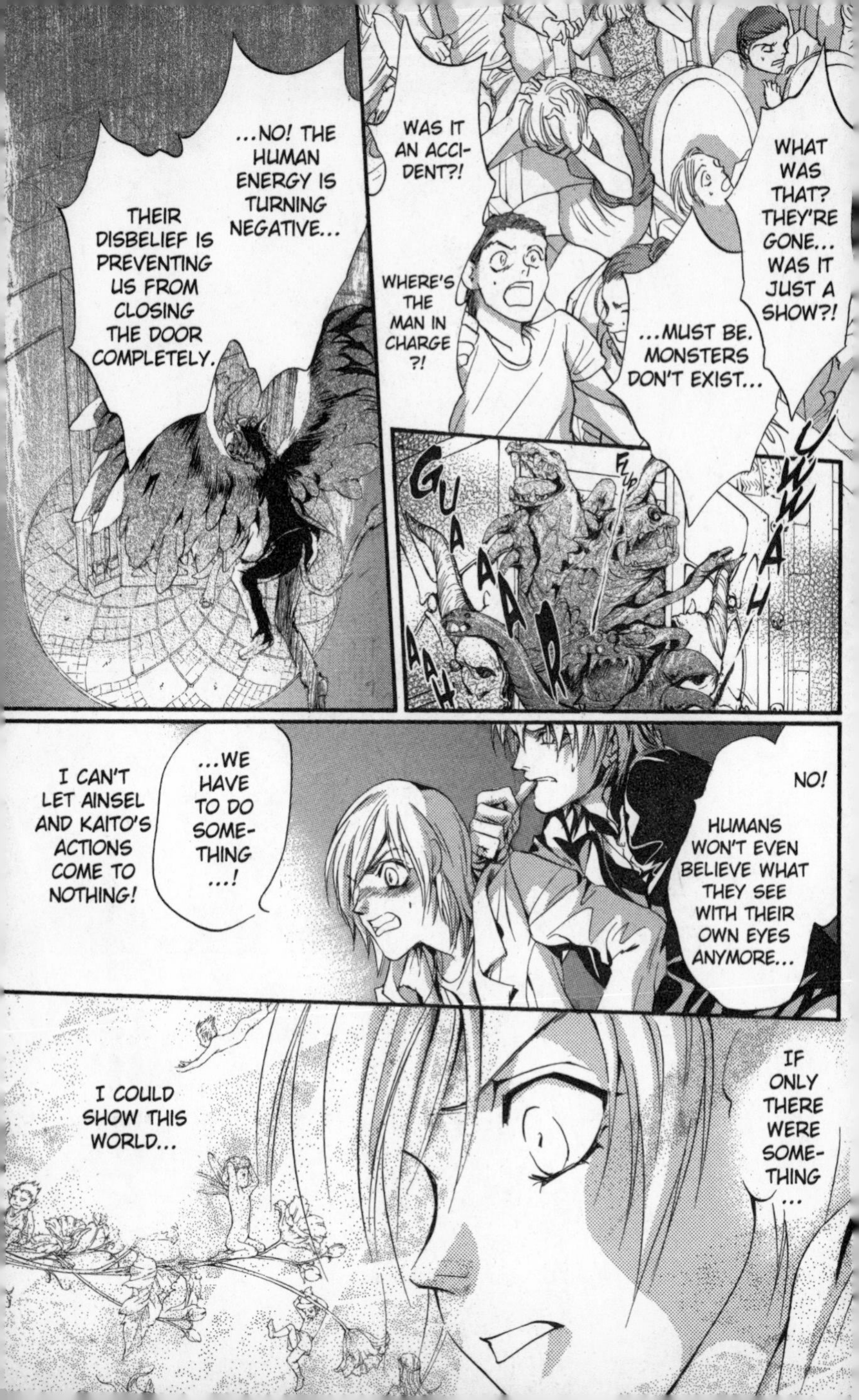
WHAT WAS THAT? THEY'RE GONE... WAS IT JUST A SHOW?!
...MUST BE. MONSTERS DON'T EXIST...
WAS IT AN ACCI-DENT?!
WHERE'S THE MAN IN CHARGE?!
UWAAAH
GUAAAAR
AAAH
...NO! THE HUMAN ENERGY IS TURNING NEGATIVE...
THEIR DISBELIEF IS PREVENTING US FROM CLOSING THE DOOR COMPLETELY.
NO!
HUMANS WON'T EVEN BELIEVE WHAT THEY SEE WITH THEIR OWN EYES ANYMORE...
...WE HAVE TO DO SOME-THING...!
I CAN'T LET AINSEL AND KAITO'S ACTIONS COME TO NOTHING!
IF ONLY THERE WERE SOME-THING...
I COULD SHOW THIS WORLD...

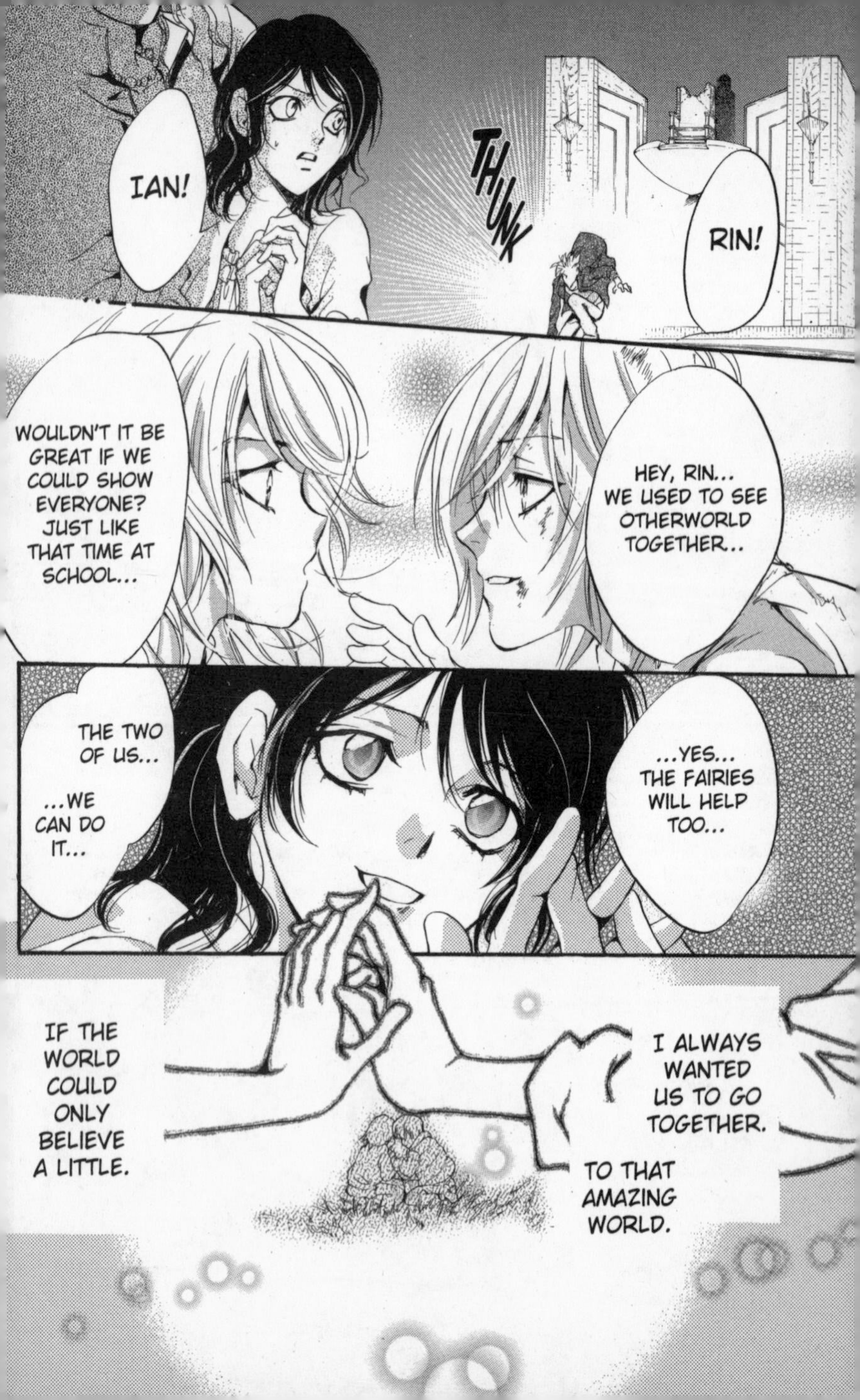
RIN!
THUNK
IAN!
HEY, RIN... WE USED TO SEE OTHERWORLD TOGETHER...
WOULDN'T IT BE GREAT IF WE COULD SHOW EVERYONE? JUST LIKE THAT TIME AT SCHOOL...
...YES... THE FAIRIES WILL HELP TOO...
THE TWO OF US...
...WE CAN DO IT...
I ALWAYS WANTED US TO GO TOGETHER.
TO THAT AMAZING WORLD.
IF THE WORLD COULD ONLY BELIEVE A LITTLE.

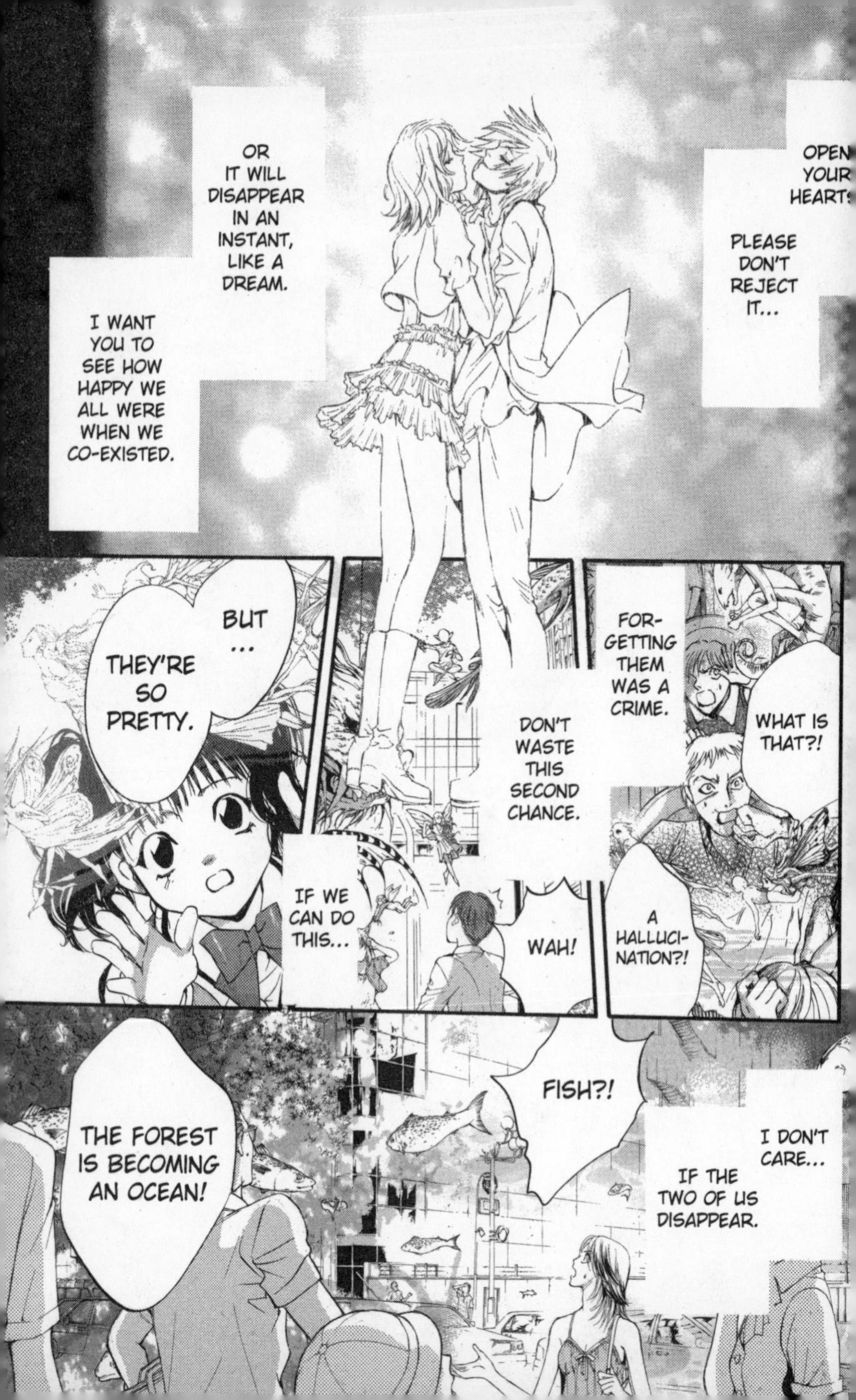
OPEN YOUR HEARTS
PLEASE DON'T REJECT IT...
OR IT WILL DISAPPEAR IN AN INSTANT, LIKE A DREAM.
I WANT YOU TO SEE HOW HAPPY WE ALL WERE WHEN WE CO-EXISTED.
FOR-GETTING THEM WAS A CRIME.
WHAT IS THAT?!
A HALLUCI-NATION?!
DON'T WASTE THIS SECOND CHANCE.
WAH!
IF WE CAN DO THIS...
BUT...
THEY'RE SO PRETTY.
I DON'T CARE...
IF THE TWO OF US DISAPPEAR.
FISH?!
THE FOREST IS BECOMING AN OCEAN!

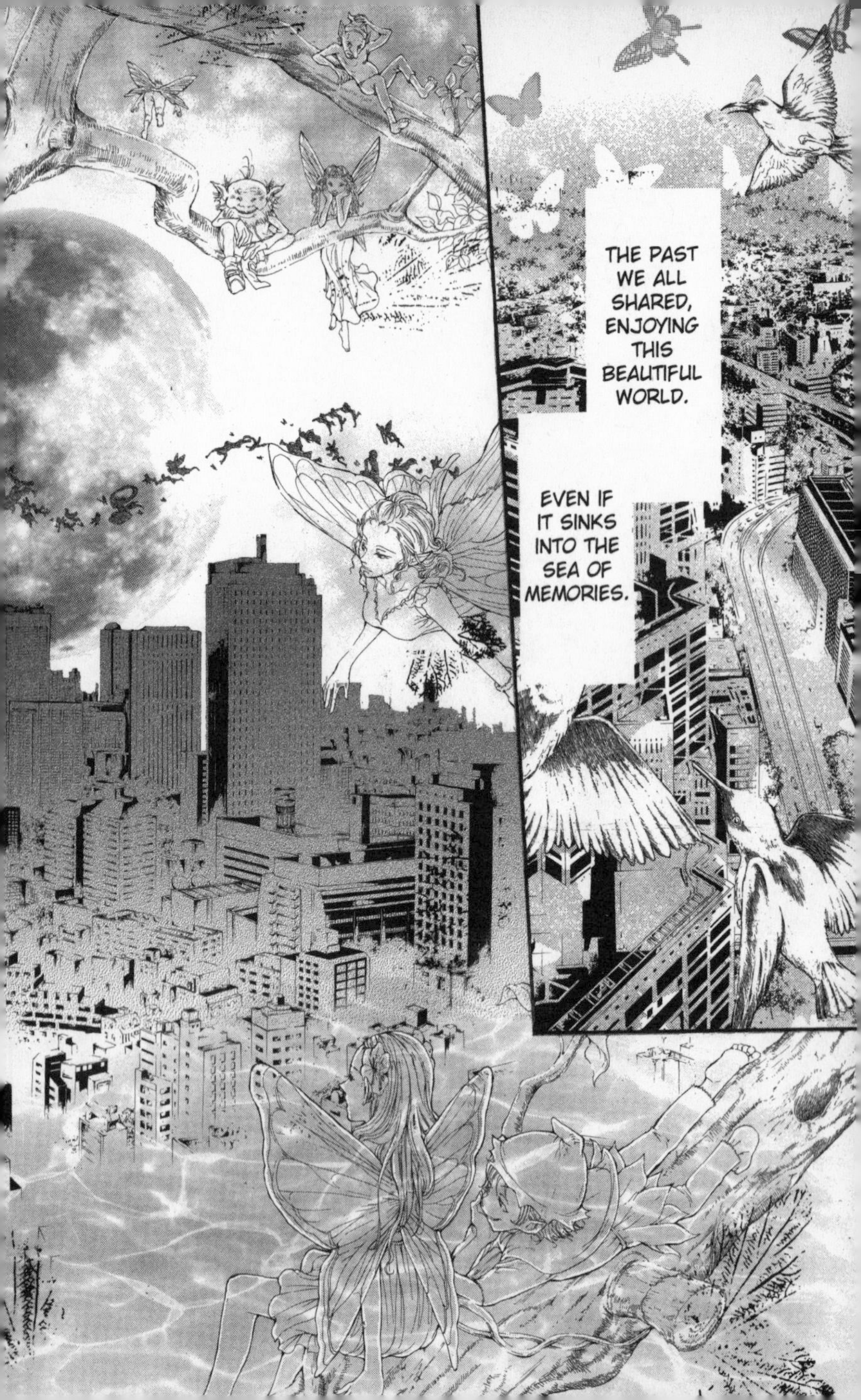
THE PAST WE ALL SHARED, ENJOYING THIS BEAUTIFUL WORLD.
EVEN IF IT SINKS INTO THE SEA OF MEMORIES.

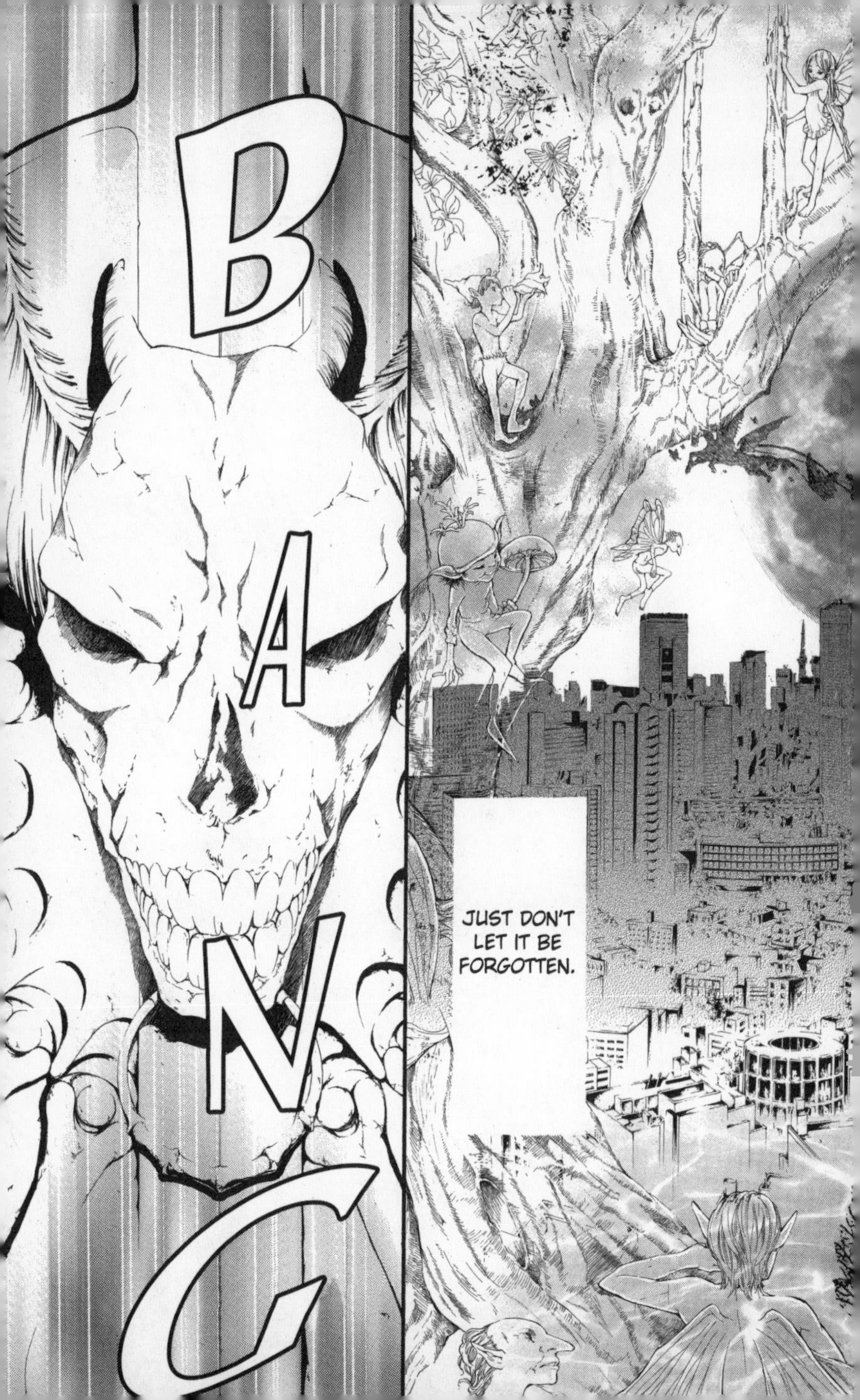
JUST DON'T LET IT BE FORGOTTEN.
BANG

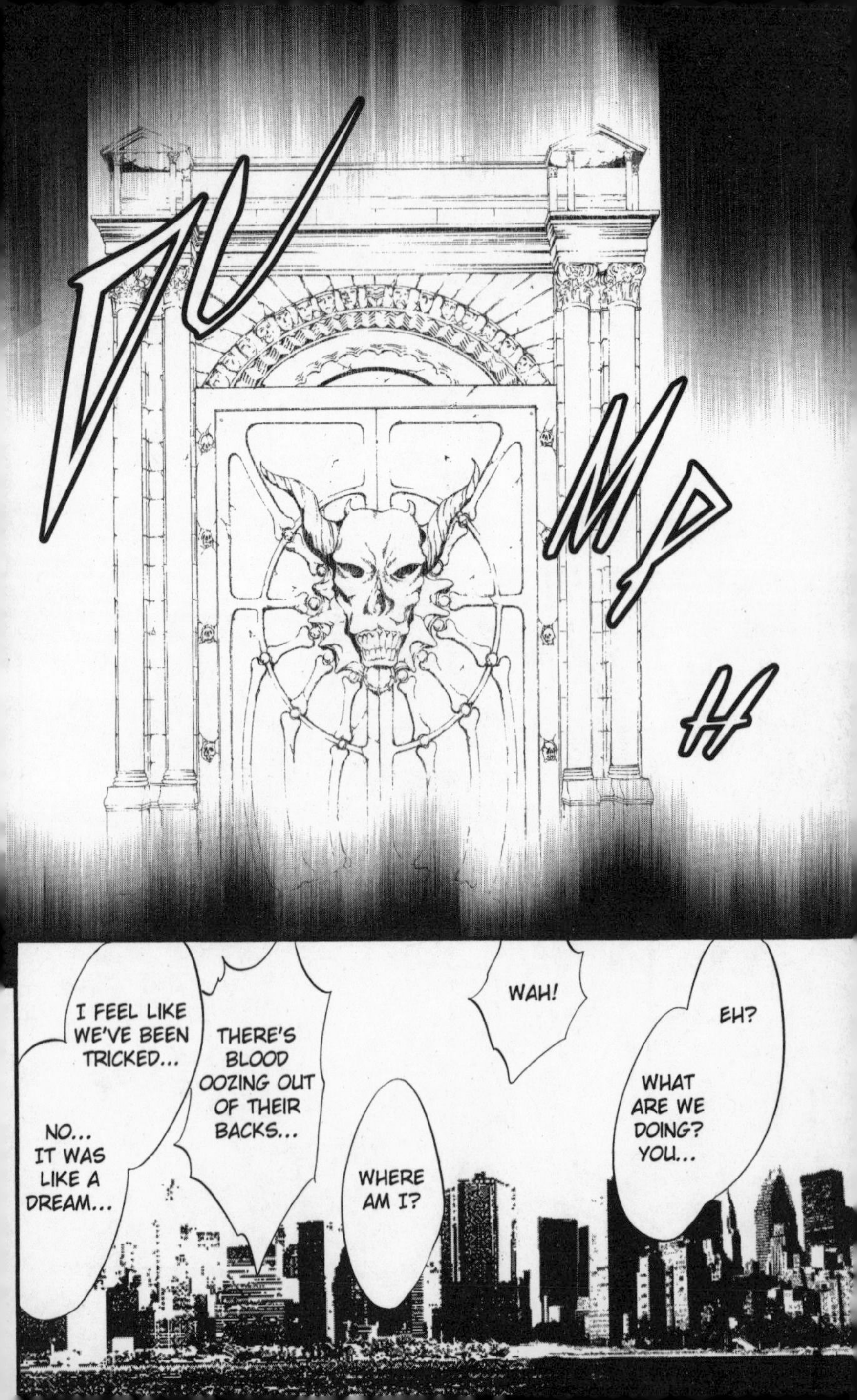
DUMPH
EH? WHAT ARE WE DOING? YOU...
WAH!
WHERE AM I?
THERE'S BLOOD OOZING OUT OF THEIR BACKS...
I FEEL LIKE WE'VE BEEN TRICKED...
NO... IT WAS LIKE A DREAM...

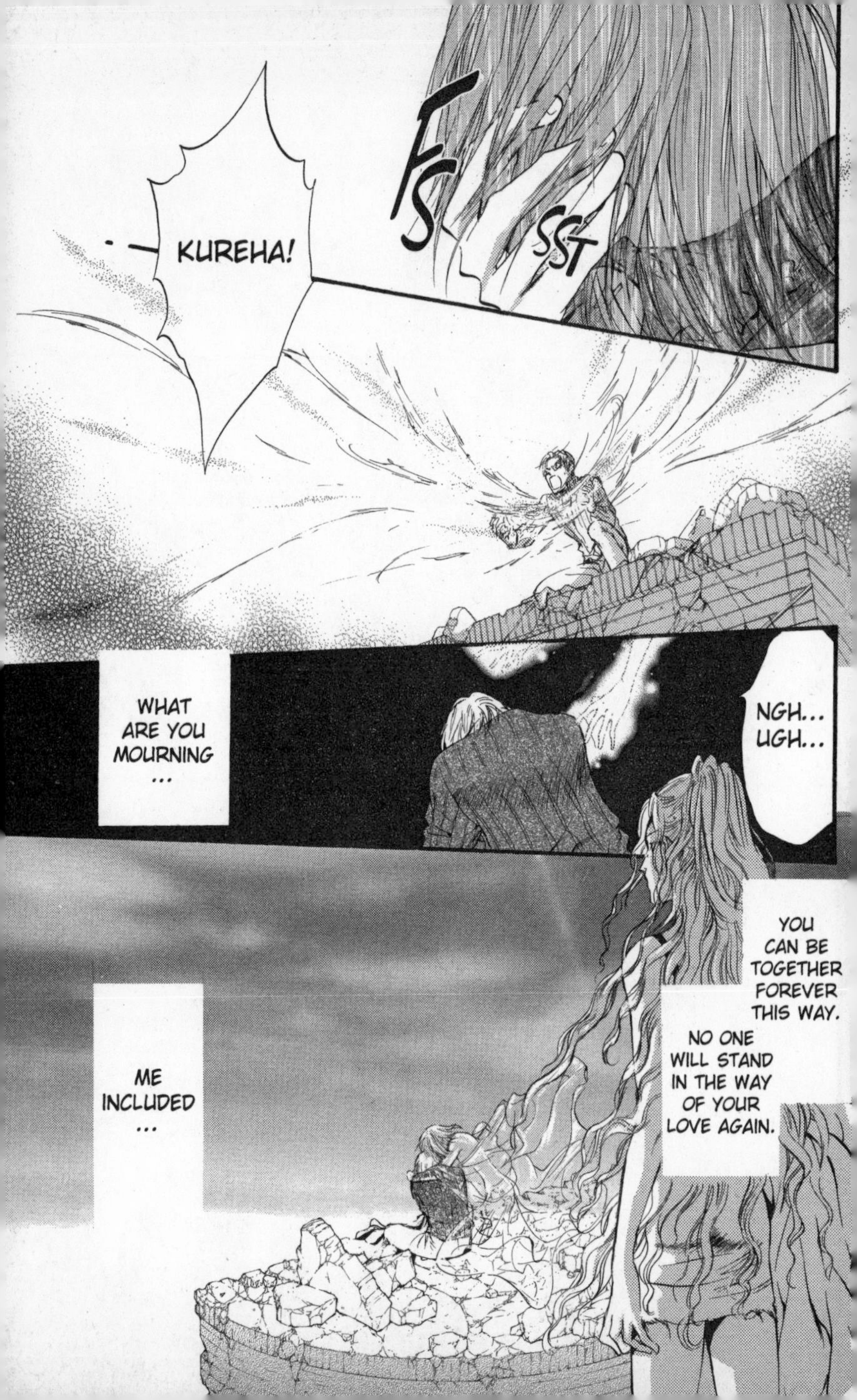

FSSST
KUREHA!
NGH... UGH...
WHAT ARE YOU MOURNING ...
YOU CAN BE TOGETHER FOREVER THIS WAY.
NO ONE WILL STAND IN THE WAY OF YOUR LOVE AGAIN.
ME INCLUDED ...

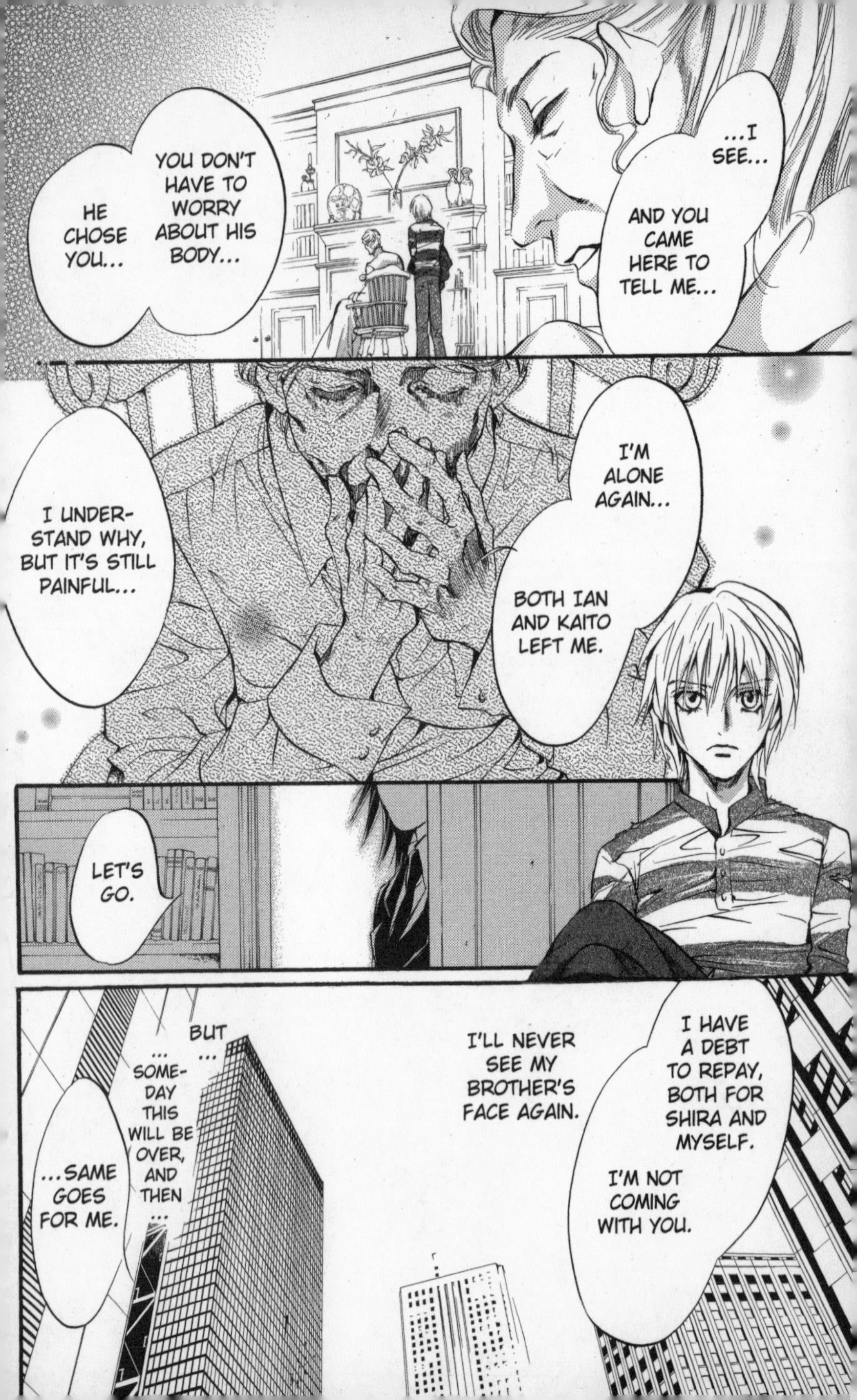
...I SEE...
AND YOU CAME HERE TO TELL ME...
YOU DON'T HAVE TO WORRY ABOUT HIS BODY...
HE CHOSE YOU...
I'M ALONE AGAIN...
BOTH IAN AND KAITO LEFT ME.
I UNDER-STAND WHY, BUT IT'S STILL PAINFUL...
LET'S GO.
I HAVE A DEBT TO REPAY, BOTH FOR SHIRA AND MYSELF.
I'M NOT COMING WITH YOU.
I'LL NEVER SEE MY BROTHER'S FACE AGAIN.
BUT ... SOME-DAY THIS WILL BE OVER, AND THEN ...
...SAME GOES FOR ME.

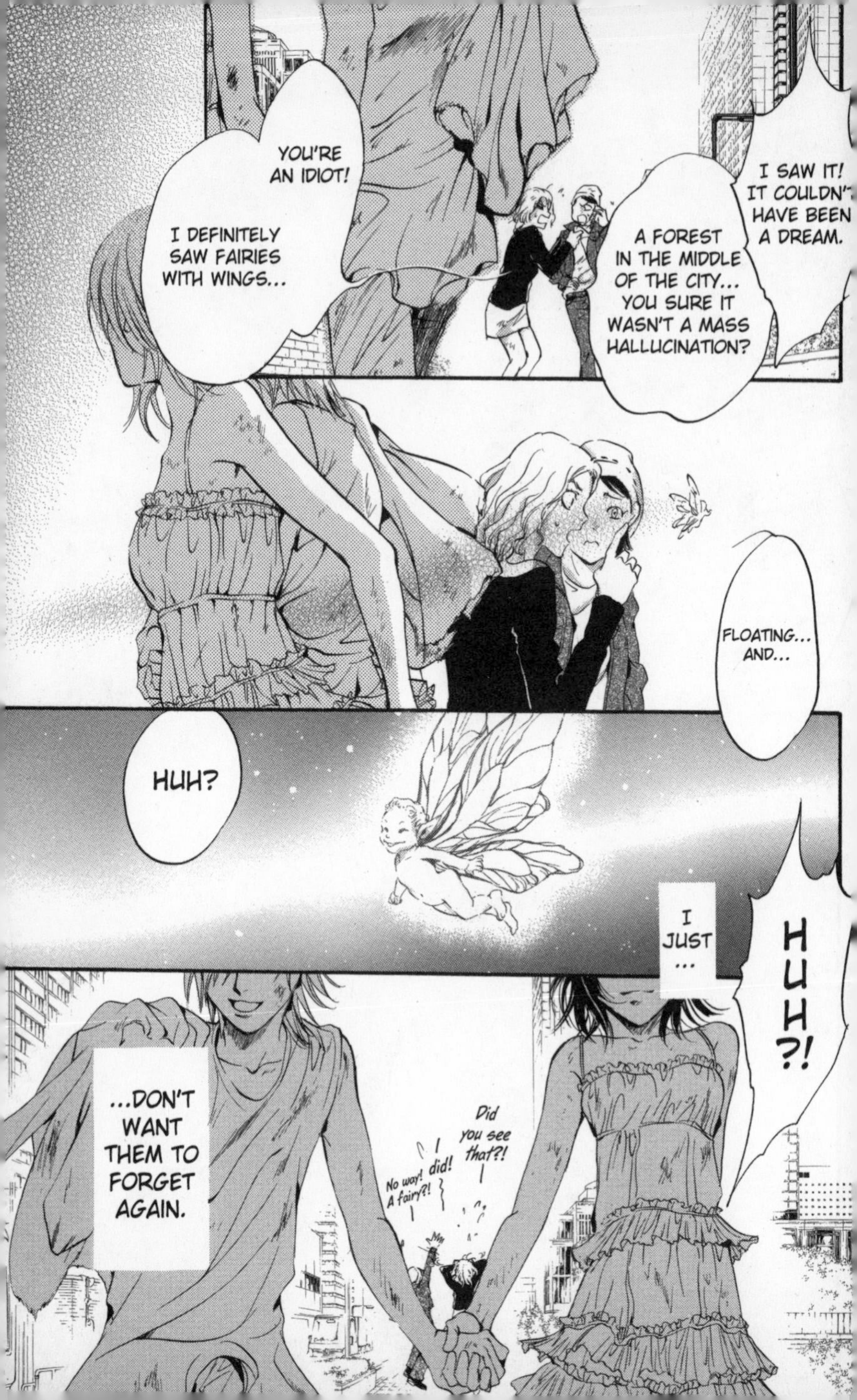
I SAW IT! IT COULDN'T HAVE BEEN A DREAM.
A FOREST IN THE MIDDLE OF THE CITY... YOU SURE IT WASN'T A MASS HALLUCINATION?
YOU'RE AN IDIOT!
I DEFINITELY SAW FAIRIES WITH WINGS...
FLOATING... AND...
HUH?
HUH?!
I JUST...
...DON'T WANT THEM TO FORGET AGAIN.
Did you see that?!
I did!
No way! A fairy?!

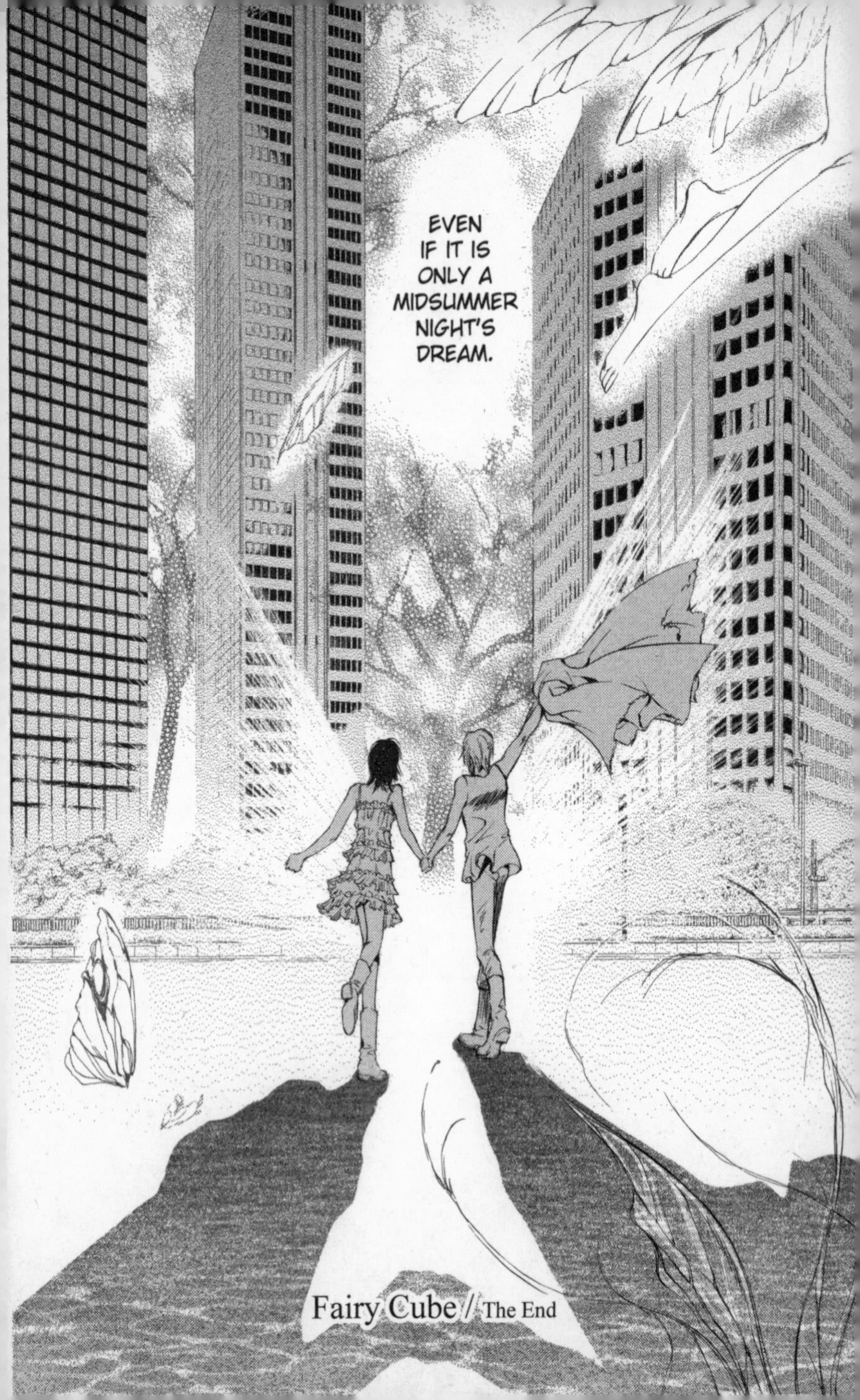
EVEN IF IT IS ONLY A MIDSUMMER NIGHT'S DREAM.
Fairy Cube // The End

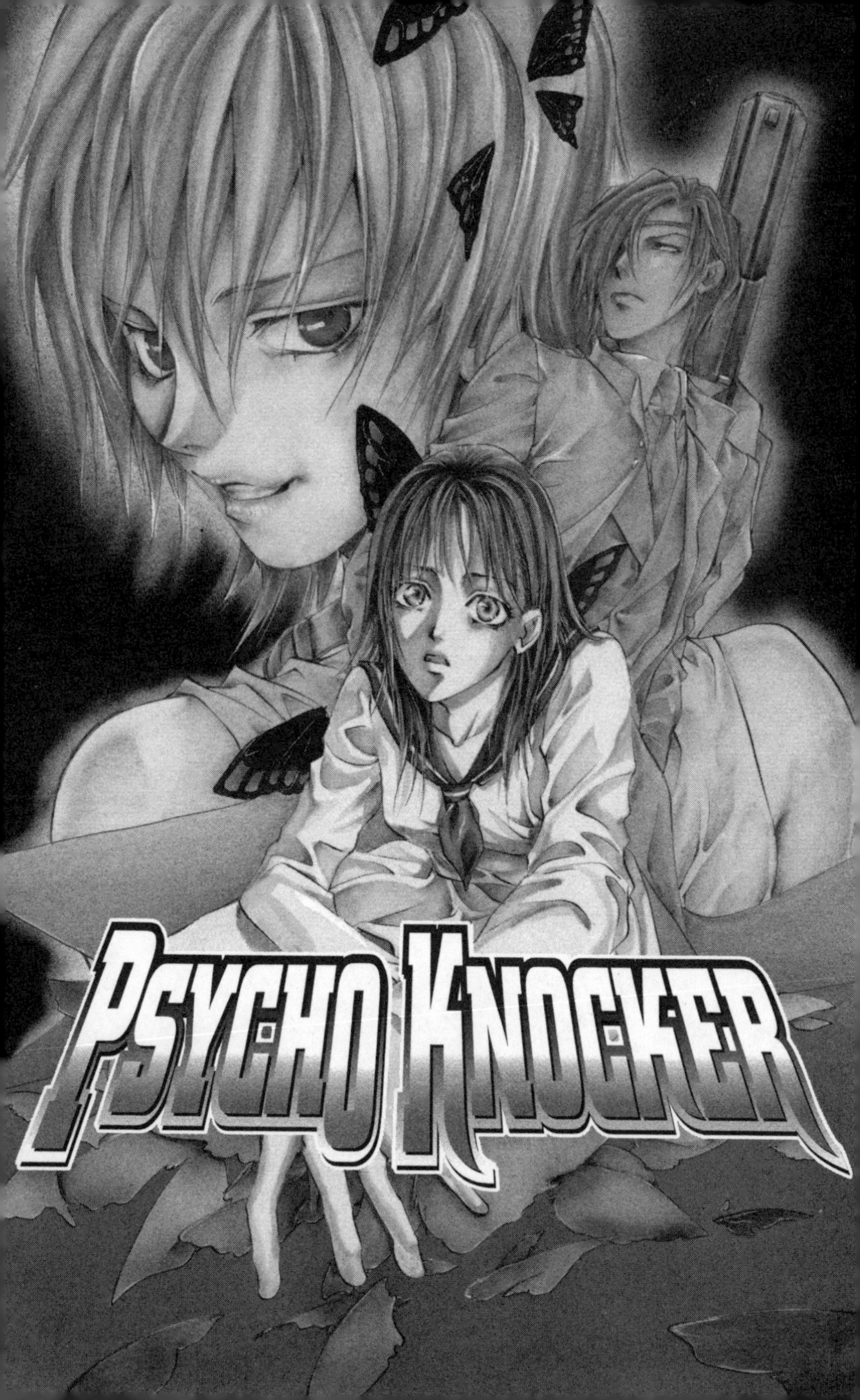
PSYCHO KNOCKER

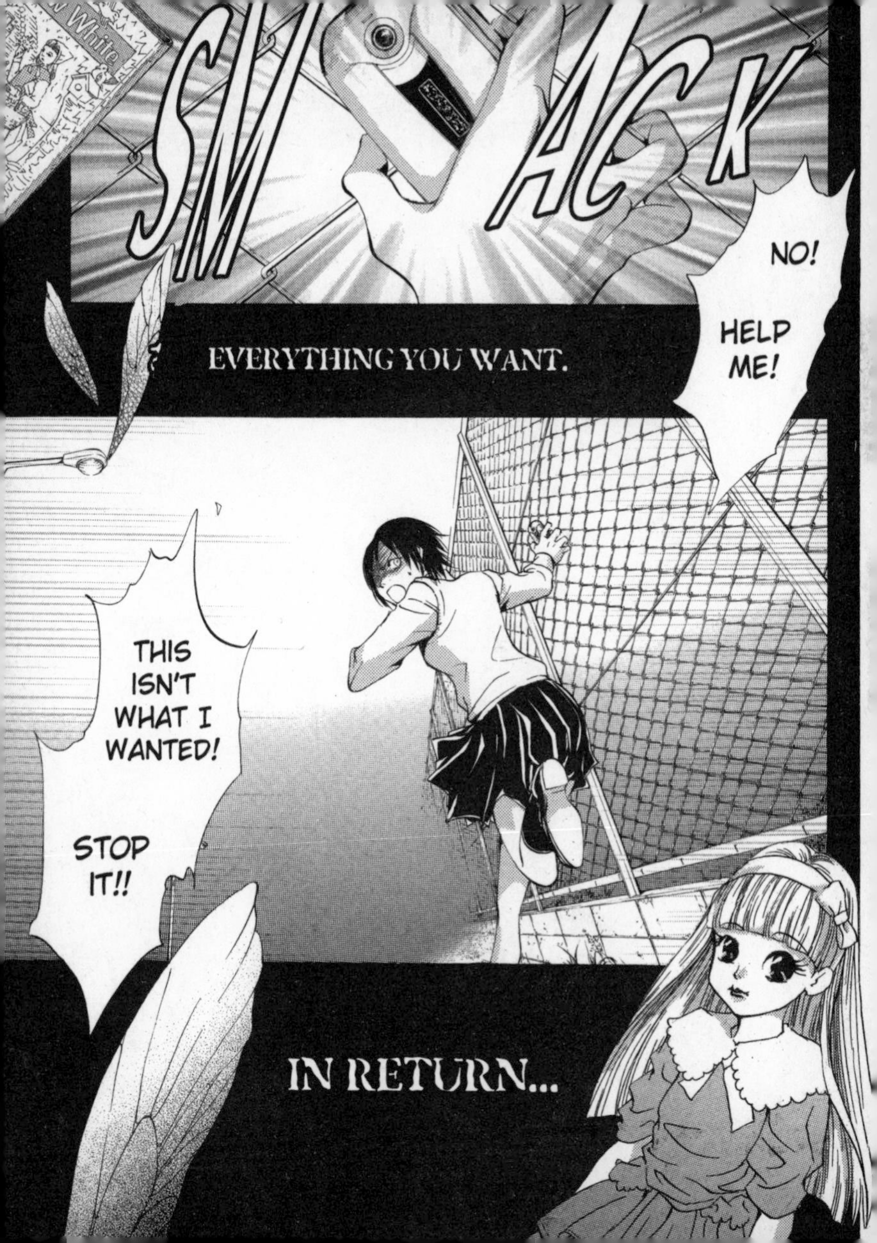
SMACK
NO!
HELP ME!
EVERYTHING YOU WANT.
THIS ISN'T WHAT I WANTED!
STOP IT!!
IN RETURN...

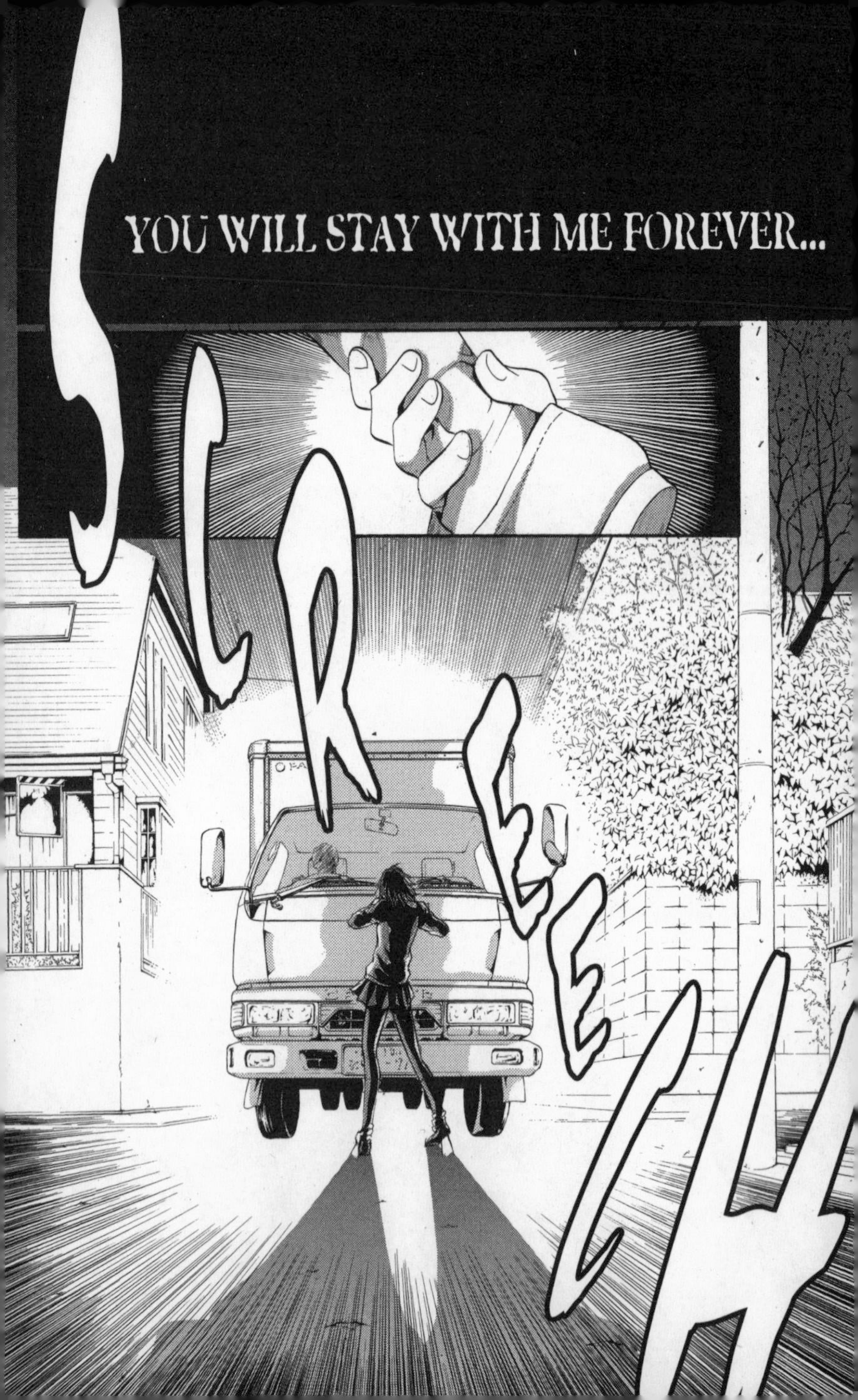
YOU WILL STAY WITH ME FOREVER...
SCREEECH

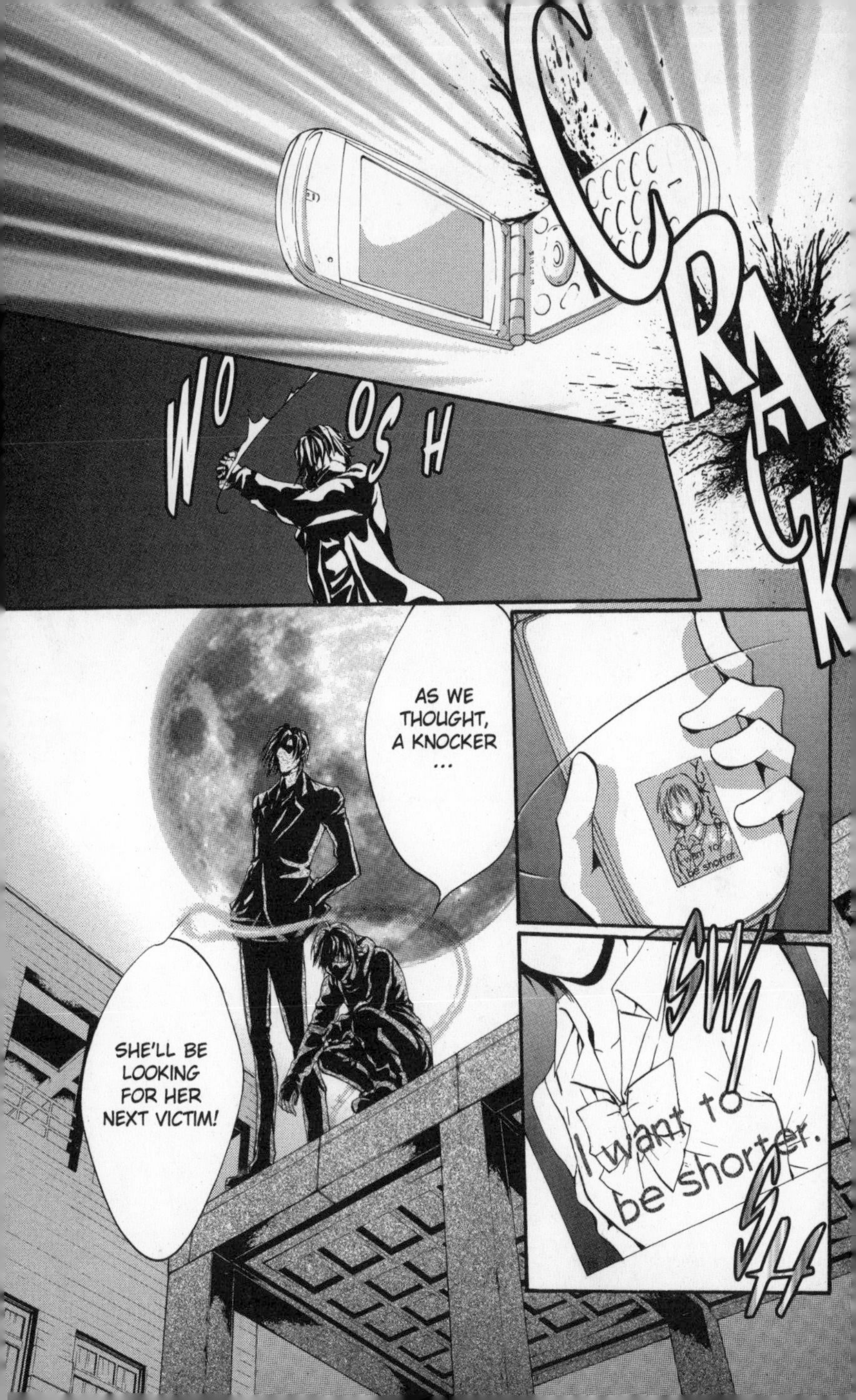
CRACK
WOOSH
YUKI
I want to be shorter.
SWISH
I want to be shorter.
AS WE THOUGHT, A KNOCKER ...
SHE'LL BE LOOKING FOR HER NEXT VICTIM!

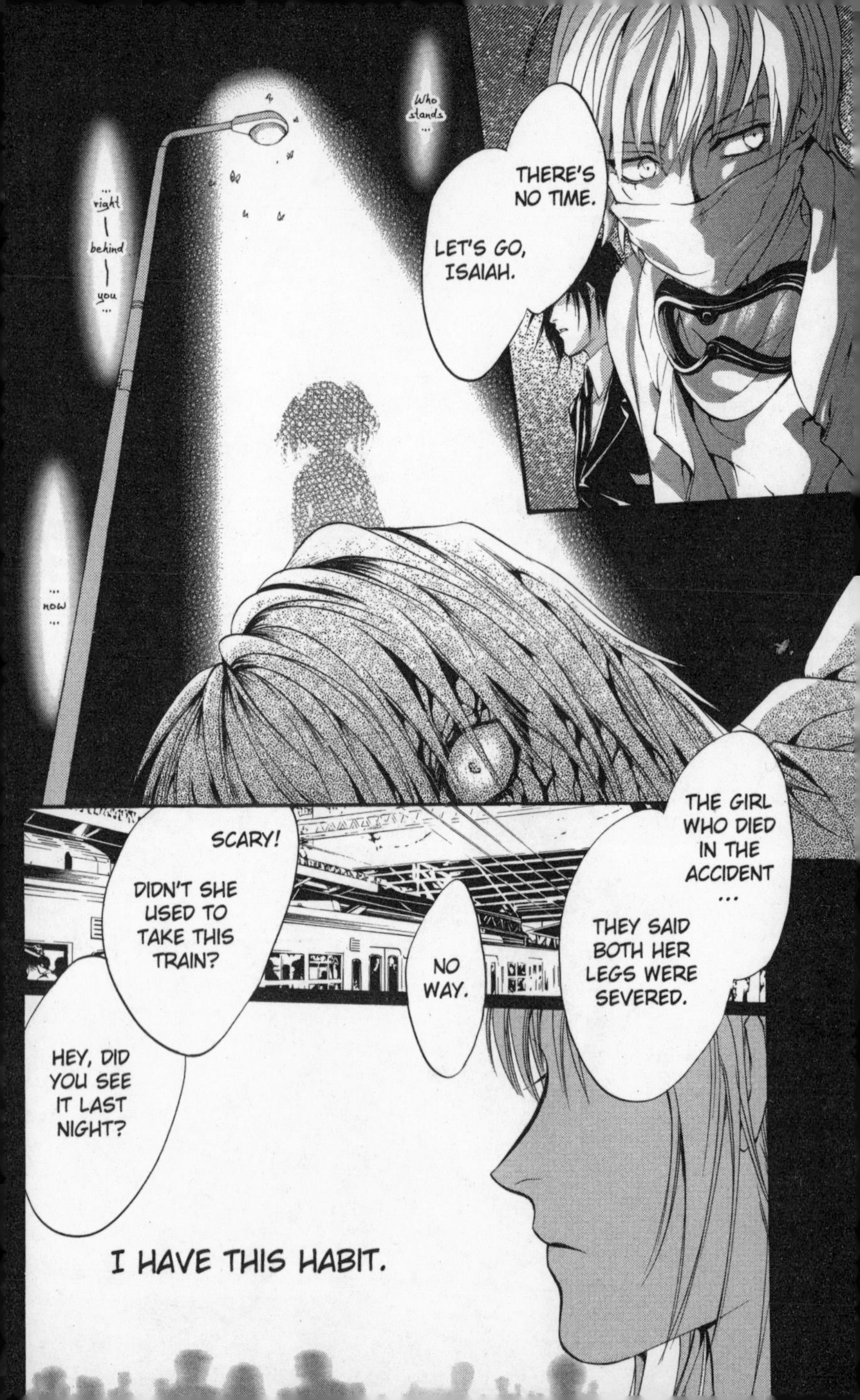
THERE'S NO TIME.
LET'S GO, ISAIAH.
Who stands ...
... right — behind — you ...
... now ...
THE GIRL WHO DIED IN THE ACCIDENT ...
THEY SAID BOTH HER LEGS WERE SEVERED.
NO WAY.
SCARY!
DIDN'T SHE USED TO TAKE THIS TRAIN?
HEY, DID YOU SEE IT LAST NIGHT?
I HAVE THIS HABIT.

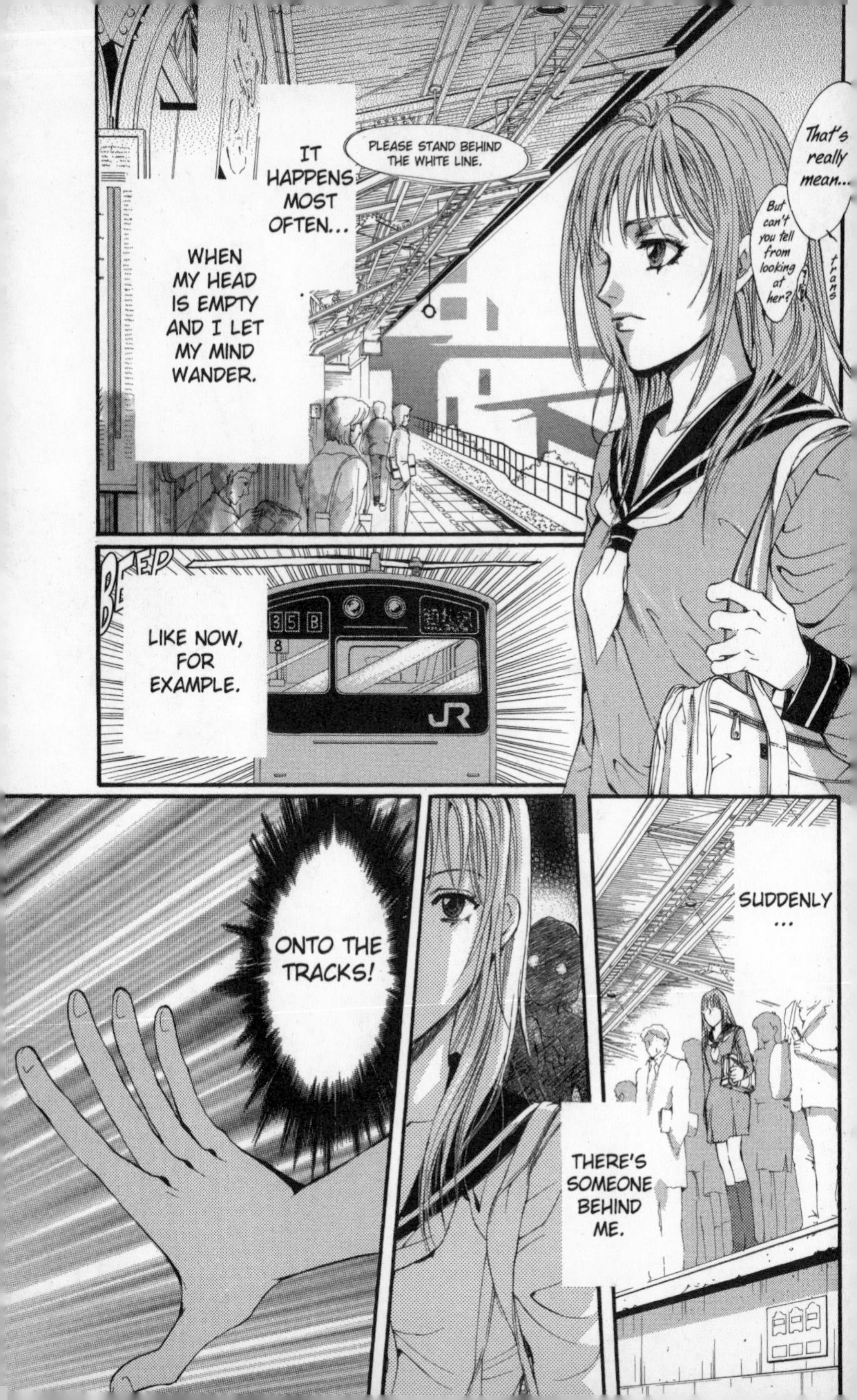

That's really mean...
But can't you tell from looking at her?
trans
PLEASE STAND BEHIND THE WHITE LINE.
IT HAPPENS MOST OFTEN...
WHEN MY HEAD IS EMPTY AND I LET MY MIND WANDER.
LIKE NOW, FOR EXAMPLE.
SUDDENLY...
THERE'S SOMEONE BEHIND ME.
ONTO THE TRACKS!

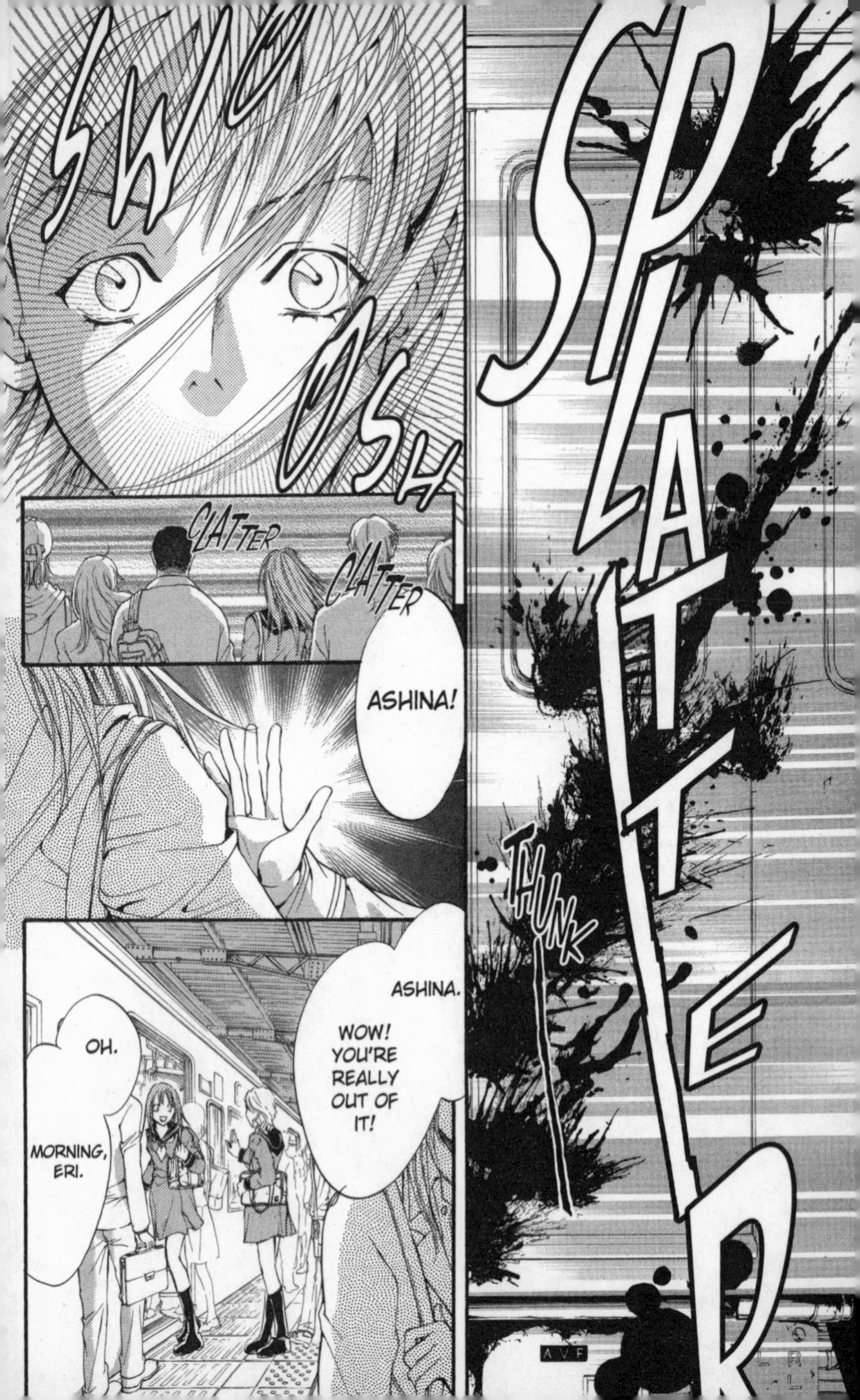
SPLATTER
THUNK
SWOOSH
CLATTER
CLATTER
ASHINA!
ASHINA.
WOW! YOU'RE REALLY OUT OF IT!
OH.
MORNING, ERI.

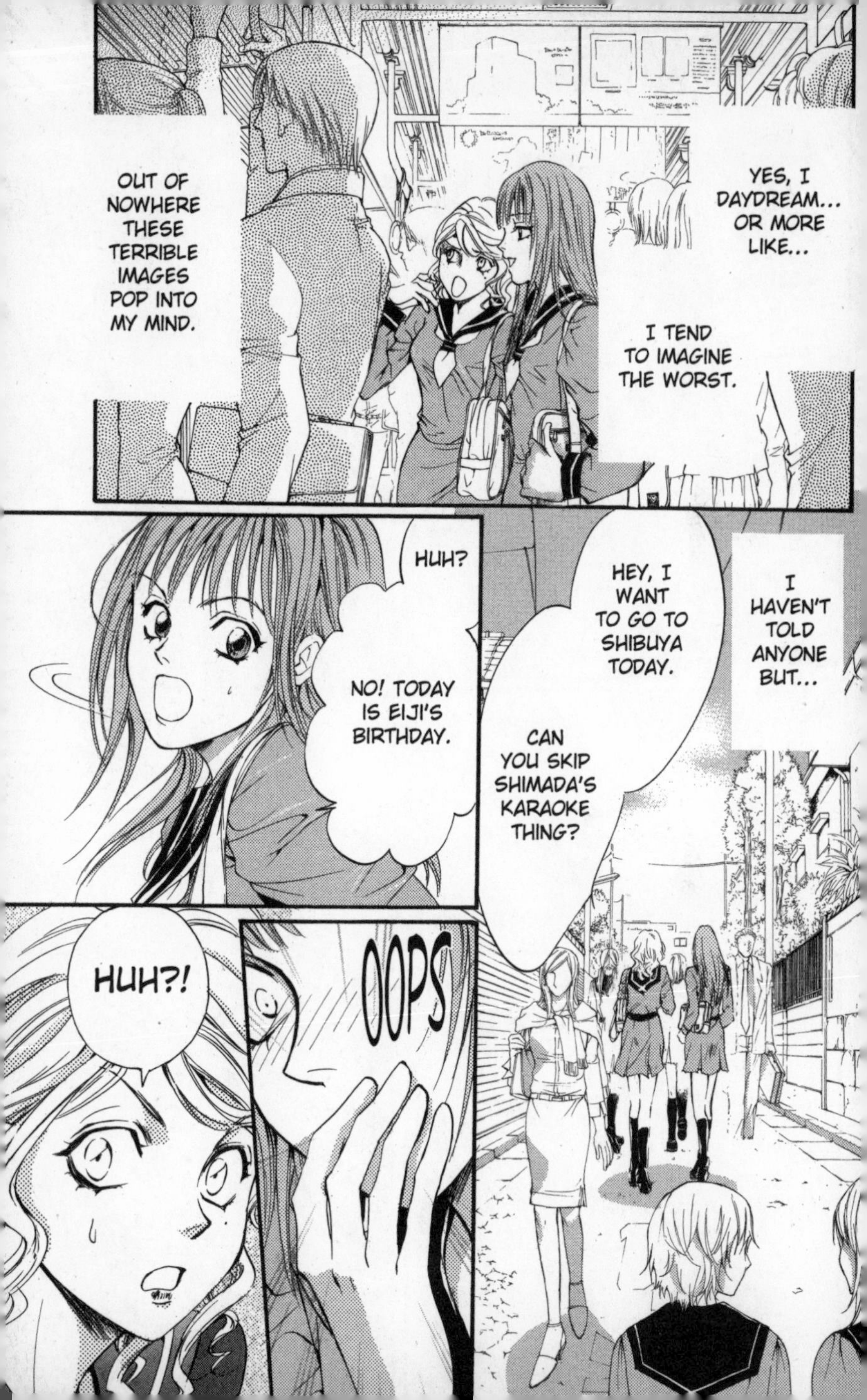
YES, I DAYDREAM... OR MORE LIKE...
I TEND TO IMAGINE THE WORST.
OUT OF NOWHERE THESE TERRIBLE IMAGES POP INTO MY MIND.
I HAVEN'T TOLD ANYONE BUT...
HEY, I WANT TO GO TO SHIBUYA TODAY.
CAN YOU SKIP SHIMADA'S KARAOKE THING?
HUH?
NO! TODAY IS EIJI'S BIRTHDAY.
OOPS
HUH?!

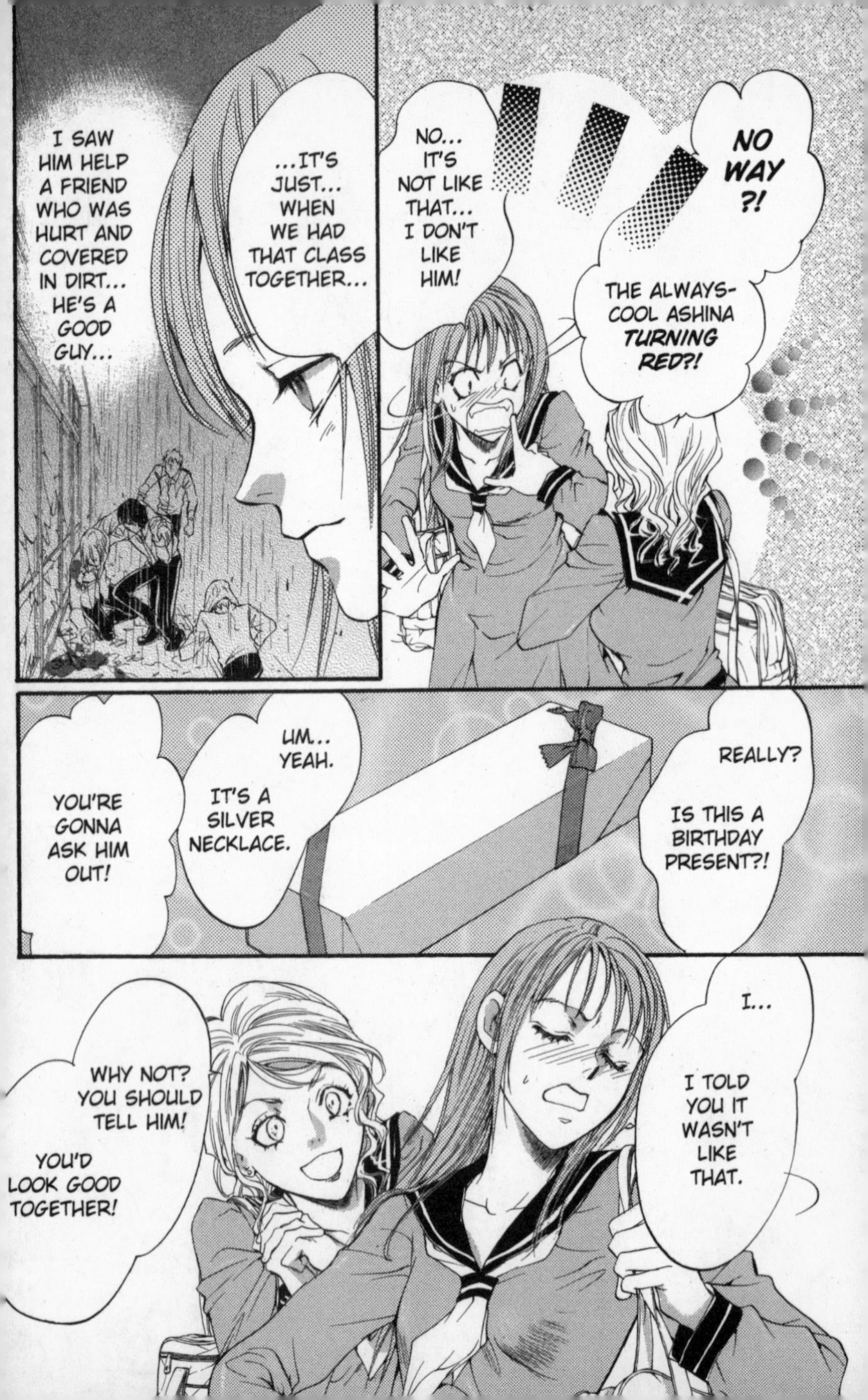

NO WAY?!
THE ALWAYS-COOL ASHINA TURNING RED?!
NO... IT'S NOT LIKE THAT... I DON'T LIKE HIM!
...IT'S JUST... WHEN WE HAD THAT CLASS TOGETHER...
I SAW HIM HELP A FRIEND WHO WAS HURT AND COVERED IN DIRT... HE'S A GOOD GUY...
REALLY?
IS THIS A BIRTHDAY PRESENT?!
UM... YEAH.
IT'S A SILVER NECKLACE.
YOU'RE GONNA ASK HIM OUT!
I...
I TOLD YOU IT WASN'T LIKE THAT.
WHY NOT? YOU SHOULD TELL HIM!
YOU'D LOOK GOOD TOGETHER!

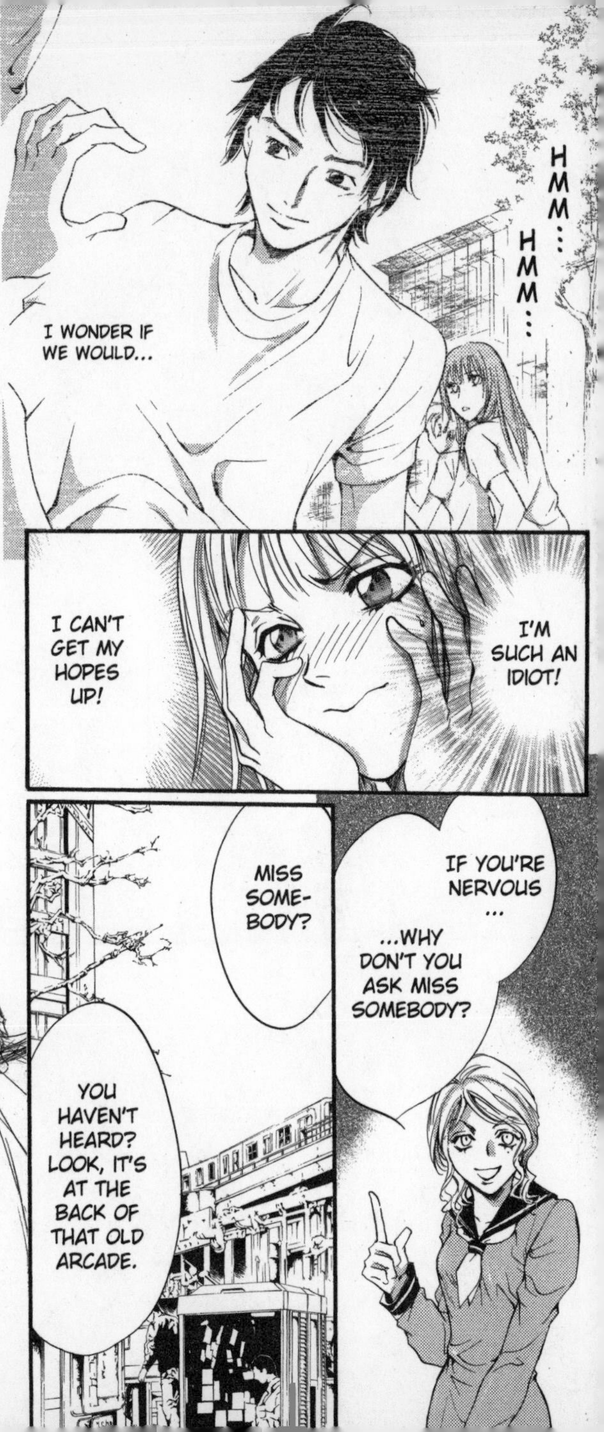
HMM... HMM...
I WONDER IF WE WOULD...
I'M SUCH AN IDIOT!
I CAN'T GET MY HOPES UP!
IF YOU'RE NERVOUS...
...WHY DON'T YOU ASK MISS SOMEBODY?
MISS SOMEBODY?
YOU HAVEN'T HEARD? LOOK, IT'S AT THE BACK OF THAT OLD ARCADE.

I'm usually not a big fan of spin-offs, but I made one!'

Isaiah and Raven are now chasing down the evil spirits that escaped from the door and sending them back where they came from. If Isaiah succeeds, he may get to see Ian again...

Isaiah's appearance has blended with Eriya's— his hair has turned blonde and his moles have disappeared. Normally his eyes are blue but sometimes they glow red.

Raven's hair has changed a little...

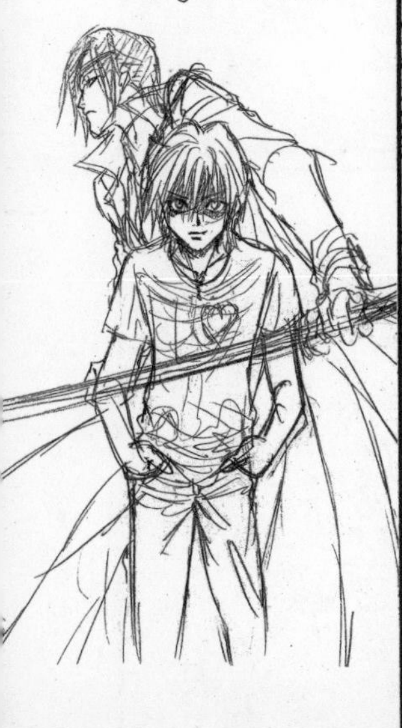

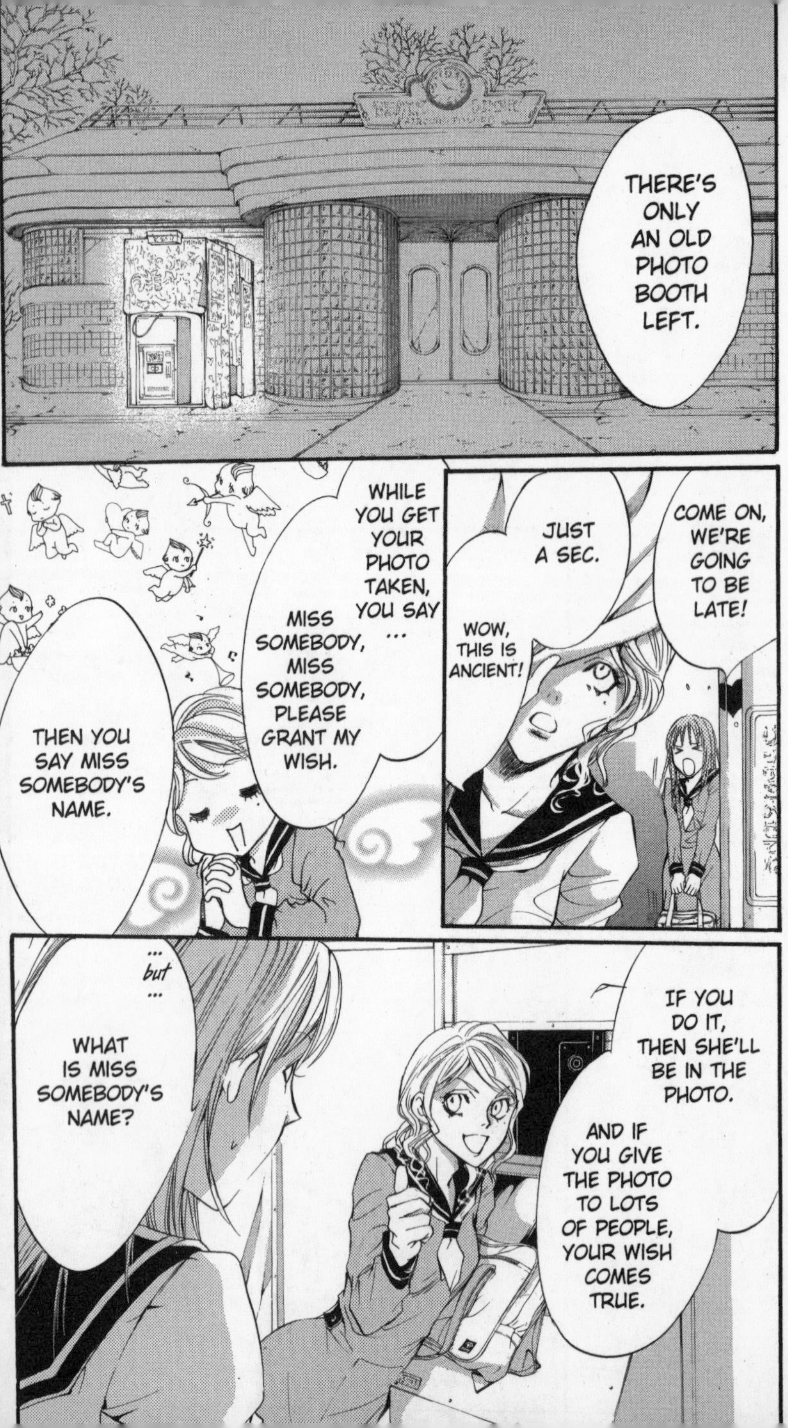

THERE'S ONLY AN OLD PHOTO BOOTH LEFT.
COME ON, WE'RE GOING TO BE LATE!
JUST A SEC.
WOW, THIS IS ANCIENT!
WHILE YOU GET YOUR PHOTO TAKEN, YOU SAY ...
MISS SOMEBODY, MISS SOMEBODY, PLEASE GRANT MY WISH.
THEN YOU SAY MISS SOMEBODY'S NAME.
IF YOU DO IT, THEN SHE'LL BE IN THE PHOTO.
AND IF YOU GIVE THE PHOTO TO LOTS OF PEOPLE, YOUR WISH COMES TRUE.
... but ...
WHAT IS MISS SOMEBODY'S NAME?

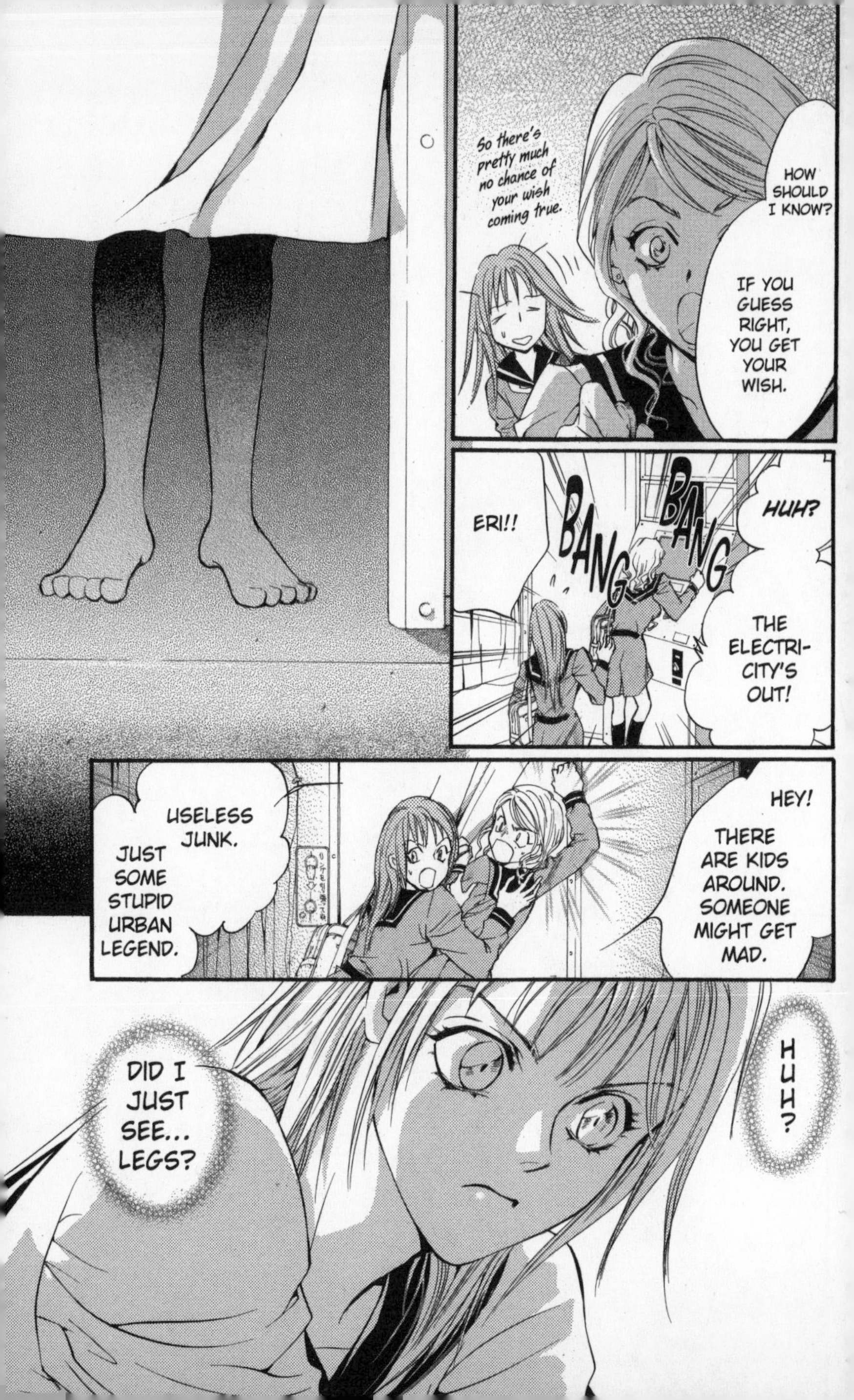

HOW SHOULD I KNOW?
IF YOU GUESS RIGHT, YOU GET YOUR WISH.
So there's pretty much no chance of your wish coming true.
HUH?
BANG BANG
BANG BANG
ERI!!
THE ELECTRI-CITY'S OUT!
HEY!
THERE ARE KIDS AROUND. SOMEONE MIGHT GET MAD.
USELESS JUNK.
JUST SOME STUPID URBAN LEGEND.
HUH?
DID I JUST SEE... LEGS?

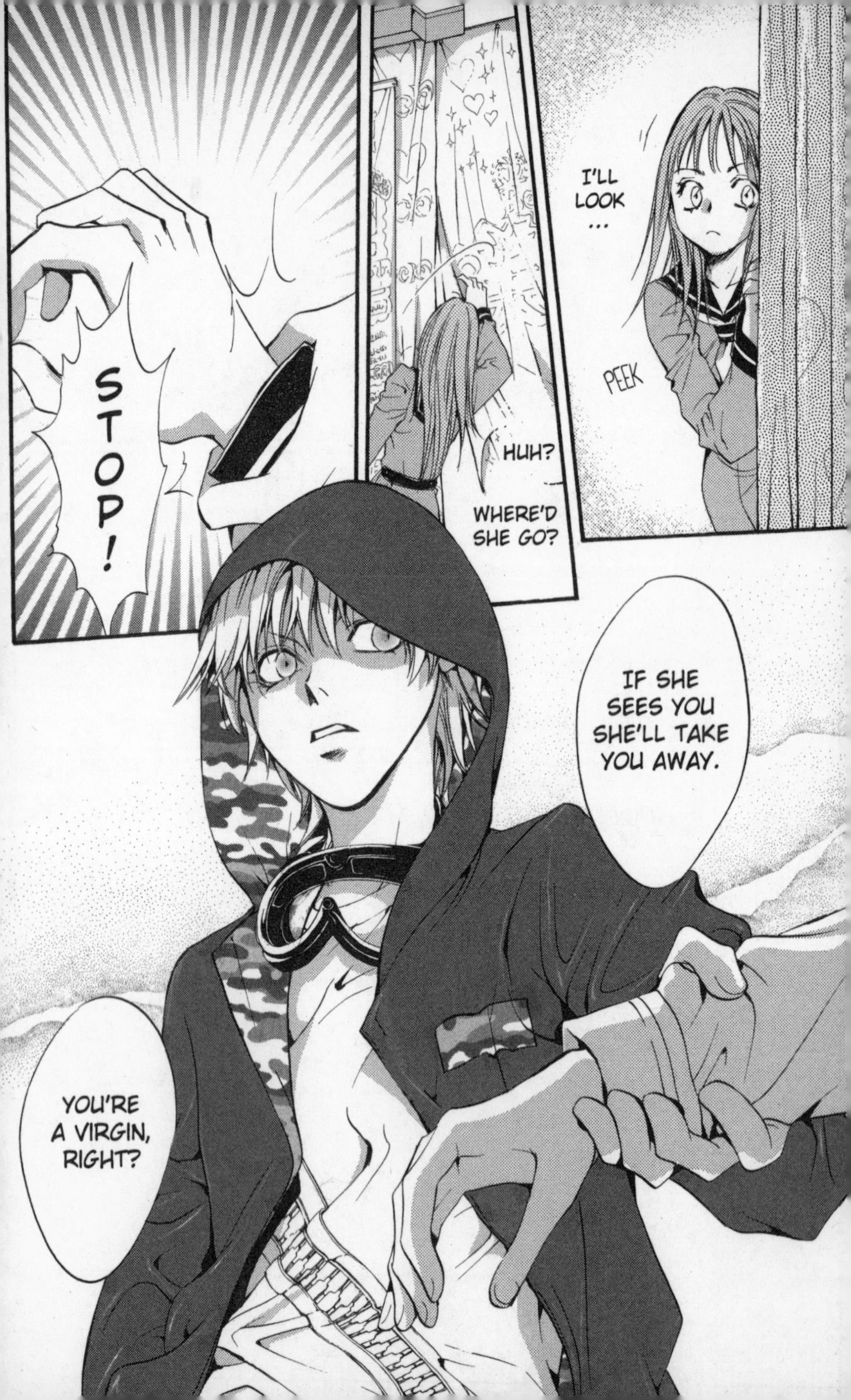
I'LL LOOK ...
PEEK
HUH?
WHERE'D SHE GO?
STOP!
IF SHE SEES YOU SHE'LL TAKE YOU AWAY.
YOU'RE A VIRGIN, RIGHT?

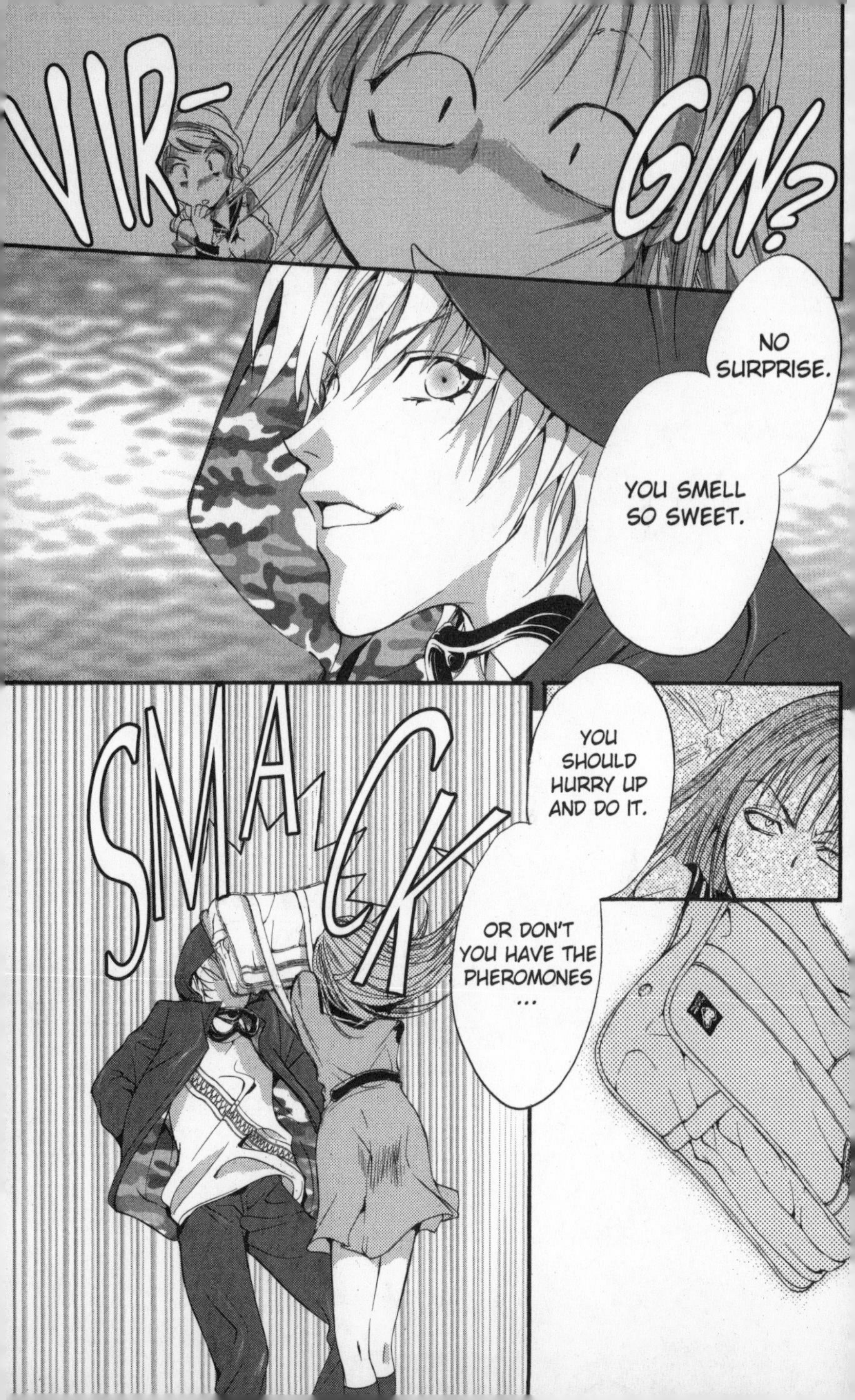
VIR-
GIN!?
NO SURPRISE.
YOU SMELL SO SWEET.
YOU SHOULD HURRY UP AND DO IT.
OR DON'T YOU HAVE THE PHEROMONES ...
SMACK

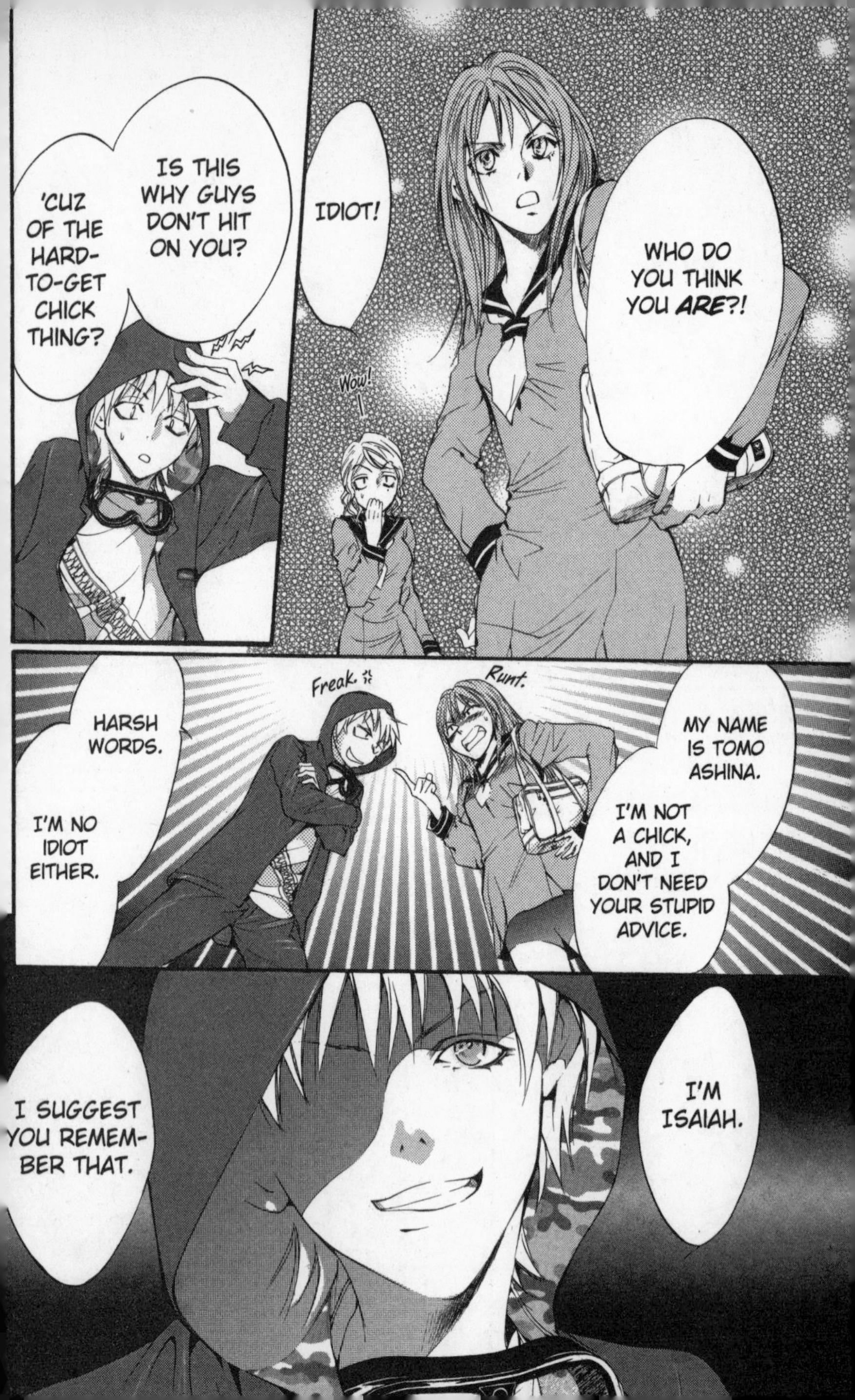
WHO DO YOU THINK YOU ARE?!
IDIOT!
Wow!
IS THIS WHY GUYS DON'T HIT ON YOU?
'CUZ OF THE HARD-TO-GET CHICK THING?
MY NAME IS TOMO ASHINA.
I'M NOT A CHICK, AND I DON'T NEED YOUR STUPID ADVICE.
Runt.
Freak.
HARSH WORDS.
I'M NO IDIOT EITHER.
I'M ISAIAH.
I SUGGEST YOU REMEMBER THAT.

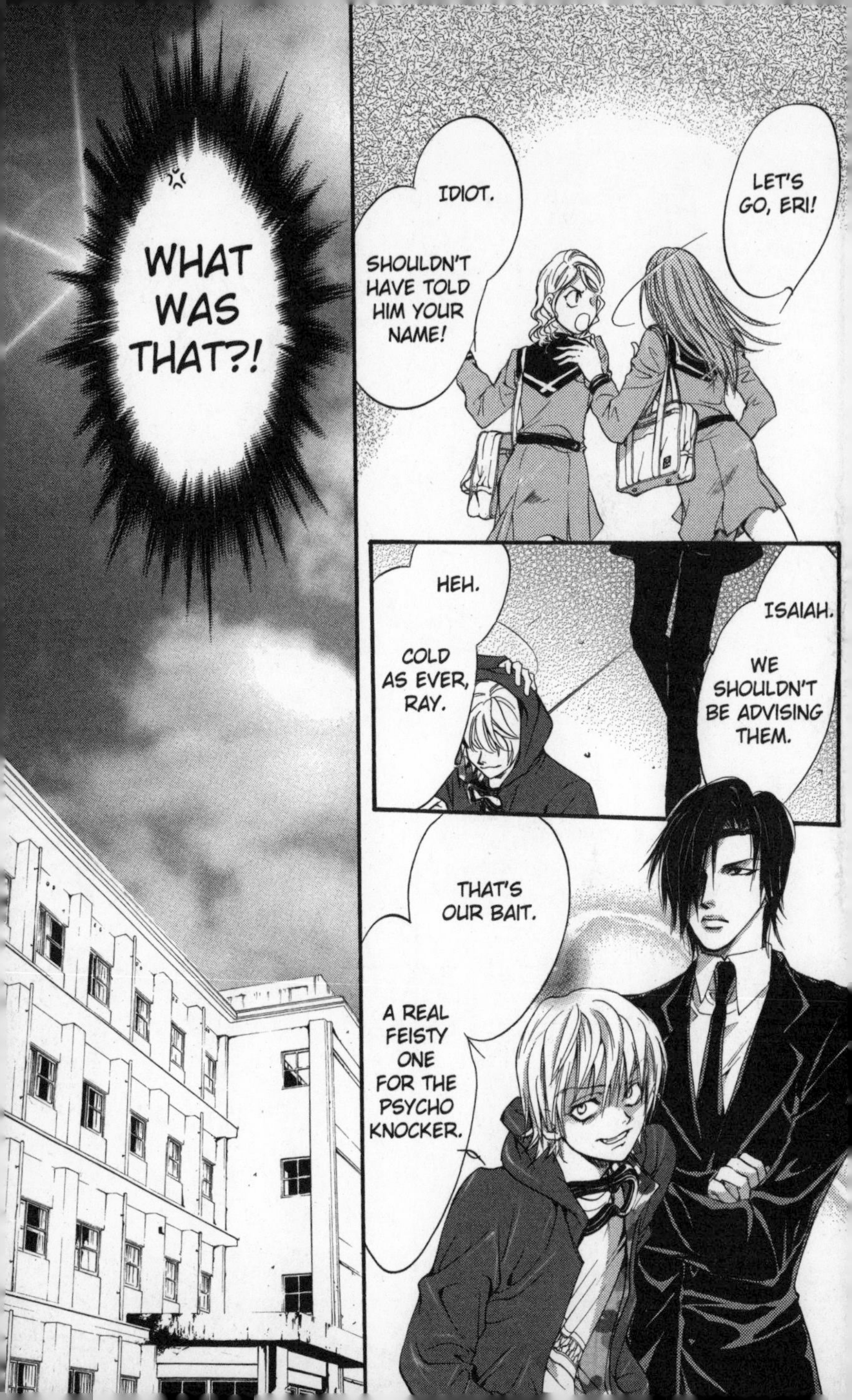
LET'S GO, ERI!
IDIOT.
SHOULDN'T HAVE TOLD HIM YOUR NAME!
ISAIAH.
WE SHOULDN'T BE ADVISING THEM.
HEH.
COLD AS EVER, RAY.
THAT'S OUR BAIT.
A REAL FEISTY ONE FOR THE PSYCHO KNOCKER.
WHAT WAS THAT?!

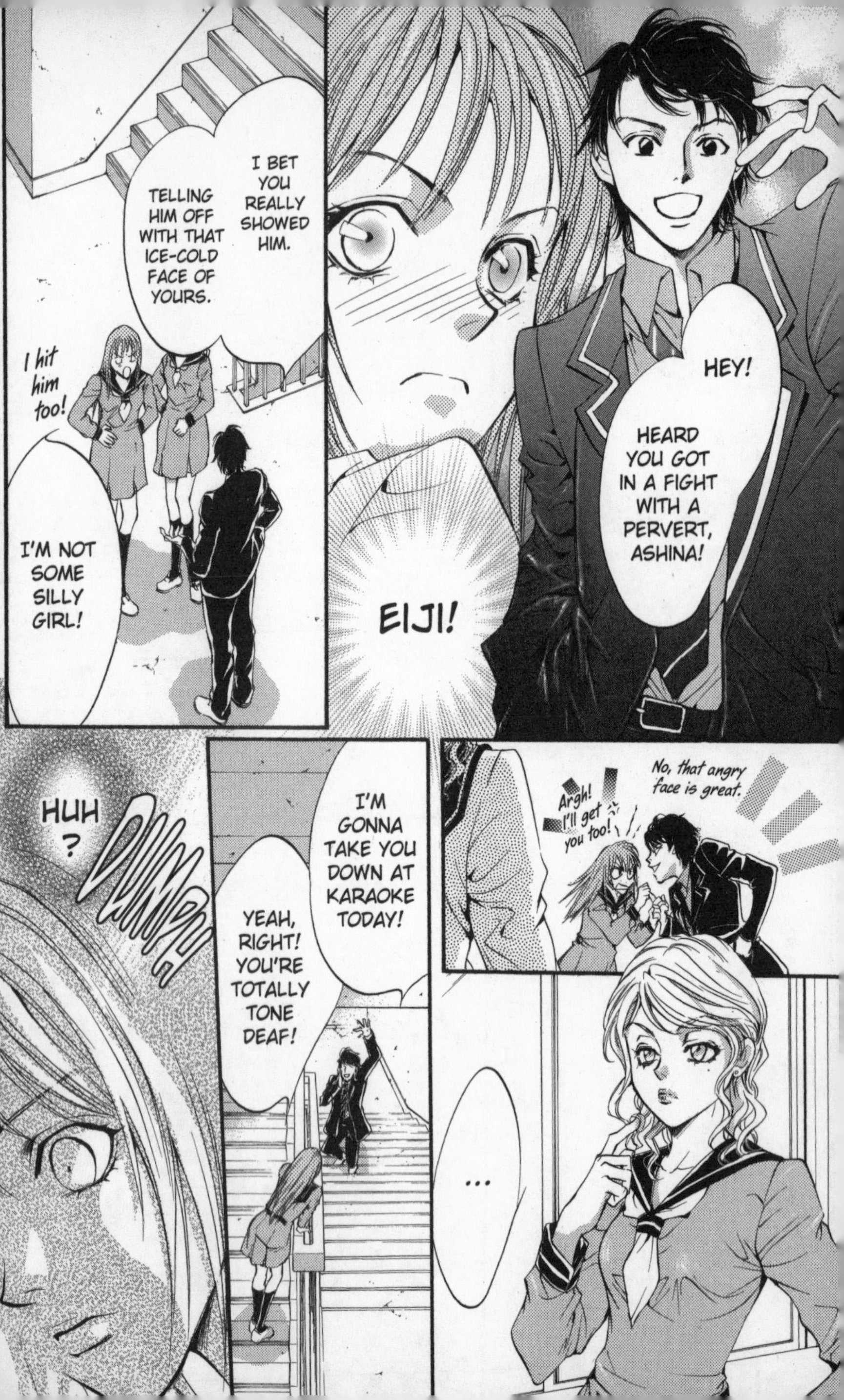
HEY!
HEARD YOU GOT IN A FIGHT WITH A PERVERT, ASHINA!
EIJI!
I BET YOU REALLY SHOWED HIM.
TELLING HIM OFF WITH THAT ICE-COLD FACE OF YOURS.
I hit him too!
I'M NOT SOME SILLY GIRL!
No, that angry face is great.
Argh! I'll get you too!
...
I'M GONNA TAKE YOU DOWN AT KARAOKE TODAY!
YEAH, RIGHT! YOU'RE TOTALLY TONE DEAF!
HUH?

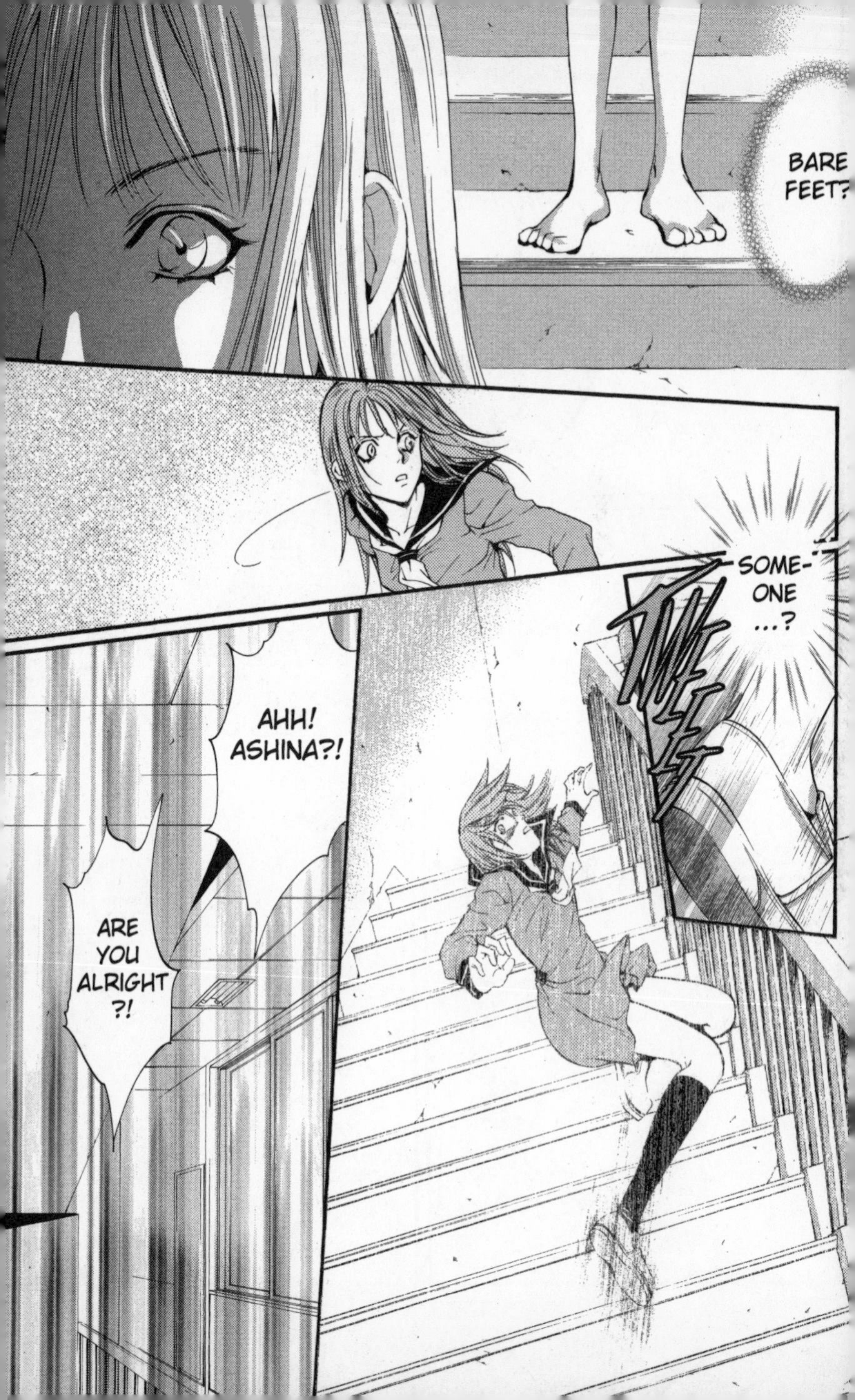
BARE FEET?
SOME-ONE ...?
AHH! ASHINA?!
ARE YOU ALRIGHT ?!

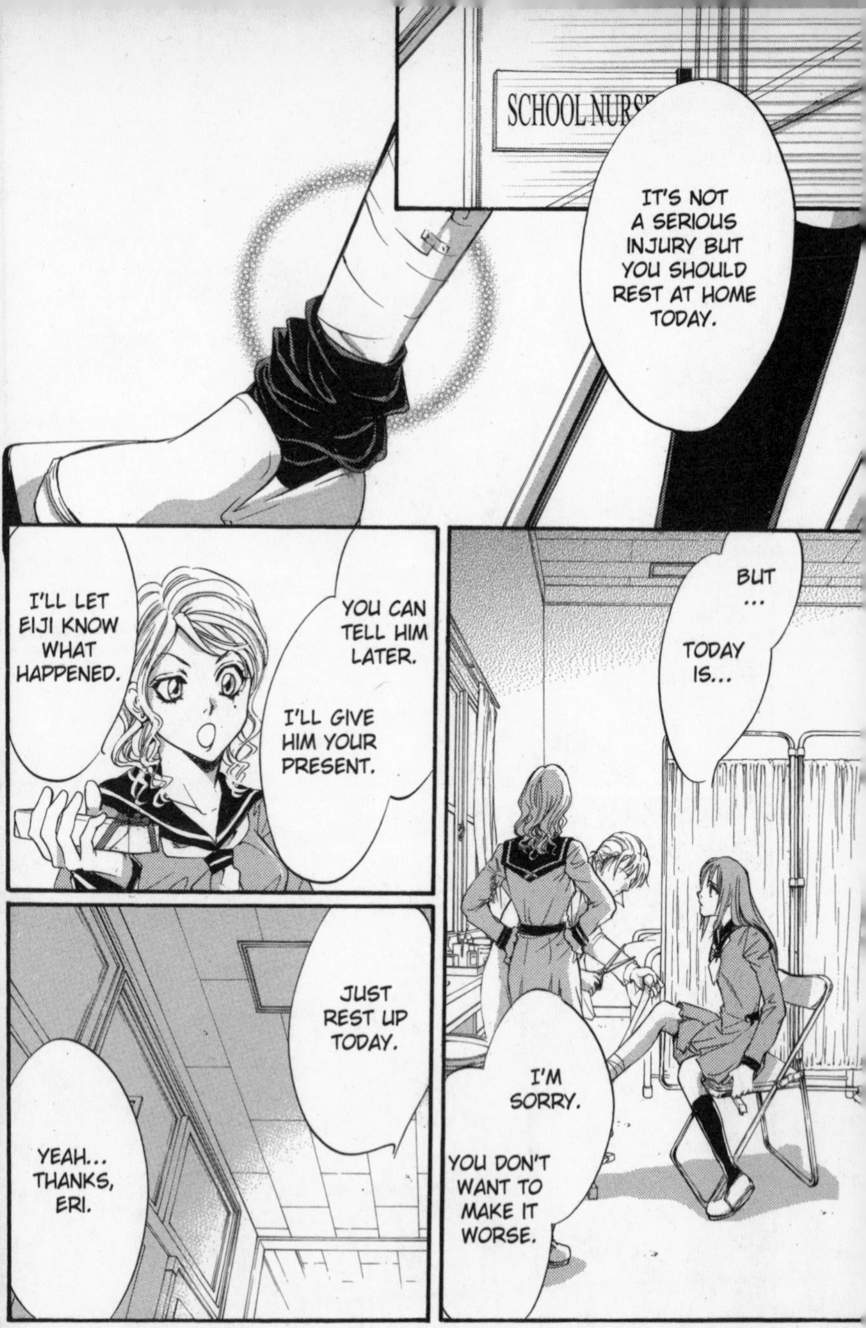
SCHOOL NURS
IT'S NOT A SERIOUS INJURY BUT YOU SHOULD REST AT HOME TODAY.
BUT ... TODAY IS...
I'M SORRY.
YOU DON'T WANT TO MAKE IT WORSE.
YOU CAN TELL HIM LATER.
I'LL GIVE HIM YOUR PRESENT.
I'LL LET EIJI KNOW WHAT HAPPENED.
JUST REST UP TODAY.
YEAH... THANKS, ERI.

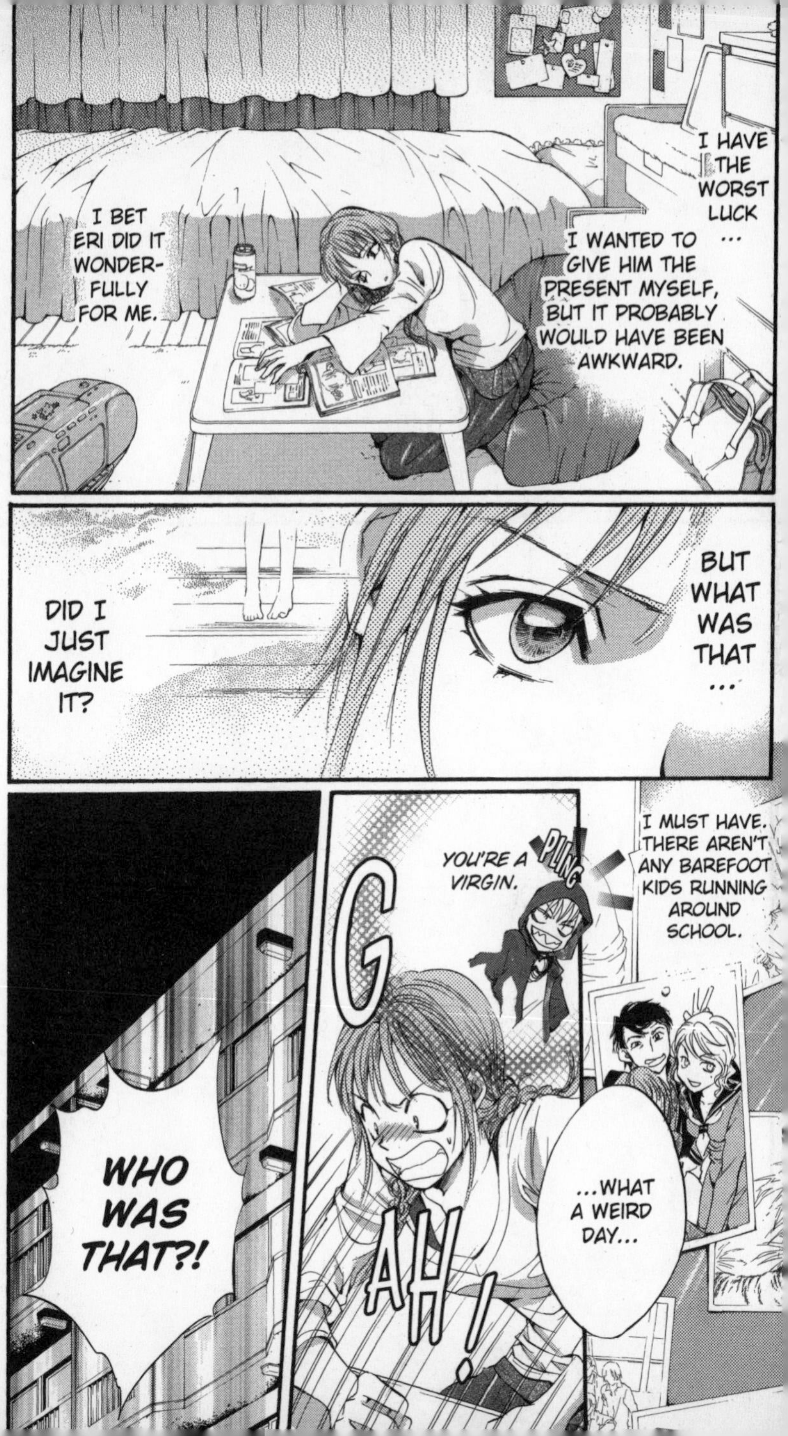
I HAVE THE WORST LUCK...
I WANTED TO GIVE HIM THE PRESENT MYSELF, BUT IT PROBABLY WOULD HAVE BEEN AWKWARD.
I BET ERI DID IT WONDERFULLY FOR ME.
BUT WHAT WAS THAT...
DID I JUST IMAGINE IT?
I MUST HAVE. THERE AREN'T ANY BAREFOOT KIDS RUNNING AROUND SCHOOL.
...WHAT A WEIRD DAY...
PLING
YOU'RE A VIRGIN.
GAH!
WHO WAS THAT?!

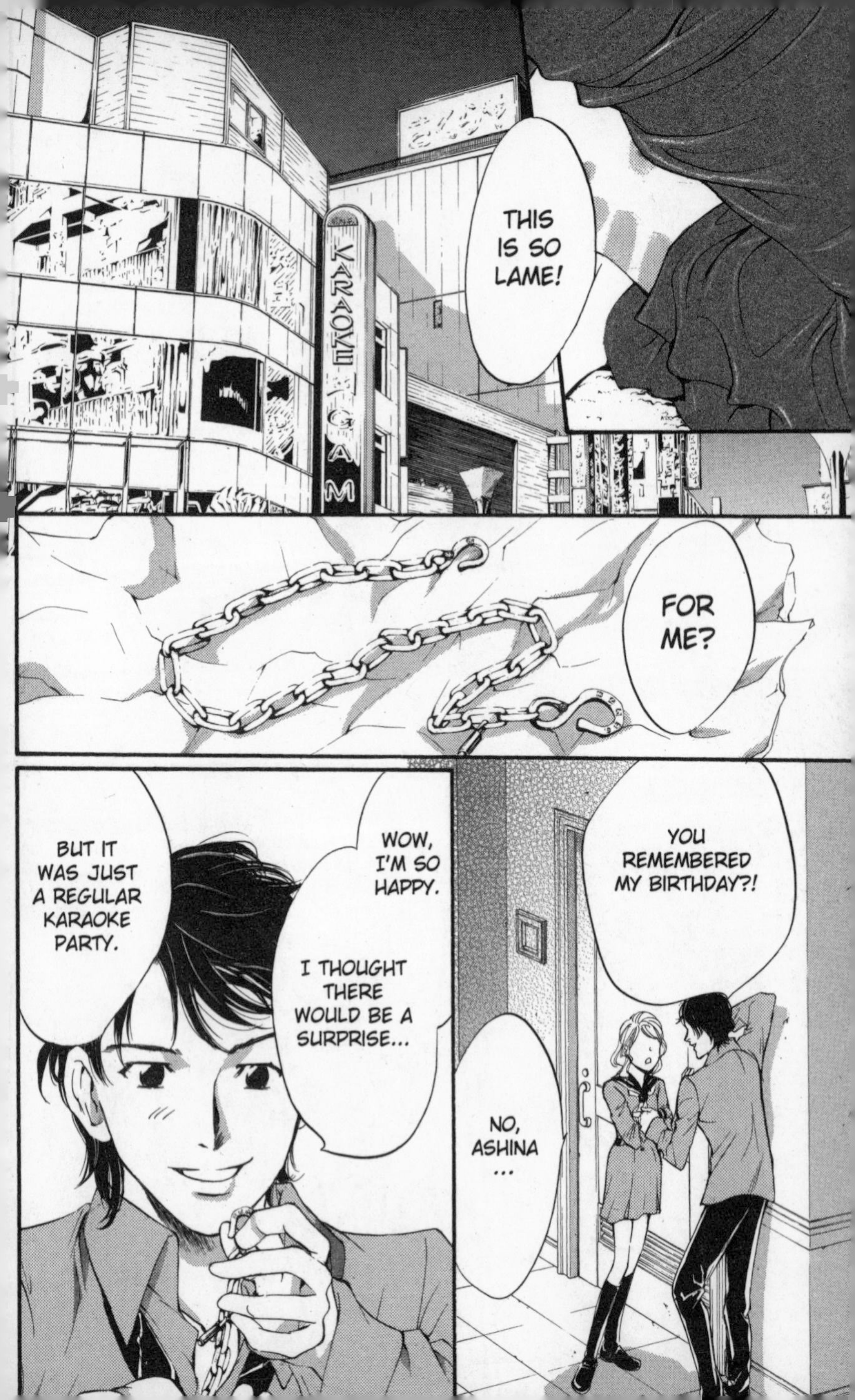
THIS IS SO LAME!
KARAOKE
GAM
FOR ME?
YOU REMEMBERED MY BIRTHDAY?!
NO, ASHINA ...
WOW, I'M SO HAPPY.
I THOUGHT THERE WOULD BE A SURPRISE...
BUT IT WAS JUST A REGULAR KARAOKE PARTY.

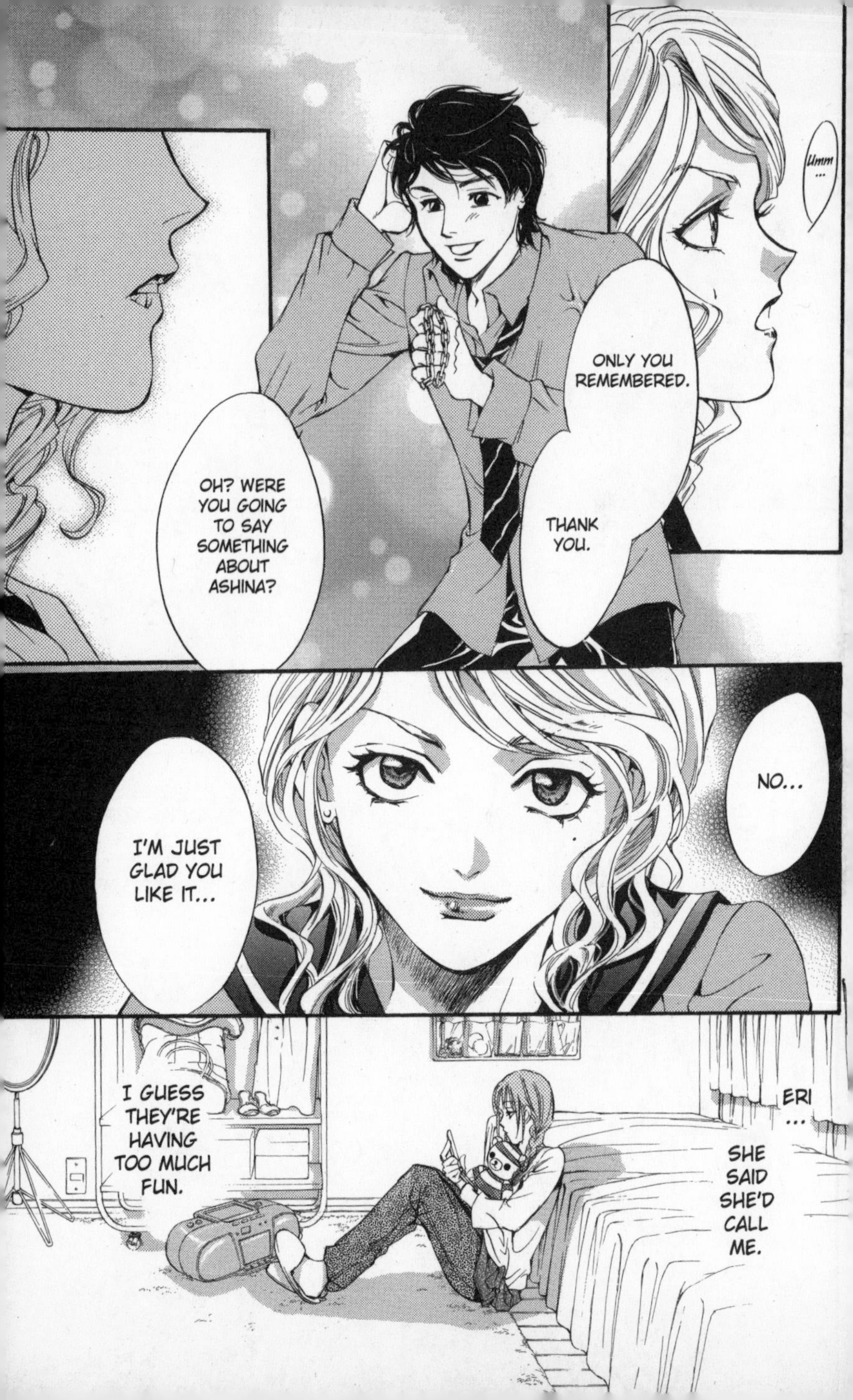
Umm...
ONLY YOU REMEMBERED.
THANK YOU.
OH? WERE YOU GOING TO SAY SOMETHING ABOUT ASHINA?
NO...
I'M JUST GLAD YOU LIKE IT...
ERI...
SHE SAID SHE'D CALL ME.
I GUESS THEY'RE HAVING TOO MUCH FUN.

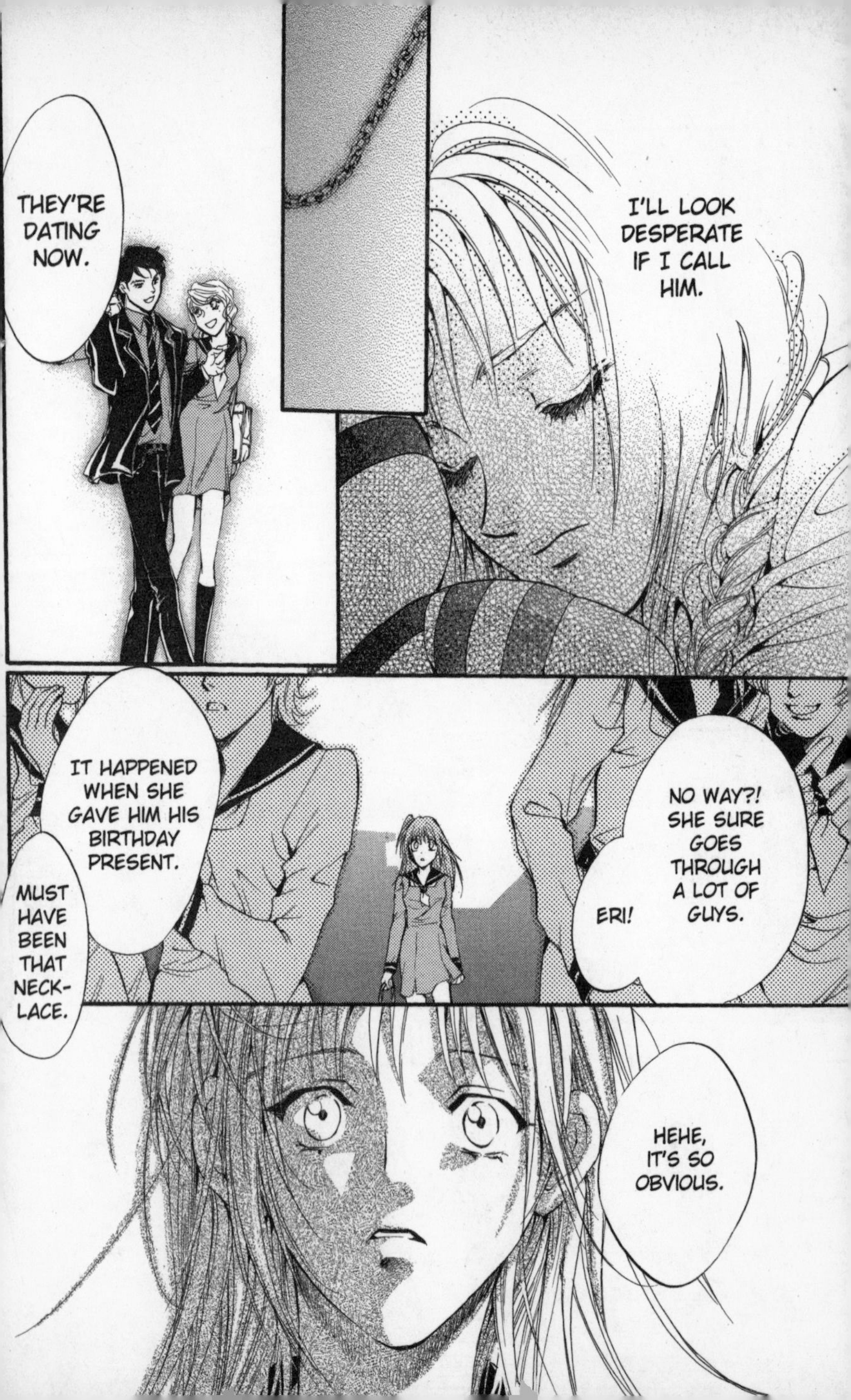
I'LL LOOK DESPERATE IF I CALL HIM.
THEY'RE DATING NOW.
NO WAY?! SHE SURE GOES THROUGH A LOT OF GUYS.
ERI!
IT HAPPENED WHEN SHE GAVE HIM HIS BIRTHDAY PRESENT.
MUST HAVE BEEN THAT NECK-LACE.
HEHE, IT'S SO OBVIOUS.

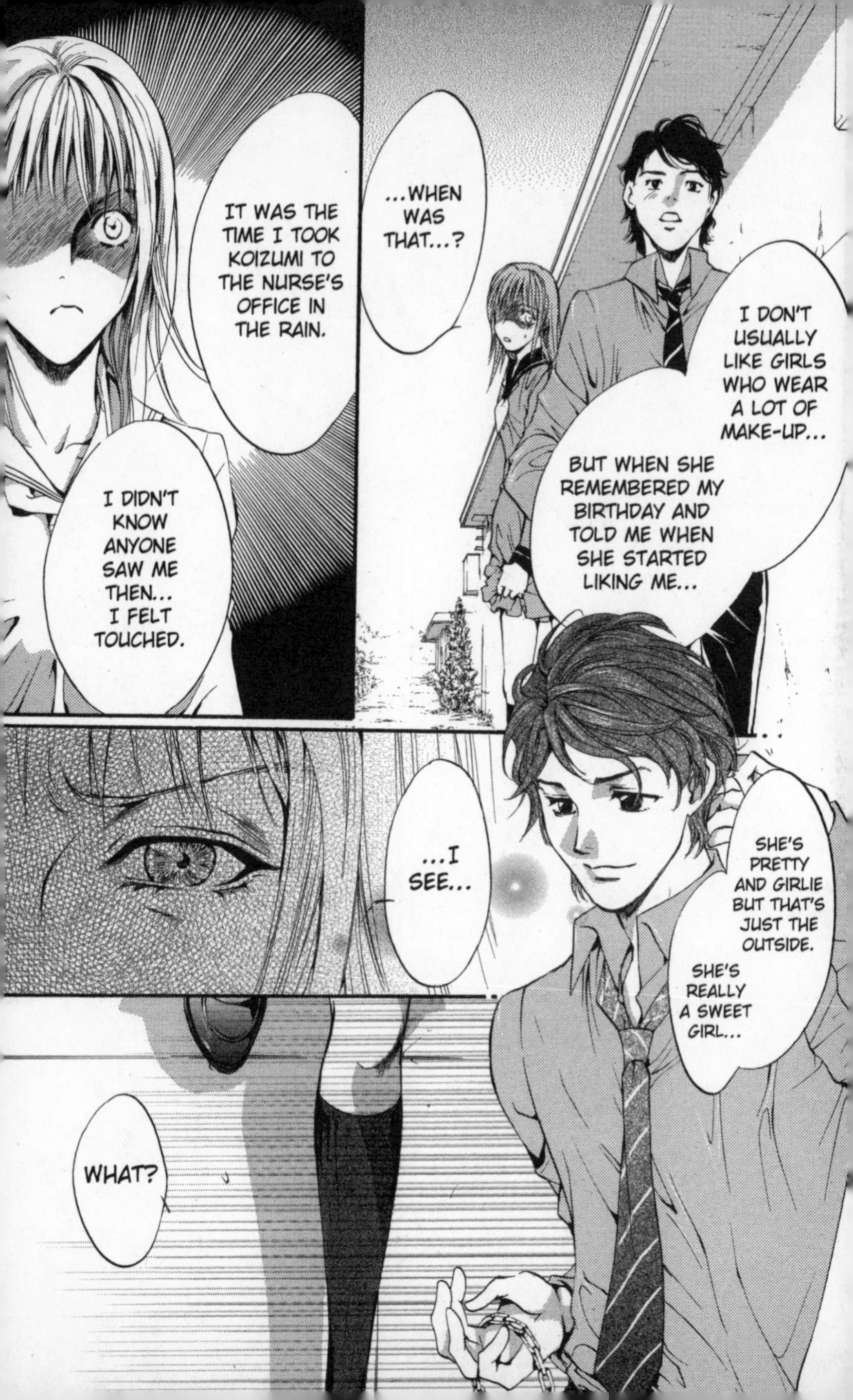
I DON'T USUALLY LIKE GIRLS WHO WEAR A LOT OF MAKE-UP...
BUT WHEN SHE REMEMBERED MY BIRTHDAY AND TOLD ME WHEN SHE STARTED LIKING ME...
...WHEN WAS THAT...?
IT WAS THE TIME I TOOK KOIZUMI TO THE NURSE'S OFFICE IN THE RAIN.
I DIDN'T KNOW ANYONE SAW ME THEN... I FELT TOUCHED.
SHE'S PRETTY AND GIRLIE BUT THAT'S JUST THE OUTSIDE.
SHE'S REALLY A SWEET GIRL...
...I SEE...
WHAT?

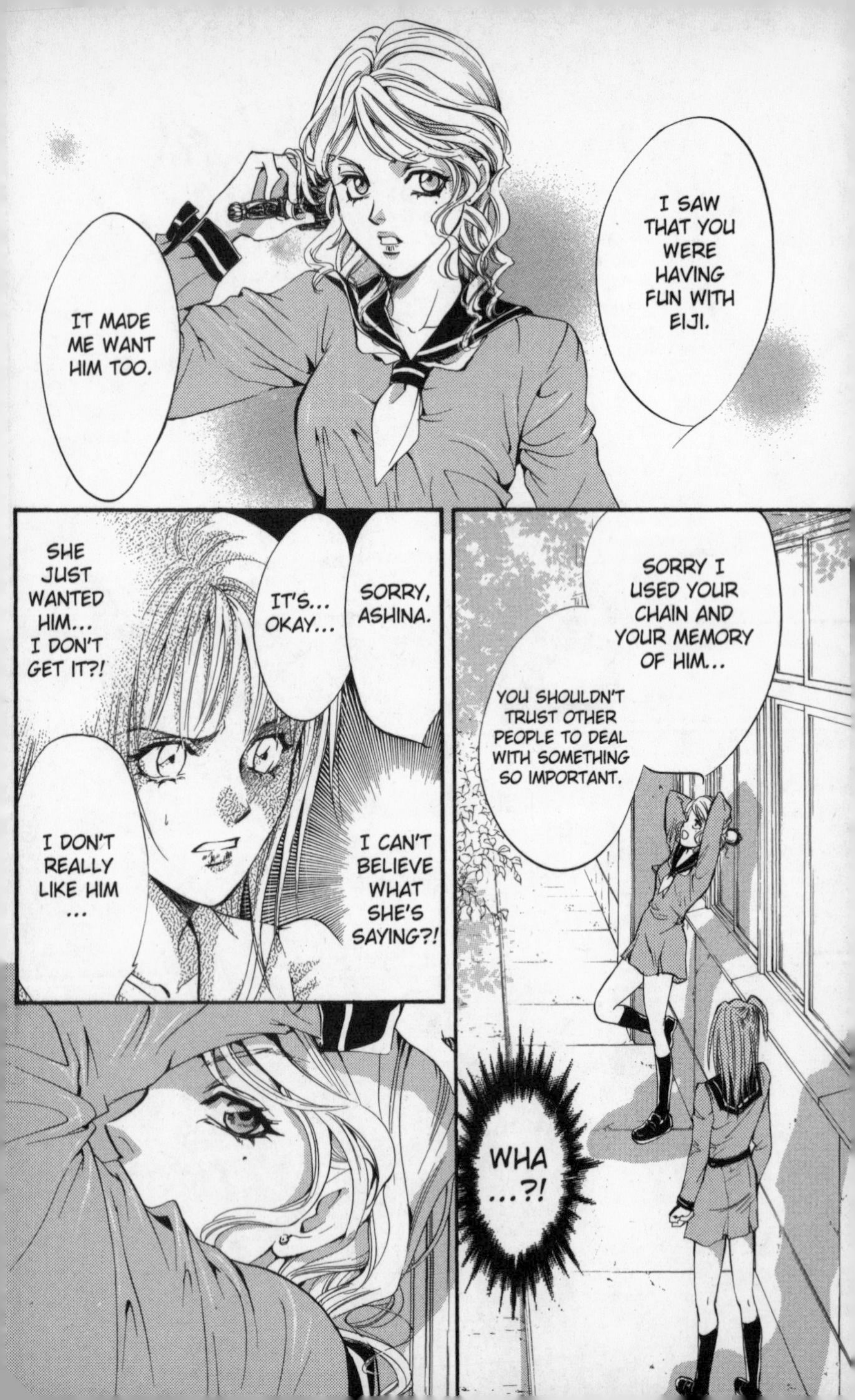
I SAW THAT YOU WERE HAVING FUN WITH EIJI.
IT MADE ME WANT HIM TOO.
SORRY I USED YOUR CHAIN AND YOUR MEMORY OF HIM..
YOU SHOULDN'T TRUST OTHER PEOPLE TO DEAL WITH SOMETHING SO IMPORTANT.
WHA ...?!
SORRY, ASHINA.
IT'S... OKAY...
SHE JUST WANTED HIM... I DON'T GET IT?!
I CAN'T BELIEVE WHAT SHE'S SAYING?!
I DON'T REALLY LIKE HIM ...

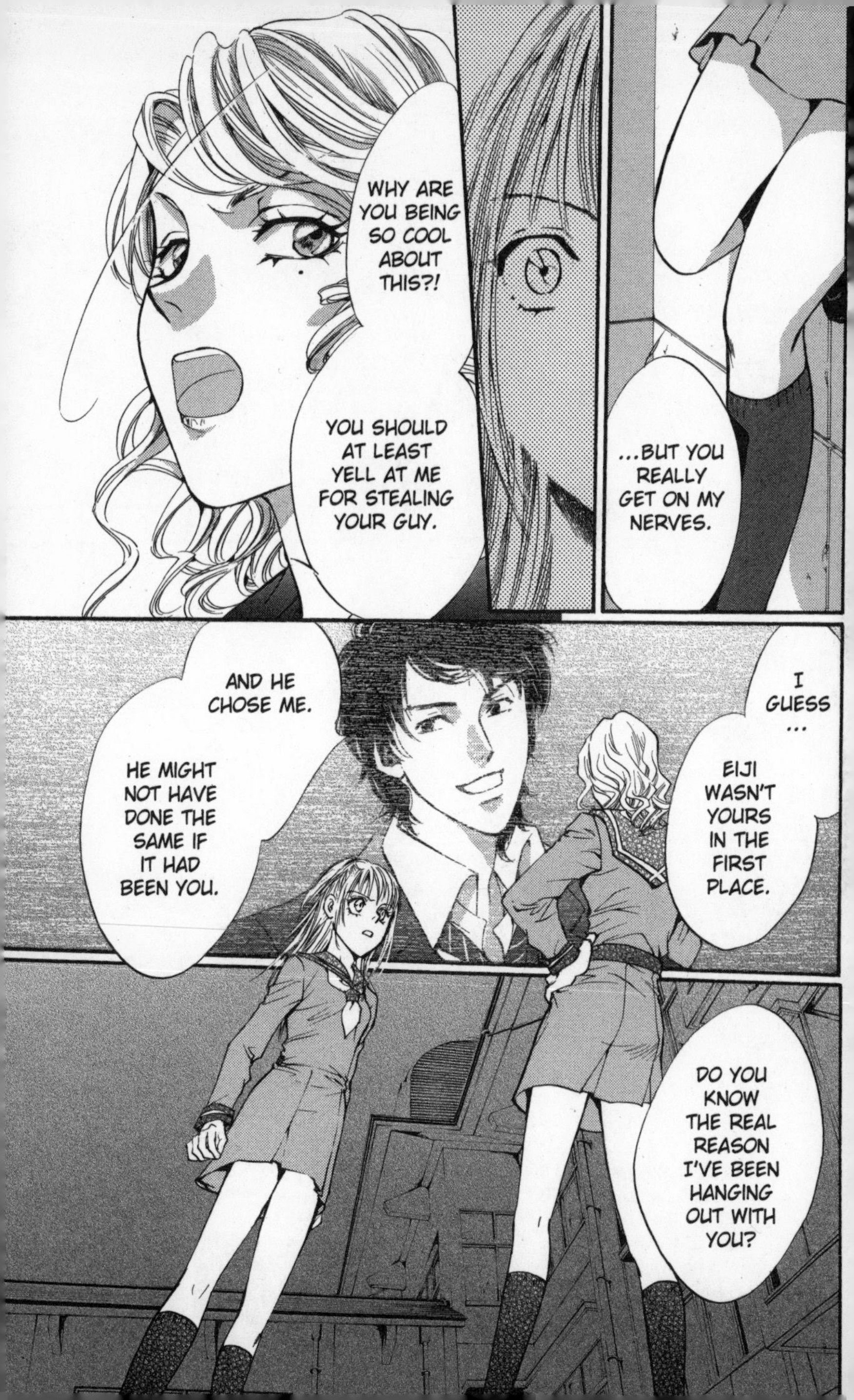
...BUT YOU REALLY GET ON MY NERVES.
WHY ARE YOU BEING SO COOL ABOUT THIS?!
YOU SHOULD AT LEAST YELL AT ME FOR STEALING YOUR GUY.
I GUESS...
EIJI WASN'T YOURS IN THE FIRST PLACE.
AND HE CHOSE ME.
HE MIGHT NOT HAVE DONE THE SAME IF IT HAD BEEN YOU.
DO YOU KNOW THE REAL REASON I'VE BEEN HANGING OUT WITH YOU?

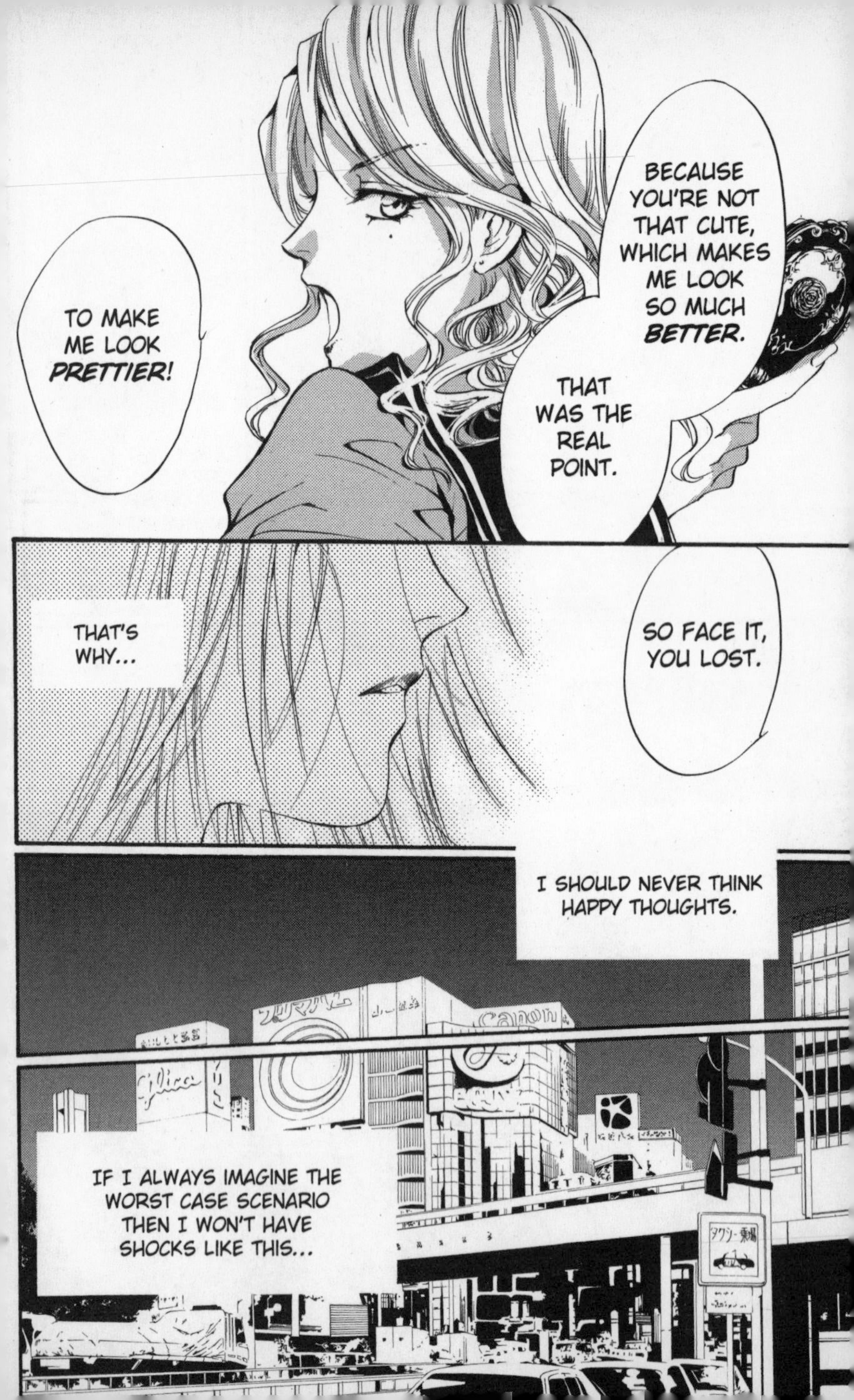
BECAUSE YOU'RE NOT THAT CUTE, WHICH MAKES ME LOOK SO MUCH *BETTER.*
THAT WAS THE REAL POINT.
TO MAKE ME LOOK *PRETTIER!*
SO FACE IT, YOU LOST.
THAT'S WHY...
I SHOULD NEVER THINK HAPPY THOUGHTS.
IF I ALWAYS IMAGINE THE WORST CASE SCENARIO THEN I WON'T HAVE SHOCKS LIKE THIS...

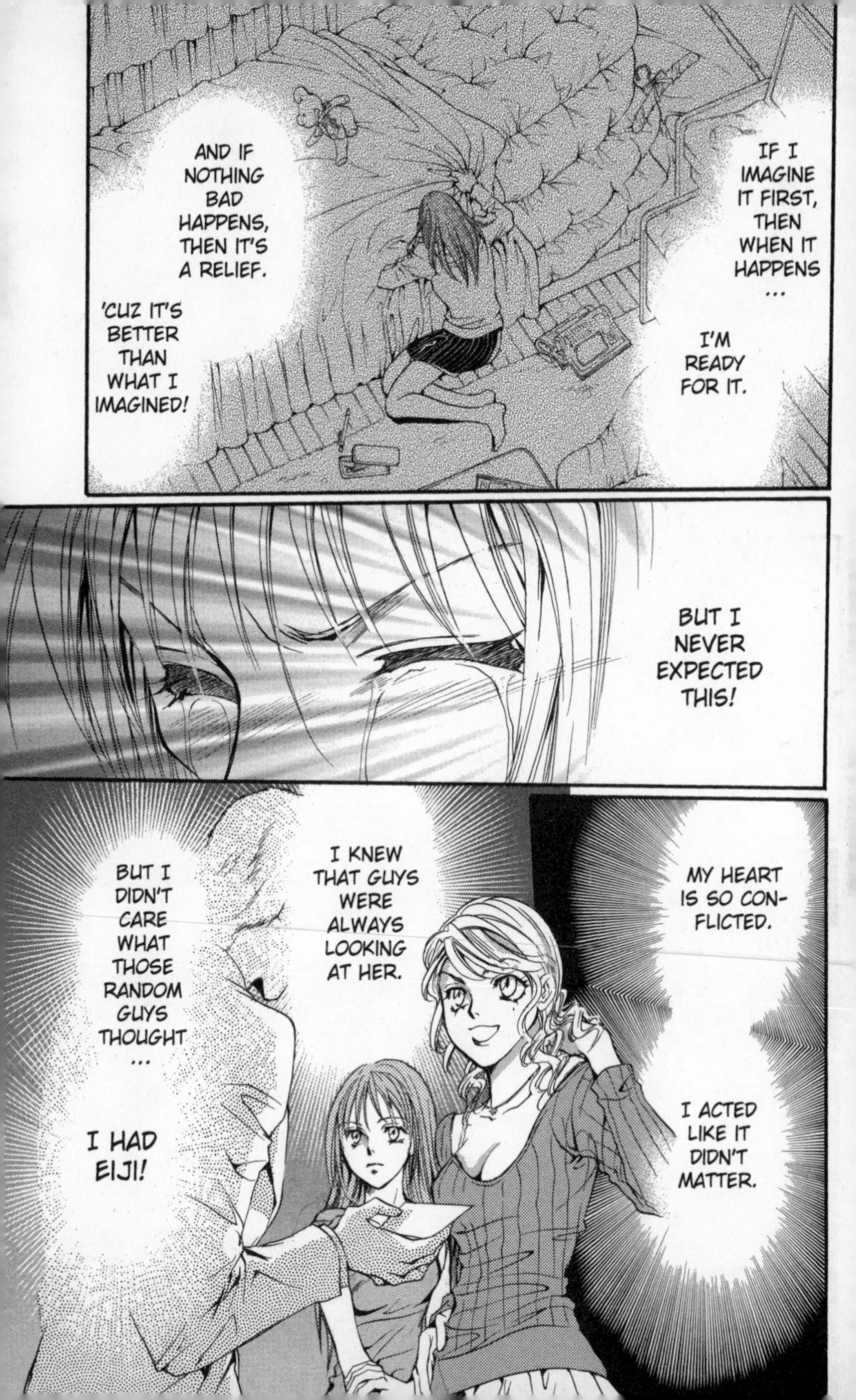
IF I IMAGINE IT FIRST, THEN WHEN IT HAPPENS...
I'M READY FOR IT.
AND IF NOTHING BAD HAPPENS, THEN IT'S A RELIEF.
'CUZ IT'S BETTER THAN WHAT I IMAGINED!
BUT I NEVER EXPECTED THIS!
MY HEART IS SO CON-FLICTED.
I ACTED LIKE IT DIDN'T MATTER.
I KNEW THAT GUYS WERE ALWAYS LOOKING AT HER.
BUT I DIDN'T CARE WHAT THOSE RANDOM GUYS THOUGHT...
I HAD EIJI!

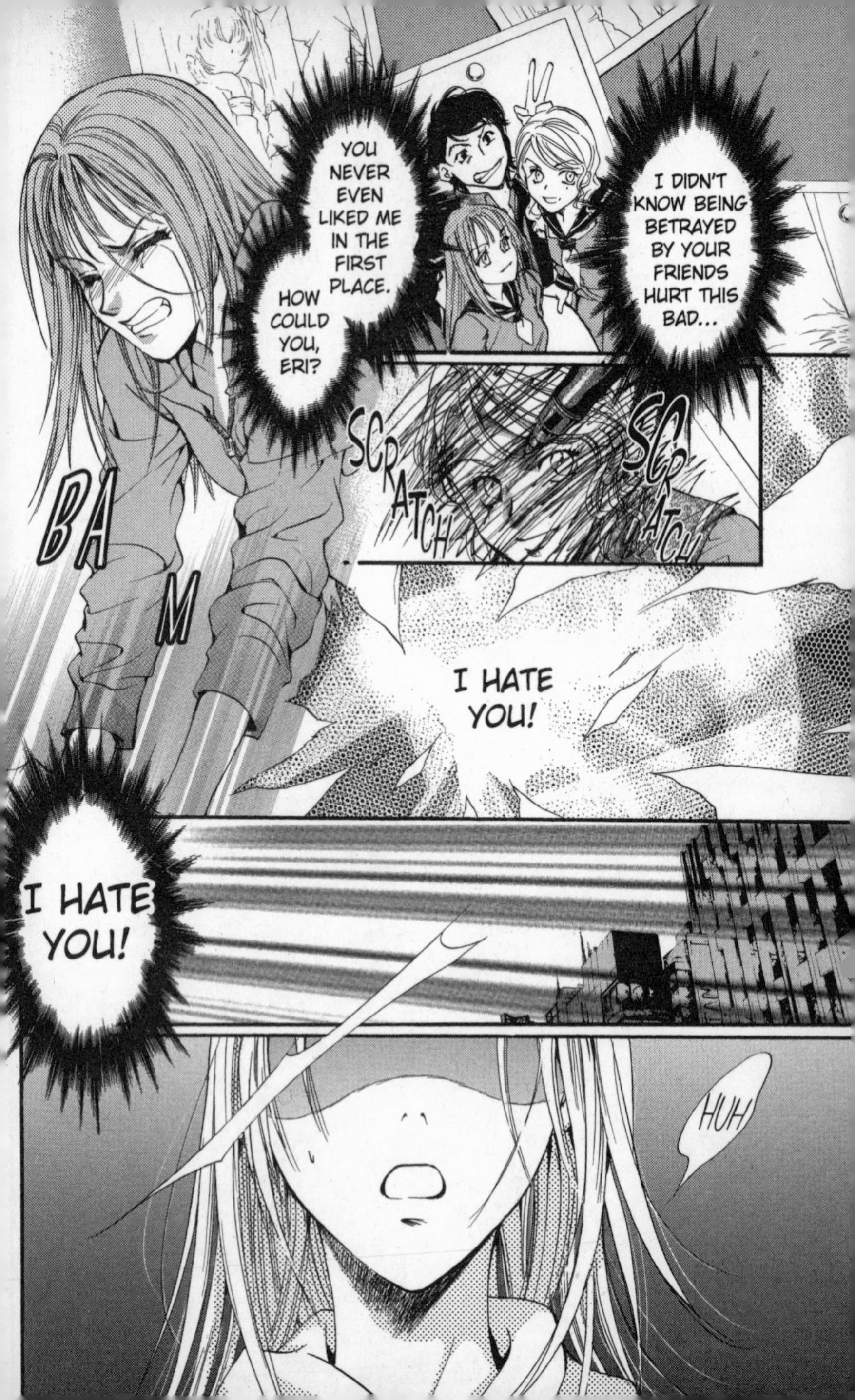
I DIDN'T KNOW BEING BETRAYED BY YOUR FRIENDS HURT THIS BAD...
YOU NEVER EVEN LIKED ME IN THE FIRST PLACE.
HOW COULD YOU, ERI?
SCRATCH
SCRATCH
BAM
I HATE YOU!
I HATE YOU!
HUH

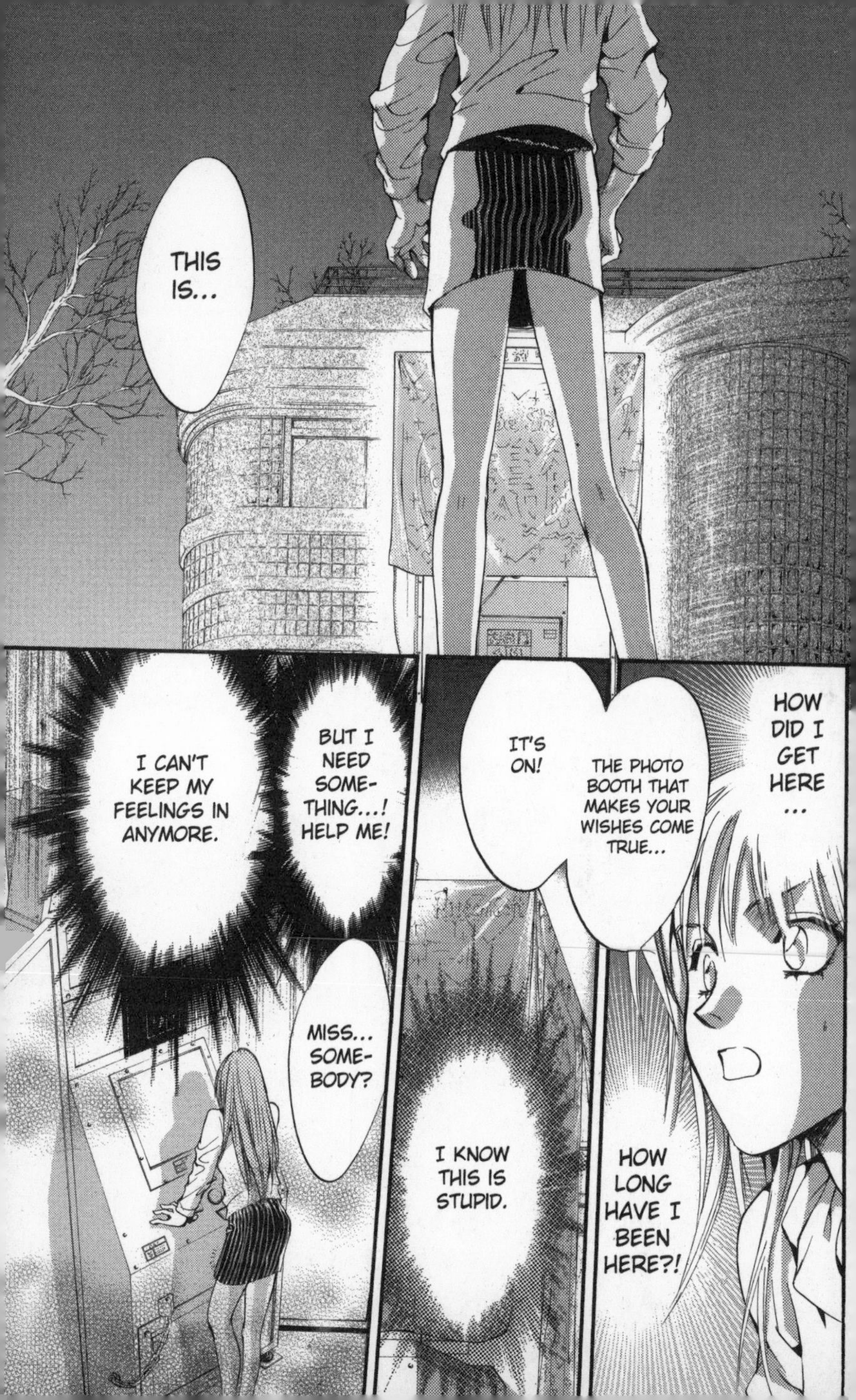
THIS IS...
HOW DID I GET HERE...
HOW LONG HAVE I BEEN HERE?!
THE PHOTO BOOTH THAT MAKES YOUR WISHES COME TRUE...
IT'S ON!
I KNOW THIS IS STUPID.
BUT I NEED SOME-THING...! HELP ME!
I CAN'T KEEP MY FEELINGS IN ANYMORE.
MISS... SOME-BODY?

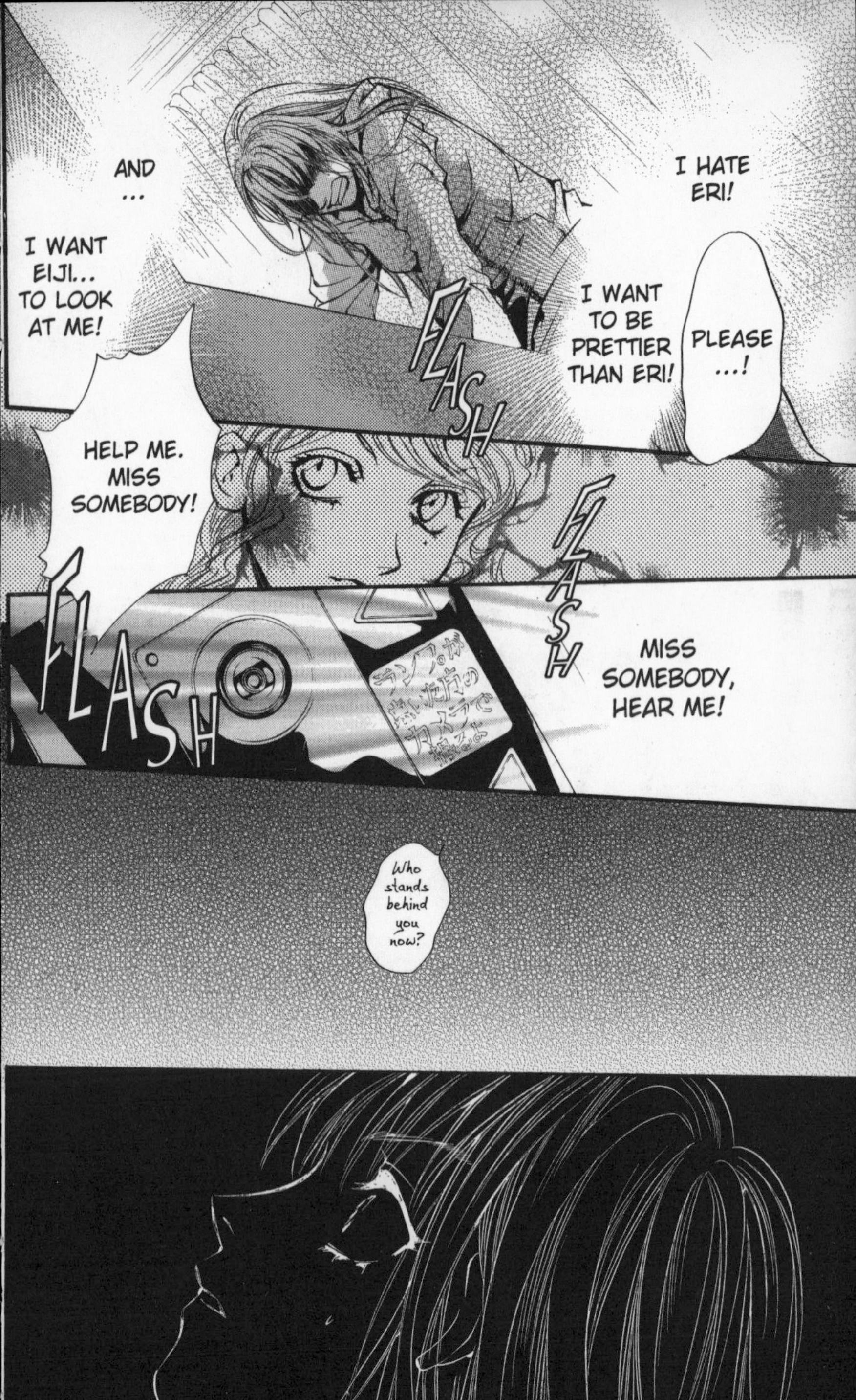
I HATE ERI!
PLEASE ...!
I WANT TO BE PRETTIER THAN ERI!
FLASH
AND ...
I WANT EIJI... TO LOOK AT ME!
FLASH
HELP ME. MISS SOMEBODY!
MISS SOMEBODY, HEAR ME!
FLASH
Who stands behind you now?

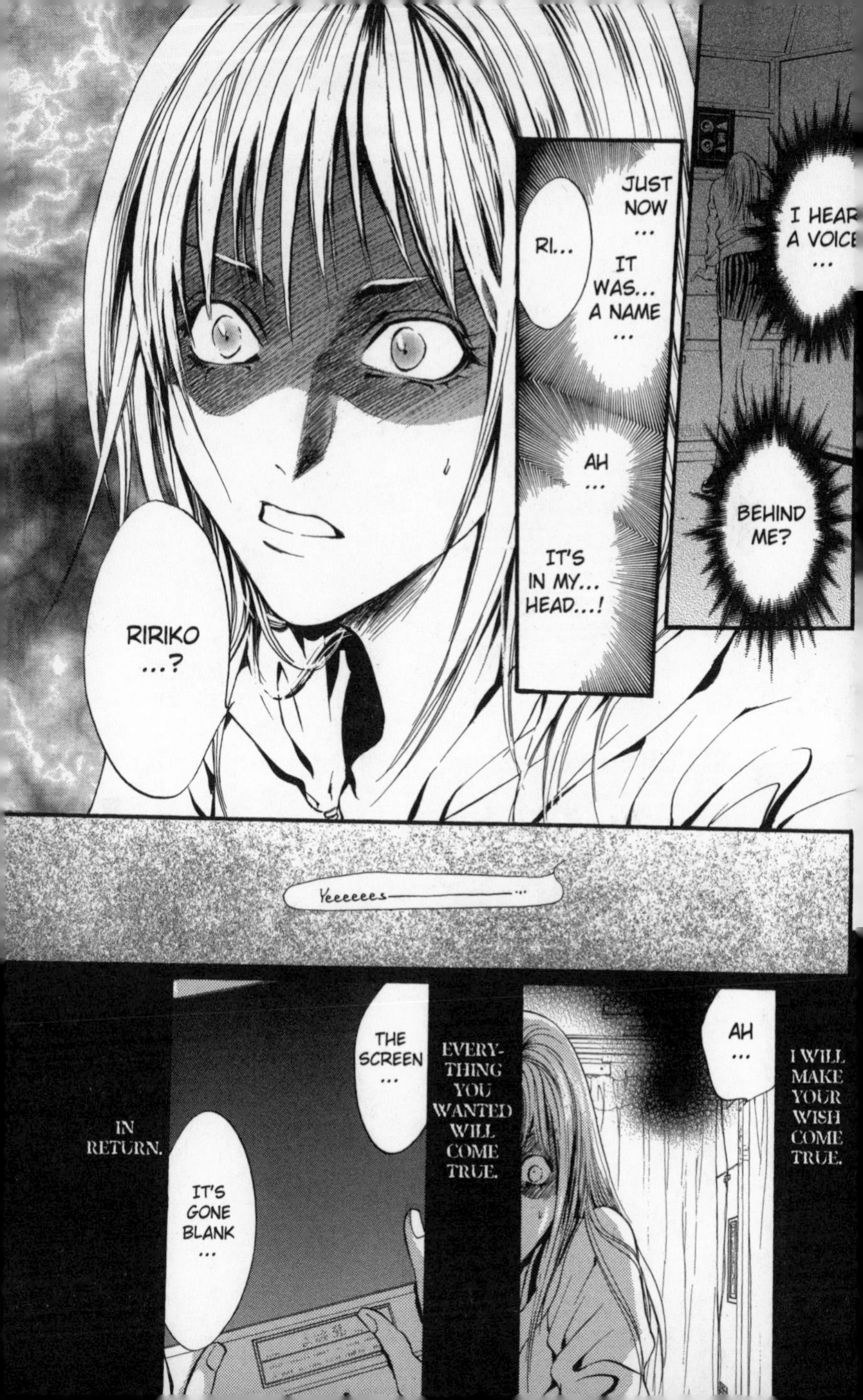

I HEAR A VOICE ...
BEHIND ME?
JUST NOW ... IT WAS... A NAME ...
RI...
AH ...
IT'S IN MY... HEAD...!
RIRIKO ...?
Yeeeeees———...
I WILL MAKE YOUR WISH COME TRUE.
AH ...
EVERY-THING YOU WANTED WILL COME TRUE.
THE SCREEN ...
IT'S GONE BLANK ...
IN RETURN.

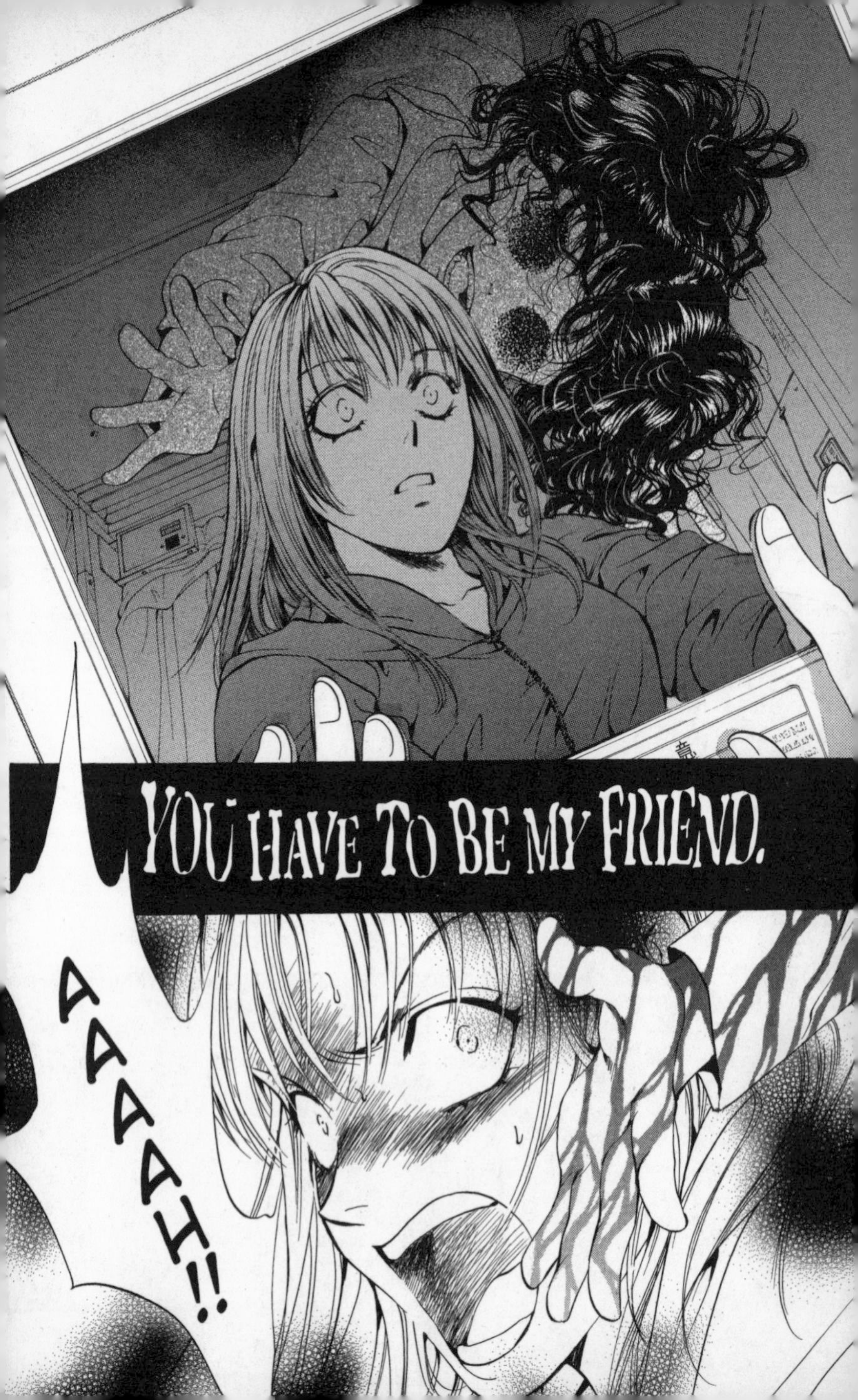
YOU HAVE TO BE MY FRIEND.
AAAAH!!

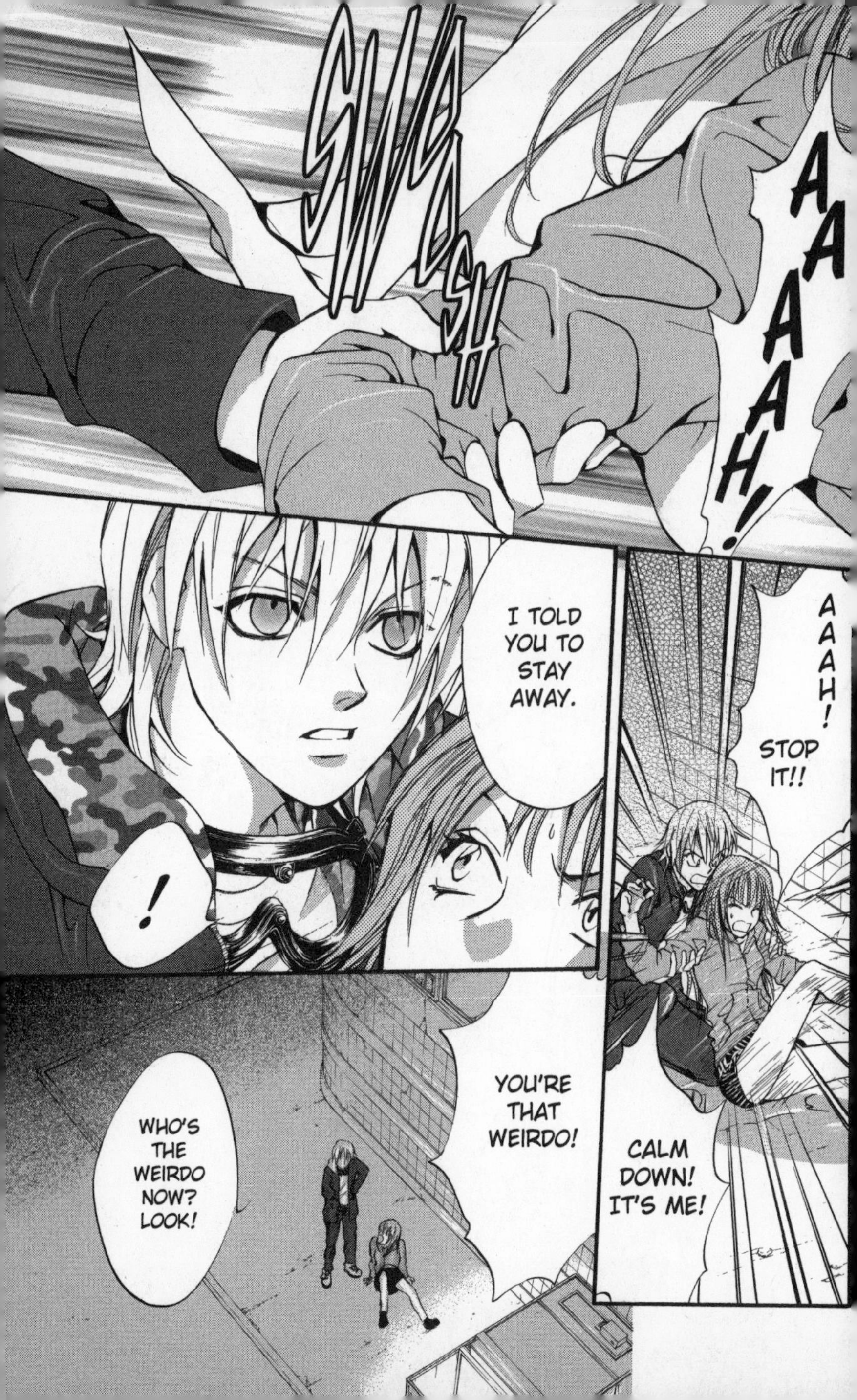
SWASH
AAAAH!
AAAH!
STOP IT!!
CALM DOWN! IT'S ME!
I TOLD YOU TO STAY AWAY.
!
YOU'RE THAT WEIRDO!
WHO'S THE WEIRDO NOW? LOOK!

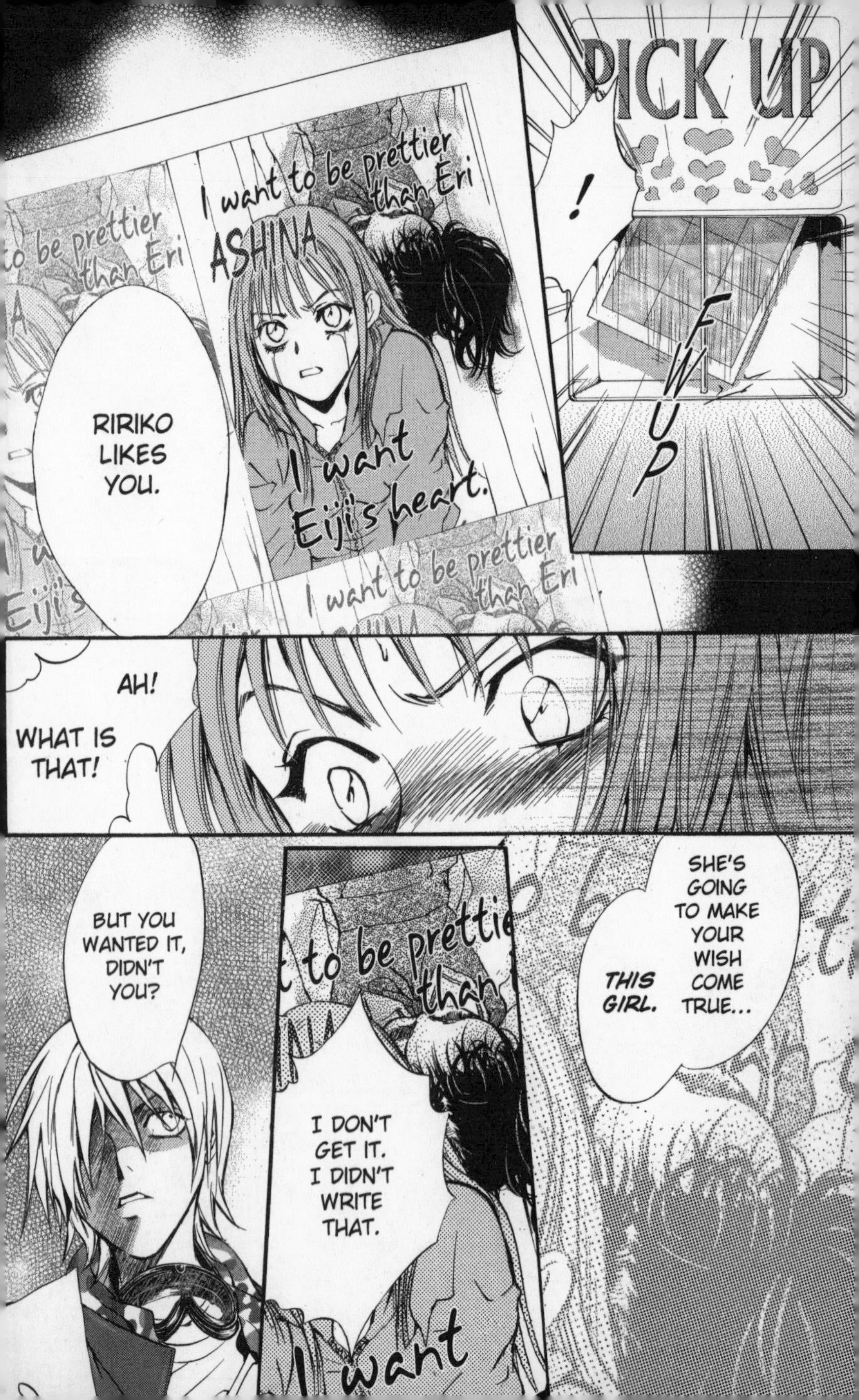
PICK UP
!
FWUP
I want to be prettier than Eri ASHINA
I want to be prettier than Eri
I want Eiji's heart.
I want to be prettier than Eri
RIRIKO LIKES YOU.
AH!
WHAT IS THAT!
SHE'S GOING TO MAKE YOUR WISH COME TRUE...
THIS GIRL.
I DON'T GET IT. I DIDN'T WRITE THAT.
BUT YOU WANTED IT, DIDN'T YOU?
I want

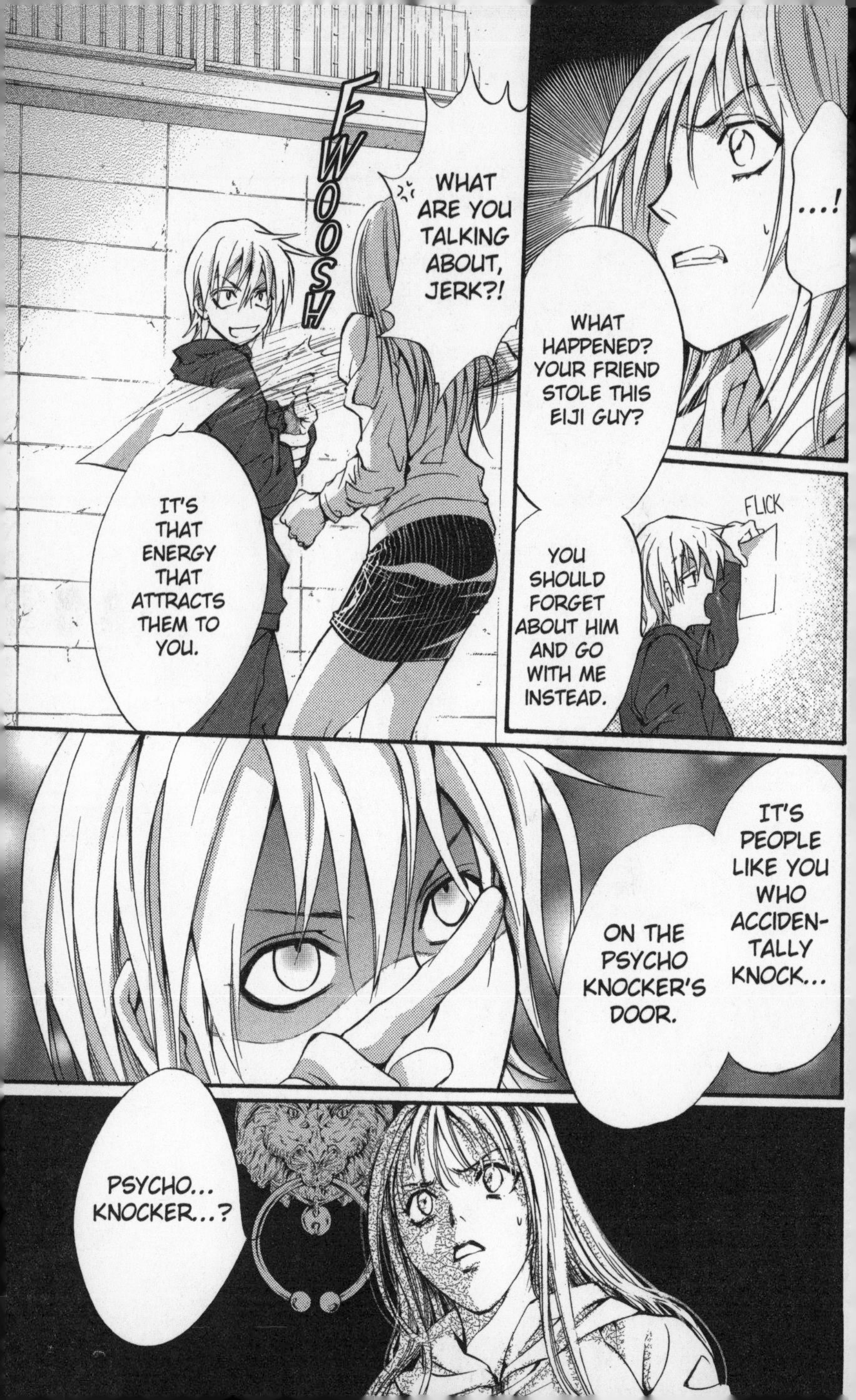
...!
WHAT HAPPENED? YOUR FRIEND STOLE THIS EIJI GUY?
YOU SHOULD FORGET ABOUT HIM AND GO WITH ME INSTEAD.
FLICK
WHAT ARE YOU TALKING ABOUT, JERK?!
FWOOSH
IT'S THAT ENERGY THAT ATTRACTS THEM TO YOU.
IT'S PEOPLE LIKE YOU WHO ACCIDEN-TALLY KNOCK...
ON THE PSYCHO KNOCKER'S DOOR.
PSYCHO... KNOCKER...?

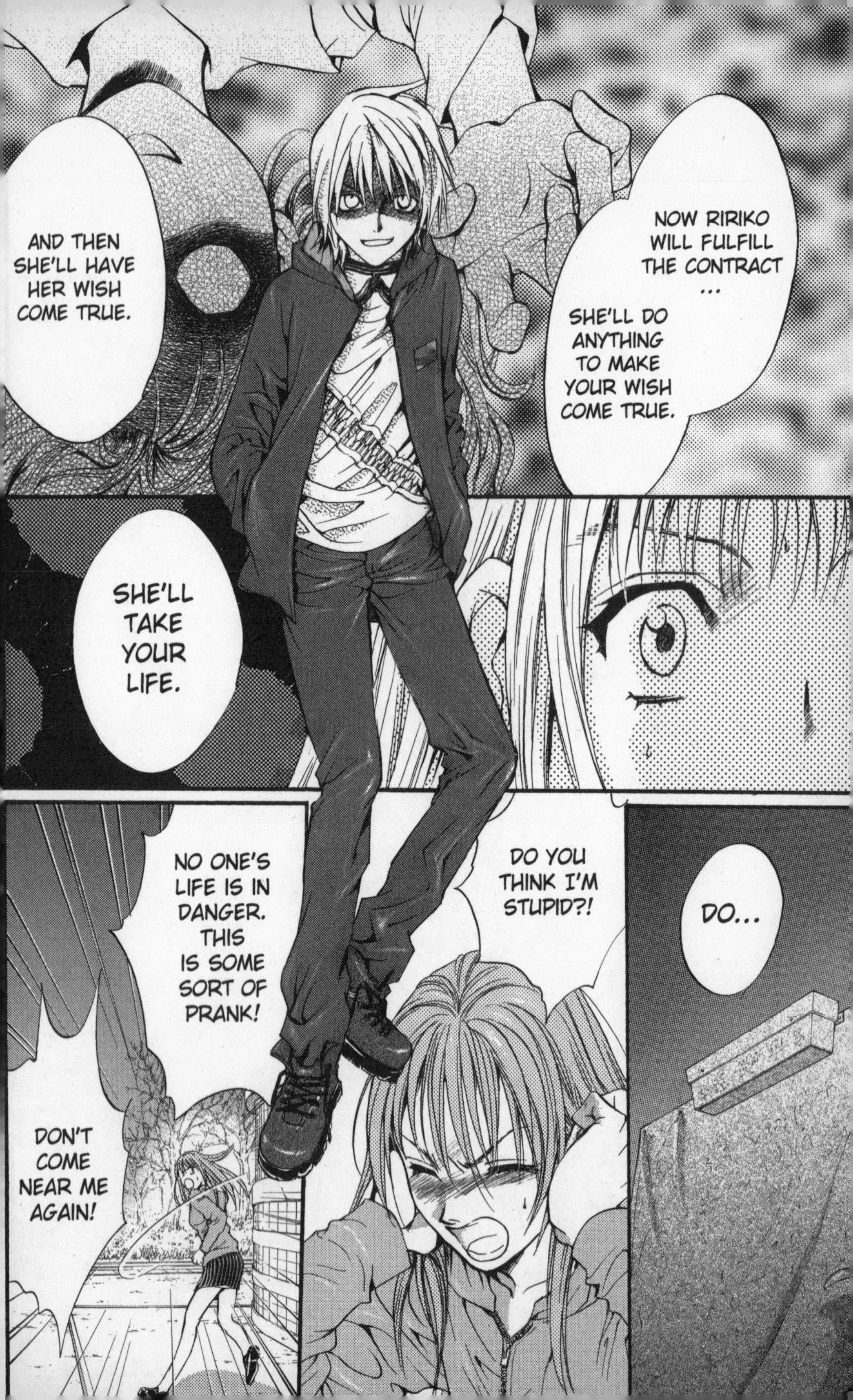
NOW RIRIKO WILL FULFILL THE CONTRACT ...
SHE'LL DO ANYTHING TO MAKE YOUR WISH COME TRUE.
AND THEN SHE'LL HAVE HER WISH COME TRUE.
SHE'LL TAKE YOUR LIFE.
DO...
DO YOU THINK I'M STUPID?!
NO ONE'S LIFE IS IN DANGER. THIS IS SOME SORT OF PRANK!
DON'T COME NEAR ME AGAIN!

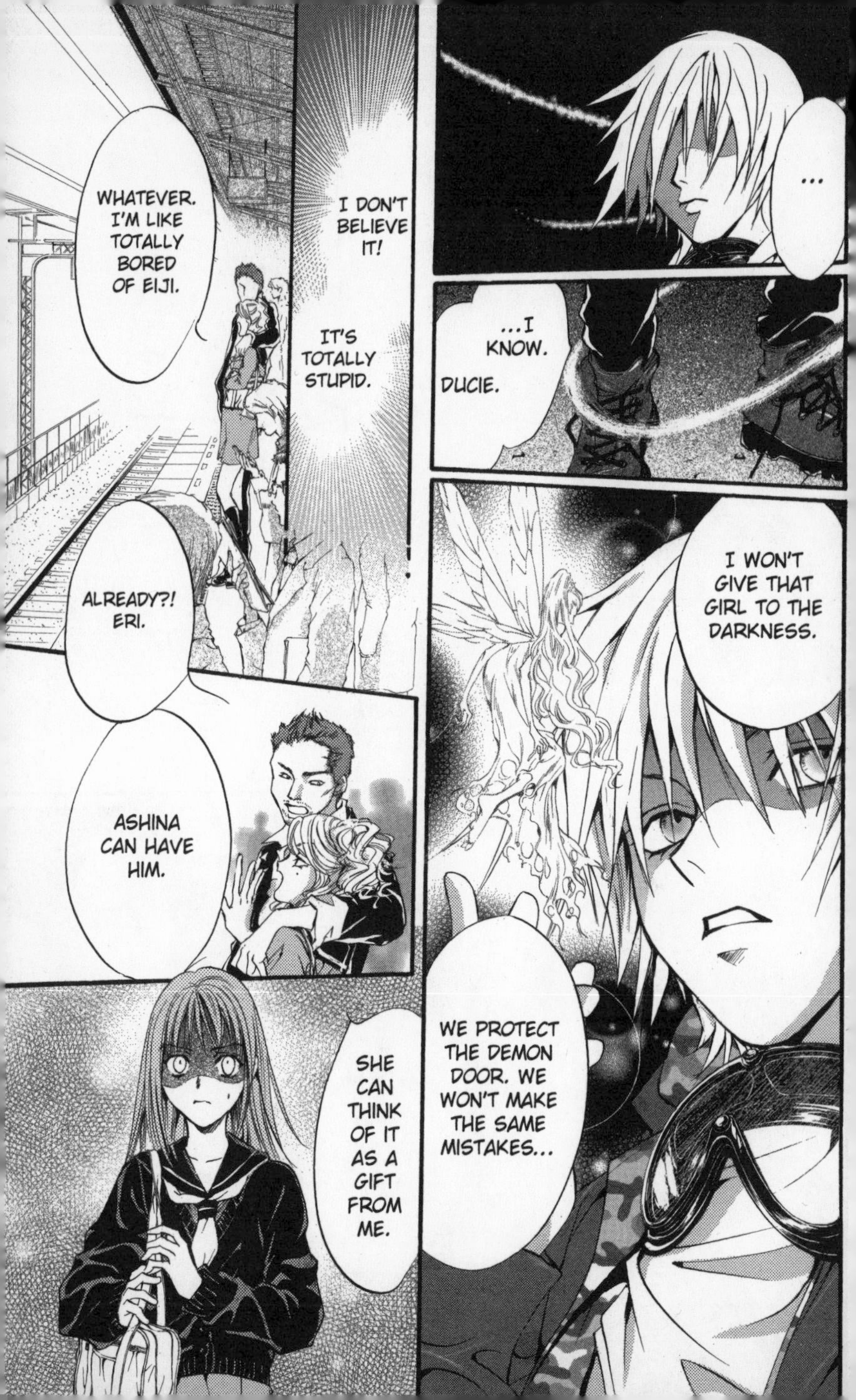
...
...I KNOW.
DUCIE.
I WON'T GIVE THAT GIRL TO THE DARKNESS.
WE PROTECT THE DEMON DOOR. WE WON'T MAKE THE SAME MISTAKES...
I DON'T BELIEVE IT!
IT'S TOTALLY STUPID.
WHATEVER. I'M LIKE TOTALLY BORED OF EIJI.
ALREADY?! ERI.
ASHINA CAN HAVE HIM.
SHE CAN THINK OF IT AS A GIFT FROM ME.

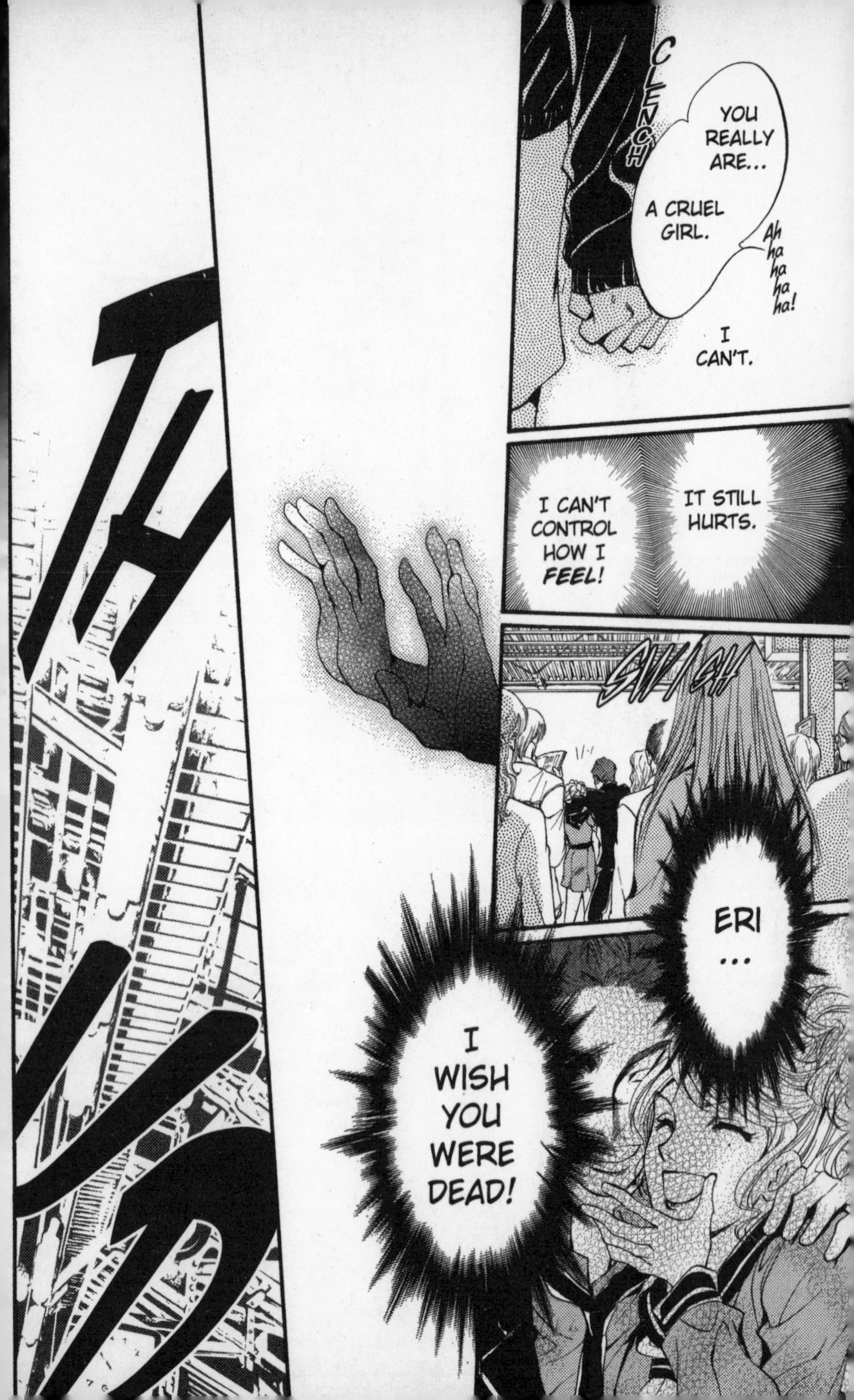
CLENCH
YOU REALLY ARE...
A CRUEL GIRL.
Ah ha ha ha ha!
I CAN'T.
IT STILL HURTS.
I CAN'T CONTROL HOW I FEEL!
SWISH
ERI...
I WISH YOU WERE DEAD!

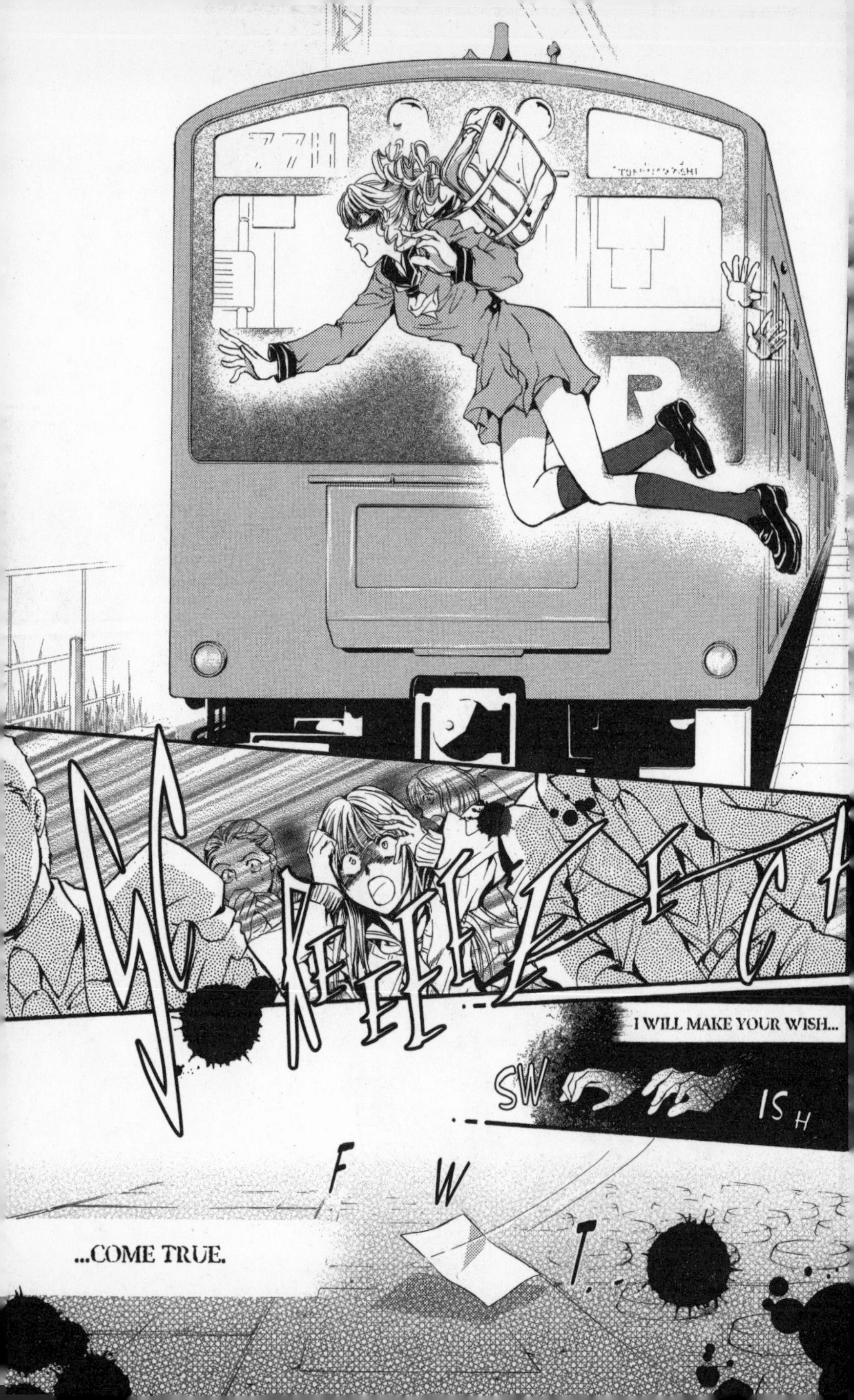
SCREEEECH
I WILL MAKE YOUR WISH...
SWISH
...COME TRUE.
FWT

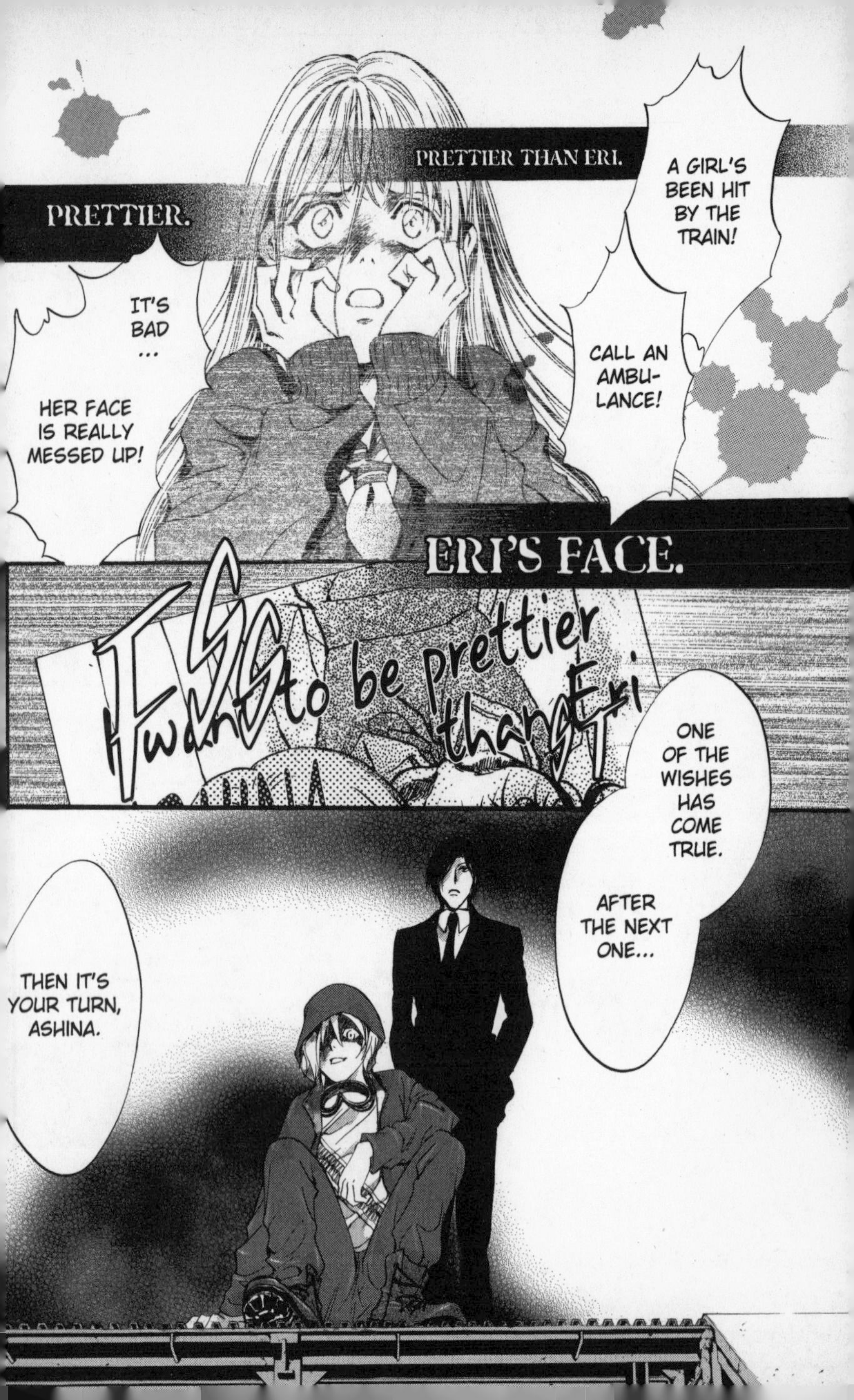
A GIRL'S BEEN HIT BY THE TRAIN!
PRETTIER THAN ERI.
PRETTIER.
CALL AN AMBULANCE!
IT'S BAD ...
HER FACE IS REALLY MESSED UP!
ERI'S FACE.
I want to be prettier than Eri
ONE OF THE WISHES HAS COME TRUE.
AFTER THE NEXT ONE...
THEN IT'S YOUR TURN, ASHINA.

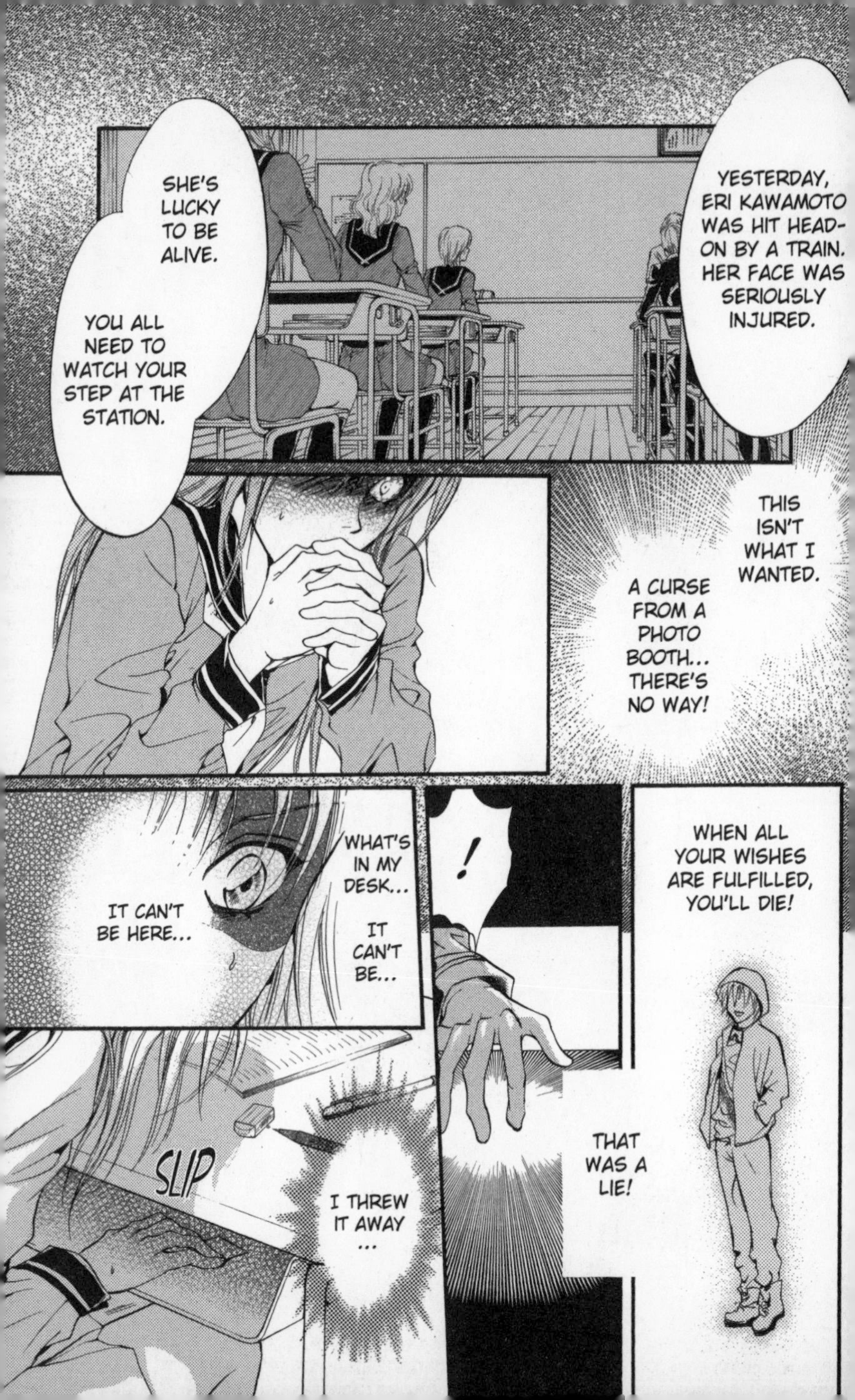
YESTERDAY, ERI KAWAMOTO WAS HIT HEAD-ON BY A TRAIN. HER FACE WAS SERIOUSLY INJURED.
SHE'S LUCKY TO BE ALIVE.
YOU ALL NEED TO WATCH YOUR STEP AT THE STATION.
THIS ISN'T WHAT I WANTED.
A CURSE FROM A PHOTO BOOTH... THERE'S NO WAY!
WHEN ALL YOUR WISHES ARE FULFILLED, YOU'LL DIE!
THAT WAS A LIE!
!
WHAT'S IN MY DESK...
IT CAN'T BE...
IT CAN'T BE HERE...
SLIP
I THREW IT AWAY ...

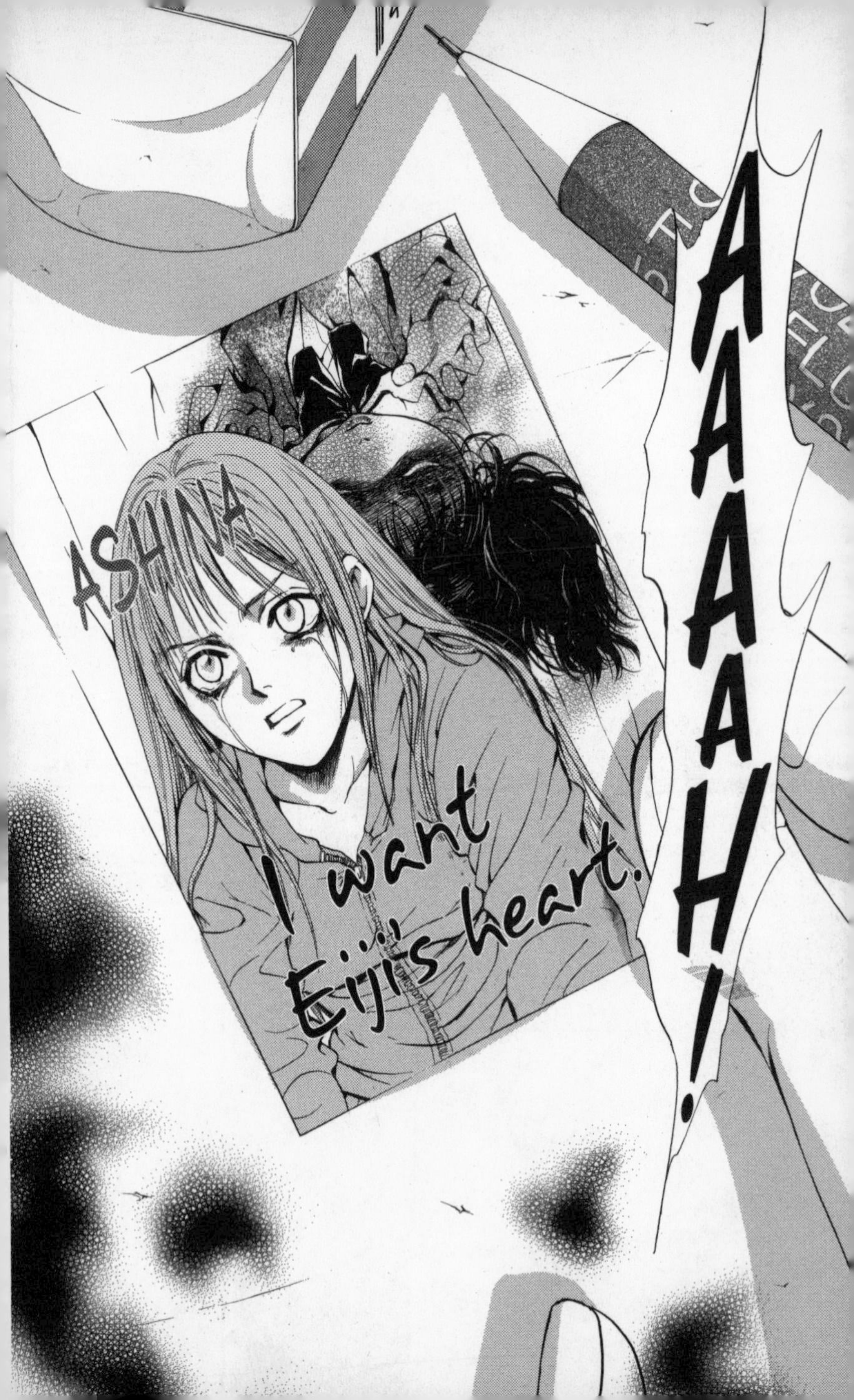
AAAAAH!!
I want... Eiji's heart.
ASHINA

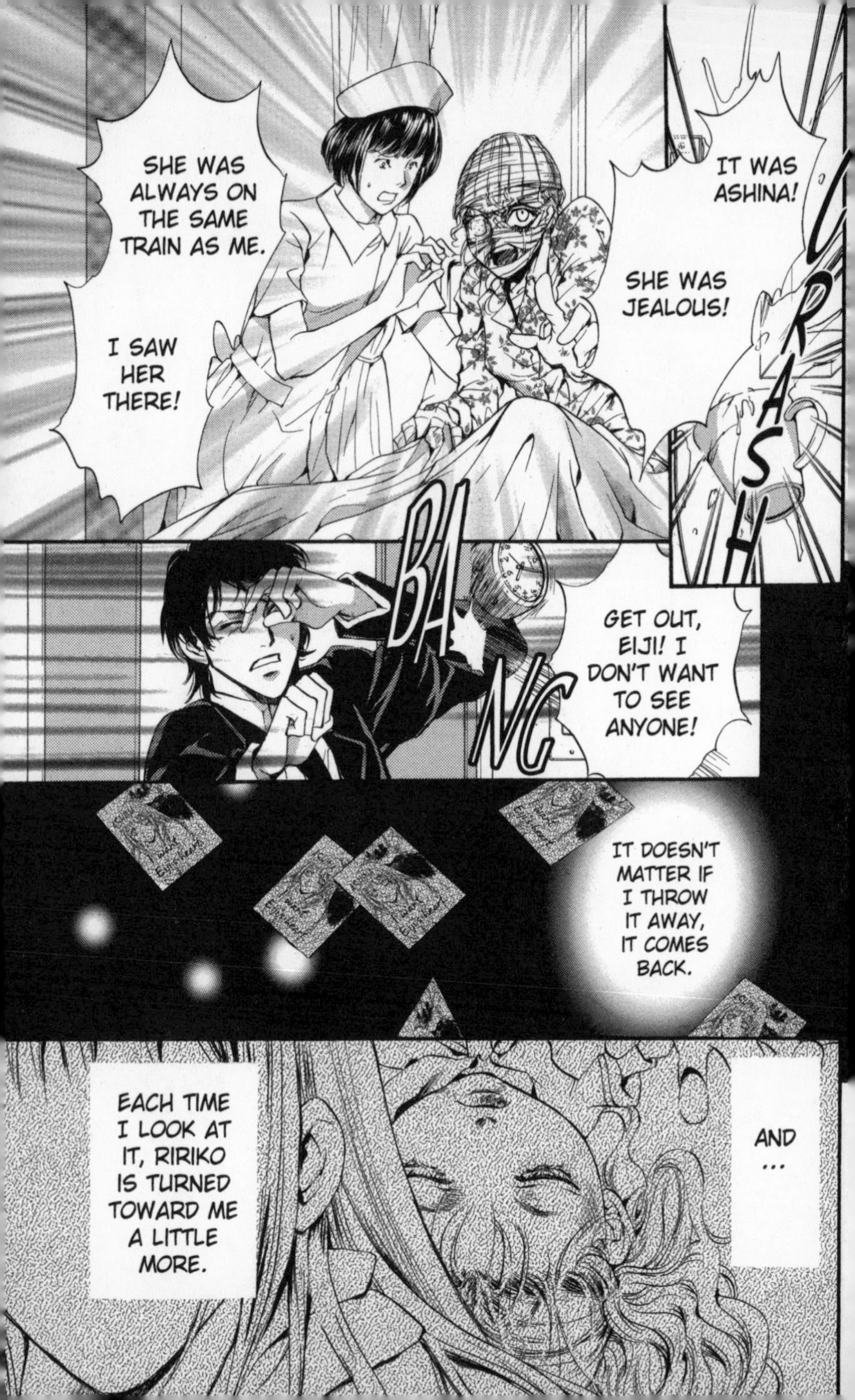
IT WAS ASHINA!
SHE WAS JEALOUS!
CRASH
SHE WAS ALWAYS ON THE SAME TRAIN AS ME.
I SAW HER THERE!
GET OUT, EIJI! I DON'T WANT TO SEE ANYONE!
BANG
IT DOESN'T MATTER IF I THROW IT AWAY, IT COMES BACK.
AND ...
EACH TIME I LOOK AT IT, RIRIKO IS TURNED TOWARD ME A LITTLE MORE.

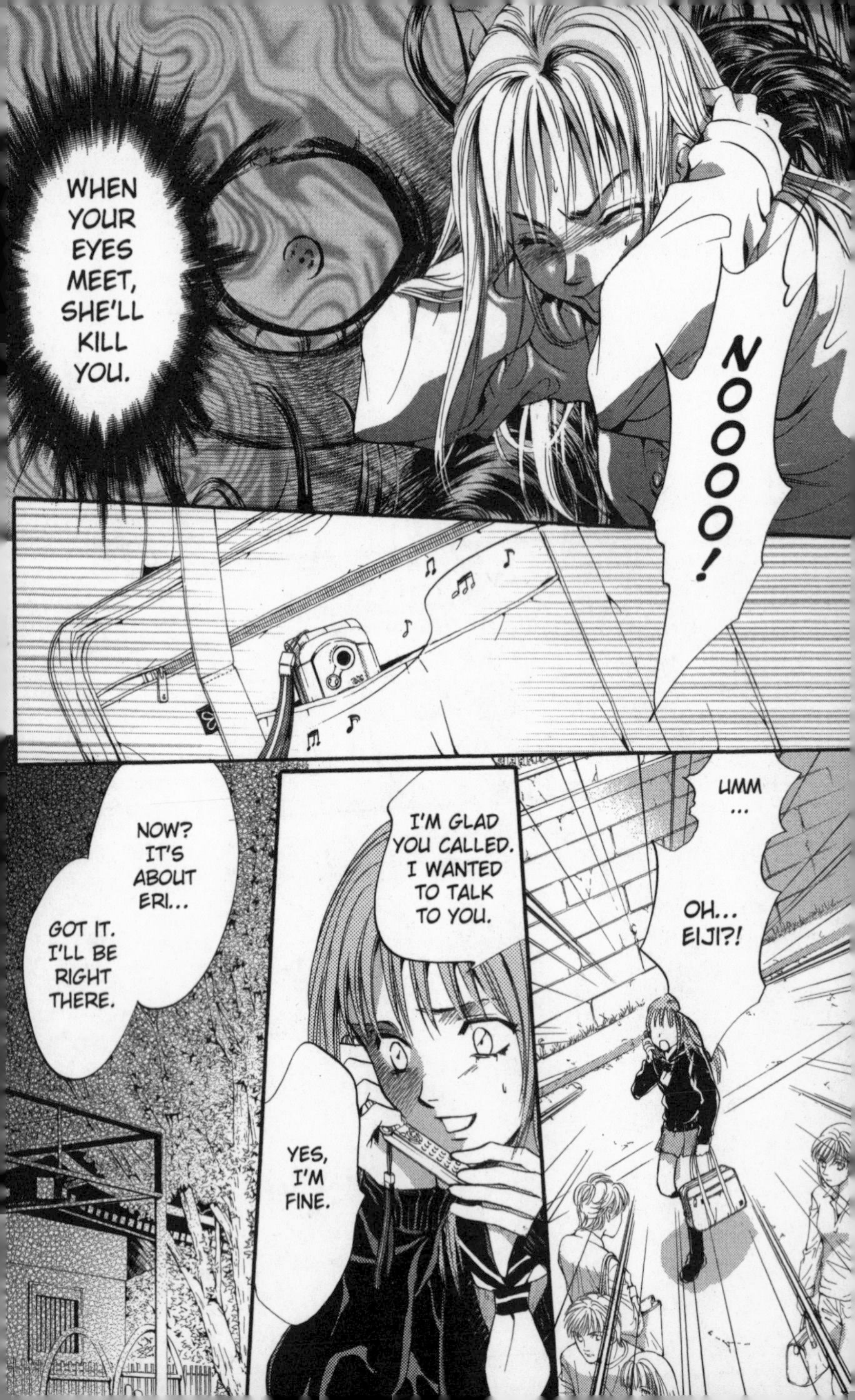
WHEN YOUR EYES MEET, SHE'LL KILL YOU.
NOOOOO!
UMM ...
OH... EIJI?!
I'M GLAD YOU CALLED. I WANTED TO TALK TO YOU.
YES, I'M FINE.
NOW? IT'S ABOUT ERI...
GOT IT. I'LL BE RIGHT THERE.

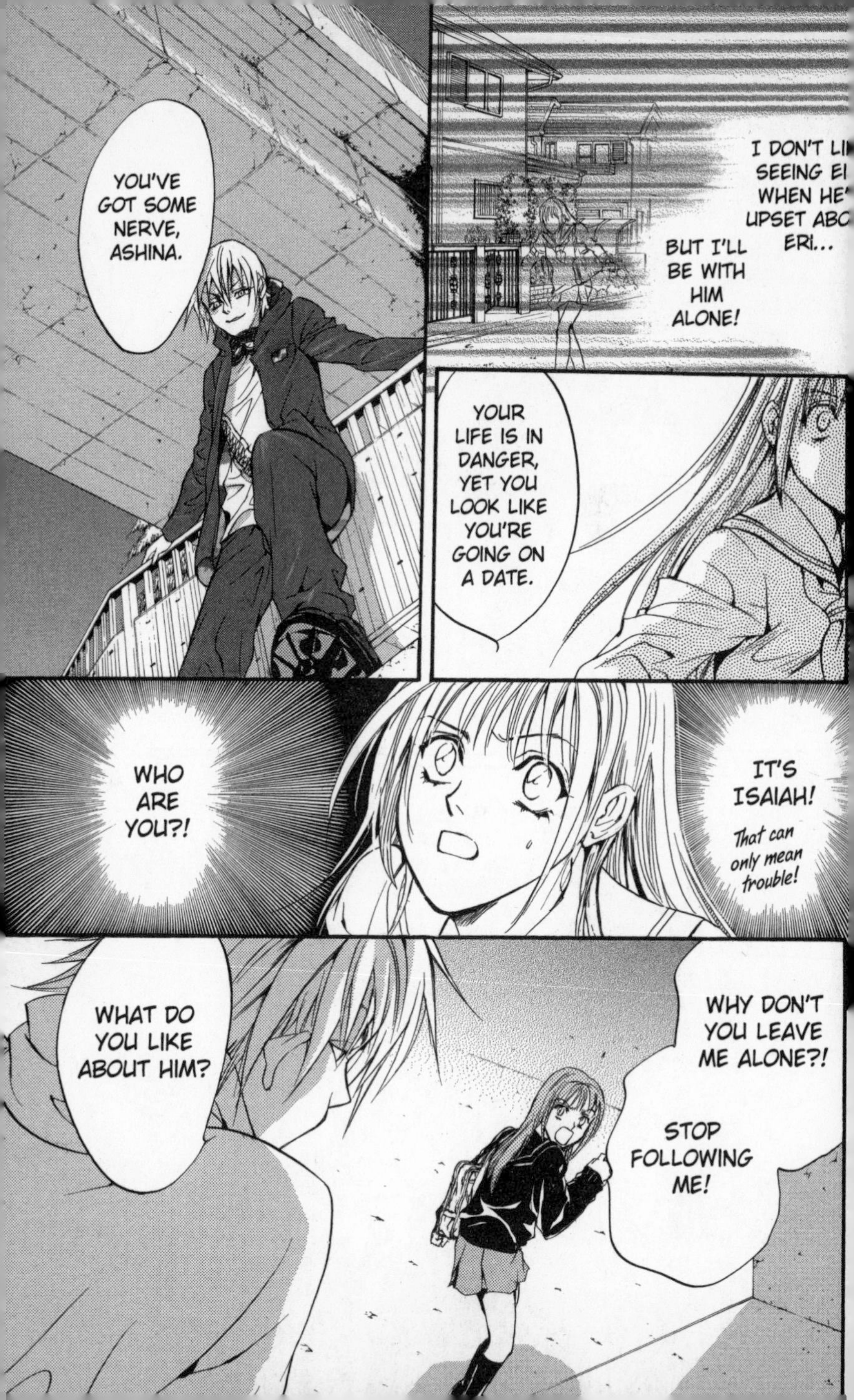

I DON'T LI SEEING EI WHEN HE' UPSET ABO ERI...
BUT I'LL BE WITH HIM ALONE!
YOUR LIFE IS IN DANGER, YET YOU LOOK LIKE YOU'RE GOING ON A DATE.
YOU'VE GOT SOME NERVE, ASHINA.
IT'S ISAIAH!
That can only mean trouble!
WHO ARE YOU?!
WHY DON'T YOU LEAVE ME ALONE?!
STOP FOLLOWING ME!
WHAT DO YOU LIKE ABOUT HIM?

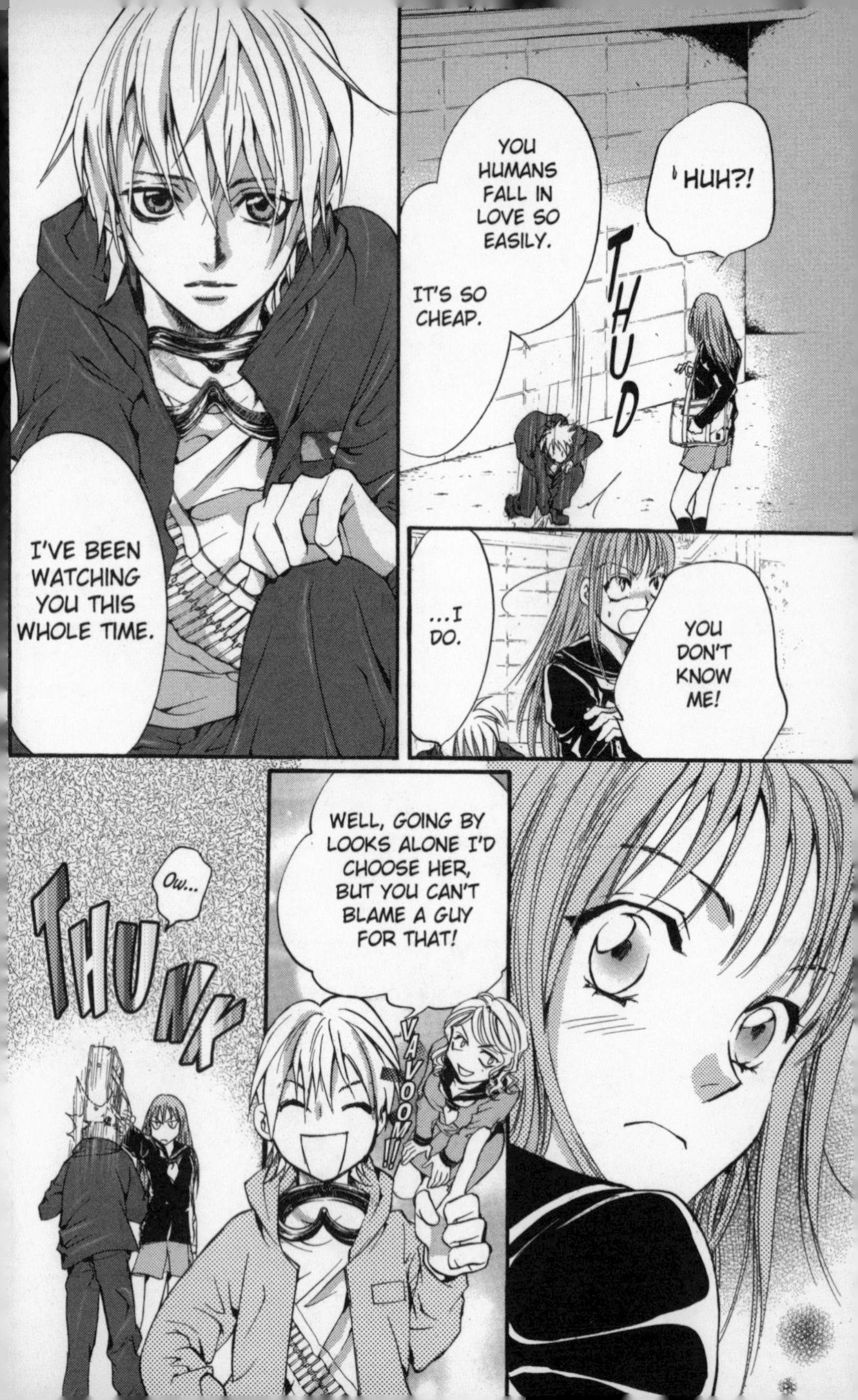
HUH?!
THUD
YOU HUMANS FALL IN LOVE SO EASILY.
IT'S SO CHEAP.
YOU DON'T KNOW ME!
...I DO.
I'VE BEEN WATCHING YOU THIS WHOLE TIME.
WELL, GOING BY LOOKS ALONE I'D CHOOSE HER, BUT YOU CAN'T BLAME A GUY FOR THAT!
VAVOOM!!
Ow...
THUNK

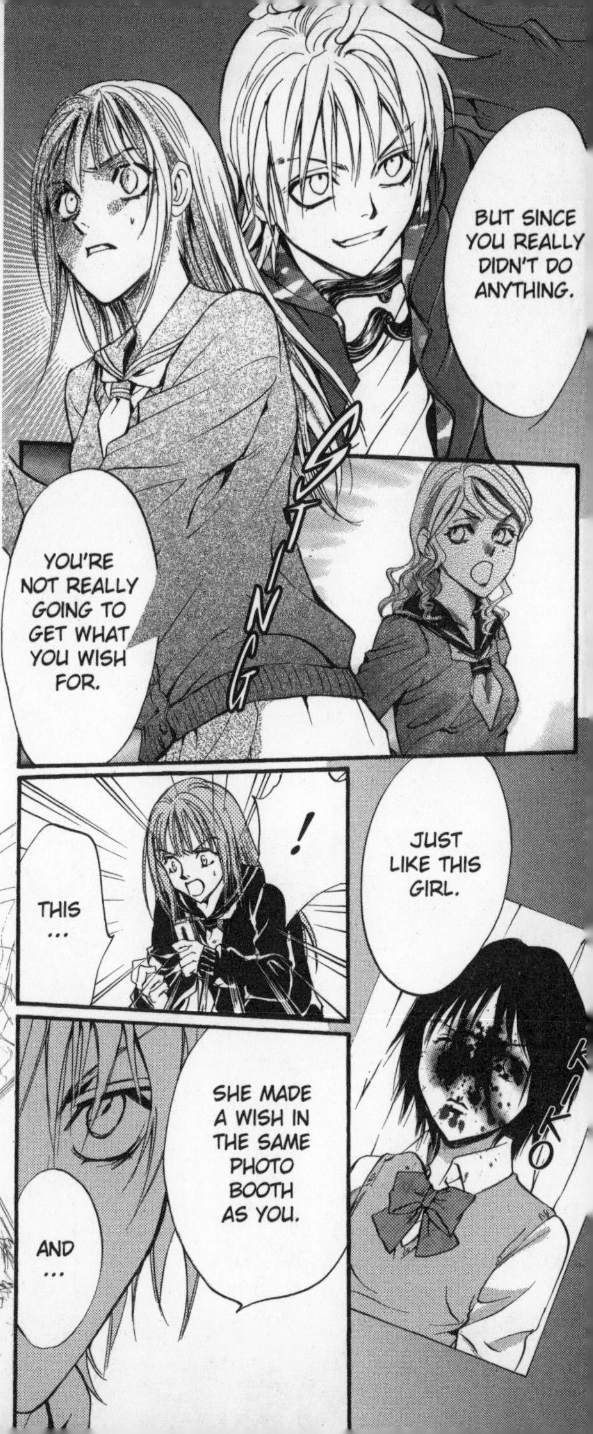
BUT SINCE YOU REALLY DIDN'T DO ANYTHING.
YOU'RE NOT REALLY GOING TO GET WHAT YOU WISH FOR.
JUST LIKE THIS GIRL.
!
THIS ...
SHE MADE A WISH IN THE SAME PHOTO BOOTH AS YOU.
AND ...

I have the same problem as Ashina. I always have a bad feeling that everything is going to go wrong. And of course nothing happens...

Because I have this super pessimistic view, I always plan for the worst case scenario. It's not good... I want to get better but it's hard. I wrote this as a lesson to myself."

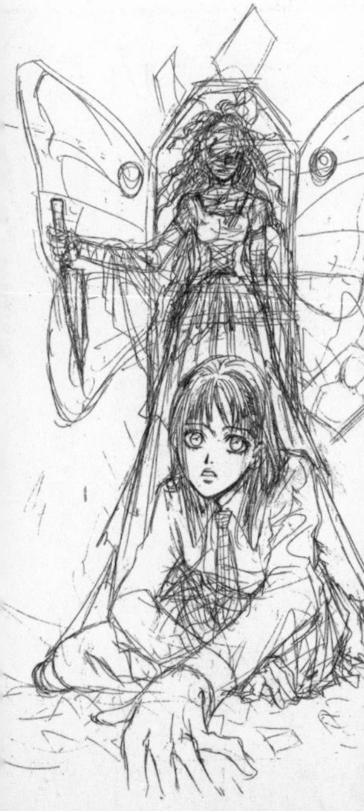

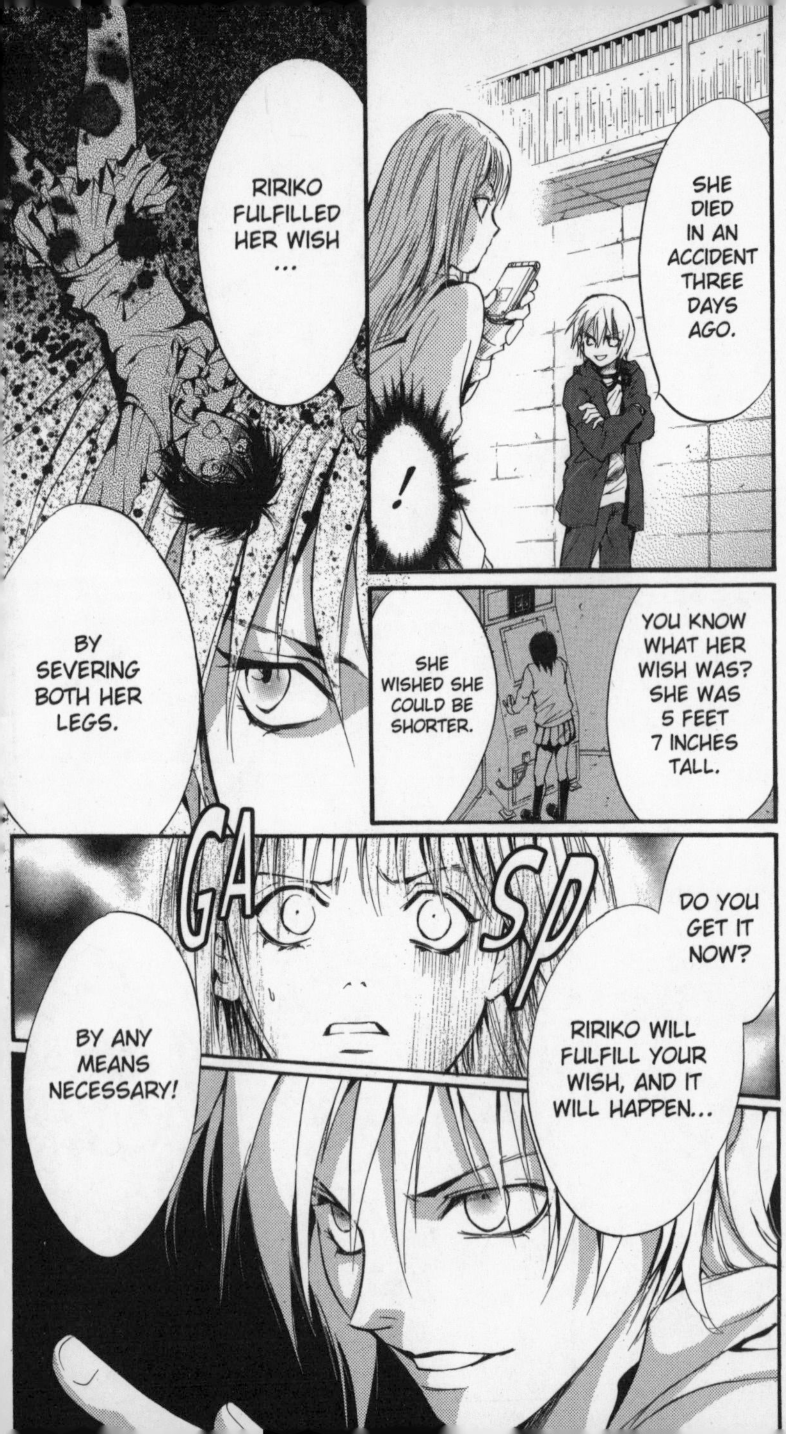
SHE DIED IN AN ACCIDENT THREE DAYS AGO.
!
YOU KNOW WHAT HER WISH WAS? SHE WAS 5 FEET 7 INCHES TALL.
SHE WISHED SHE COULD BE SHORTER.
RIRIKO FULFILLED HER WISH ...
BY SEVERING BOTH HER LEGS.
GASP
DO YOU GET IT NOW?
RIRIKO WILL FULFILL YOUR WISH, AND IT WILL HAPPEN...
BY ANY MEANS NECESSARY!

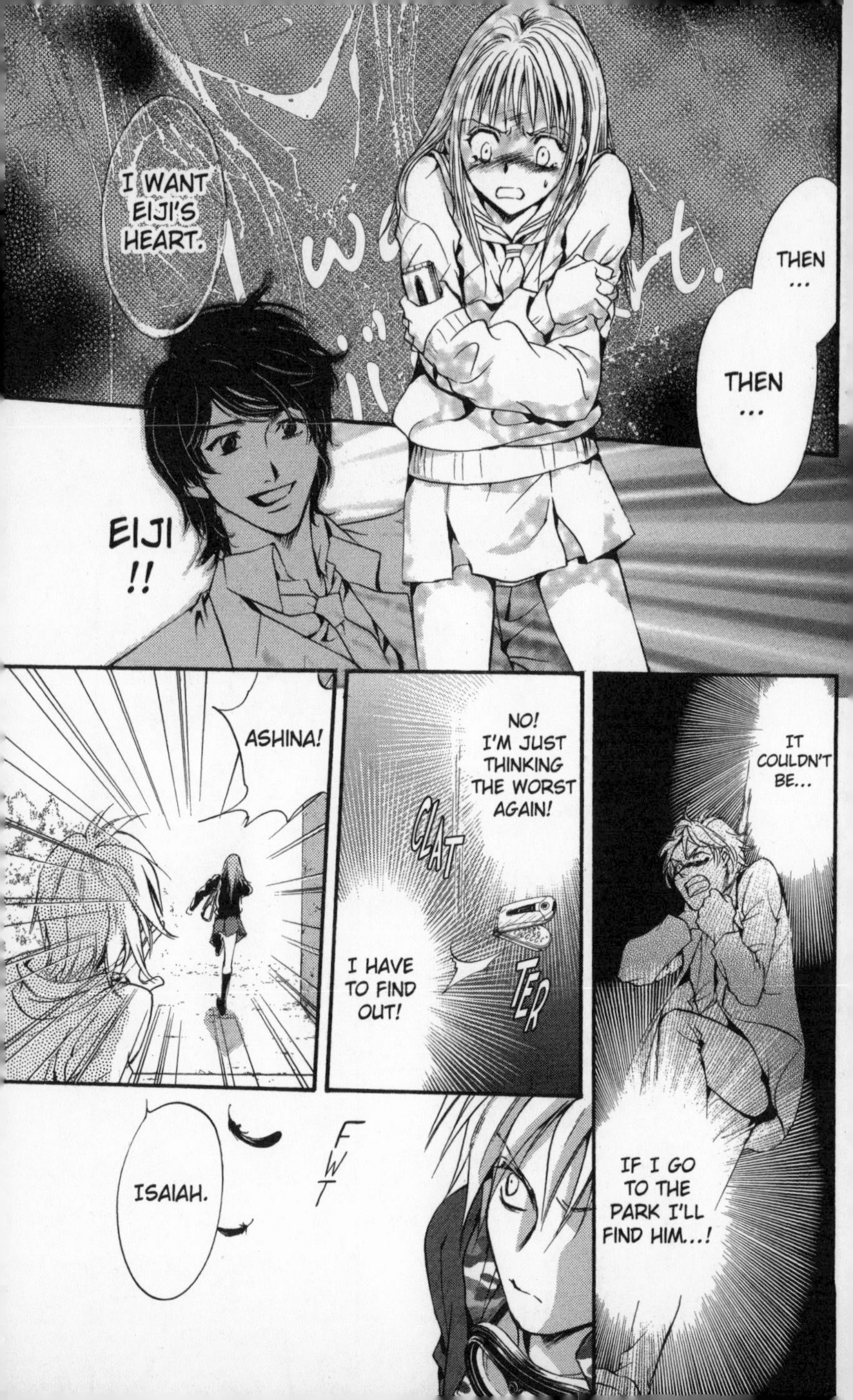
THEN...
THEN...
I WANT EIJI'S HEART.
EIJI!!
IT COULDN'T BE...
IF I GO TO THE PARK I'LL FIND HIM...!
NO! I'M JUST THINKING THE WORST AGAIN!
CLATTER
I HAVE TO FIND OUT!
ASHINA!
FWT
ISAIAH.

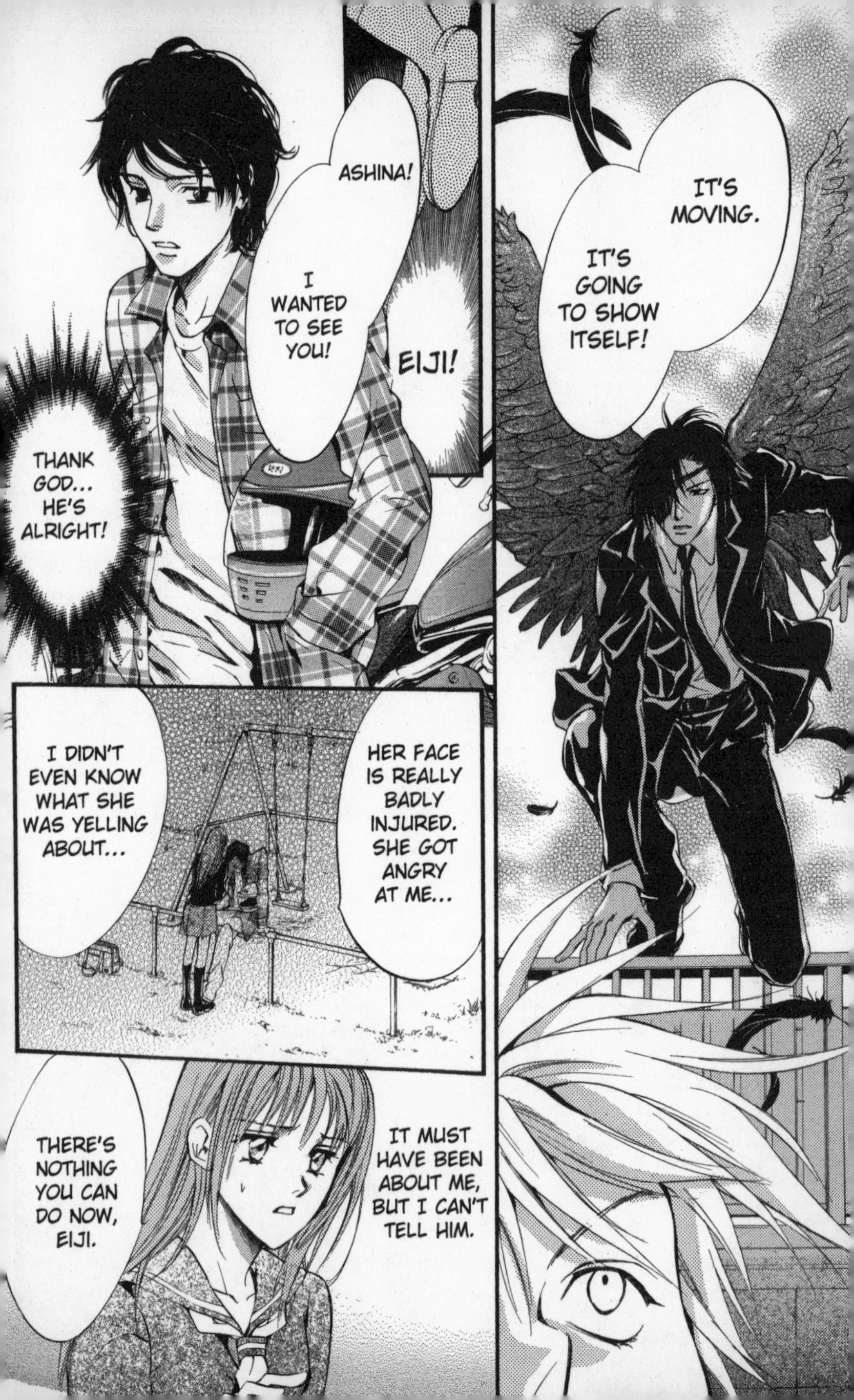
IT'S MOVING. IT'S GOING TO SHOW ITSELF!
ASHINA! I WANTED TO SEE YOU!
EIJI!
THANK GOD... HE'S ALRIGHT!
HER FACE IS REALLY BADLY INJURED. SHE GOT ANGRY AT ME...
I DIDN'T EVEN KNOW WHAT SHE WAS YELLING ABOUT...
IT MUST HAVE BEEN ABOUT ME, BUT I CAN'T TELL HIM.
THERE'S NOTHING YOU CAN DO NOW, EIJI.

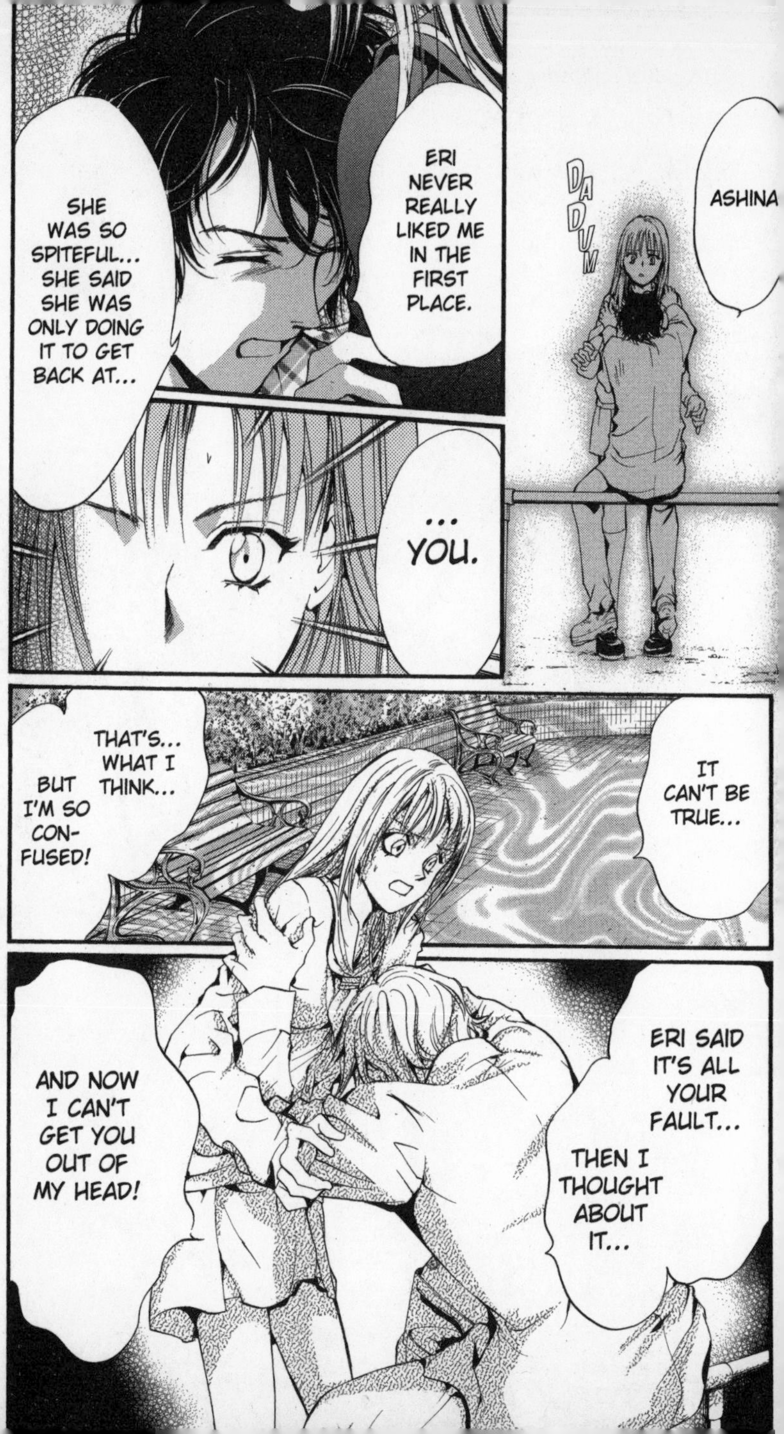
ASHINA
DADUM
ERI NEVER REALLY LIKED ME IN THE FIRST PLACE.
SHE WAS SO SPITEFUL... SHE SAID SHE WAS ONLY DOING IT TO GET BACK AT...
... YOU.
IT CAN'T BE TRUE...
THAT'S... WHAT I THINK...
BUT I'M SO CON-FUSED!
ERI SAID IT'S ALL YOUR FAULT...
THEN I THOUGHT ABOUT IT...
AND NOW I CAN'T GET YOU OUT OF MY HEAD!

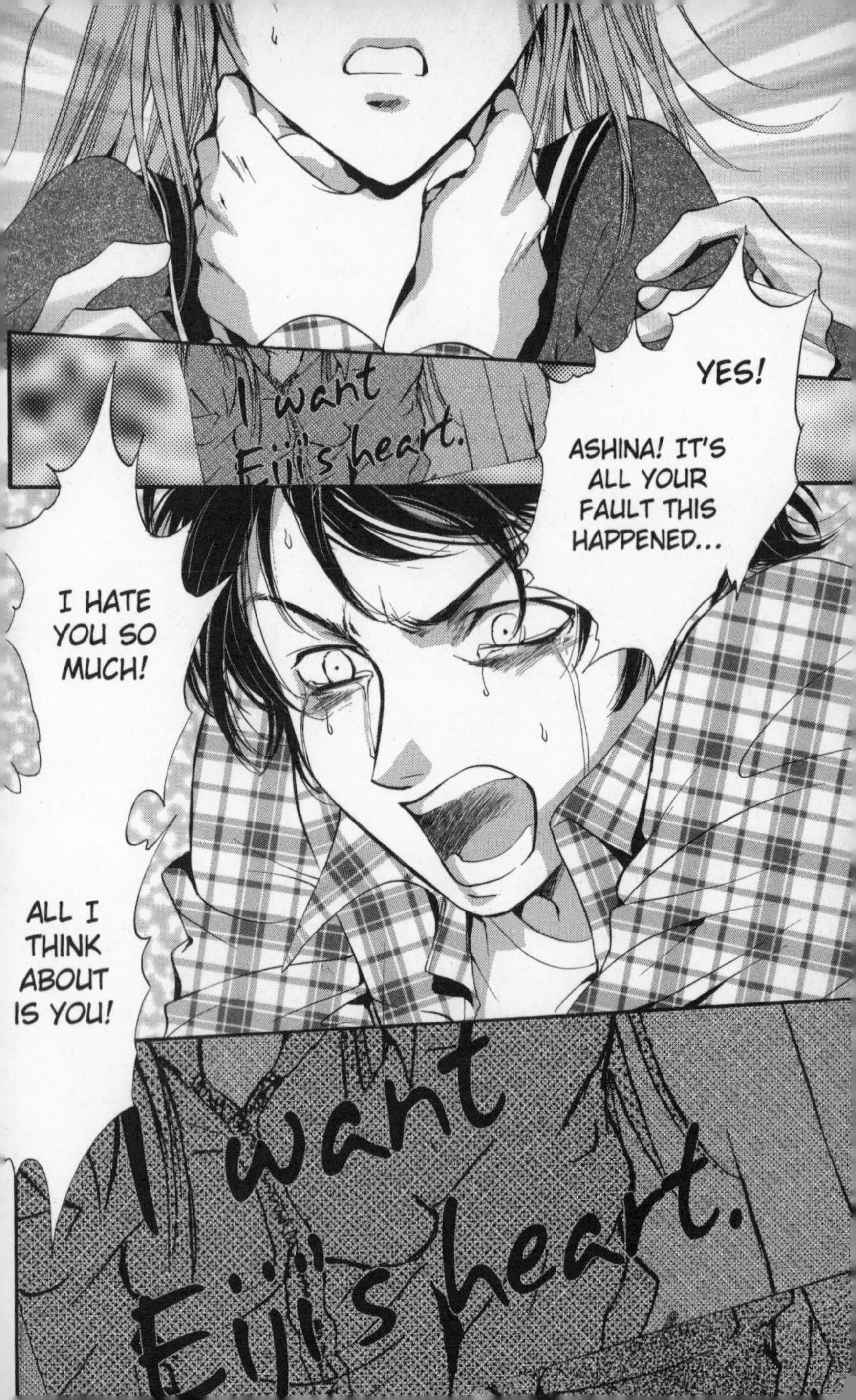
YES!
ASHINA! IT'S ALL YOUR FAULT THIS HAPPENED...
I want Eiji's heart.
I HATE YOU SO MUCH!
ALL I THINK ABOUT IS YOU!
I want Eiji's heart.

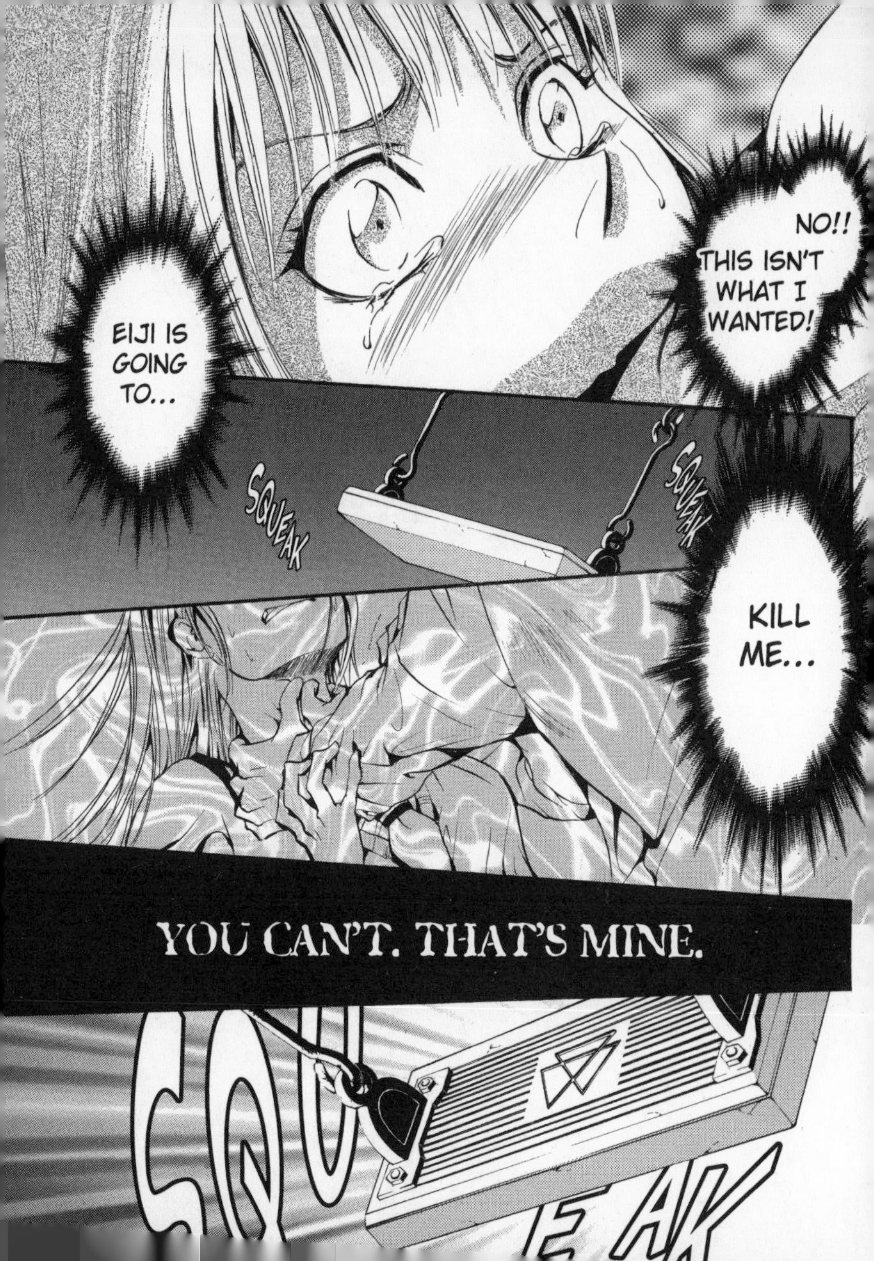
NO!! THIS ISN'T WHAT I WANTED!
EIJI IS GOING TO...
SQUEAK
SQUEAK
KILL ME...
YOU CAN'T. THAT'S MINE.
SQUEAK

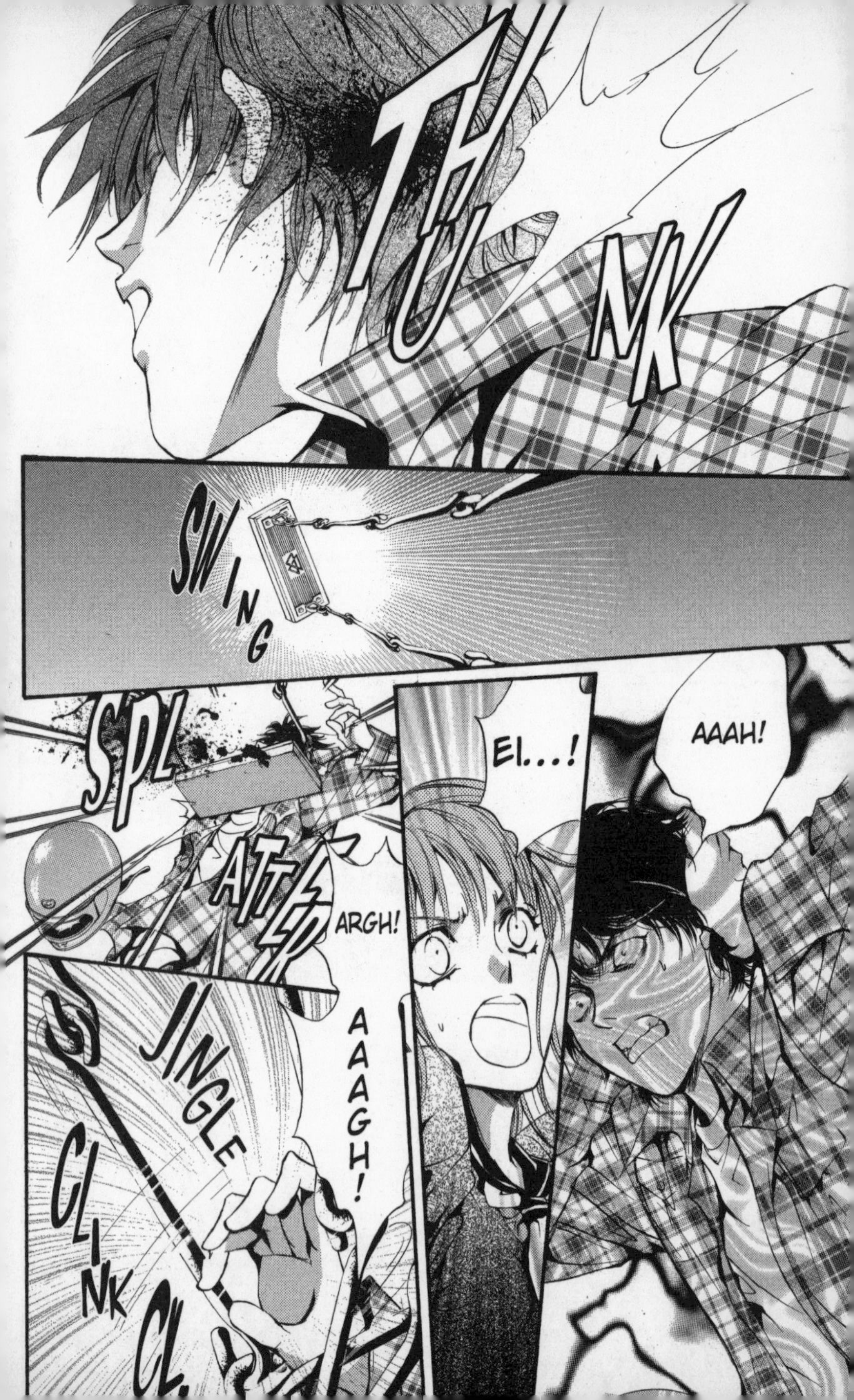
THUNK
SWING
AAAH!
EI...!
SPLATTER
ARGH!
AAAAGH!
JINGLE
CLINK
CL.

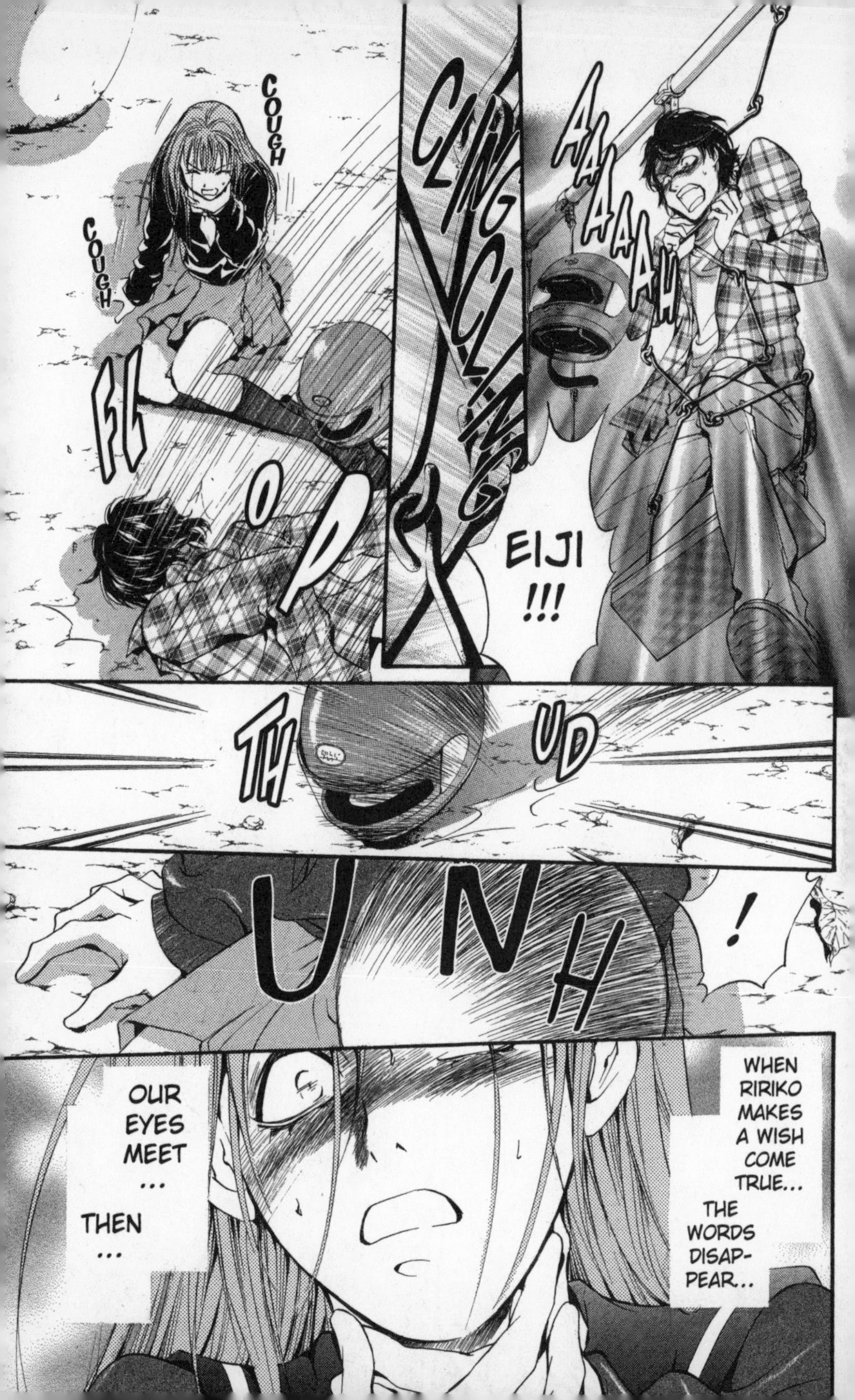
AAAAAAH
EIJI!!!
CLING CLING CLING
COUGH COUGH
COUGH COUGH
FLOP
THUD
UNH!
WHEN RIRIKO MAKES A WISH COME TRUE...
THE WORDS DISAPPEAR...
OUR EYES MEET...
THEN...

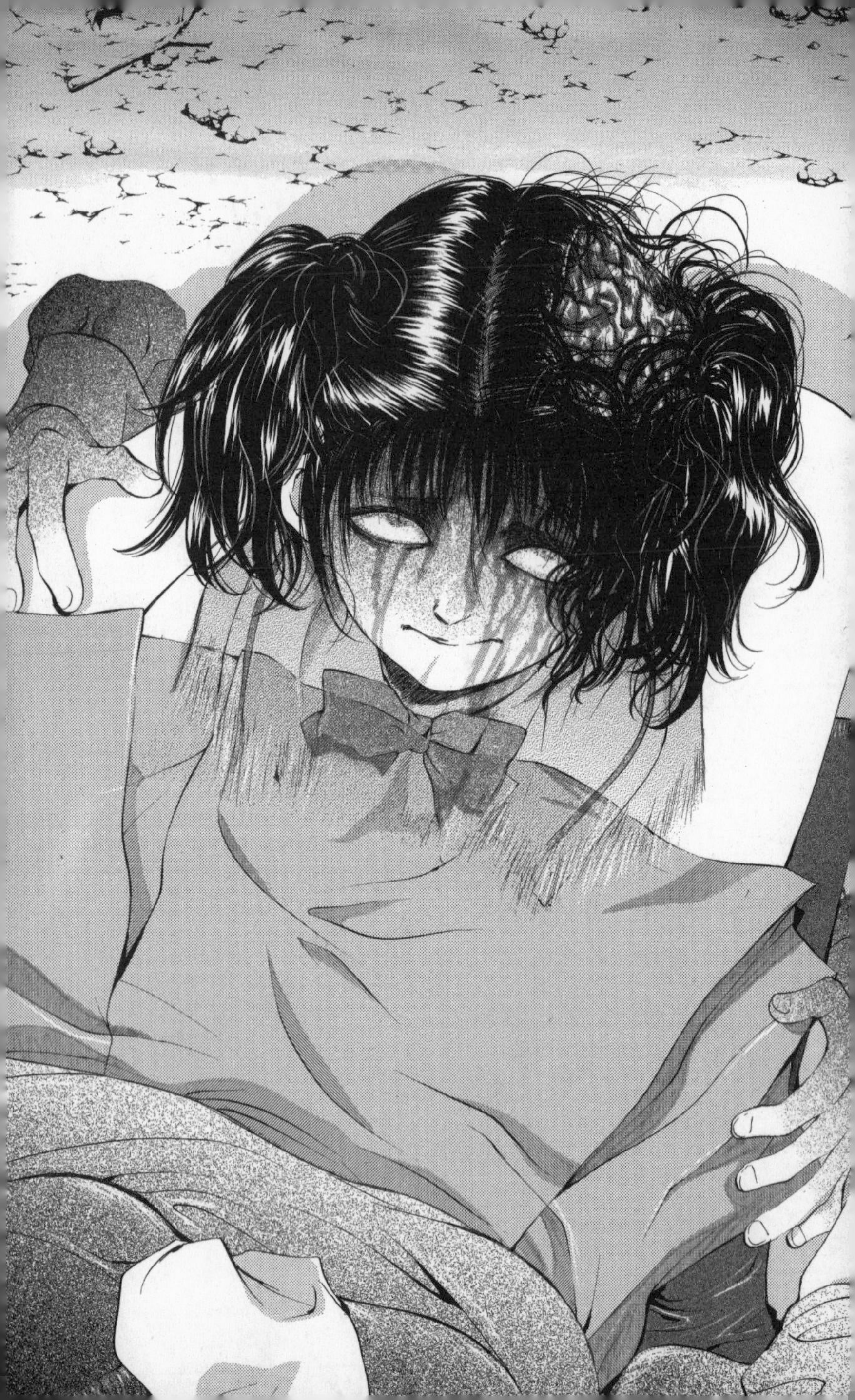

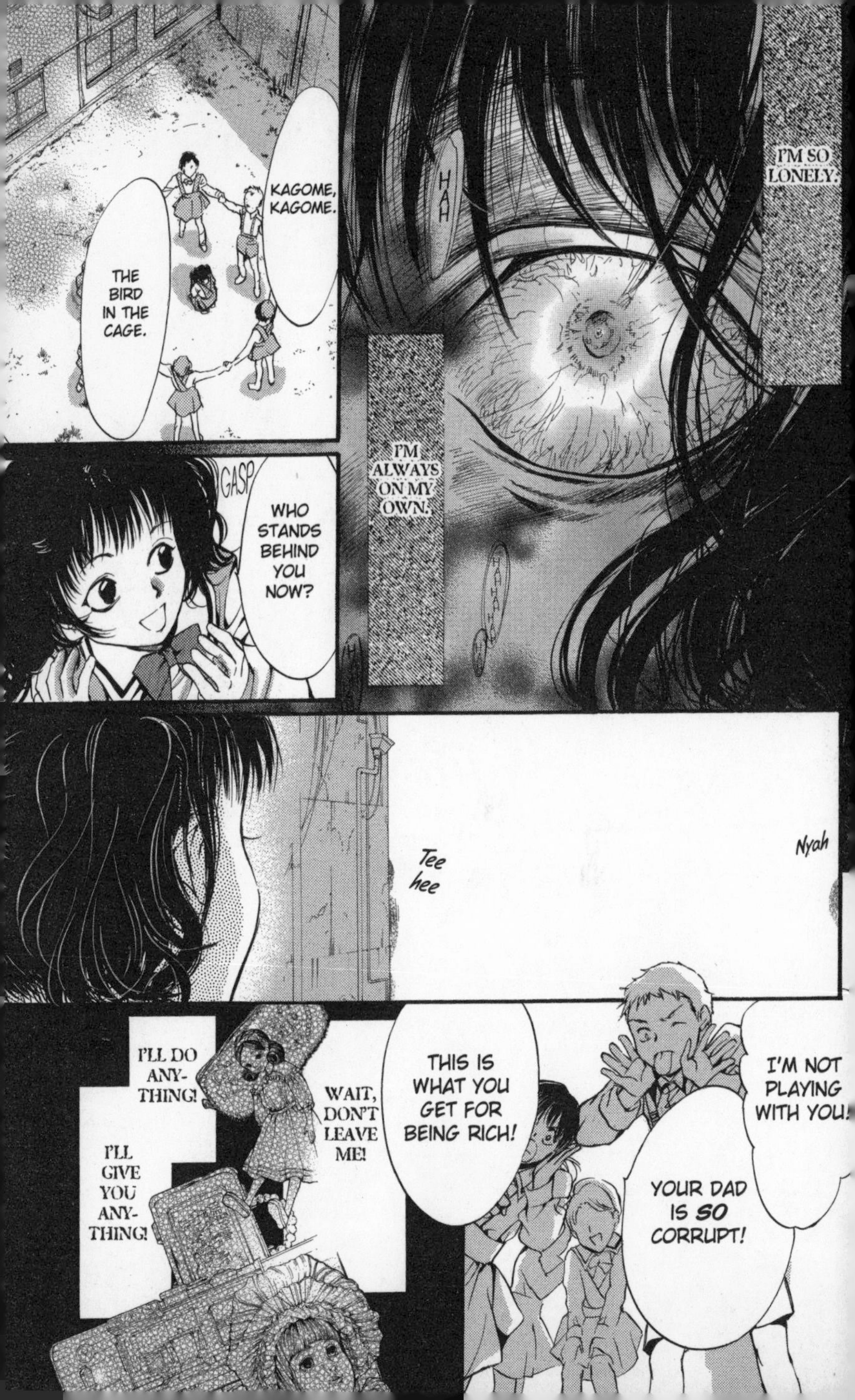
I'M SO LONELY.
HAH
I'M ALWAYS ON MY OWN.
KAGOME, KAGOME.
THE BIRD IN THE CAGE.
GASP
WHO STANDS BEHIND YOU NOW?
Nyah
Tee hee
I'M NOT PLAYING WITH YOU!
YOUR DAD IS *SO* CORRUPT!
THIS IS WHAT YOU GET FOR BEING RICH!
WAIT, DON'T LEAVE ME!
I'LL DO ANY-THING!
I'LL GIVE YOU ANY-THING!

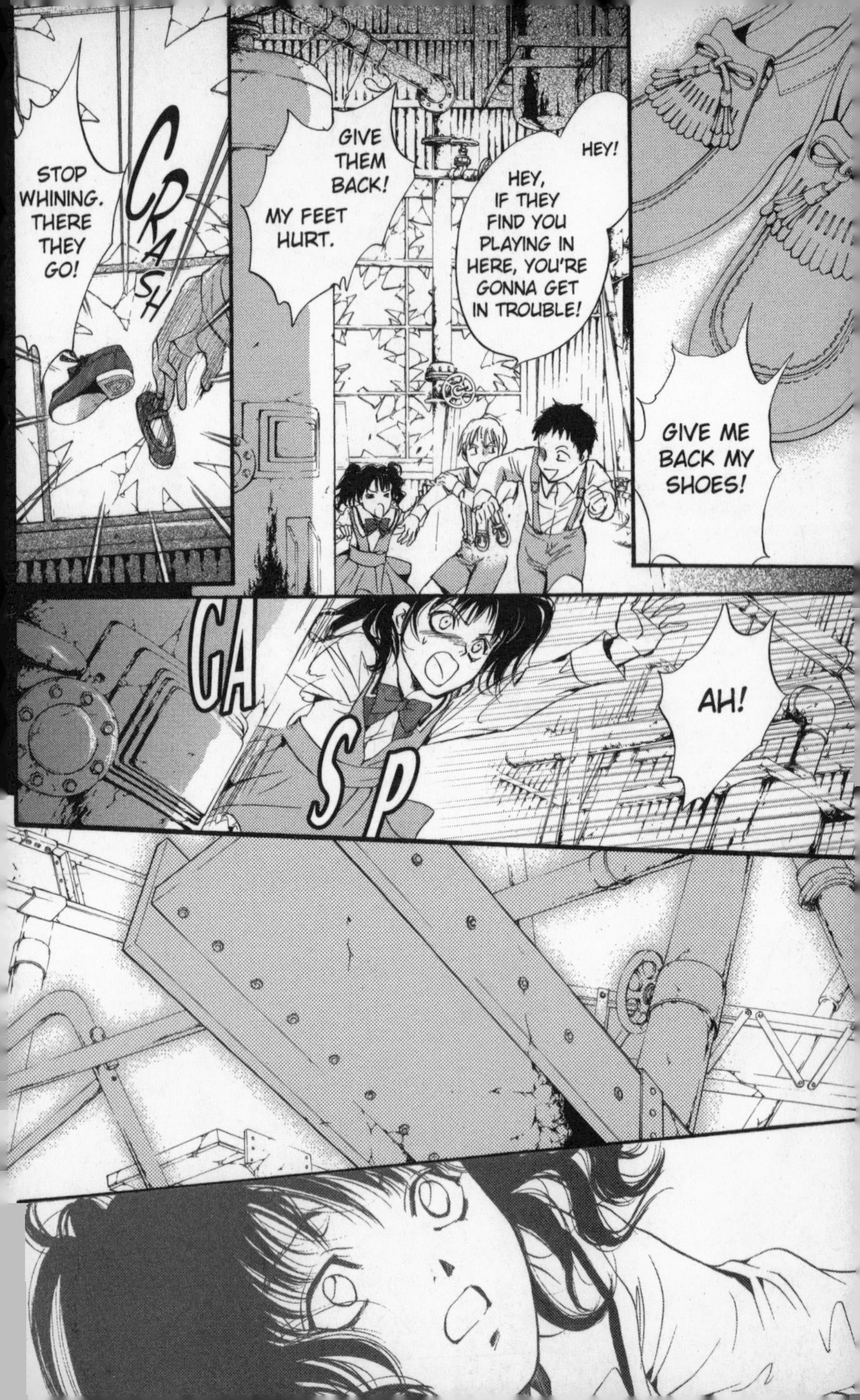

GIVE ME BACK MY SHOES!
HEY!
HEY, IF THEY FIND YOU PLAYING IN HERE, YOU'RE GONNA GET IN TROUBLE!
GIVE THEM BACK!
MY FEET HURT.
CRASH
STOP WHINING. THERE THEY GO!
AH!
GASP

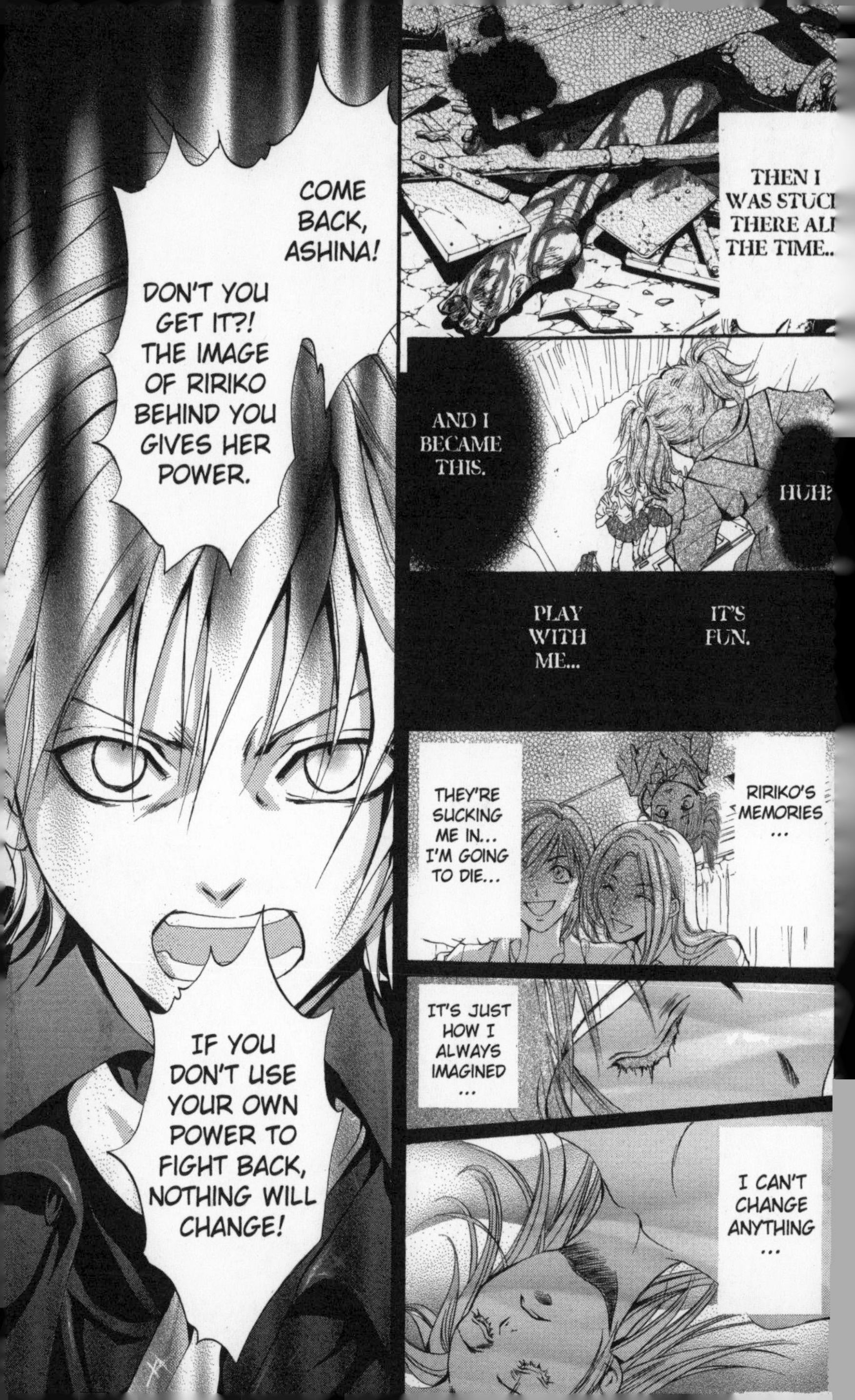
THEN I WAS STUC THERE AL THE TIME..
HUH?
AND I BECAME THIS.
IT'S FUN.
PLAY WITH ME...
RIRIKO'S MEMORIES...
THEY'RE SUCKING ME IN... I'M GOING TO DIE...
IT'S JUST HOW I ALWAYS IMAGINED...
I CAN'T CHANGE ANYTHING...
COME BACK, ASHINA!
DON'T YOU GET IT?! THE IMAGE OF RIRIKO BEHIND YOU GIVES HER POWER.
IF YOU DON'T USE YOUR OWN POWER TO FIGHT BACK, NOTHING WILL CHANGE!

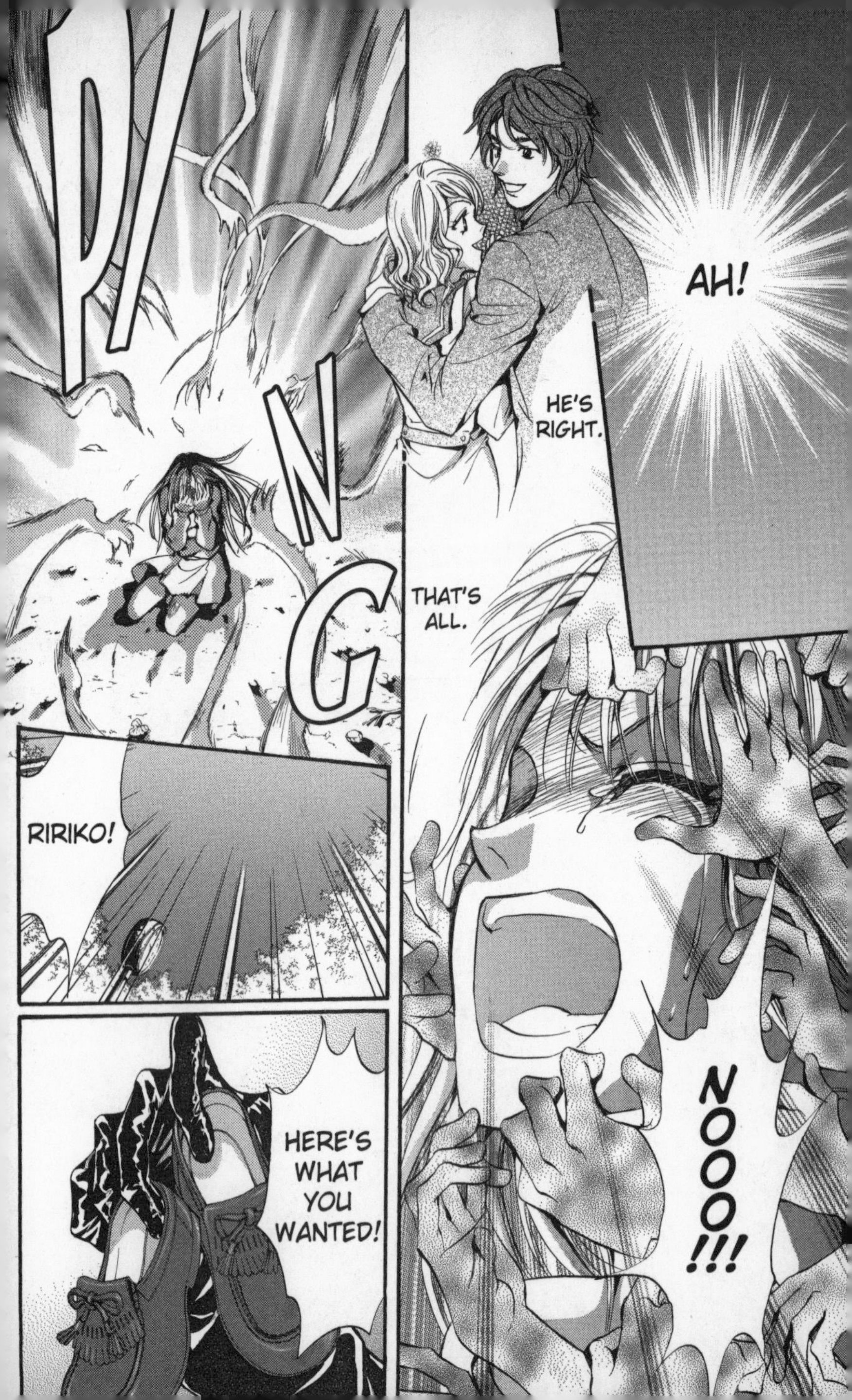
AH!
HE'S RIGHT.
THAT'S ALL.
NOOOO!!!
PING
RIRIKO!
HERE'S WHAT YOU WANTED!

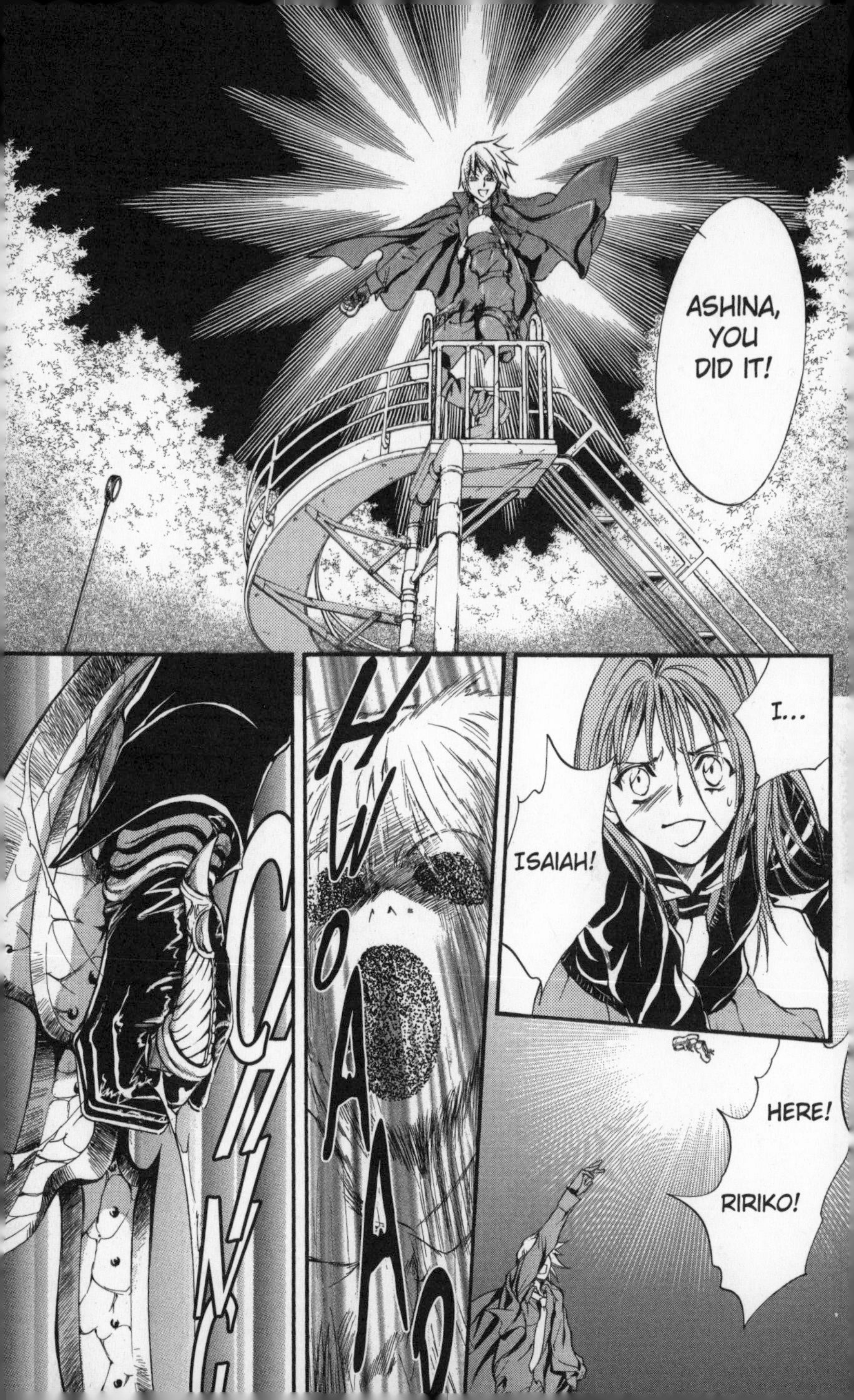
ASHINA, YOU DID IT!
I...
ISAIAH!
HERE!
RIRIKO!

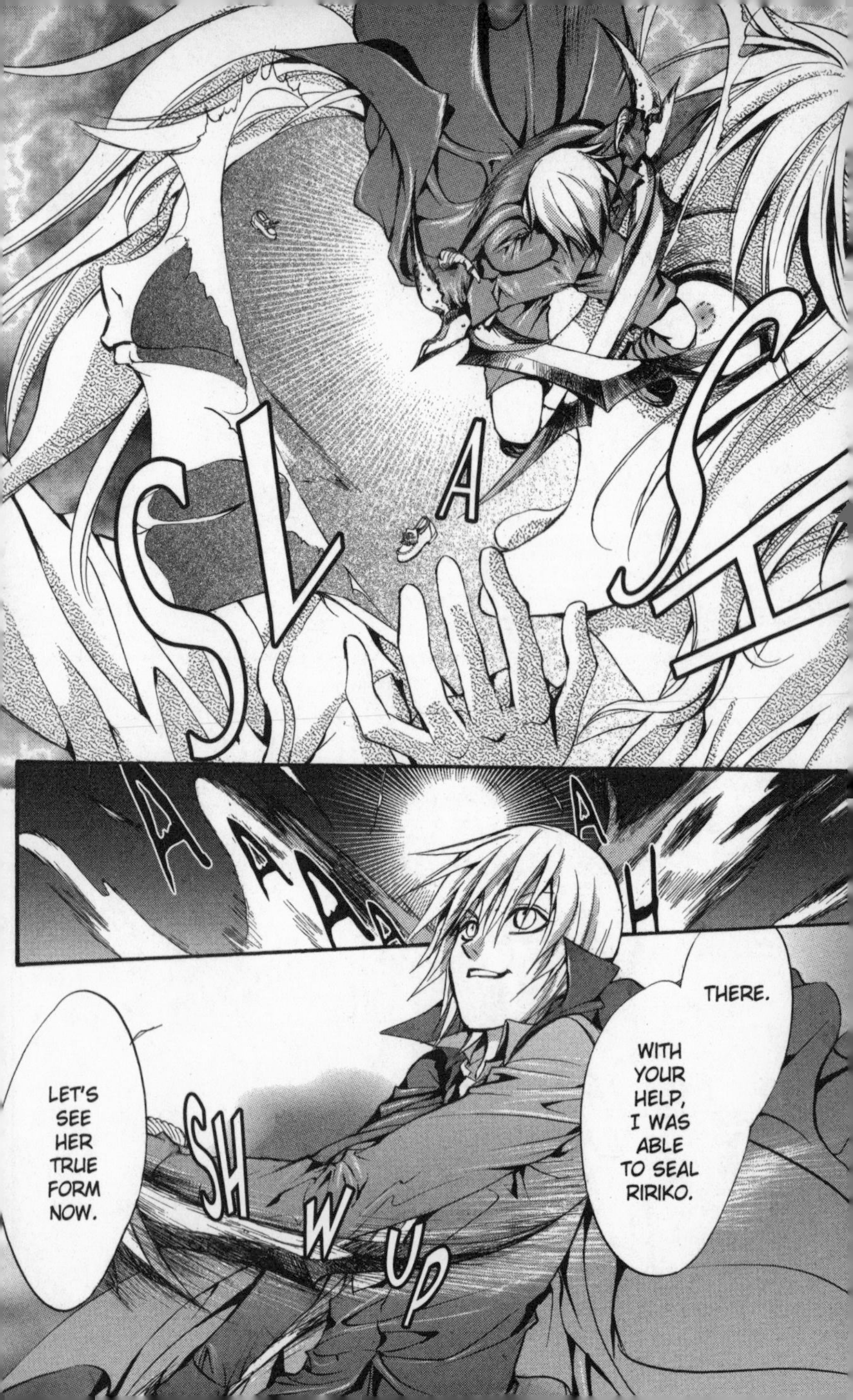
SLASH
AAAAAAH
THERE.
WITH YOUR HELP, I WAS ABLE TO SEAL RIRIKO.
SHWUP
LET'S SEE HER TRUE FORM NOW.

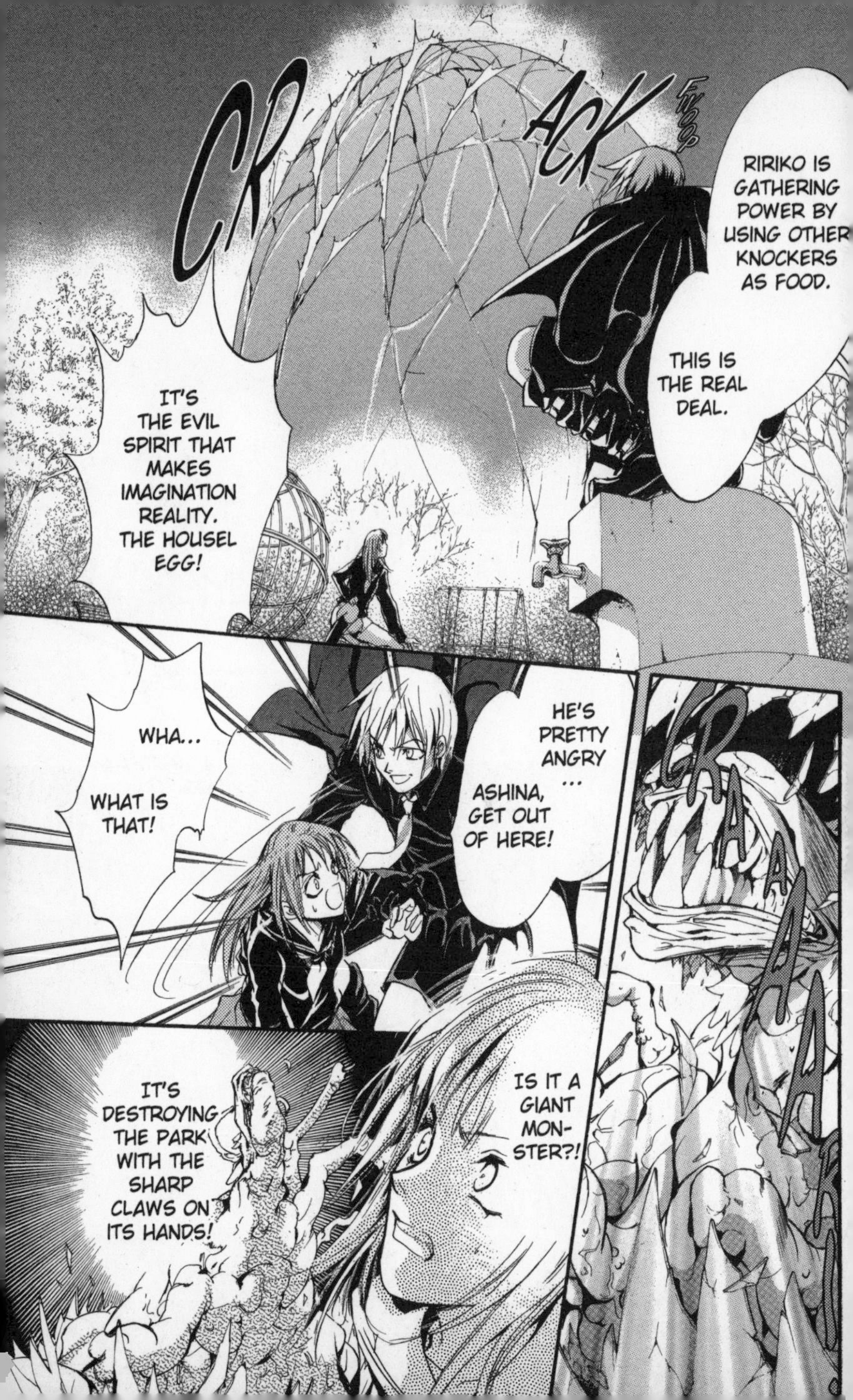
CRACK
FWOOP
RIRIKO IS GATHERING POWER BY USING OTHER KNOCKERS AS FOOD.
THIS IS THE REAL DEAL.
IT'S THE EVIL SPIRIT THAT MAKES IMAGINATION REALITY. THE HOUSEL EGG!
CRAAAA
HE'S PRETTY ANGRY...
ASHINA, GET OUT OF HERE!
WHA...
WHAT IS THAT!
IS IT A GIANT MON-STER?!
IT'S DESTROYING THE PARK WITH THE SHARP CLAWS ON ITS HANDS!

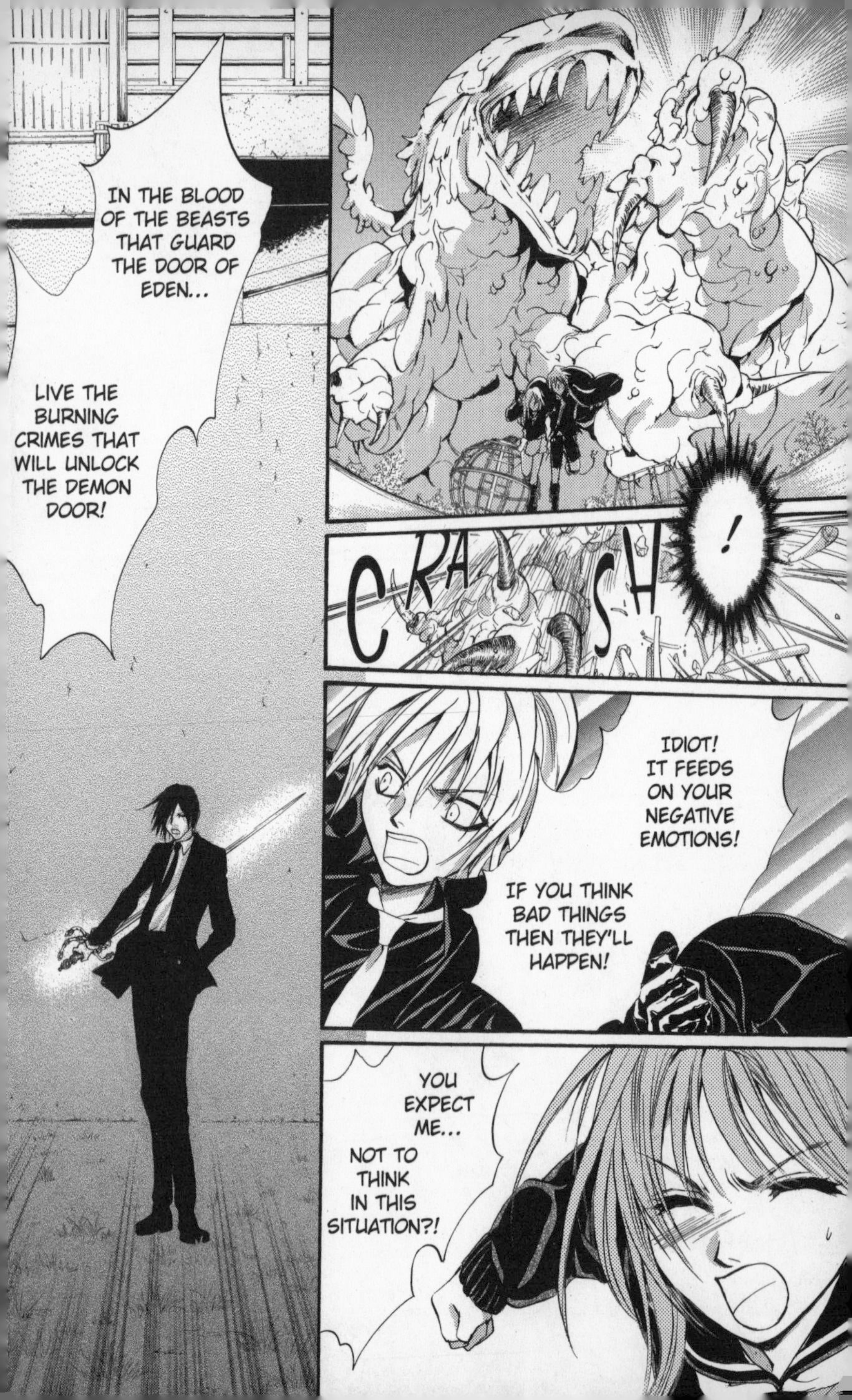

!
CRASH
IDIOT! IT FEEDS ON YOUR NEGATIVE EMOTIONS!
IF YOU THINK BAD THINGS THEN THEY'LL HAPPEN!
YOU EXPECT ME...
NOT TO THINK IN THIS SITUATION?!
IN THE BLOOD OF THE BEASTS THAT GUARD THE DOOR OF EDEN...
LIVE THE BURNING CRIMES THAT WILL UNLOCK THE DEMON DOOR!

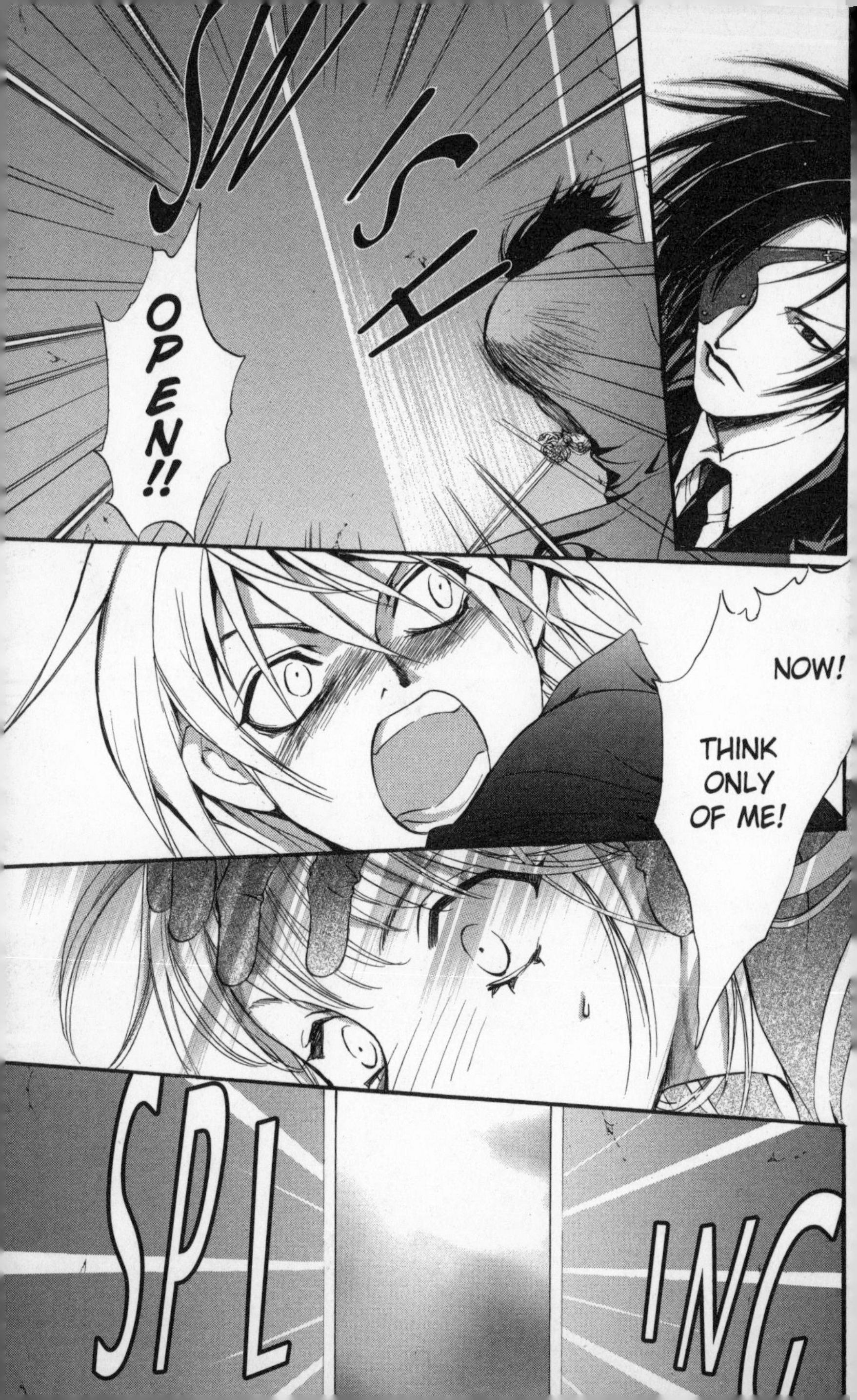
SWISH
OPEN!!
NOW!
THINK ONLY OF ME!
SPL ING

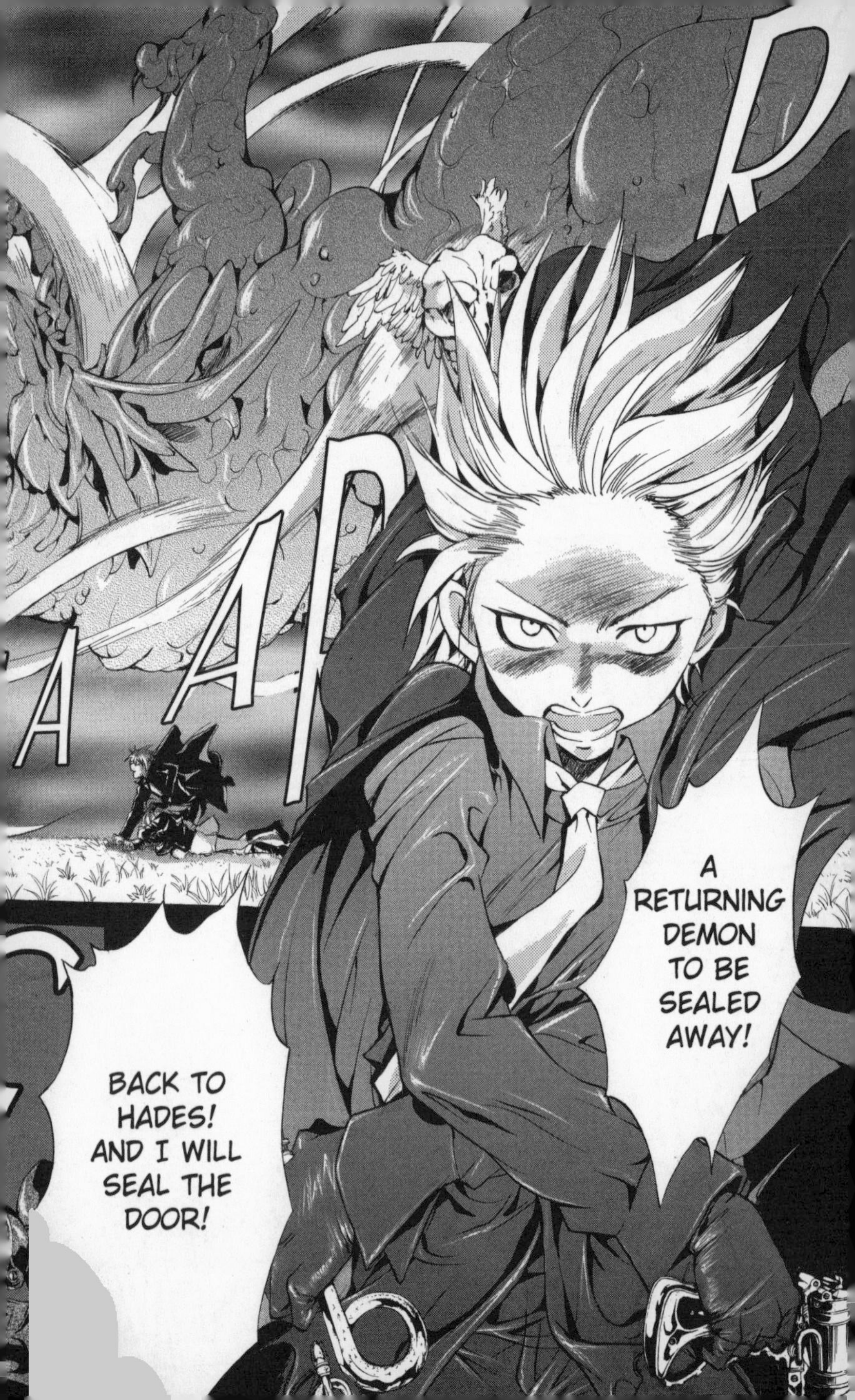
RAAA
A RETURNING DEMON TO BE SEALED AWAY!
BACK TO HADES! AND I WILL SEAL THE DOOR!

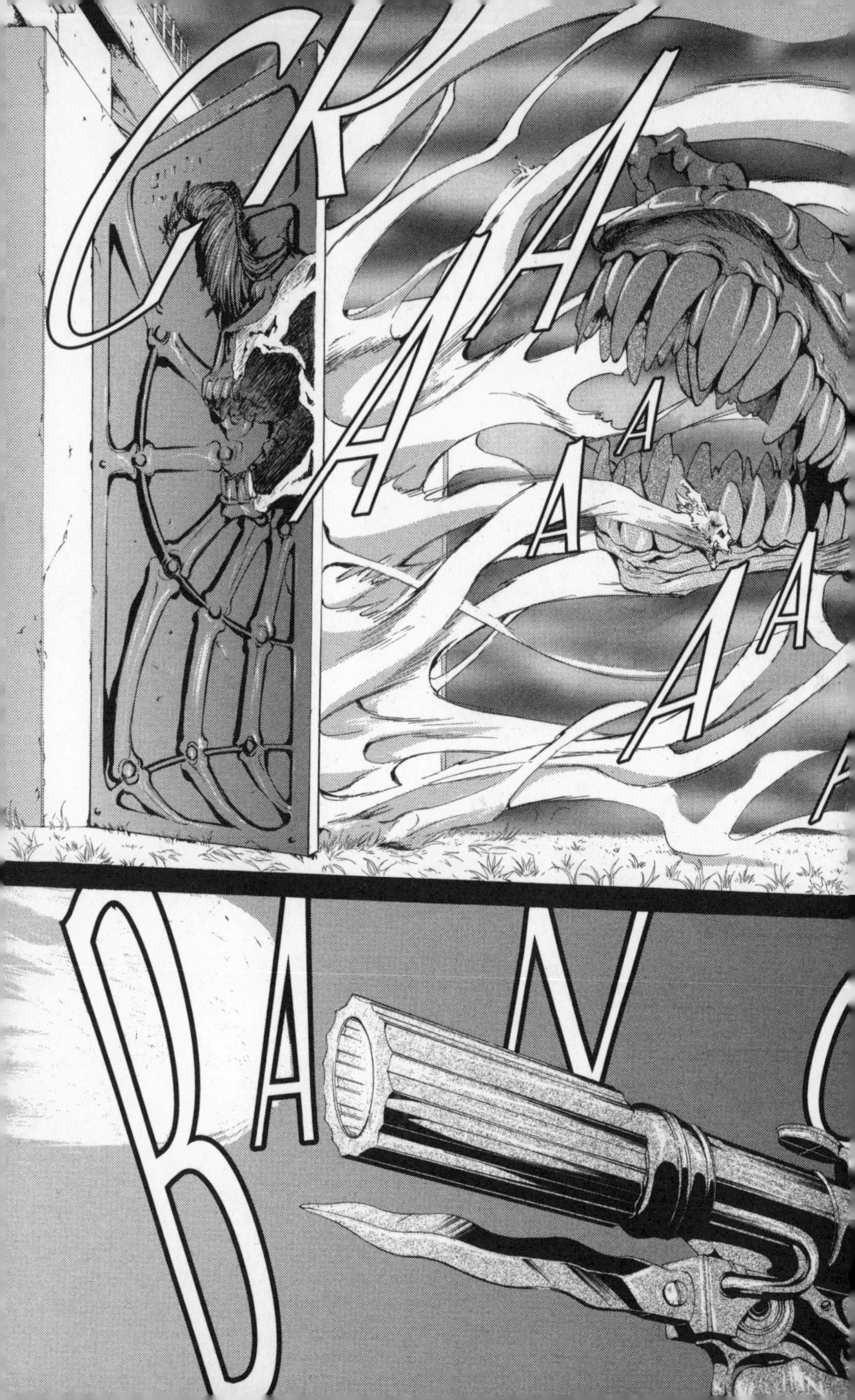
CKHAAAAAAA
BAN

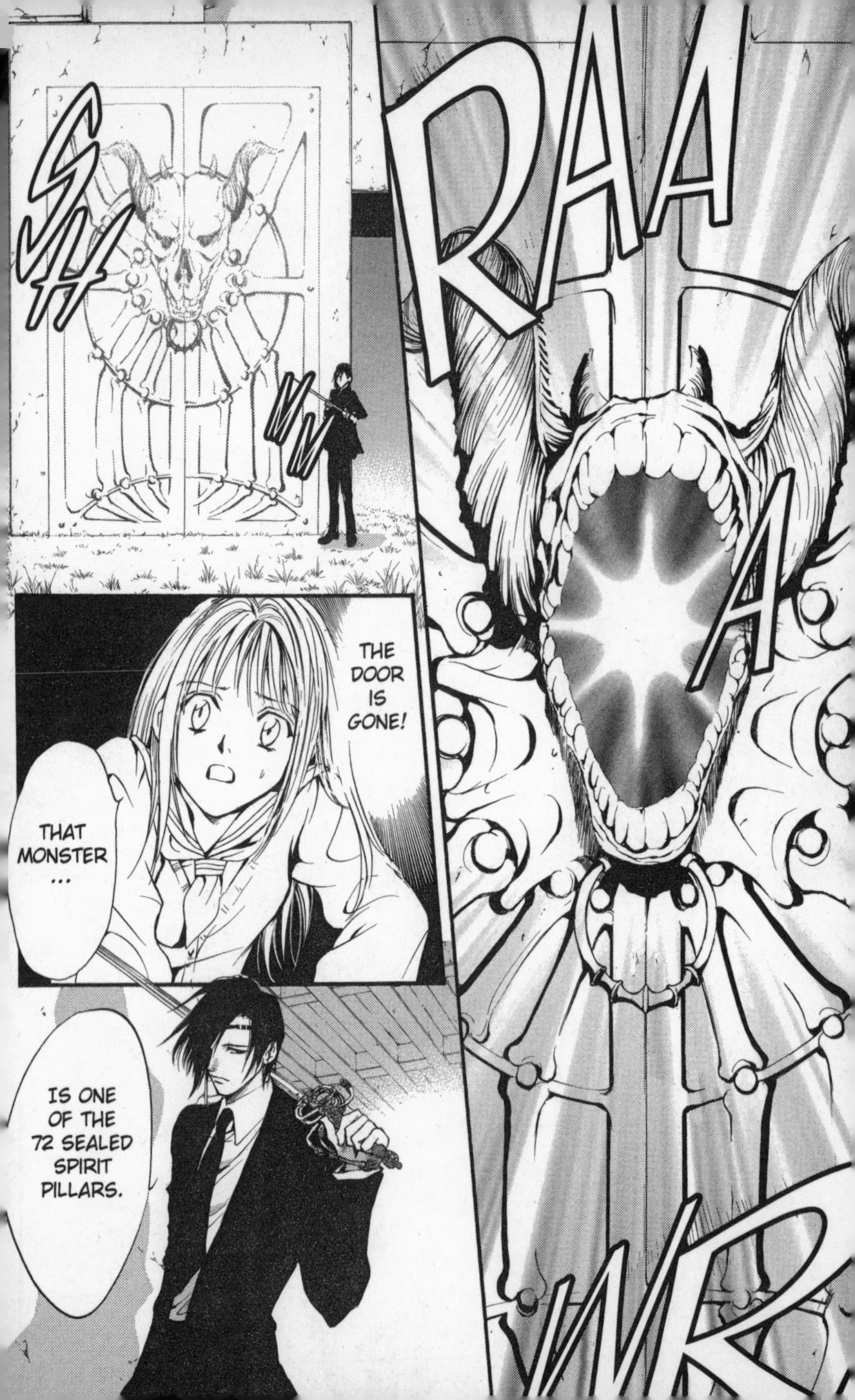
RAAAWR
SH
THE DOOR IS GONE!
THAT MONSTER ...
IS ONE OF THE 72 SEALED SPIRIT PILLARS.

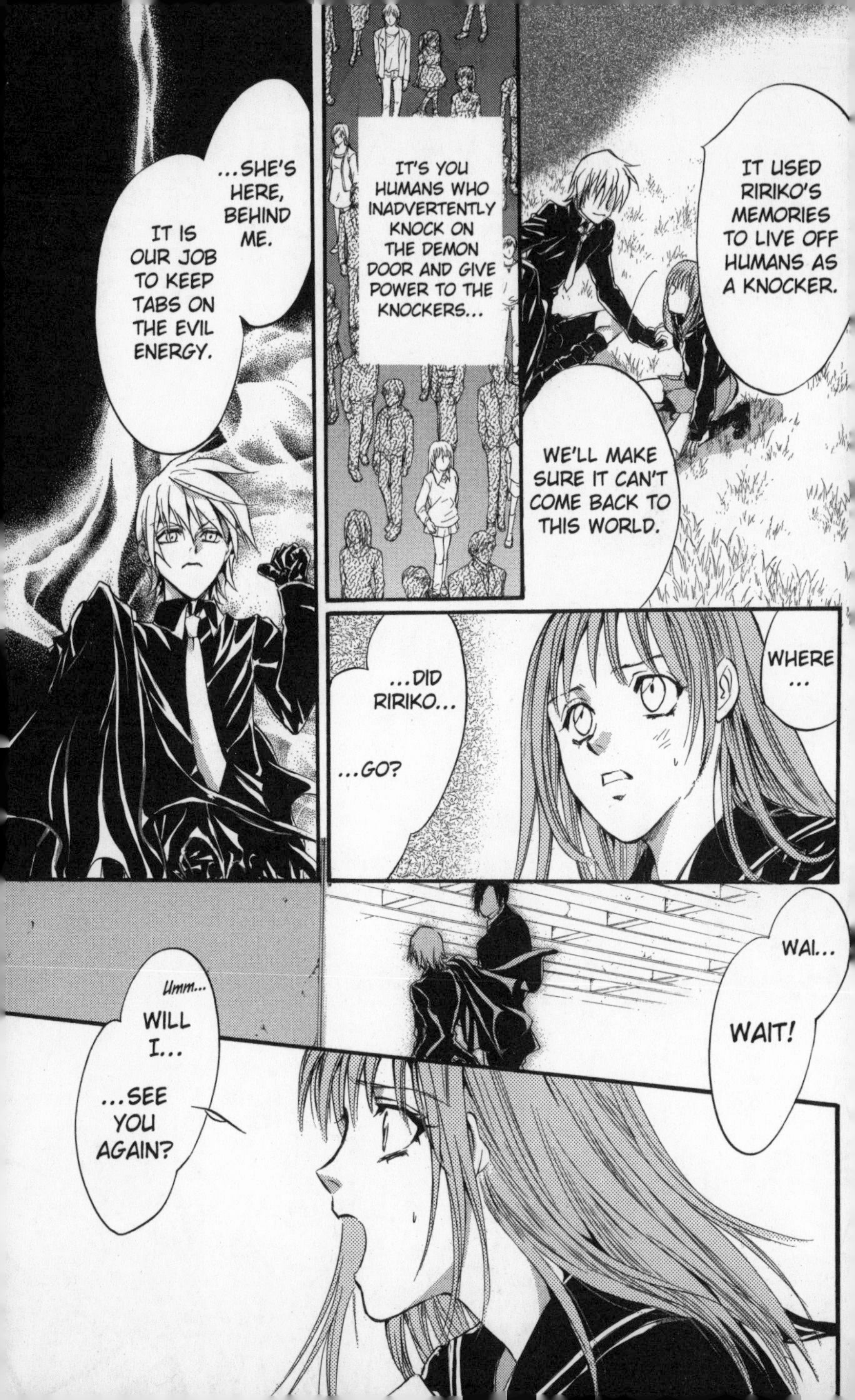
IT USED RIRIKO'S MEMORIES TO LIVE OFF HUMANS AS A KNOCKER.
WE'LL MAKE SURE IT CAN'T COME BACK TO THIS WORLD.
IT'S YOU HUMANS WHO INADVERTENTLY KNOCK ON THE DEMON DOOR AND GIVE POWER TO THE KNOCKERS...
WHERE...
...DID RIRIKO...
...GO?
...SHE'S HERE, BEHIND ME.
IT IS OUR JOB TO KEEP TABS ON THE EVIL ENERGY.
WAI...
WAIT!
Umm...
WILL I...
...SEE YOU AGAIN?

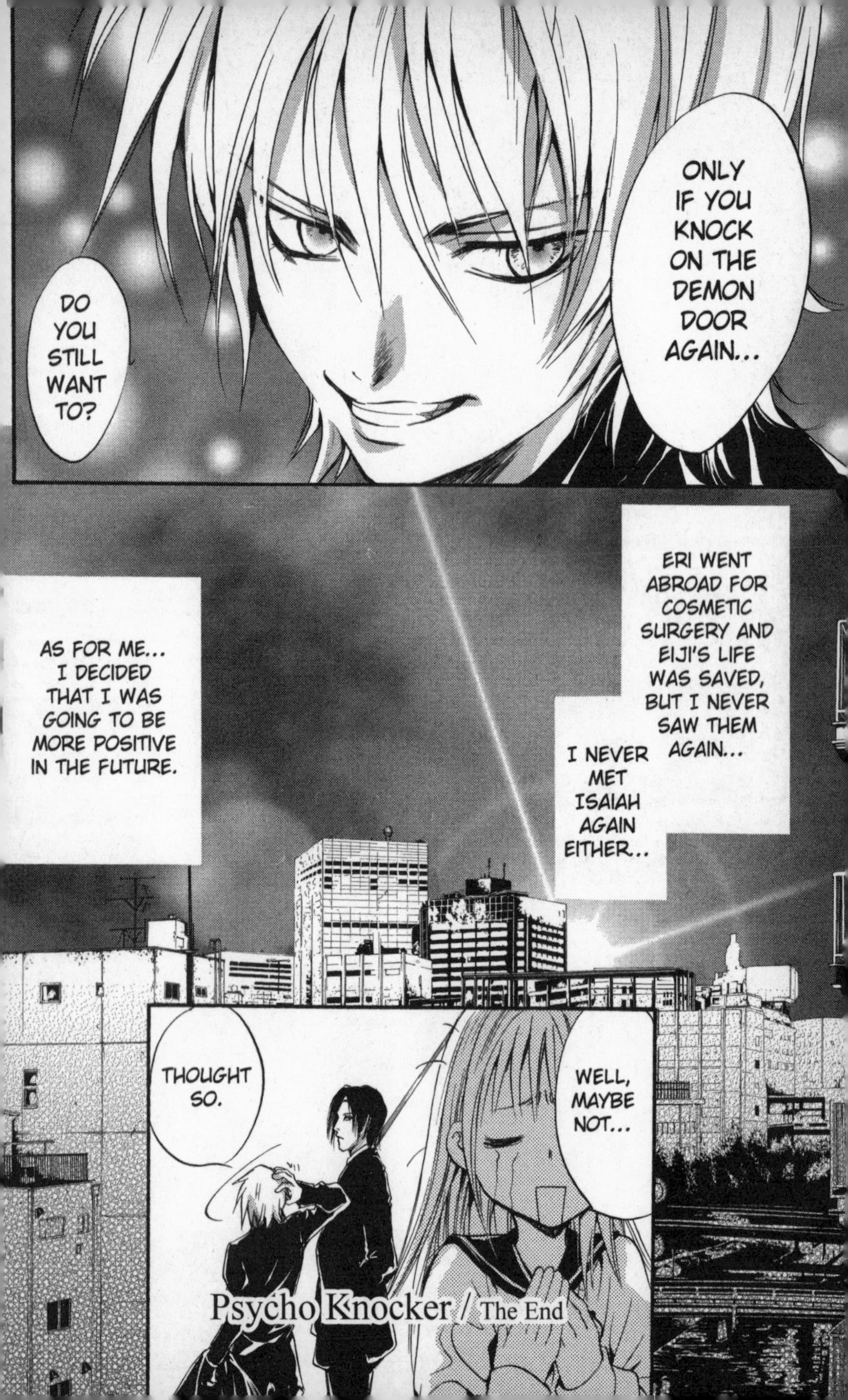
ONLY IF YOU KNOCK ON THE DEMON DOOR AGAIN...
DO YOU STILL WANT TO?
ERI WENT ABROAD FOR COSMETIC SURGERY AND EIJI'S LIFE WAS SAVED, BUT I NEVER SAW THEM AGAIN...
I NEVER MET ISAIAH AGAIN EITHER...
AS FOR ME... I DECIDED THAT I WAS GOING TO BE MORE POSITIVE IN THE FUTURE.
WELL, MAYBE NOT...
THOUGHT SO.
Psycho Knocker / The End

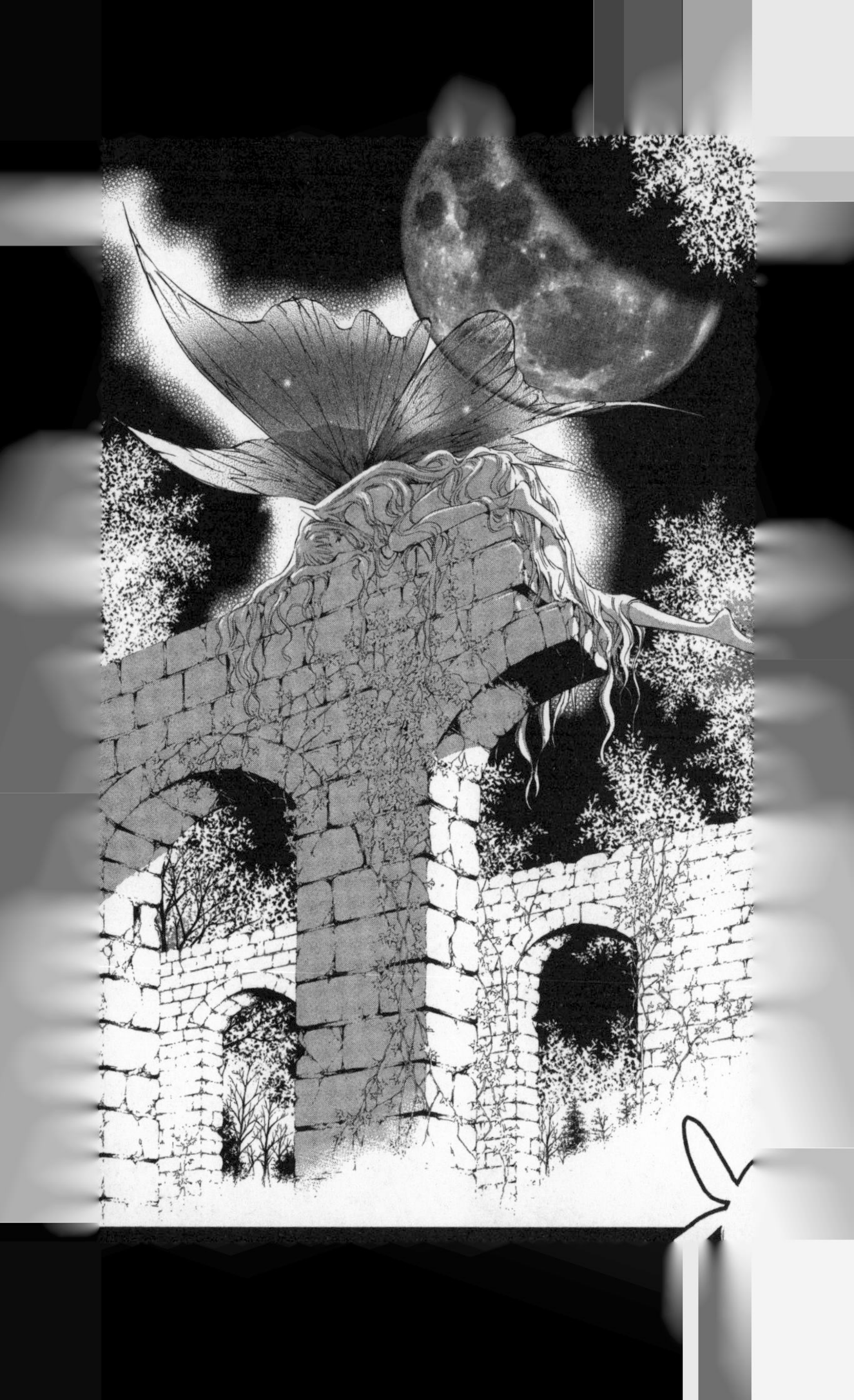

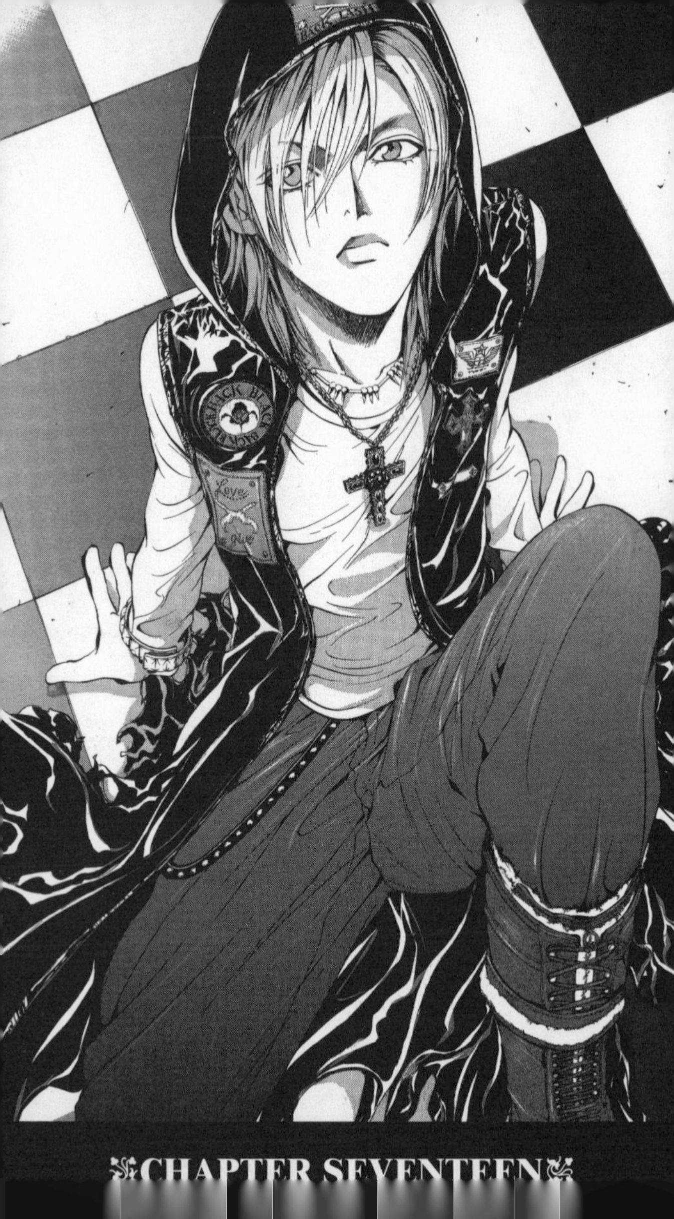

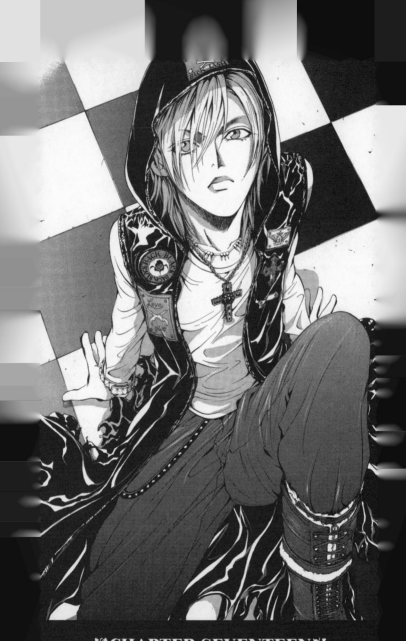

CHAPTER SEVENTEEN

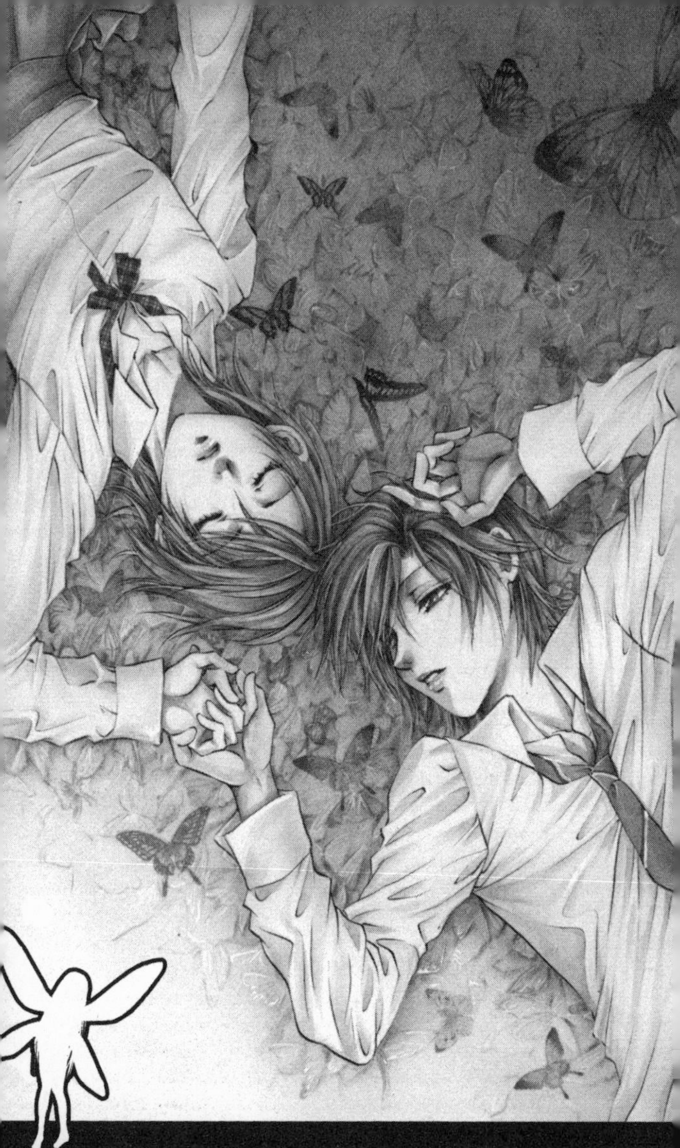

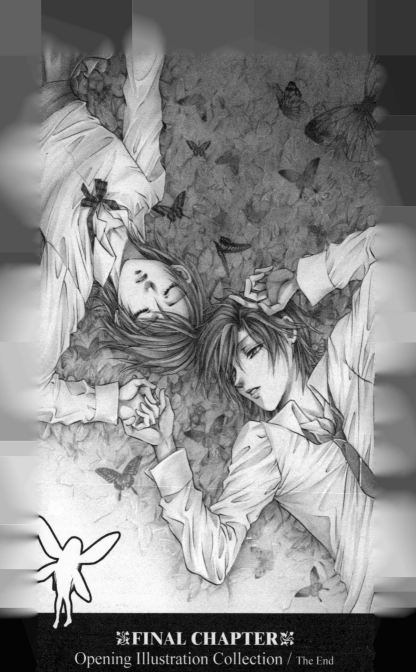

FINAL CHAPTER

Opening Illustration Collection / The End

Final Bonus Strip

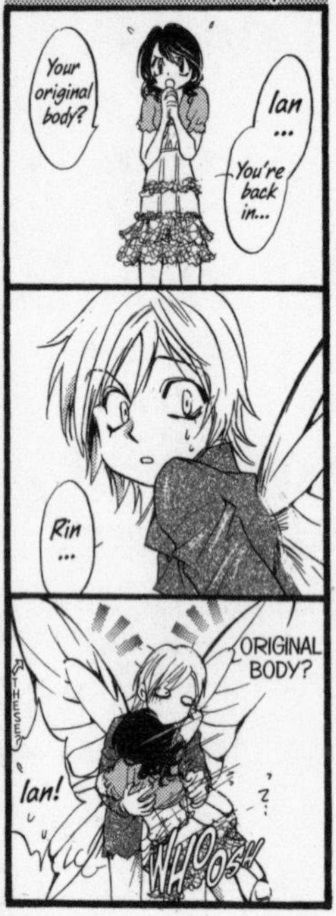
Ian ... You're back in...
Your original body?
Rin ...
ORIGINAL BODY?
Ian!
WHOOSH!

THE END

This face I drew looked more human than Fairylike. Maybe it's just this picture.

←This was my first rough drawing of Ian. I developed him from this... I hope to see you all again soon!♡

I only had a certain number of pages in the magazine, but I managed to fit a lot into part three, plus *Psycho Knocker.* Was it too much? It would have been nice if there were more on Ian and Tokage (Isaiah) making friends. But the main plot was Ian and Rin.° I thought about writing a sadder ending (with the door using Ian and Rin as a seal), but I didn't want to leave a nasty aftertaste. Well... I actually do like sad endings. But I really wanted to draw the fairies as one big happy family. Sea and water fairies and gray earth fairies. The Dullahan, or Headless Horseman, is really cool too!

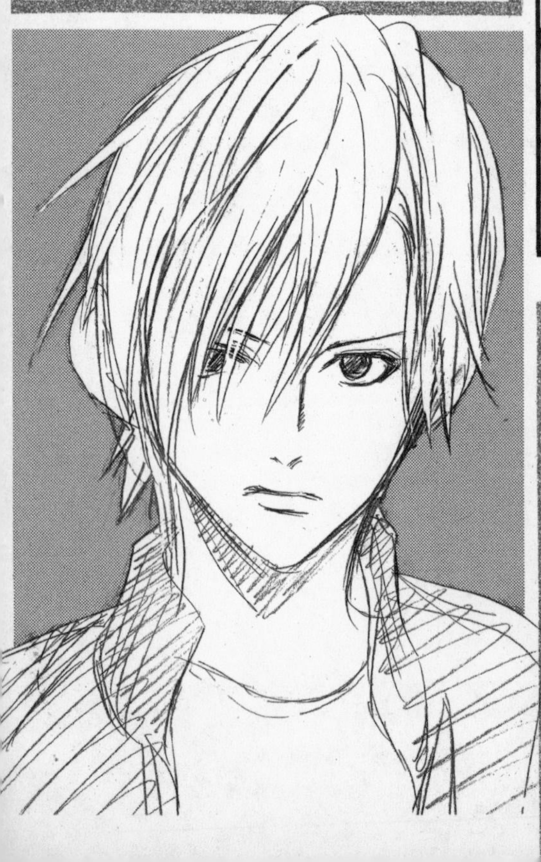

Creator: Kaori Yuki

Date of Birth: December 18

Blood Type: B

Major Works: *Angel Sanctuary* and *Godchild*

Kaori Yuki was born in Tokyo and started drawing at a very early age. Following her debut work *Natsufuku no Erie* (Ellie in Summer Clothes) in the Japanese magazine *Bessatsu Hana to Yume* (1987), she wrote a compelling series of short stories: *Zankoku na Douwatachi* (Cruel Fairy Tales), *Neji* (Screw), and *Sareki Ōkoku* (Gravel Kingdom).

As proven by her best-selling series *Angel Sanctuary* and *Godchild*, her celebrated body of work has etched an indelible mark on the gothic comics genre. She likes mysteries and British films and is a fan of the movie *Dead Poets Society* and the television show *Twin Peaks*.

FAIRY CUBE

VOL. 3
The Shojo Beat Manga Edition

STORY AND ART BY KAORI YUKI

Translation/Gemma Collinge
English Adaptation/Kristina Blachere
Touch-up Art & Lettering/James Gaubatz
Design/Courtney Utt
Editor/Joel Enos

Editor in Chief, Books/Alvin Lu
Editor in Chief, Magazines/Marc Weidenbaum
VP of Publishing Licensing/Rika Inouye
VP of Sales/Gonzalo Ferreyra
Sr. VP of Marketing/Liza Coppola
Publisher/Hyoe Narita

Fairy Cube by Kaori Yuki © Kaori Yuki 2004. All rights reserved.
First published in Japan in 2006 by HAKUSENSHA, Inc., Tokyo.
English language translation rights arranged with
HAKUSENSHA, Inc., Tokyo.

Printed in Canada

Published by VIZ Media, LLC
P.O. Box 77010
San Francisco, CA 94107

Shojo Beat Manga Edition
10 9 8 7 6 5 4 3 2 1

First printing, November 2008

Love Kaori Yuki?

Read the rest of VIZ Media's Kaori Yuki Collection!

Angel Sanctuary
Rated T+ for Older Teen
20 Volumes

The angel Alexiel loved God, but she rebelled against Heaven when she saw how disgracefully the other angels were behaving. She was finally captured and, as punishment, sent to Earth to live an endless series of tragic lives. She now inhabits the body of Setsuna Mudo, a troubled teen in love with his sister Sara.

The Cain Saga
Rated M for Mature Readers
5 Volumes

Delve into the tortured past of Earl Cain C. Hargreaves, charismatic heir to a wealthy family full of secrets, lies and unthinkable crimes. The prequel to the *Godchild* series, *The Cain Saga* follows the young Cain as he attempts to unravel the secrets of his birth, all the while solving each new mystery that comes his way.

Godchild
Rated T+ for Older Teen
8 Volumes

In 19th century London, dashing young nobleman Earl Cain Hargreaves weaves his way through the shadowy cobblestone streets that hide the dark secrets of aristocratic society. With his young sister Mary Weather and his constant companion Riff, Cain sets out to solve the dangerous mystery of his disturbing lineage.

The Art of Angel Sanctuary:
Angel Cage

The Art of Angel Sanctuary 2:
Lost Angel

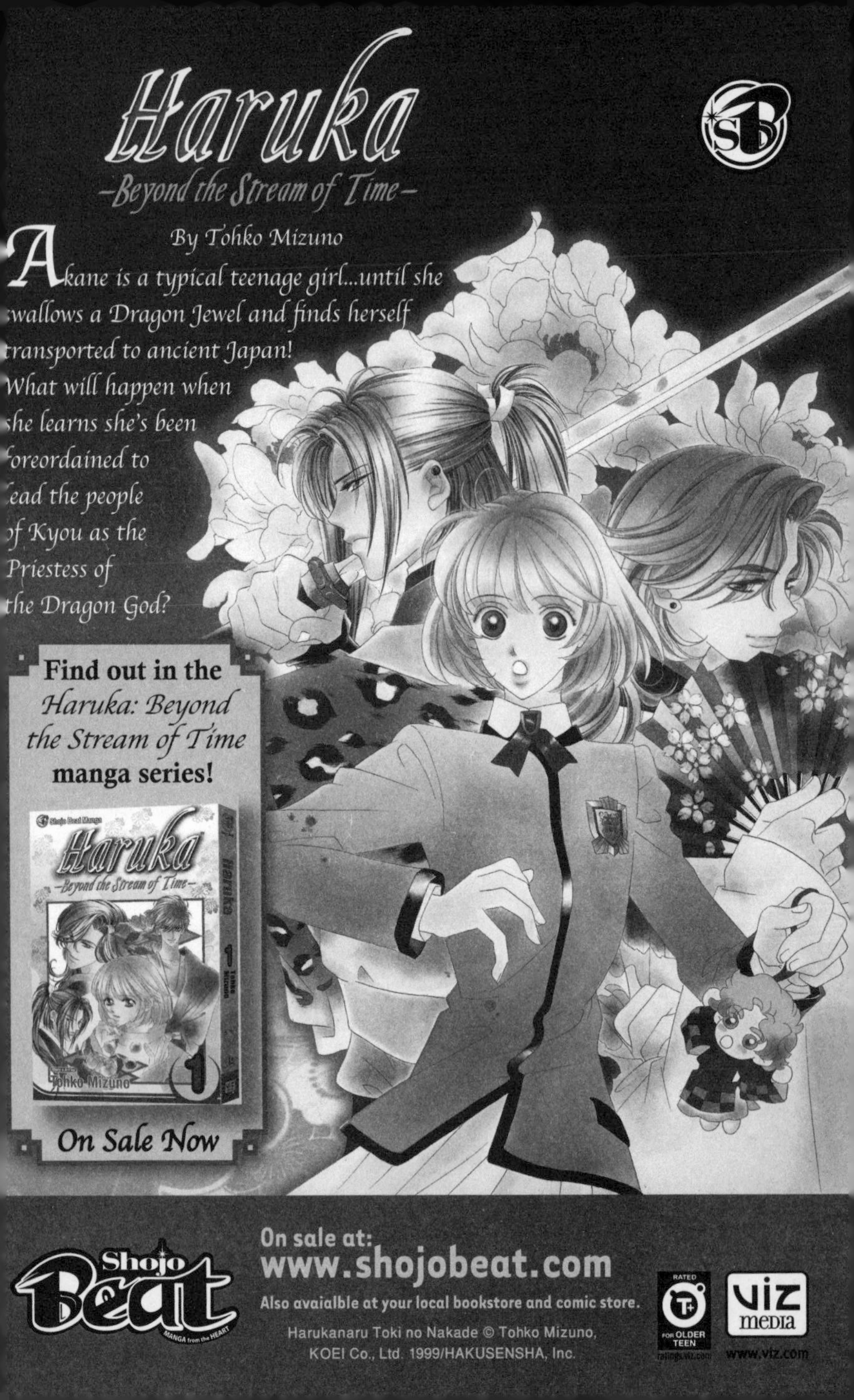
Haruka
-Beyond the Stream of Time-
By Tohko Mizuno
Akane is a typical teenage girl...until she swallows a Dragon Jewel and finds herself transported to ancient Japan! What will happen when she learns she's been foreordained to lead the people of Kyou as the Priestess of the Dragon God?
Find out in the Haruka: Beyond the Stream of Time manga series!
Shojo Beat Manga
Haruka
-Beyond the Stream of Time-
Tohko Mizuno
1
On Sale Now
Shojo Beat
MANGA from the HEART
On sale at:
www.shojobeat.com
Also avaialble at your local bookstore and comic store.
Harukanaru Toki no Nakade © Tohko Mizuno, KOEI Co., Ltd. 1999/HAKUSENSHA, Inc.
RATED
T+
FOR OLDER TEEN
ratings.viz.com
viz media
www.viz.com

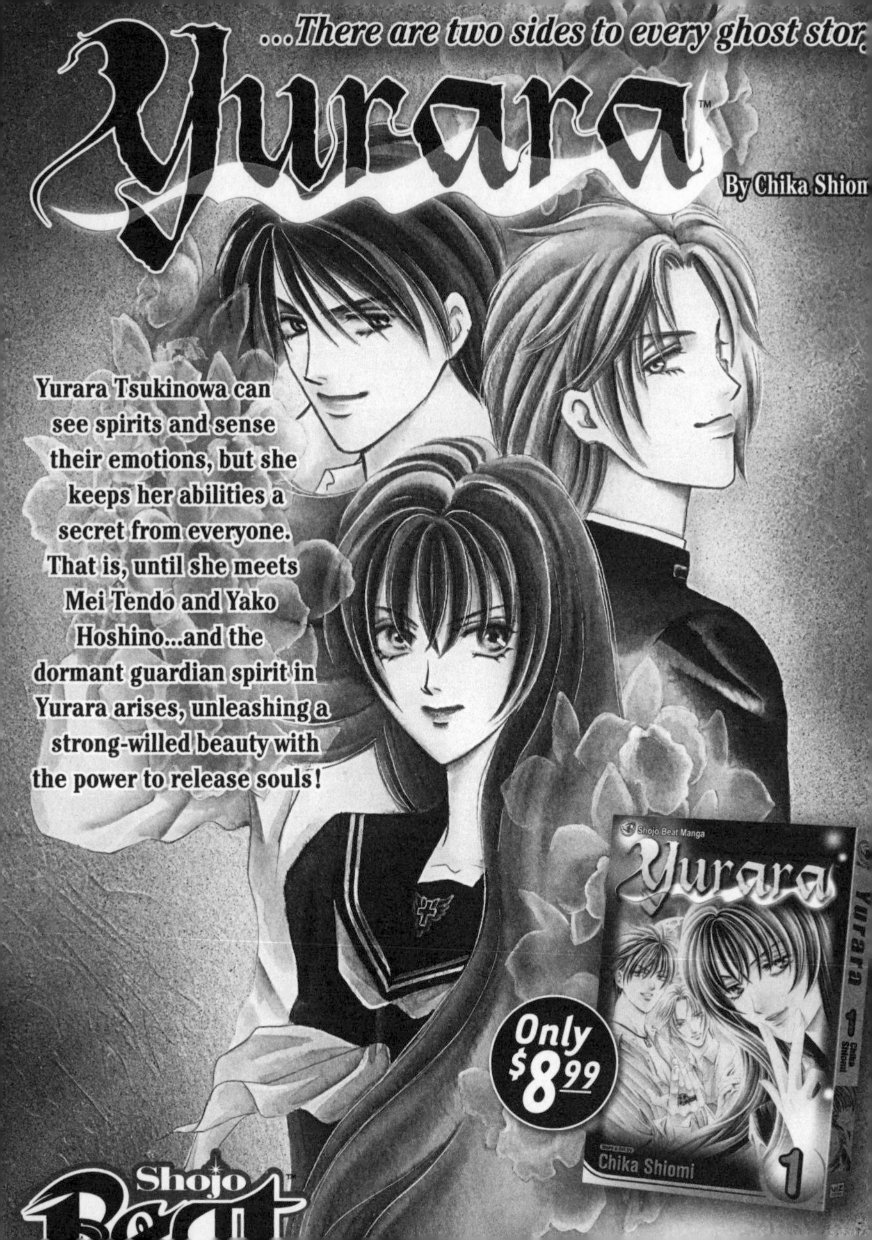
...There are two sides to every ghost stor
Yurara™
By Chika Shiom
Yurara Tsukinowa can see spirits and sense their emotions, but she keeps her abilities a secret from everyone. That is, until she meets Mei Tendo and Yako Hoshino...and the dormant guardian spirit in Yurara arises, unleashing a strong-willed beauty with the power to release souls!
Shojo Beat Manga
Yurara
Chika Shiomi
1
Only $8.99
Shojo Beat™

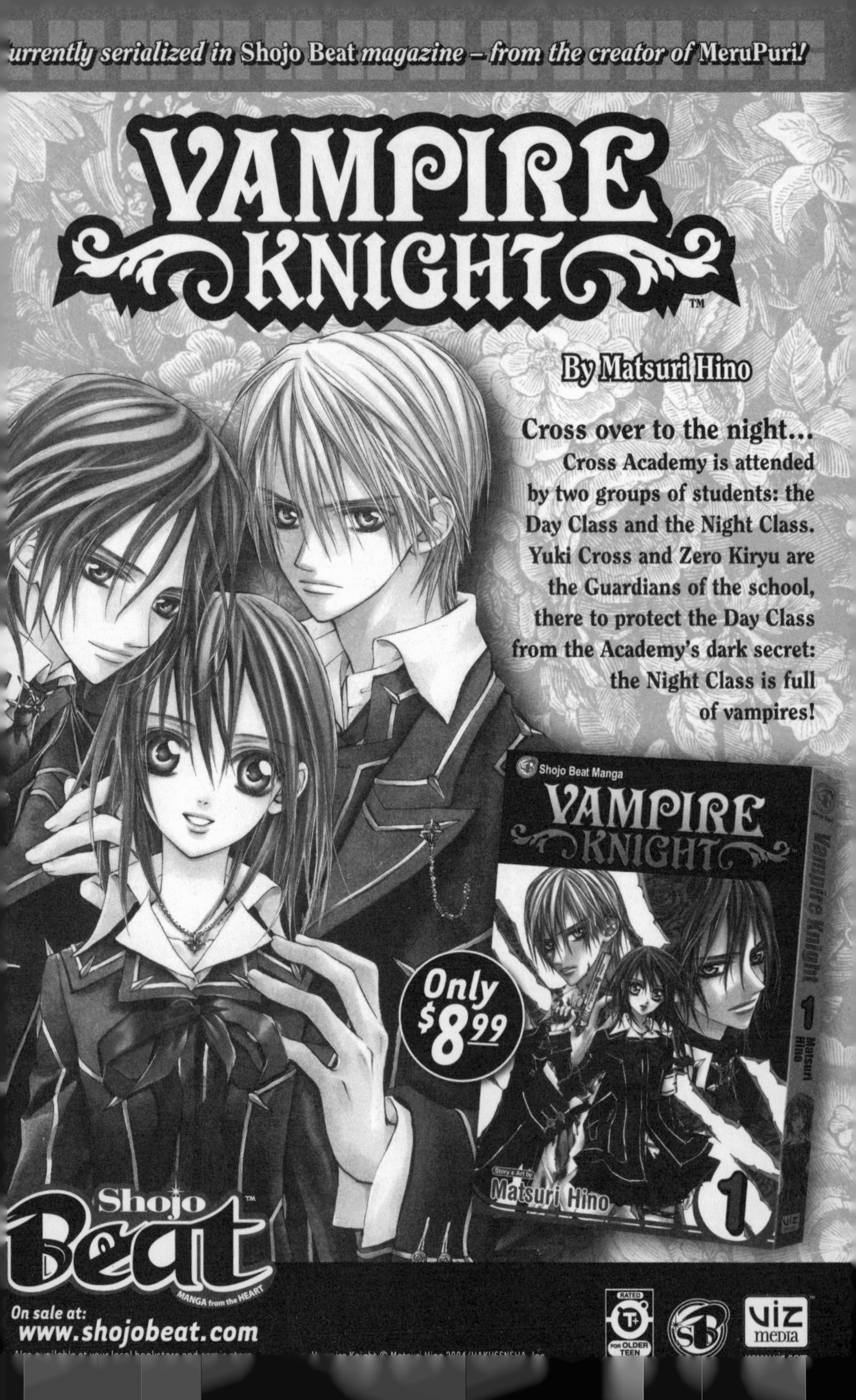
urrently serialized in Shojo Beat magazine – from the creator of MeruPuri!
VAMPIRE KNIGHT™
By Matsuri Hino
Cross over to the night...
Cross Academy is attended by two groups of students: the Day Class and the Night Class. Yuki Cross and Zero Kiryu are the Guardians of the school, there to protect the Day Class from the Academy's dark secret: the Night Class is full of vampires!
Shojo Beat Manga
VAMPIRE KNIGHT
Vampire Knight 1 Matsuri Hino
Story & Art by Matsuri Hino
1
Only $8.99
Shojo Beat™
MANGA from the HEART
On sale at:
www.shojobeat.com
RATED T+ FOR OLDER TEEN
VIZ media

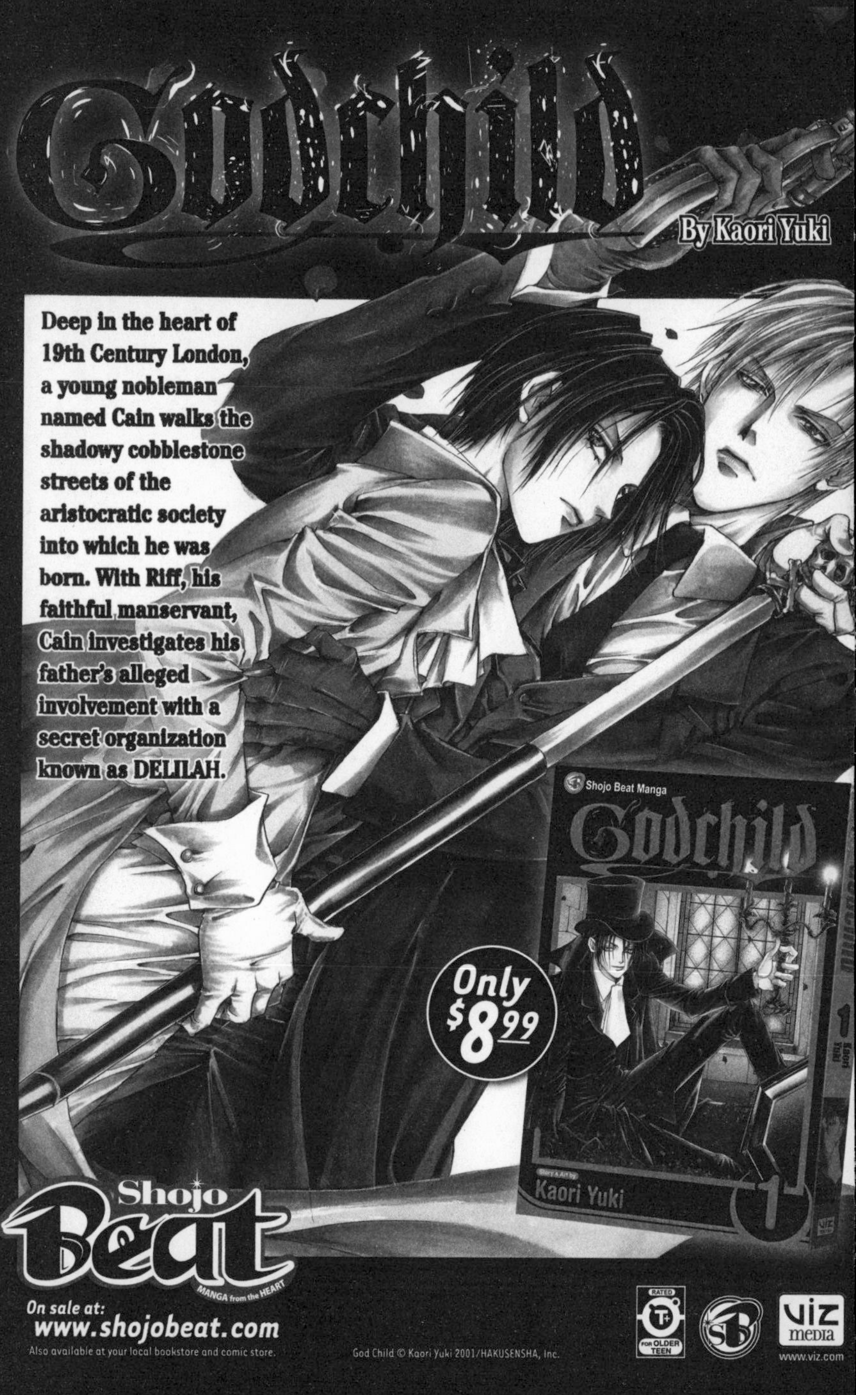
Godchild
By Kaori Yuki
Deep in the heart of 19th Century London, a young nobleman named Cain walks the shadowy cobblestone streets of the aristocratic society into which he was born. With Riff, his faithful manservant, Cain investigates his father's alleged involvement with a secret organization known as DELILAH.
Shojo Beat Manga
Godchild
Story & Art by
Kaori Yuki
Only $8.99
Shojo Beat
MANGA from the HEART
On sale at:
www.shojobeat.com
Also available at your local bookstore and comic store.
God Child © Kaori Yuki 2001/HAKUSENSHA, Inc.
RATED T+ FOR OLDER TEEN
VIZ media
www.viz.com

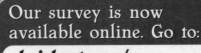